In *The Amateur Strategist,* James DeNardo explores how the everyday person reasons about nuclear strategy. His data reveal surprising patterns of thinking on basic issues from the Strategic Defense Initiative, arms control, and proliferation to the end of the Cold War. The book describes a fascinating cast of players, including "Nice Hawks" like Ronald Reagan, who wanted to give SDI to the Russians, and the "NIFFs," whose procurement rule, expressed simply, was: "If they have it, we don't want it, but if they don't have it, we should get it." To explain his remarkable evidence, Professor DeNardo presents an innovative theory of intuitive deterrence reasoning. He then confronts the theory with data from professional nuclear strategists. His sophisticated demonstration that professional strategists reason like novices – that we are *all* Amateur Strategists – challenges the intellectual foundations of modern deterrence theory, public opinion studies, and game theory.

THE AMATEUR STRATEGIST

THE AMATEUR STRATEGIST

Intuitive Deterrence Theories and the Politics of the Nuclear Arms Race

JAMES DENARDO

University of California, Los Angeles

CAMBRIDGE
UNIVERSITY PRESS

Published by the Press Syndicate of the University of Cambridge
The Pitt Building, Trumpington Street, Cambridge CB2 1RP
40 West 20th Street, New York, NY 10011-4211, USA
10 Stamford Road, Oakleigh, Melbourne 3166, Australia

First published 1995

Printed in the United States of America

Library of Congress Cataloging-in-Publication Data
DeNardo, James, 1949–
The amateur strategist : intuitive deterrence theories and the
politics of the nuclear arms race / James DeNardo.
  p.   cm. – (Cambridge studies in political psychology
and public opinion)
Includes index.
ISBN 0-521-48121-X (hard). – ISBN 0-521-48446-4 (pbk.)
1. Nuclear arms control.   2. Deterrence (Strategy) – Psychological
aspects.   I. Title.   II. Series.
    JX1974.7.D444   1995
  327.1'74 – dc20   94–40411
                             CIP

A catalog record for this book is available from the British Library.

ISBN 0-521-48121-X Hardback
ISBN 0-521-48446-4 Paperback

For my favorites,
Laura and Carol

Contents

Acknowledgments

As you will shortly discover, *The Amateur Strategist* does not fit neatly into any of the conventional niches that organize academic life in the social sciences. It combines security studies, game theory, cognitive psychology, democratic theory, and social statistics in a rather unconventional blend. Such research would be difficult to pursue in many universities, where resources are allocated to narrowly focused "fields" and short time horizons preclude efforts to immerse oneself in new things. I have been lucky to find a home at UCLA that actively encourages boundary-crossing research. My work has been nurtured by wonderfully supportive colleagues and friends, who worked together to create an exceptionally stimulating intellectual atmosphere. It is a pleasure, now, to recall their kindnesses and to express my gratitude to them.

For stimulating discussions and thoughtful readings of the manuscript: Stephen Ansolabehere, Robert Axelrod, Kathleen Bawn, Jan DeLeeuw, Michael Doyle, Joshua Epstein, Jeffrey Frieden, Andrew Gelman, Terri Givens, Miriam Golden, Jack Hirshleifer, Michael Intriligator, Shanto Iyengar, Ker Chau Li, Susanne Lohmann, Mathew McCubbins, Robert Powell, Robert Putnam, Douglas Rivers, Ronald Rogowski, Richard Rosecrance, Thomas Schwartz, David Sears, George Tsebelis, Michael Wallerstein, Kenneth Watman, Dean Wilkening, Don Ylvisaker, and John Zaller.

For engaging forums and group discussions: Institute des Hautes Etudes, Geneva, Switzerland; Princeton Center for Environmental and Strategic Studies; The Jacob Marschak Colloquium; The Princeton Seminar for the Study of Political Change; The University of Lisbon; The CISA Seminar Series; UCLA's Political Economy Luncheon Group; the Executive Lunch Seminar at TRW Corporation; the UCLA Seminar in Statistics and Data Analysis; The RAND Corporation Seminar in International Studies.

For painstaking research assistance: Rob Mellen, Devi Bricker, Rupen Cetinyan, John Medearis, and Kevin Hashizume. Terri Givens went far beyond the call of duty in preparing the tables and figures for publication.

For guiding the manuscript toward publication: Alex Holzman, Susan Thornton, and Janis Bolster.

For research and financial support: The Academic Senate of UCLA; The Center for International and Strategic Affairs, Michael Intriligator and Richard Rosecrance, directors; Richard Sisson; David Sears; Ronald Rogowski; and Leonard Binder.

And, of course, for their love and kindness, my two favorites, Carol and Laura.

1

Introduction

When the world's first great nuclear arms race finally reversed course, Americans reacted with the same wary ambivalence that seems to overtake survivors of shipwrecks, plane crashes, and wars. That a nuclear catastrophe had been avoided and a dangerous adversary removed from the world stage naturally brought relief, exhilaration, and an eagerness to get on with life. But mixed with the euphoria was unmistakable anxiety about the future, and a weakened sense that we controlled our own destinies. Would the former Soviet Union become a benign liberal democracy, or degenerate into a malignant "Weimar Russia"? Would the exhaustion of the superpowers persuade others that arms racing is folly, or merely propel a sell-off of nuclear materials and expertise? Would the post–Cold War world become a stable and prosperous one, or were the ugly wars in the Gulf and the Balkans a portent of impending chaos? In the face of complex events on a vast scale, it was easy to feel like a witness to history and hard to feel like its master.

The same mixed feelings are now very much at work in the weary fields of security studies and arms control. After World War II, strategists and arms controllers struggled for nearly 50 years to contain the staggering cost of the nuclear arms race, to rationalize the deployment of weapons, and to reduce the potential for nuclear war. The artful intellectual blueprints for these efforts were largely completed in the 1950's by pioneers like Thomas Schelling, Albert Wohlstetter, and Bernard Brodie. But as it turned out, the blueprints of the founding fathers were difficult to follow in practice. The trouble was that neither the Soviet Union nor the United States showed much resistance to new weapons technologies, however dangerous or destabilizing they might be. After the A-bomb came the H-bomb, miniaturized bombs, rapid delivery launchers, precision guidance systems, MIRVs, cruise missiles, electronic warfare, exotic space weapons, stealth, and more. About the only systems that didn't get built were those that didn't work or that cost too much, like the ABM. Otherwise, attempts at arms control were largely ineffectual until the early 1990's when the Soviet economic and political systems unexpectedly collapsed, and the Soviet threat to NATO disintegrated.

Had the Cold War arms race concluded with a rationally deliberated treaty for mutual cooperation, arms controllers could take pride in having conquered a perverse dynamic in modern world politics. In fact, the arms race was accelerating sharply when the Cold War crash landed, leaving one "superpower" on the brink of chaos and the other badly depleted. Though the arms controllers' traditional policy agenda was suddenly resolved, the end came by *deus ex machina* and not without strings. Nothing typified the disconcerting tenor of the times more than the frightening Gulf War, which appeared out of the blue amid learned discourse about "The End of History," the "obsolescence of war," and the "peace dividend." No sooner had the Cold War been declared "won" than the United States found itself coping with a dramatic failure of deterrence against an almost-nuclear adversary that it had unwittingly nurtured and developed. Far from vindicating our theories of arms control and international cooperation, the Cold War's sorry finale in Russia and Kuwait precipitated a conceptual crisis of confidence that now leaves the field groping for moorings.

This book presents new evidence about three questions that I believe go to the heart of our failure to control the nuclear arms race during the Cold War, to anticipate its collapse, and to comprehend its aftermath. Broadly speaking, the questions go like this:

- How do everyday citizens think and reason about nuclear strategy, nuclear deterrence, and the arms race?
- Does the strategic novice approach such questions differently than a trained expert would?
- How has the end of the Cold War affected thinking about nuclear weapons and national security?

I realize that after the collapse of Communism, many people wonder why we should care about such things anymore. After spending more than a trillion dollars on the nuclear arms race, there is understandable eagerness to move on to urgent domestic problems. That the nuclear arms race subsided only after one adversary dropped from exhaustion should nevertheless give pause. As long as weapons of mass destruction and hostile relationships coexist in world politics, the question of deterrence will not go away. Neither then does the need to understand what deters, what drives armaments competitions, and what steps can be taken to manage them. That we survived the first great nuclear arms race is certainly cause for celebration, but hardly inspires confidence that we have mastered the nuclear predicament. Lest we become like the survivors of shipwrecks who drift ashore and then dismiss navigation as a "solved problem," we should exploit the current respite to reflect and learn from a dangerous and poorly understood experience.

In that spirit then, let me explain how evidence about the three questions listed above might contribute to resolving important conceptual problems in security studies, and to fixing our bearings in the uncertain and dynamic environment of the post–Cold War.

THEORETICAL TRENDS IN STRATEGIC STUDIES

During the Cold War, the guiding theories of national security described how strategically calculating states could exploit threats of nuclear retaliation to deter attacks on their homelands and protect their international interests. By explaining what deters, and what makes deterrence stable, these theories provided a blueprint for designing nuclear forces and for anticipating how rational players would react to each other's moves. In this way, a set of fundamental precepts about the logic of deterrence supported a constellation of derivative theories about the arms race and arms control. The trouble is that these corollary theories provide a very poor description of actual behavior. Their empirical shortcomings were noticed early in the Cold War, they became glaring during the Reagan and Gorbachev years, and there still exists no consensus about how to repair them. The search for a fix proceeds on every level of Kenneth Waltz's famous hierarchy of causes in international relations, addressing the psychology of individual decision makers, the internal politics of states, and the dynamics of international systems.

One line of development proceeds on the highest level of Waltz's hierarchy where rational state actors interact in an anarchic international environment. Here there has been a new wave of formal studies about deterrence, the balance of power, and international cooperation that all seek to rejuvenate the dominant paradigm by refining the concept of strategic rationality. The new generation of theories deploy improved methodologies for understanding games of incomplete information, iterated play, evolutionary equilibria, and sophisticated bargaining behavior. On display is the latest in analytical high technology, much of it imported from neighboring fields, in hopes of cracking fundamental intellectual puzzles about threats and promises, signalling, reputation, credibility, and cooperation.[1]

1 For good examples, see Robert Powell, *Nuclear Deterrence Theory: The Search for Credibility* (Cambridge: Cambridge University Press, 1990); Emerson Niou, Peter Ordeshook, and Gregory Rose, *The Balance of Power* (Cambridge: Cambridge University Press, 1989); Robert Axelrod, *The Evolution of Cooperation* (New York: Basic Books, 1984); George Downs and David M. Rocke, *Tacit Bargaining, Arms Races, and Arms Control* (Ann

A second line of development seeks to check the hyper-formal rationalism of the system-level, or "third image," theories by providing more realistic psychological and political microfoundations for state behavior. This trend has a decidedly less abstract, more historical flavor, focusing on cognitive, organizational, and political pathologies that compromise rationality in national policy making. Here the stock in trade are historical case studies that describe surprise attacks and deterrence breakdowns, spirals of misperceptions, imperial overextensions, "group think," intelligence failures, standard operating procedures, organizational parochialism, partisan politics, and "cults of the offensive" – dynamics that all elevate "bounded rationality" to theoretical center stage. Along somewhat different lines, the discovery, or rediscovery, that liberal states don't go to war with each other has renewed interest in the ideological foundations of security, and the domestic political origins of foreign relations. Theories with a domestic focus confound rationalist stories too, by replacing "unitary state actors" with coalitions of competing political interest groups, organizations, and factions.[2]

Arbor: University of Michigan Press, 1990); Robert Powell, "Absolute and Relative Gains in International Relations Theory," *American Political Science Review* 85, No. 4 (December 1991); and Duncan Snidal, "Relative Gains and the Pattern of International Cooperation," *American Political Science Review* 85, No. 3 (September 1991). For reviews of the recent literature, see Barry O'Neill, "Game Theory and the Study of the Deterrence of War," in Paul C. Stern, et al., eds., *Perspectives on Deterrence* (New York: Oxford University Press, 1989), or George W. Downs, "Arms Races and War," in Philip E. Tetlock, et al., eds., *Behavior, Society, and Nuclear War*, Vol. 2 (New York: Oxford University Press, 1991).

2 Kenneth N. Waltz, *Man, the State and War* (New York: Columbia University Press, 1954), and Graham T. Allison, *Essence of Decision* (Boston: Little Brown, 1971), distinguish among international relations theories that focus on the strategic behavior of states, domestic political origins of state behavior, and the psychology of decision makers. The works listed below pursue Waltz's "first" and "second" images, concentrating on the psychological and domestic origins of state behavior: Steven Kull, *Minds at War: Nuclear Reality and the Inner Conflicts of Defense Policymakers* (New York: Basic Books, 1988); Michael W. Doyle, "Kant, Liberal Legacies, and Foreign Affairs," Parts I and II, *Philosophy and Public Affairs* 12 (Summer and Fall 1983); Jack Snyder, *The Ideology of the Offensive* (Ithaca: Cornell University Press, 1984); Barry Posen, *The Sources of Military Doctrine* (Ithaca: Cornell University Press, 1984); Robert Jervis, *Perception and Misperception in International Politics* (Princeton: Princeton University Press, 1977); Bruce Russett, *Controlling the Sword: Democratic Governance of National Security* (Cambridge: Harvard University Press, 1990); Stephen Van Evera, "The Cult of the Offensive and the Origins of the First World War," *International Security* 9 (1984); Jack Snyder, *Myths of Empire* (Ithaca: Cornell University Press, 1991); Robert Jervis, Richard Ned Lebow, and Janice Gross Stein, *Psychology and Deterrence* (Baltimore: Johns Hopkins University Press, 1985); Alexander George and Richard Smoke, *Deterrence in American Foreign Policy: Theory and Practice* (New York: Columbia University Press, 1974); Richard K. Betts, *Surprise Attack* (Washington, D.C.: Brookings Institution, 1982); John Steinbruner, *The Cybernetic Theory of Decision* (Princeton: Princeton University Press, 1974); Deborah Welch Larson, *Origins of Containment: A Psychological Explanation* (Princeton: Princeton University Press, 1985); and Jeffrey Freiden, *Debt, Development, and Democracy: Modern Political Economy and Latin America, 1965–1985* (Princeton: Princeton University Press, 1991).

While both lines of development originate from a common sense of frustration, it is surprising how much tension exists between them and how difficult it has been to reconcile their main results. The psychologically and historically-minded scholars argue that rational deterrence theory and its corollary models of the arms race overestimate the cognitive sophistication of decision makers and underestimate their domestic political motivations. The formal theorists, on the other hand, remain deeply skeptical about their critics' inductive inferences. Historical case studies rarely exploit an explicit scheme for assessing the relative importance of different factors, and remain open to pointed statistical criticisms about selection bias (non-random sampling), underidentification (too many variables, not enough cases), and errors-in-variables (unreliable, unsystematic measurements).[3] And, as Reinhard Selten sardonically points out: "High powered theorists tend to feel uncomfortable with a theory without theorems."[4]

The testy methodological exchanges between rational choicers and their critics highlight the fundamental role played by the assumption of rationality in strategic theory, and the very great reluctance among theorists to let it go. Here one must understand that rationality allows for tremendous theoretical simplifications by imposing a fundamental symmetry on strategic interactions. When the theorist can assume that everyone shares a common and predictable scheme of reckoning, and that everybody knows as much – that the players all perceive the game the same way and approach it with the same logic – the possibilities for powerful deductive reasoning grow enormously. Indeed, you could argue that economists and game theorists have played the dominant role in shaping security studies because their assumption of symmetric rationality was the only one that produced sharp results when a guiding theory was badly needed.

By pressing cognitive constraints and domestic factional politics into the story, the psychological and historical revisionists jeopardize the basic simplifying assumption of the ruling paradigm. Each line of criticism is highly plausible, but they are hard to cope with for essentially the same reason. Because rationality can be bounded in so many different ways, and because domestic politics admits ill-defined and heterogeneous preferences, both arguments open a Pandora's box by breaking the symmetry that underlies the classical framework. The basic source of friction, then, is not the substantive ideas that the revisionists present, but the lack of a ready theoretical framework in which to handle them.

With no compelling theory of boundedly rational behavior in sight, the

---

3 A good survey of the issues appears in the *World Politics* special issue on "The Rational Deterrence Debate" (January 1989).
4 Reinhard Selten, "Bounded Rationality," *Journal of Institutional and Theoretical Economics* 146 (1990).

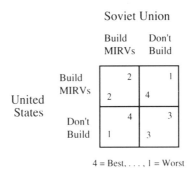

Figure 1.1 A nuclear Prisoner's Dilemma

two main lines of development remain very much at loggerheads in international studies (as they do in the supporting disciplines of decision theory, game theory, and psychology). There remains, to say the least, an enormous conceptual distance still to be closed between theoretical studies of finite automata playing iterated games or learning behavior in artificial neural networks and the historical data on deterrence failures in World War II or 1914. For the most part, research in the rational and historical traditions proceeds on separate tracks with concepts and evidence that hardly make contact. So far, the efforts to bridge and integrate the levels of Waltz's hierarchy have been limited and tentative. A basic purpose of this book is to break the impasse by providing the foundation for a truly multileveled understanding of the arms race.

THE NUCLEAR THINKING DATA

As you will discover shortly, my own loyalties in this debate are very much divided. You could say that my heart is with the rational approach but my head is with the psychologists and the historians. One experience that deeply affected my thinking occurred in early 1988 when I was teaching a class on the nuclear arms race. I had intended to persuade the students that the arms race could be understood as a Prisoner's Dilemma by introducing them to the classical game illustrated in Figure 1.1.

The entries beside the matrix are the *players'* potential moves, and the numbers inside (called *payoffs*) rank the possible outcomes of the game from each player's point of view. In this game, the United States (lower left payoffs in each cell) and the Soviet Union both approach the decision to

MIRV in the same way. (MIRVs are multiple, independently targetable, reentry vehicles – the hydra headed nuclear missiles that created intense pressures in the arms race.) Because building is always the best response to the other side's move, each country has a *dominant strategy* to deploy the multiple warhead missiles. If, for example, the Soviet Union does not MIRV, the United States prefers by 4 to 3 to build anyway. If the Soviet Union does MIRV, the United States will too, preferring parity to inferiority by 2 to 1. The same calculation applies from the Soviet perspective. The strategy combination [*Build, Build*] is the unique dominant strategy equilibrium in the game. The dilemma occurs because both sides find themselves worse off after building than they would have been under a treaty that banned MIRVs (then the payoffs for both sides are 3 rather than 2). The dominant strategy equilibrium is *Pareto-inefficient* because arms control increases the payoffs of both players. Unfortunately, arms control is not a stable equilibrium in the game, because either player can raise its payoffs unilaterally by *defecting* from the treaty and building on the sly. The problem then is how to achieve mutually beneficial cooperation when both sides are motivated to defect, when neither trusts the other to keep its word, and there is no overarching authority to enforce their treaties. Even though arms control is collectively rational, cooperation is in neither side's individual best interest.

At the time, these characteristics of the Prisoner's Dilemma seemed to capture the maddening intractability of the arms race, which both sides avidly pursued even as it made them worse off. There were, I thought, many good reasons for undergraduates to study the game. The Prisoner's Dilemma had attracted enormous theoretical attention, and was the main platform for a multidisciplinary research program about the origins of social cooperation (both international and otherwise). As one game theorist suggested, "Whenever you observe individuals in a conflict that hurts all of them, your first thought should be of the Prisoner's Dilemma."[5] The game also exemplifies the state-level, rational choice paradigm on which modern deterrence theory rests. In this game, like most other models of the arms race, the states are unified rational actors with homogeneous and symmetric preferences. And finally, the model provides an interesting and accessible laboratory for discussing theories of arms control. When the game is played just once, the dilemma appears intractable. But when the players interact repeatedly, and conditions are right, a

5 Eric Rasmusen, *Games and Information* (New York: Basil Blackwell, 1989), p. 29. Robert Axelrod, *The Evolution of Cooperation* (New York: Basic Books, 1984), and Kenneth Oye, ed., *Cooperation Under Anarchy* (Princeton: Princeton University Press, 1986), gave the Prisoner's Dilemma tremendous prominence in international studies during the late 1980's.

cooperative equilibrium can be sustained. We can rationally reject defection today for fear of jeopardizing the long-term benefits of ongoing cooperation.

So far, so good. In fine Socratic style, I planned to launch my lecture by first placing an empty matrix for the MIRVing game on the board, and then inviting the class to fill in the payoffs for each cell. After they derived the preference profile for the Prisoner's Dilemma, I would explain the perverse and self-defeating character of the game. And when the story became grim and demoralizing, I would introduce the idea of iteration to show light at the end of the tunnel. This surefire plan quickly turned into a pedagogical nightmare when every cell in the matrix produced a tooth and nail struggle over how to assign the payoffs. With my lecture going down in flames, I tried to bully the class into accepting the Prisoner's Dilemma rankings, only to be rebuffed by protests that "you can't say that." "Take out a paper and fill in your own preference orderings," I replied, completing an inspired build-up to what had to be the least convincing lecture ever given about the arms race as Prisoner's Dilemma.

When I reviewed the students' preference profiles afterwards, I got my first glimpse of the complex and intriguing patterns that occupy much of this book. Though I had no explanation for their responses, and wouldn't for a long time, it was obvious that these bright and politically engaged students did not think about the arms race at all as the Prisoner's Dilemma theorists said they should – or as I had so casually assumed they must. It occurred to me that the same kind of data, if appropriately designed, could provide an effective litmus test for all kinds of deterrence theories, each with its corollary model of the arms race.

Theories of nuclear deterrence are notorious for their Strangelovian complexity, much of which resides in convoluted scenarios about limited wars, escalation ladders, missile attrition dynamics, targeting doctrines, and tacit bargaining. But the core issue, lurking behind all the elaborate conjectures and calculations, is how to design nuclear forces. The theorist first reasons about why nuclear wars would be fought and how they would unfold, and then deduces how they could be deterred by configuring nuclear forces in the right way. By identifying security-maximizing configurations of nuclear forces, deterrence theories effectively define policy preferences in arms racing games like the one in Figure 1.1. Arms race modellers reason in much the same way, starting from a premise about strategic motivation – in essence, from an axiom about what deters or an assumption about what "security" means to each side – and then deducing which arrangements of forces will provide mutual security, and what kinds of technology should be avoided. Game theoretic arms race models like the Prisoner's Dilemma, the Security Dilemma, or Deadlock proceed from an explicit description of preferences. Eliciting preferences about weapon systems like MIRVs therefore provides revealing information for deciding whether any particular theory captures the respondent's thinking about nuclear security and the arms race.[6]

With these considerations in mind, I elaborated my classroom exercise into a survey questionnaire and began collecting data systematically – mainly at first from strategic novices. The questionnaire doesn't seek out the underlying rationale for different weapons deployments, but rather addresses the end-product of such reasoning. Since preferences about what weapons to build and what weapons to avoid ultimately determine the course of the arms race, this tack seemed politically interesting as well as theoretically telling. The critical items in the questionnaire I used before the collapse of the Soviet Union appear in Figure 1.2. You should go ahead and complete them now, filling in "the former Soviet Union" or "Russia" where appropriate.

Since games like the Prisoner's Dilemma provide the conceptual foundation for our leading theories about deterrence, arms races, and arms control, not to mention about social cooperation generally, it was surprising to discover that virtually no empirical data had been collected to check whether the structures of preference analyzed by theorists actually described real people's understanding of these games. As I had myself assumed in class, the theorists seemed confident that they could derive preferences from the "structure of the problem" or the "logic of the situation." This pattern of reasoning is hardly unique to international studies, I should add, but typifies rational choice theories in general. Preferences are the point of departure in formal models of choice, and virtually never a direct object of study in applied work.[7]

At the same time, I also discovered that the major commercial and aca-

---

6 In fact, such preference data can address a much wider class of armaments models than those driven strictly by considerations of "national security" in the traditional sense. They can reveal, for example, whether people's preferences in the arms race are parochially driven by motives of personal profit. They can also accommodate conceptions of security that extend beyond purely military considerations to issues of, say, economic or environmental well-being.

7 Ariel Rubinstein describes the situation this way: "There exists a widespread myth in game theory, that it is possible to achieve a miraculous prediction regarding the outcome of interaction among human beings using only data on the order of events, combined with a description of the players' preferences over the feasible outcomes of the situation. For forty years, game theory has searched for the grand solution which would accomplish this task. The mystical and vague word 'rationality' is used to fuel our hopes of achieving this goal. I fail to see any possibility of this being accomplished. . . . Missing are data describing the processes of reasoning adopted by the players when they analyze the game." "Comments on the Interpretation of Game Theory," *Econometrica* 59, No. 4 (July 1991), p. 923.

Reinhard Selten has also expressed profound discomfort with "the rationalistic tradition of deriving behavior from abstract principles without any reference to empirical evidence, an attempt which is doomed to fail." "Bounded Rationality," *Journal of Institutional and Theoretical Economics* 146 (1990), p. 651.

How would you evaluate the following outcomes (some actual, others potential) of the arms competition between the United States and Soviet Union? Give numerical values to each of the four alternatives, assigning ties when the choices seem about equal. [Rankings like {4,3,2,1} or {4,1,1,1} are both perfectly o.k.]

4 = Most Desirable   3 = Next best   2 = Next to last   1 = Least Desirable.

A. How about a race to develop an effective means to search out and destroy ballistic missile submarines?

_____ Both Sides have it   _____ Only the U.S. has it
_____ Only the U.S.S.R. has it _____ Neither Side has it

B. To develop ballistic missile defenses covering the entire national territory? [Suppose the defenses are less than perfect but not trivial either.]

_____ Both Sides have it   _____ Only the U.S. has it
_____ Only the U.S.S.R. has it _____ Neither Side has it

C. To develop highly accurate, multiple warhead ICBMs like the MX?

_____ Both Sides have it   _____ Only the U.S. has it
_____ Only the U.S.S.R. has it _____ Neither Side has it

D. To develop effective technologies for protecting nuclear forces from preemptive attack?

_____ Both Sides have it   _____ Only the U.S. has it
_____ Only the U.S.S.R. has it _____ Neither Side has it

Figure 1.2 Core items on the nuclear thinking questionnaire

demic surveys about security issues invariably failed to elicit the respondents' nuclear preferences in a strategically telling format. As one example, consider the typical Likert scale questionnaire item, which would address the arms racing game in Figure 1.1 by asking whether you support MIRVed ICBMs 'strongly,' 'somewhat,' 'very little,' or 'not at all.' The item provides a sense of the respondents' positions on an important policy question, but doesn't come close to identifying their preference ordering over the alternative outcomes in the game. In particular, such data don't reveal how policy preferences about MIRVing might depend on the adversary's move. The question format therefore does not conform with the core assumption of modern security studies or of game theory generally. As Kenneth Waltz explained nearly 40 years ago:

There is in international politics no simple rule to prescribe just how belligerent, or how peaceful, any given state should strive to appear in order to maximize its chances of living at peace with neighboring states. One cannot say in the abstract that for peace a country must arm, or disarm, or compromise, or stand firm. . . . The peace strategy of any one country must depend on the peace or war strategies of all other countries. [*Man, the State and War* (New York: Columbia University Press, 1954), p. 222]

The same idea is emphasized by Thomas Schelling in his seminal study of deterrence:

Game theory is concerned with situations . . . in which the best course of action for each participant depends on what he expects the other participants to do. A deterrent threat meets this definition nicely; it works only because of what the other player expects us to do in response to his choice of moves, and we can afford to make the threat only because we expect it to have an influence on his choice. [Thomas Schelling, *The Strategy of Conflict* (New York: Oxford University Press, 1960), p. 10]

Unless preferences about strategic policies are measured in a way that reveals their dependency on the other side's moves, public opinion data cannot provide any sharp test of theories about deterrence, the arms race, or international cooperation. We have a great deal of survey data about nuclear attitudes and defense issues, but amazingly, virtually none of them meets this simple test.[8]

The upshot of these peculiar disciplinary habits is that an enormous body of strategic theory rests upon an unnecessary leap of faith. Why assume that preferences take a particular form in political games, rather than measuring directly how real players rank the alternative outcomes? Since preferences play a defining role in any game, and support the whole chain of theoretical deductions about rational behavior, treating them as a self-evident point of departure – as if they were mathematical axioms – is surely a dangerous methodological tactic.

In fact, such an analytical strategy creates the potential for big surprises, of the kind that have been all too common during the Cold War and its aftermath. A basic purpose of the chapters ahead is to persuade you that *all* of our important theories of deterrence and the arms race – including not just the Prisoner's Dilemma, but the Richardsonian action–reaction models, the Security Dilemma, the classical MAD theories, the conservative "war fighting" theories, and many more – drastically misspecify preferences in the games they describe. Descriptive accounts that reduce strategic preferences to shopworn categories like "hawks, doves, and owls" or "hardliners and softliners" similarly fail to capture the richness, the diver-

---

8 The same criticism can be leveled against commonplace analytical categories like "hawks and doves" or "hardliners and softliners" that people impute to politicians to describe their strategic preferences.

sity, or the anomalies that characterize real nuclear preferences. That our conceptual apparatus fails so dramatically, and on such a fundamental level, was the first great surprise in an exciting intellectual journey that I shall describe in the chapters ahead.

Such conclusions are rather strong, to say the least, and I resisted them myself for a long time. Because my early respondents were strategic novices, it was hard to know at first what to make of their complex and often mystifying preference profiles. Were the preference data interpretable signal or simply noise? Did they have any general significance, or were they simply a local curiosity? Two kinds of validation finally convinced me that novice nuclear thinking had substantial implications for understanding nuclear strategy and the arms race – during the Cold War and after.

The first task was to see whether the strange patterns I was seeing could be explained by a plausible theory of nuclear thinking. After many false starts, I eventually devised a model of *intuitive deterrence theories* that exploits a formal heuristic algorithm to account for the novices' puzzling strategic preferences. The *intuitive nuclear calculus,* as I sometimes call the model described in Chapter 6, is squarely located in the bounded rationality school. It assumes that cognitively simple rules of thumb govern people's preferences about nuclear weapon systems – what Reinhard Selten calls a *superficial analysis* – not the intricate strategic calculations that appear in the expert literature. That politicians and voters should rely on an intuitive strategic calculus seems plausible enough, but this one predicts a pattern of nuclear preferences completely unlike the ones you will find in any familiar theory. That the model's predictions could be validated in remarkable detail, in sample after sample, with carefully constructed measurements and statistical tests, was the second great surprise of my intellectual journey. I regret that these tests may strain the patience of the non-technical reader (they appear in Chapter 7). It is nevertheless important to demonstrate the range of inferences that these data can support. Unlike more conventional survey measurements, the strategic preference data are rich enough to test a surprising array of theoretical ideas and to reconstruct a complicated cognitive algorithm. After you see what can be done with them, I hope that you'll agree that they are unusually fertile and interesting, and ought to be used more widely in public opinion studies.

At the time I was wrestling with these early datasets, my principle concern was understanding why arms control was so difficult to achieve. It suddenly seemed obvious – at least after seeing the data – that important decisions in the arms race had always been controlled by amateur strategists, including not just legions of voters, congressmen, and apparatchiks, but national leaders like Lyndon Johnson, Ronald Reagan, and Mikhail Gorbachev. If amateurs were in fact playing a pivotal role, and their preferences deviated sharply from theoretical assumptions, then little wonder that real behavior deviated sharply from theoretical prescriptions. Because a critical component in our analytical machinery had been poorly designed, the tenets of arms control theory simply didn't take in the political arena.

How much to make of these conjectures clearly depended on whether they could be generalized beyond the novice respondents in my samples. Would similar patterns appear in populations that were closer to the levers of power? Did the precepts of prescriptive deterrence theory describe expert nuclear thinking any better than it did the novice's? If novices controlled important strategic decisions, would their behavior really deviate from the experts'? All of these questions invited direct comparisons with sophisticates, and opened up the second phase of my study.

THE EXPERT SAMPLES

Very shortly after I collected the first data from novices, I began sampling nuclear experts and decision makers, including senior executives from giant aerospace companies and defense contractors, defense analysts at the RAND Corporation, government officials, and academic specialists in nuclear strategy and arms control. The expert data raised fascinating new questions that often ranged beyond security studies into broader issues of cognitive science, political psychology, and public opinion. In fact, many of the core questions in these disciplines turn on the relationship between expert and novice reasoning. Cognitive scientists study why grandmasters play better chess than novices do because they want to understand what dynamics drive learning and induction, and how to build intelligent machines. Social and political psychologists study the relationship between expert and lay opinion because they want to understand the origins of mass belief systems, the cognitive sophistication of voters, the stability of public opinion, and the quality of democratic decision making.[9]

Much of this theorizing supports the idea that experts' thinking is more coherent than novices', more economical, more abstract, and more connected from issue to issue. It also suggests that lay opinion often amounts to a garbled assimilation of expert ideas – ideas that are fractured during transmission from elite to mass. To the extent that nuclear decisions are strongly influenced by strategic amateurs, such findings naturally become highly salient to strategic studies. If amateur strategists really control such fateful

9 For influential discussions that compare expert and novice reasoning, see Herbert A. Simon, *Models of Thought* (New Haven: Yale University Press, 1979); Philip E. Converse, "The Nature of Belief Systems in Mass Publics," in David Apter, ed., *Ideology and Discontent* (New York: Free Press, 1964); and J. Holland, K. J. Holyoak, R. E. Nisbet, and P. R. Thagard, *Induction* (Cambridge: The MIT Press, 1989).

decisions, are the objectives of arms control less likely to be achieved? Are the configurations of nuclear forces that amateurs devise more likely to be destabilizing? Do amateurs behave more quixotically and less predictably than experts would? Such questions certainly seemed relevant in the Reagan years, when the President of the United States and the First Secretary of the CPSU both pursued nuclear strategies that deviated sharply from the experts' prescriptions. They seem no less important today as weapons of mass destruction continue to fall into new and inexperienced hands around the world.

The nuclear thinking data are unusual in providing a direct comparison of expert and novice responses to questions that, at least in strategic theory, have well defined, prescriptive "right answers." In Chapter 8, we'll see how the experts' preference profiles contain the biggest surprises of all, defying expectations at every turn. From the perspective of security studies, no theory of deterrence that I'm aware of comes close to capturing the baroque diversity of the experts' strategic preferences. From the perspective of political and cognitive psychology, it does not appear at all that novice nuclear thinking is a blurry image of the expert's. In the first place, the novice's opinions are not nearly as garbled or "aschematic" as they first appear. To the contrary, their weird structures can be explained in great detail by an orderly heuristic calculus. And in the second place, it appears that the novice's heuristic calculus places an indelible stamp on expert thinking. Far from superseding the novices' crude intuitive calculations, the experts' nuclear preferences display the same anomalous patterns and underlying heuristic structure. This evidence constitutes the heart of my case that in the face of bewildering social and political complexity we are *all* amateur strategists.

These observations, if correct, have fairly sweeping implications – not only for security studies, but for game theory, public opinion studies, and democratic theory more generally. In the strategy field, we are led toward a theory of unitary actors (states who deploy weapons or not, as a collective action) but heterogeneous decision makers (fluid coalitions, composed of disparate, boundedly-rational individuals). The data support a rich set of inferences about who will coalesce with whom, on what weapon systems and arms control packages, as a function of the other side's behavior. Such a theory has the appealing property of linking together all three levels of Waltz's causal hierarchy, sustaining a unified discussion of political psychology, domestic politics, and international strategy.

The new techniques for measuring opinions and the models of heuristic thinking also invite applications to a broader class of policy issues that are essentially game-theoretic in character. A defining feature in many of our great public debates is that the policy choice one favors depends on what strategy "the other guy" follows. Examples include trade policy (NAFTA, relations with the EEC, trade sanctions against the Japanese), law enforcement (gun control, the death penalty, mandatory sentencing), education (busing, voucher schemes, magnet schools), and environmental cooperation. That conventional survey techniques do not address the contingent, strategic element of public opinion is a serious weakness, inherited from longstanding psychometric scaling traditions. The additional information provided by measuring *preference profiles* creates a direct link between public opinion studies and game theory, enriching both fields at once. At the same time, such data support refined inferences about the cognitive foundations of public opinion. I believe that a model of opinion formation rooted in intuitive social heuristics will find wide application. Such a model reverses the usual top-down flow of opinion from elites to mass, and forces us to rethink normative theories that give the "deliberative" opinions of experts a privileged role in democratic decision making.

For all of these reasons, I hope that the discussion to follow will be interesting to many readers outside the nuclear strategy field. Certainly, I would never have discovered the reasoning and analytical methods described in this book had I not been immersed in the nuclear debate. But the nuclear debate shares a striking resemblance to many other economic, political, religious, educational, and legal controversies. By studying its mysteries and uncovering its secrets, we can learn a lot about human thinking and political conflict in the face of daunting social complexity.

A TRANSFORMED ADVERSARY AND THE DEMOCRATIZATION OF THE ARMS RACE

Little did I realize, as I grappled with these difficult problems, that events of historic magnitude were about to unfold. In late 1989 the inconceivable happened when communism collapsed in Eastern Europe and the Cold War unraveled at breakneck speed. As one remarkable event followed the next, I continued to sample both novices and experts, gathering their reactions to the monumental happenings. Living in California, I felt something like a geologist who had developed a sensitive seismic instrument and set it running, when all of a sudden The Big One arrived. By pure serendipity, my study entered a third phase that focused on the end of the Cold War, how it occurred, and what it implied. The before-after data from experts and novices provide what may be unique evidence about the effect on strategic preferences when "the enemy" is radically transformed. They are a powerful lens, too, for studying the political dynamics that preceded and followed the undoing of the Cold War.

It is ironic that our highest hopes and deepest forebodings about the end of the Cold War both turn on the "democratization" of the nuclear arms race. The ascendancy of democratic forces in the former Soviet Union has surely been the most auspicious development in nuclear politics since 1945, propelling a build-down of nuclear forces that no one imagined possible just a few years ago. On the other hand, nobody seems to like democratization when it comes to nuclear forces. The idea that the Ukraine and Kazakhstan should become major nuclear powers leaves us deeply chilled. So does evidence that Soviet nuclear capabilities are being auctioned to the highest bidder. That we should be wary about the disintegration of Soviet military organizations, the emergence of autonomous republican governments, and the diffusion of Soviet nuclear know-how clearly reflects our fear that nuclear weapons are falling under "popular" control.

For better or worse, the popularization of nuclear authority seems to be one of the basic dynamics in contemporary armaments politics. One element of the process became evident during the Reagan and Gorbachev years, when conspicuous nuclear amateurs not only commanded the two highest positions of nuclear decision making, but actively defied the advice of nuclear experts. By exploiting bold "unilateral initiatives," including the Star Wars program, military demobilizations, and calls for complete nuclear disarmament, the two leaders rallied mass political support to outmaneuver nuclear specialists who opposed their unorthodox policies. A second aspect is evident within the former Soviet Union itself, where nuclear authority has now fallen into the hands of autonomous republics and democratically elected parliaments. Decisions that once were taken by officers and commissars are now in the hands of elected officials. And finally, the dangerous and frightening Gulf War demonstrated the ineffectiveness of our proliferation controls and the speed with which nuclear capabilities are spreading around the world. In many different ways, then, we see nuclear authority devolving from relatively centralized control into more and different hands.

No one has captured our conflicted feelings about nuclear populism more beautifully than the disgruntled Russian official Vladimir Bukovsky.

When thousands of nuclear weapons aimed at the West were in the hands of ruthless, ideologically motivated Communist dictators, when the Soviet Union was an omnipotent superpower with global ambitions, the West was not particularly alarmed.

Today, when the old archenemy is disintegrating, when it has lost its ambitions and power, while dreaded nuclear weapons seem to be in the hands of elected leaders accountable to the elected parliaments, the Western public has been stricken with panic . . . . What a nightmare: for the first time nuclear weapons are not under control of a Communist but of pro–Western democrats. [Vladimir Bukovsky, "Goodbye, Gorby, and Good Riddance," *N.Y. Times* Op–Ed, 12/18/91]

The answer to Bukovsky's riddle appears in a somber document from Harvard University, ominously entitled "Soviet Nuclear Fission."

Proliferation in successor states would put nuclear weapons in the hands of inexperienced and possibly unstable governments, which are likely to be populated by people new to the problem of security policy. (p. 60)

It is worth questioning whether the canons of strategic stability as they evolved over 45 years of U.S.-Soviet standoff are so universal as to be pertinent to the nuclear relationship between the successor states of the Soviet Union and other nuclear powers around the world. (p. 31) [K. M. Campbell, A. B. Carter, S. E. Miller, C. A. Zraket, *Soviet Nuclear Fission: Control of the Nuclear Arsenal in a Disintegrating Soviet Union,* Harvard University, John F. Kennedy School of Government: CSIA Studies in International Security, No. 1, November 1991]

The dark side of nuclear democracy, it seems, is the ascendancy of amateur strategists – people who are innocent about the subtleties of deterrent stability, and who we fear will be incompetent, irrational, impetuous, or worse still, "undeterrable."

Our profound ambivalence about nuclear democratization explains, I believe, much of the strategic confusion after the Cold War. While we celebrate the overthrow of the old Soviet tyranny, we recoil from the irrationality of the revolutionary "mob." Perhaps the darkest fear of all is that we no longer understand what game we're in. The evidence contained in the chapters ahead suggests that this fear is ironic and belated, but nevertheless well worth attending to. Because our leading theories have systematically neglected the amateur strategist, they provide little guidance for navigating in a strategic environment where nuclear authority is devolving rapidly both across and within countries. Without understanding of how novices think and reason about weapons of mass destruction, it will become more and more difficult to predict the consequences of our own policies, or to anticipate anyone else's.

2

A Primer on the Cold War Nuclear Debate

The literature on nuclear strategy is the obvious point of departure for anyone interested in nuclear thinking. Many excellent studies dissect the debate and classify its arguments into competing schools of thought. What I find most interesting about these classifications is how many different kinds there are, and how difficult it is to devise simple strategic categories that capture the theorists' arguments. However one slices the problem, there always seem to be glaring exceptions to the rules of classification.

The data and reasoning presented below will explain, I think, why simple classifications of nuclear thinking are doomed to failure. But to understand what these data mean requires some fluency in strategic concepts and vocabulary. To help readers who might not be specialists, I have prepared a short primer on the nuclear debate as it stood near the end of the Cold War, when my study of nuclear thinking began. Like most classifying schemes in the literature, my composite sketch divides the debaters into two main schools of thought. In this way, it reproduces the commonplace distinction between "hawks and doves" or "hardliners and softliners" that informs so much discussion about armaments politics. The critical point to notice is how competing nuclear deterrence theories generate different menus of weapons preferences. In the chapters ahead, these distinctive theoretical signatures will become our handle for investigating whether prescriptive deterrence theories capture real nuclear thinking in the political arena.[1]

1 A good sampling of classifications can be found in the following sources: Lawrence Freedman, *The Evolution of Nuclear Strategy* (New York: St. Martin's Press, 1983); L. Eden and S. E. Miller, eds., *Nuclear Arguments: Understanding the Strategic Nuclear Arms and Arms Control Debates* (Ithaca: Cornell University Press, 1989); Robert A. Levine, *The Arms Debate* (Cambridge: Harvard University Press, 1963); Robert Jervis, *The Illogic of American Nuclear Strategy* (Ithaca: Cornell University Press, 1984) and *The Meaning of the Nuclear Revolution* (Ithaca: Cornell University Press, 1989); Fred Kaplan, *The Wizards of Armageddon* (New York: Simon and Schuster, 1983); S. E. Miller, ed., *Strategy and Nuclear Deterrence* (Princeton: Princeton University Press, 1984); George H. Quester, "Cultural Barriers to an Acceptance of Deterrence," in R. Kolkowicz, ed., *The Logic of Nuclear Terror* (Boston: Allen and Unwin, 1987); Graham T. Allison, Albert Carnesale, and Joseph S. Nye, Jr., eds., *Hawks, Doves, and Owls: An Agenda for Avoiding Nuclear War* (New

THE CLASSICAL THEORY OF NUCLEAR DETERRENCE

When the Soviet Union detonated an atomic bomb in 1949, American strategic theorists faced an alarming and unprecedented crisis. The overriding question in national security was how to prevent a nuclear attack on the United States. The problem attracted some of the best strategic minds of a generation, who devised what might be called the classical theory of nuclear deterrence. Many people describe the classical theory as the conceptual foundation of our national security policy and the strategic conventional wisdom. It remains an important intellectual beacon even today as we enter new and uncharted strategic waters.[2]

Deterrence Not Defense

The classical strategists concluded immediately that a defense against nuclear attack would be out of the question. The problem is not just that nuclear weapons are incredibly destructive, but that they are small and cheap. Atomic warheads can be delivered in such large numbers, all at once, and at such high velocity that the offense becomes overwhelming. Nuclears, it was claimed, were "the absolute weapon." Forty years later, nobody has devised a nuclear defense that is both reliable and affordable. But even if a defense were nearly perfect, a nuclear attack of middling size would still be calamitous. Because effective defenses seemed out of reach, the classical strategists concluded that national security must rest on deterrence.[3]

York: W. W. Norton, 1985); Spurgeon M. Keeny, Jr., and Wolfgang K. H. Panofsky, "MAD versus NUTS," *Foreign Affairs* 60 (Winter 1981–82); Charles L. Glaser, *Analyzing Strategic Nuclear Policy* (Princeton: Princeton University Press, 1990); Aaron Friedberg, "A History of the U.S. Strategic 'Doctrine' – 1945 to 1980," *Journal of Strategic Studies* (December 1980); and Adam M. Garfinkle, "The Politics of Space Defense," *Orbis* 28 (Summer 1984).

2 Among the canons of the classical literature are Bernard Brodie et al., *The Absolute Weapon* (New York: Harcourt, Brace, 1946); Thomas Schelling, *The Strategy of Conflict* (New York: Oxford University Press, 1960) and *Arms and Influence* (New Haven: Yale University Press, 1966); Albert Wohlstetter, "The Delicate Balance of Terror," *Foreign Affairs* 37 (January 1959); Bernard Brodie, *Strategy in the Missile Age* (Princeton: Princeton University Press, 1959); Daniel Ellsberg, "The Crude Analysis of Strategic Choices," RAND P-2183, 1959. Some skillful applications and extensions of the classical viewpoint include Robert Jervis, *The Illogic of American Nuclear Strategy* (Ithaca: Cornell University Press, 1984); Herbert Scoville, *MX: Prescription for Disaster* (Cambridge: The MIT Press, 1981); Sidney Drell, Philip J. Farley, and David Holloway, *The Reagan Strategic Defense Initiative: A Technical, Political, and Arms Control Assessment*, Stanford University Center for International Security and Arms Control, July 1984; and George Rathjens, "The Dynamics of the Arms Race," *Scientific American* April 1969.

3 The following passages capture the classical attitude: "The significance of nuclear weapons . . . depends above all on the possibilities of defense against them in strategic attack. When we stress their utterly revolutionary and potentially annihilistic effects, in international politics as well as in strategy, we are implicitly assuming that the prognosis for defense is not good." Bernard Brodie, *Strategy in the Missile Age* (Princeton: Princeton University

Classical Axiom I: Nuclear weapons convey an insuperable advantage to the offense.

Secure Second Strikes and Credible Central Deterrence

The pivotal idea in classical deterrence theory can be expressed in a second simple axiom:

Classical Axiom II: What deters is not the ability to strike first, but to strike second.

To fathom why classical strategists defended ballistic missile submarines but not the MX missile, why they promoted the mobile Midgetman but opposed SDI and civil defenses, and why they preferred invulnerable nuclear arsenals to complete nuclear disarmament – even after the Cold War collapsed – it is necessary to unravel both clauses in this pithy formula.

In order to deter the Soviet Union, the theorists reasoned, the United States had to make the following threat credible: If you launch a nuclear attack on us, your country will be destroyed in turn. If the leaders of the Soviet Union believed the threat, and they were rational, they would be deterred from attacking by the expectation of devastating retaliation. What deters the Soviets' *first strike* is the anticipation of an American *second strike*. Threatening to strike the Soviets first, on the other hand, would not only fail to deter, but might actually trigger a nuclear war. If the other side concludes that we are going to strike first, then their choices are reduced to two unpleasant alternatives. They can absorb the full brunt of our strategic arsenal or try to blunt the blow by striking first themselves and destroying as many nuclear weapons as possible. In this way, first strike threats become anti-deterrents, inviting the opponent to strike before you do. Stable deterrence requires an ability to strike second, *after* being struck first.[4]

The deterrence problem boils down, then, to making the retaliatory threat

Press, 1959), p. 173. "The only way to protect our country from nuclear war is to prevent nuclear war." Gerard Smith, *Arms Control Today* 16 (March 1986).

4 In a seminal article called "The Delicate Balance of Terror," Albert Wohlstetter brought the crucial distinction between strike-first and strike-second capabilities to wide public attention: "Since sputnik, the United States has made several moves to assure . . . that we will match or over-match Soviet technology and, specifically, Soviet offensive technology. . . . This has meant confusing deterrence with matching or exceeding the enemy's ability to strike first. To deter an attack means being able to strike back in spite of it. It means, in other words, a capability to strike second. In the last year or two, there has been a growing awareness of the distinction between "strike-first" and "strike-second" capability. "The Delicate Balance of Terror," *Foreign Affairs* 37 (January 1959). In *The Strategy of Conflict*, Thomas Schelling expressed the same idea: "It is not our existing capacity to destroy Russia that deters a Russian attack against us, but our capacity to retaliate after being attacked ourselves. . . . There is a difference between a balance of terror in which *either* side can obliterate the other and one in which *both* sides can do it no matter who strikes first." *The Strategy of Conflict* (New York: Oxford University Press, 1960).

credible. On the face of things, credibility seems to require two capabilities. You must first demonstrate the *technical wherewithal* to strike second, after the opponent's first strike, and then the *political will* to carry out the threat, should the occasion arise. In the domain of *central deterrence* – the deterrence of attacks on supreme national interests like the urban-industrial base – the political element of the problem seems easy. Who could doubt that the United States would retaliate, if it were able to, after a nuclear attack on its cities? The trickier problem is finding the technical wherewithal to retaliate. The trouble is that anyone launching a surprise attack would surely try to destroy the victim's nuclear arsenal in the process, before it could be fired back in retaliation. A rational nuclear first strike necessarily entails a *counterforce* attack on the adversary's strategic forces. The key to making the deterrent threat credible is to ensure that a counterforce attack can't succeed. The country needs, in other words, a *secure second strike* – a nuclear force that can weather a determined first strike and still deliver devastating retaliation.

Mutual Fear of Surprise Attack

We can now see that the first clause in the second classical axiom implies a sobering message – the existence of nuclear arsenals *per se* does not necessarily guarantee stable deterrence. The mere ability to drop nuclear bombs on the enemy's country ("the ability to strike first" in a literal sense) provides no deterrent at all, if those nuclear forces are vulnerable to preemptive attack. Even worse, the "ability to strike first" in a politically rational sense entails a counterforce capability that threatens the other side's deterrent. If the two adversaries simply build large stockpiles of nuclear bombers or missiles, without securing them from nuclear attack, the result would be the antithesis of stable deterrence, or what was called *the mutual fear of surprise attack*. Neither side could deter the other, and both could eliminate a mortal peril by striking first. Even if nobody wanted a nuclear war, everyone would be tempted to start one in such an environment. By rewarding the side who strikes first, vulnerable counterforce weapons generate *first-strike instability* – the cardinal problem to be avoided in the classical theory.

Deterrence Must Be Mutual

An interesting question, if we accept this line of reasoning, is whether it would be adequate to secure our own second strike, even if the opponent does not do so. In fact, wouldn't it be better to secure a second strike for ourselves *and* to hold the enemy's nuclear forces at risk? To this question, the classical theorists answered a resounding NO. To be stable, they insisted, deterrence must be mutual.

Suppose that political leaders conclude during a major crisis that their nuclear forces are vulnerable to an absolutely disarming or *splendid first strike*, while the other side's forces are mostly invulnerable. What does one do when the enemy can launch a nuclear attack with impunity? As soon as the political leaders conclude that an attack is coming, their opponent's secure second strike becomes irrelevant. Deterrence has already failed. At that point, the problem is no longer avoiding attack, but limiting the damage it will do. If the threatened side fears the worst, and it has any capability to limit damage by striking first itself, then it might become desperate enough to use it. But now the superior side, realizing the inferior side's dilemma, would have all the more reason to strike first itself – even if it had no such intention in the first place. But this thinking gives the inferior side all the more reason to become desperate. And so on, back and forth. So long as the inferior side's nuclear forces provide some *damage limiting* capability, their vulnerability creates an incentive for *both* sides to strike first. To be stable, then, deterrence must be mutual. Both sides must have a secure second strike.[5]

Classical Axiom III: Deterrence must be mutual.

MAD

We can now see that the notorious acronym MAD – for *mutual assured destruction* – actually represents the classical solution to the mutual fear of

5 Seminal expositions of these ideas include Daniel Ellsberg, "The Crude Analysis of Strategic Choices" (Santa Monica: RAND P-2183, 1959), and Thomas Schelling, *The Strategy of Conflict*. Schelling argues: "The balance [of terror] is stable only when *neither*, in striking first, can destroy the other's ability to strike back. . . . If *each* side were confident that its own forces could survive an attack, but also that it could not destroy the other's power to strike back – there would be no powerful temptation to strike first." *The Strategy of Conflict* (New York: Oxford University Press, 1960), 233–234. Elsewhere Schelling argues for mutuality this way: "If in fact we have either no intention or no political capacity for a first strike, it would usually be helpful if the enemy were confidently assured of this. His own manifest invulnerability to our first strike could be to our advantage if it relieved him of a principal concern that might motivate him to try striking first. If *he* has to worry about the exposure of *his* strategic force to a surprise attack by *us*, *we* have to worry about it too." *The Strategy of Conflict*, p. 238.

The forcefulness of the early formulations can be appreciated in many recent works like Herbert Scoville's *MX: Prescription for Disaster*. Scoville states the classical argument this way: "Deterrence had to be two-sided or mutual in order to ensure that neither American or Soviet leaders would have any incentive to launch a nuclear strike. Thus paradoxically it was in the U.S. interest for the Soviets also to have an invulnerable strategic deterrent force because this would reduce incentives for them to unleash their nuclear weapons in a time of crisis. . . . If there is a situation where they see we could gain great advantage by a first strike, they might decide to launch a preemptive strike in a period of high tension." *MX: Prescription for Disaster* (Cambridge: The MIT Press, 1981).

surprise attack. When *both* sides possess a secure second strike, the anticipation of certain retaliation (or assured destruction) deters each one from starting a nuclear war. If either side lacks a secure retaliatory force, on the other hand, two noxious forms of instability arise:

• Arms Race Instability
  When either side threatens the other's deterrent, the endangered party will be forced to build more or better nuclear forces to ensure a sufficient retaliatory response. Technologies that undermine second strikes therefore propel the arms race.

• Crisis or "First-Strike" Instability
  Technologies that undermine secure second strikes (and therefore reward preemption) trigger the mutual fear of surprise attack during crises, and increase the probability of a nuclear exchange.

The overriding objective in classical deterrence theory is to avoid these instabilities by designing nuclear forces *on both sides* to discourage first strikes.

Strike-First and Strike-Second Weapons

From the fundamental axioms of deterrence, the classical strategists derived two basic principles for designing nuclear forces:

> Design Principle 1: Avoid technologies that undermine second strikes.
> Design Principle 2: Deploy technologies that secure second strikes.

Good technologies, or *strike-second forces*, secure retaliatory forces from preemptive attack. Bad technologies, or *strike-first forces,* neutralize the opponent's deterrent threat. According to the classical logic, the best weapons are those that can survive a first strike, but are themselves useless for striking first.

To put these principles into practice, it was necessary to derive the technical requirements for a secure second strike. As a matter of logic, it follows that each side needs several capabilities:

• Survivability (or invulnerable platforms)
  Deterrent forces must be able to survive a determined preemptive attack. Albert Wohlstetter's central concern in "The Delicate Balance of Terror" was the vulnerability of bomber bases built in the 1950s. The same issue reemerged during the late 1970s when silo-based ICBMs became potentially vulnerable to preemptive attack. The so-called WINDOW OF VULNERABILITY was a focus of intense debate during that time.

• Penetrability
  To reach their targets, second strike forces must not only survive preemptive attack, but penetrate any defenses that the adversary places in their way.

• Sufficiency
  Preemptive attack and nuclear defenses are the two generic threats to a secure second strike. After these threats have taken their toll, there must survive a

sufficient number of warheads to inflict devastating retaliation. How much destruction will be sufficient to deter depends on the opponent's scheme of values. Robert McNamara proposed one famous criterion for assured destruction. He believed that a capability to destroy 25% of the Soviet's population and 50% of its industrial capacity would deter any conceivable attack.

- Postive Control
  Beyond the physical systems for striking second, it is also necessary to secure the command organizations that control nuclear weapons. To maintain POSITIVE CONTROL – the ability to launch a retaliation on command – demands a secure system of *command, control, communication, and intelligence* (C³I). Otherwise the adversary can design a *decapitation attack* to destroy the organizations that control the nuclear arsenals.

These considerations suggest that technologies like the following would contribute to stable deterrence by securing second strikes:

- The Nuclear Triad
  By locating retaliatory forces on platforms that present different obstacles to the attacker – for example, on bombers, submarines, and hardened silos – a coordinated first strike becomes very difficult to achieve. An important application of this reasoning is the famous Scowcroft Commission Report, which discounted the Window of Vulnerability by invoking the confounding properties of the nuclear triad.
- Early Warning Systems
  Early warning against nuclear attack allows retaliatory forces to fly out from under the attack, before they are destroyed on the ground.
- Spy Satellites
  Spy satellites, in addition to providing early warning, ensure that each side can enumerate its adversary's arsenal, and therefore calculate the kind of first strike it can muster. Both sides can then take adequate measures to secure second strikes.
- Hardened Silos and Mobile Launchers
  Measures that defend or hide nuclear platforms from preemptive attack help secure second strikes.
- Submarine Launched Ballistic Missiles (SLBMs)
  Submarines provide virtually invulnerable platforms for ballistic missiles. For a long time, however, they did not allow sufficient accuracy to threaten hardened missile silos. In these ways, they epitomized the idea of a strike-second weapon.
- Careful Plans for the Devolution of Command Authority
  To avoid a paralyzing decapitation attack, provisions must be made for transferring command authority if the President is killed or incapacitated.

Classical principles also forbid strike-first weapons. The technological elements of a preemptive capability are taboo in classical theory because they set in motion the mutual fear of surprise attack:

- No Counterforce
  Systems that threaten to destroy the opponent's nuclear forces in a surprise attack are *destabilizing*. *Counterforce* weapons, especially *prompt hard-target killers* or *silo-busters* (highly accurate, stealthy, rapid delivery weapons) are what first-strikers need to destroy nuclear arsenals before they can be fired in retaliation. To

retaliate against unprotected societal assets like urban centers, industrial facilities, and agricultural lands only requires *countervalue* weapons (slow, dirty, inaccurate bombs). Countervalue weapons are fine for retaliating against cities, but are
unusable for nuclear first strikes.

Schelling's classic discussion goes this way: "It is precisely the weapons most
destructive of people that an anti–surprise attack scheme seeks to preserve – the
weapons of retaliation, the weapons whose mission is to punish rather than to fight,
to hurt the enemy afterwards, not to disarm him beforehand. A weapon that can
only hurt *people*, and cannot possibly damage the other side's striking force, is
profoundly defensive: it provides the possessor no incentive to strike first. It is the
weapon that is designed or deployed to destroy 'military' targets – to seek out the
enemy's missiles and bombers – that can exploit the advantage of striking first and
therefore provide a temptation to do so." [*The Strategy of Conflict*, p. 233]

Schelling's profile of a "pure strike-back weapon" had a profound influence on
arms controllers: ". . . the relatively inaccurate vehicle with a super-dirty bomb
that can kill just about everything in the enemy's country except a well-protected
or well-hidden retaliatory force, and that itself is so well-protected or well-hidden
as to be invulnerable to any weapons the other side might possess. Ideally, this
weapon would suffer no disadvantage in waiting to strike second and gain no
advantage in striking first." [*The Strategy of Conflict*, p. 240]

• No National Defenses Against Nuclear Attack
It's fine to build defenses for your retaliatory forces (like *hard point defenses* of
missile silos or mobile submarine platforms), but destabilizing to defend your
societal assets. A *national area defense* defeats the adversary's capability to retaliate, and therefore compromises its deterrent threat. Countries whose national
assets remain exposed to retaliation, on the other hand, clearly don't intend to
strike first. Both SDI and civil defense are bad ideas, classical theorists argue,
because they undermine the *mutual hostage relationship* that supports stable deterrence. In classical theory, one defends weapons not people.

• Negative Control
If you can't maintain *negative control* – the ability to prevent accidental or unau-
thorized launch – the other side can't be sure that you (or your agents) are
deterred. But if they fear you will strike first – for whatever reason – then they
might do so. In this way, a breakdown of negative control feeds the mutual fear of
surprise attack.

These considerations made the following technologies prime targets for
classical critics (and prime candidates for arms control bans):

• Highly Accurate, Silo-Based, MIRVed ICBMs (like the American MX missile or
the Soviet SS-18)
A missile with Multiple, Independently-targetable Reentry Vehicles (MIRVs)
carries several warheads, each of which can be aimed at separate targets. When a
single missile can threaten several missiles of the other side, a disarming first
strike can become feasible – provided the warheads are accurate and reliable
enough, and the opponent's missiles are vulnerable to nuclear attack.

Suppose both sides locate 1000 missiles in vulnerable silos, each armed with a
single highly accurate warhead. Since no engineering system is ever perfect (missile systems are roughly 80% reliable), neither side can count on destroying more
than 800 or so of its opponent's missiles in an all out first strike. That leaves 200

available for a devastating retaliation. If each missile carries 10 warheads, on the other hand, *both* sides can destroy all 1000 of their opponent's missiles with virtual certainty, and still have several hundred missiles left over.

For these reasons, classical thinkers were steadfast opponents of the heavily MIRVed, silo-based MX missile. An outstanding classical critique is Herbert Scoville, *MX: Prescription for Disaster* (Cambridge: The MIT Press, 1981).

• SDI
Classical thinkers violently opposed SDI. A space-based defense against ballistic missiles would defend not just nuclear forces but the whole national territory. Unless such systems were absolutely leakproof – which seems impossible – they could deprive both sides of their nuclear deterrent against a first strike. Civil defenses for populations would have the same destabilizing effect. Defenses of cities undermine the *mutual hostage relationship* that provides the foundation of stable deterrence.

• Anti-Submarine Warfare (ASW)
The ability to seek out and destroy ballistic missile submarines would erode the sea-based leg of the nuclear triad. Since submarines are the most secure platform against a nuclear first strike, an effective means of anti-submarine warfare would be potentially extremely destabilizing.

Thomas Schelling described ASW this way: "The Navy is urgently seeking a better system of defense against submarines. . . . We have to try to detect submarines because we can't afford to let the Russians find a technique that we do not know. Yet perhaps we ought simultaneously to hope that the problem is insoluble. If it were insoluble, . . . stable deterrence might be technologically possible." [*The Strategy of Conflict*, p. 238]

• Anti-Satellite Warfare (ASAT)
An ability to destroy spy satellites could blind the opponent to a nuclear first strike.

• Nuclear Disarmament
Because nuclear weapons can not be "uninvented," complete nuclear disarmament might be highly destabilizing. Neither side would possess a deterrent if the other decided to rearm covertly, and only a few extra weapons on either side would make a huge difference. Classical theorists prefer the robust mutual deterrence provided by large invulnerable arsenals to the chancier prospects of mutual disarmament.

Shelling argues as follows: "For anything like equal numbers on both sides, the likelihood of successfully wiping out the other side's missiles becomes less and less as the missiles on both sides increase. And the *tolerance* of the system increases too . . . . Neither side needs to worry if it falls behind a little bit, and neither has any great hope that it could draw far enough ahead to have the kind of dominance it would need. . . . Within the logic of stable deterrence, [it] is *not* a foregone conclusion that disarmament, in the literal sense, leads to stability." [*The Strategy of Conflict*, p. 237]

Summary on Classical Weapon Preferences

The disarmingly simple axioms of classical deterrence theory support a rich set of preferences about nuclear forces and arms control. Since the earliest days of the nuclear era, the goal of classical theorists has been to configure the nuclear arsenals for stable mutual deterrence. The key idea is to maintain secure second strikes on both sides, while avoiding technologies that undermine them. Classical thinking informs arms control agreements even to this day, including the recent START II treaty to eliminate land-based (but not sea-based) MIRVed ballistic missiles.

ANTI-CLASSICAL DETERRENCE THEORIES

The controlling idea of anti-classical deterrence theories can also be put in a nutshell – MAD is BAD. A sharp antipathy toward the MAD philosophy of deterrence is the unifying thread in a large and diverse literature whose gist can be gathered from the following examples:

No matter how cataclysmic the threatened "assured destruction," those calculated decisions which our deterrent seeks to prevent are not the sole processes that could lead to nuclear war. [Fred Charles Iklé, "Can Nuclear Deterrence Last Out the Century?" *Foreign Affairs* 51, No. 2 (January 1973)]

Although it is commonly called a "strategy," "assured destruction" was by itself the antithesis of strategy. Unlike any strategy that ever preceded it throughout the history of armed conflict, it ceased to be useful precisely where military strategy is supposed to come into effect: at the edge of war. [Benjamin S. Lambeth, *Selective Nuclear Options in American and Soviet Strategic Policy* (Santa Monica: RAND, R-2034-DDRE, December 1976)]

MAD's perfectly sound logic is based on very implausible psychological assumptions: the attacker is supposed to be safely deterred by his cautious calculations of the losses that retaliation would inflict upon him, while the victim is supposed to be entirely reckless in unleashing the reflex-like retaliation MAD calls for. This reverses the usual character attributes of victims and aggressors. [Edward Luttwak, "Nuclear Strategy: The New Debate," in *Strategy and Politics: Collected Essays* (New Brunswick, N.J.: Transaction Books: 1980), p. 38]

The principal intellectual culprit in our pantheon of false strategic gods is the concept of stability. The still-authoritative and inhibiting ideas of crisis and arms race instability . . . have misinformed the structure of our thinking. First and foremost, the Soviet leadership fears defeat, not the suffering of damage. [Colin Gray, "Nuclear Strategy: A Case for a Theory of Victory," in Steven E. Miller, ed., *Strategy and Nuclear Deterrence* (Princeton: Princeton University Press, 1984)]

In the event of a Soviet counterforce attack, we could forgo a counterforce response and devote all of our remaining forces to an attack on Soviet population and industry. But is it desirable for a future president to be in the position of having no other useful option? . . . The Soviets see the importance of deterring the deterrent; in other words, they wish to be able, after a counterforce attack, to maintain sufficient reserve megatonnage to hold U.S. population and industry hostage in a wholly asymmetrical relationship. . . . The objective [should be] to deny to the Soviet Union the possibility of a successful war-fighting capability. [Paul Nitze, "Deterring Our Deterrent," *Foreign Policy* 25 (Winter 1976–77)]

Mutual assured destruction thinking . . . virtually ensures self-deterrence and denies us the freedom of strategic-nuclear action that is a premise of NATO's strategy of flexible response. . . . There can be no evading the requirement [for] nuclear employment options that a reasonable political leader would not be self-deterred from ever executing. [Colin Gray, "Nuclear Strategy: A Case for a Theory of Victory," in Steven E. Miller, ed., *Strategy and Nuclear Deterrence* (Princeton: Princeton University Press, 1984)]

. . . . Those who espouse MAD rarely go beyond the assumption that the attacker's purpose is to strike preemptively before he is attacked. . . . What if the Soviets launch a nuclear attack, but one directed solely at our allies and which avoids any damage to the U.S.? How long can an explicitly suicidal nuclear response remain a credible threat in the eyes of our allies or the Soviet Union? [Fred S. Hoffman, "The SDI in U.S. Nuclear Strategy," *International Security* 10, No. 1 (Summer 1985)]

Extended Not Central Deterrence

The point of departure for anti-classical writers invariably boils down to the same troubling question: What if deterrence fails – not absolutely, but in some less-than-total way? If the Soviets launched an attack on our allies in Europe, on our interests in the Middle East, or even against our vulnerable missile silos (but nothing else), what would we do? The concern lurking behind the question is that a classical force posture would leave us without any tenable options, save for surrender.

The anti-classical scenarios raise the problem of *extended nuclear deterrence*. How can we extend a *nuclear umbrella* to cover our less-than-vital interests? Naturally, if the Soviets believed that any attack against American interests would trigger *massive retaliation* upon their cities and society, they would be deterred from every conceivable aggression. But could such threats remain credible if we designed our nuclear forces according to classical principles? By deploying dirty, inaccurate, countervalue weapons and by forgoing nuclear defenses of our national territory, a classical design carefully preserves the invulnerability of the Soviet's nuclear arsenal and our vulnerability to it. In a condition of mutual vulnerability, responding massively to a limited Soviet aggression would only produce a response in kind. As long as the Soviets' initial attack did not immediately jeopardize our national survival, a deterrent threat that entailed mutual destruction would be grossly irrational to carry out – and therefore politically *incredible*.

These objections drove two long-standing and acrimonious debates about national security strategy during the Cold War. One concerned our deterrent umbrella in Europe, where for a long time the Soviet's substantial conventional superiority apparently precluded meeting a ground attack on its own terms. Recognizing the West's conventional inferiority, NATO doctrine threatened a *nuclear first use* after a Soviet invasion. But if an "assured destruction" retaliation against Soviet territory would simply be met in kind, the President's choices would be reduced to "surrender or suicide." Since no rational American leader would willingly "sacrifice New York for Paris," the MAD posture did not seem a credible deterrent against the Soviet conventional threat.

The same kind of reasoning was even applied to a nuclear first strike against vulnerable missile silos on American territory. The former Secretary of Defense, James Schlesinger, pressed this argument during the middle 1970's after Soviet force modernization began to present a silo-busting capability. In the *Schlesinger scenario*, the Soviets preemptively disarm the land-based leg of the American triad, and then present the American President with a *fait accompli* – accept your relative nuclear inferiority (and perhaps our seizure of some prize like the Middle Eastern oil fields) and we will do nothing more. If you retaliate against Soviet cities with your remaining slow bombers or inaccurate SLBMs, we will destroy your cities in turn:

A President of the United States under those circumstances where, as a result of an attack against the ICBM sites, there are already approximately 800,000 fatalities, would know that if he responds by destroying the urban industrial base of the Soviet Union approximately 95 million American fatalities would be added to that number. [James Schlesinger, Testimony before the Senate Committee on Foreign Relations, September 1975]

A threat of *massive retaliation*, it seemed evident, would be deterred by the prospective Soviet third strike – or to apply the misnomer that became popular, we would be *self-deterred* by the inappropriate design of our nuclear forces and doctrine. The retaliatory threat implied by the MAD doctrine seemed "logically incredible" whenever American cities were not the direct target of a first strike.

Since we ourselves find it difficult to believe that we would actually implement the threat of assured destruction in response to a limited attack on military targets that caused relatively few civilian casualties, there can be no certainty that, in a crisis, prospective opponents would be deterred from testing our resolve. [James Schlesinger, Department of Defense Annual Report, FY 1975]

Limited Nuclear Options, Flexible Response, and Limited War Doctrines

In order to extend credible deterrence to less-than-vital interests, anti-classical theorists argued that the United States needed a capability for less-than-total nuclear retaliation. To avoid provoking a nuclear cataclysm, it needed a menu of *limited nuclear options* or *flexible responses* that tailored punishments to fit the crime (actually, to fit all the possible crimes). As

James Schlesinger put it, "In order to deter you must have a threat that you are prepared to implement, and that your opponent perceives that you are prepared to implement."

What made these reasonable-sounding proposals controversial were the nuclear force prescriptions that typically came bundled with them. Time and again, the systems advocated for credible extended deterrence directly violated the classical canons of stable central deterrence. The tensions between the two kinds of deterrence can be seen in the debate about the Schlesinger scenario:

Flexibility of response is essential because, despite our best efforts, we cannot guarantee that deterrence will never fail. Many types of targets can be pre-programmed as options. . . . In some circumstances, a set of hard targets might be the most appropriate objective for our retaliation, and I realize this is a subject fraught with great emotion. To enhance deterrence, we may also want a *more efficient hard-target-kill capability* than we now possess. [James Schlesinger, Department of Defense Annual Report, FY 1975] [Emphasis added]

To understand why theorists of extended deterrence often prescribed weapons that defied classical principles, it is necessary to explore the murky intellectual swamp called theories of "limited nuclear war."

As soon as either side crosses the nuclear threshold with a "flexible response" to some limited aggression, the problem of controlling escalation immediately becomes an overwhelming concern. During the Cold War, the usual plan advocated by the defenders of flexible response was to retaliate directly against Soviet military and nuclear forces, while withholding attacks against the Soviet cities. The object was to target the means of aggression directly, to intimidate the Soviets into backing down, to preserve a deterrent against further Soviet escalation, to avoid committing genocide against innocent civilians, and to avoid provoking attacks against our own cities.[6]

Such a strategy seems especially attractive when our side enjoys a measure of *escalation dominance* so that the Soviets can not simply match our flexible response tit-for-tat. If we could deploy a series of intermediate nuclear capabilities like battlefield nuclear weapons, short range nuclear missiles, and tactical nuclear fighters – capabilities the Soviets didn't have

---

6 The *no cities* strategies evolved in the 1950's after the Soviets began to develop their own nuclear forces and the Dulles doctrine of *massive retaliation* appeared less and less credible. Gradually the new doctrine moved toward *counterforce no cities*. Important early discussions appear in Bernard Brodie, "Nuclear Weapons: Strategic or Tactical?," *Foreign Affairs* (January 1954); William W. Kaufmann, "Limited Warfare," in W. W. Kaufmann, ed., *Military Policy and National Security* (Princeton: Princeton University Press, 1956); Herman Kahn, *On Thermonuclear War* (Princeton: Princeton University Press, 1960) and *On Escalation* (New York: Praeger, 1965); Henry A. Kissinger, *Nuclear Weapons and Foreign Policy* (New York: Harper, 1957); Robert E. Osgood, *Limited War* (Chicago: University of Chicago Press, 1957); and Klaus Knorr and Thornton Read, *Limited Strategic War* (New York: Praeger, 1962). Dulles' speech on massive retaliation is reprinted in the *Department of State Bulletin* 25 (January 1954).

themselves – then they would be deterred from engaging in lower levels of violence by the prospect of becoming militarily inferior at higher levels. The Soviets would realize that if they tried to prevail in a game of one-upsmanship, the process would eventually lead to a rung on the *escalation ladder* where they would be outgunned. At that point their choices would be reduced to submitting or escalating toward full blown strategic exchanges. Looking ahead to that level of the game, and realizing that submission would become the only possible choice, they would be dissuaded from playing in the first place.

Flexible response eventually became the official strategy of NATO, which proceeded to deploy a vast quantity of nuclear artillery, mines, fighters, and short-range forces. The trouble was that the Soviets stubbornly refused to concede escalation dominance. Whenever NATO created a new category of nuclear weaponry, the Soviets matched with deployments of their own. As they did so, the escalation ladder became more and more elaborate, with fewer clear discontinuities between limited nuclear war and unconstrained city exchanges. In the process, it became less and less evident how escalation could ever be controlled to our advantage, especially when the Soviets enjoyed superiority on the conventional first rung. Without some physical asymmetry in the two nuclear arsenals, the game of escalation boiled down to a deadly war of nerves resembling the *game of chicken*. At each stage of the game, the choice would be to submit (by swerving) or to continue on a collision course in the hope that the other guy might have the lower threshold of nerve (or pain). Who might chicken out first, if indeed anyone would, seemed hard to predict. Since neither side could observe the other's *resolve*, and since defeat would be a political disaster for the leaders who accepted it (as it proved to be in the Cuban Missile Crisis and Vietnam), it seemed possible that rational players might slowly but surely escalate into oblivion, each hoping that the next turn of the screw would induce the other side to quit.[7]

The anti-classical theorists were propelled by these prospects toward the kind of counterforce and defensive capabilities that classical theory had declared *verboten*. On one hand they were convinced that flexible response was the only way to achieve credible extended deterrence. At the same time, they believed that the Soviet Union was far more reckless and cold-blooded than the United States. The prospect of engaging the Soviets from a position of parity in a game of nuclear chicken therefore seemed to be an uninviting

---

7 Formal game theoretic analysis shows that the escalation game need not even favor the side with the greater resolve. Because the other side's resolve remains uncertain, the better bluffer can win the game, as in the game of poker. For a careful discussion, see Robert Powell, *Nuclear Deterrence Theory: The Search for Credibility* (Cambridge: Cambridge University Press, 1990).

and unreliable foundation for national security. The anti-classicals much preferred the kind of manifest military superiority that provided escalation dominance. America's strength, they argued, was its technological, economic, and scientific prowess, not its recklessness and aggressiveness. A prudent strategy should exploit those strengths, not forsake them.

As the Soviets gradually matched the American moves at the lower rungs of the nuclear ladder, the quest for escalation dominance naturally proceeded toward the hardened strategic arsenals that composed the Soviet's central nuclear deterrent. The goal was to achieve the kind of *damage limiting* counterforce and defensive capabilities that would give the United States an unbeatable trump card at the highest levels of nuclear violence. Only then would our threats of limited nuclear retaliation be credible and compelling deterrents.[8]

To cement the argument, the anti-classicals produced much evidence that the Soviets followed a crude anti-classical logic themselves. Soviet military doctrine, they argued, rejected any concept of mutual deterrence or limited war. Instead, the Soviets believed in striking decisively, with everything they had, as soon as a war seemed inevitable. Their military doctrine emphasized fighting to win, and their nuclear deployments reflected that objective. By procuring as much counterforce and defensive potential as possible, the Soviets seemed to approach nuclear war in the old-fashioned way – seeking ways to minimize damage to themselves and to defeat the other side's military forces.

The guidelines of Soviet nuclear strategy . . . resulted in the unequivocal rejection of the notion of the "absolute weapon" and all the theories that U.S. strategists had deduced from it. Those who had control of Soviet Russia's nuclear arsenal were not

---

8 The quest for dominance up the escalation ladder is better understood, perhaps, as an important conceptual trend in anti-classical thinking, rather than as a literal chronological sequence. Some theorists advocated a *damage limiting* nuclear posture from the very outset of the nuclear era. Other anti-classicals stopped short of advocating a full blown counterforce threat to the Soviet central arsenal, emphasizing countermilitary capabilities instead. A common theme was that nuclear weapons did have military utility, beyond merely deterring themselves, and that active plans should be made to use them.

The conceptual trend toward strategic counterforce is evident in the following exchange between James Schlesinger and Senator Muskie:

> Senator: May I say I understand the need for a conventional deterrence in Europe as well, but that in-between is where I cannot get the feeling.
> Schlesinger: Of course, we have an in-between deterrent in the sense that we have war plans that contemplate the employment of tactical nuclear weapons in Europe. What we are doing here is to apply the same selectivity with regard to strategic forces as has been historically contemplated with regard to the tactical nuclear force. [Testimony Before Senate Committee on Foreign Relations, September 1975]

Many writers have described the tension between classical deterrence postures and damage-limiting capabilities. A clear discussion appears in George Rathjens, "Dynamics of the Arms Race," *Scientific American* (April 1969).

thinking in terms of mutual deterrence. The strategic doctrine adopted by the USSR calls for a policy diametrically opposite to that adopted in the United States by the predominant community of civilian strategists: not deterrence but victory, not sufficiency in weapons but superiority, not retaliation but offensive action. The doctrine has five related elements: (1) preemption (first strike), (2) quantitative superiority in arms, (3) counterforce targeting, (4) combined arms operations, and (5) defense. [Richard Pipes, "Why the Soviet Union Thinks It Could Fight and Win a Nuclear War," *Commentary* (July 1977), p. 31]

To deter an adversary that's fighting to win on the nuclear battlefield, the anti-classicals insisted, nothing could be worse than a doctrine that guarantees the survival of the Soviet's nuclear forces, that targets civilian rather than military capabilities, and that assumes from the start that nuclear wars are "unwinnable." When the opponent only respects military superiority, the last thing one wants are countervalue weapons that have no military value, and a defenseless posture that guarantees vulnerability to threats of escalation. Threatening the Soviet's cities with slow, dirty, horrendous bombs does nothing to stop their armies, nor anything to prevent their nuclear forces from hitting you back. A MAD strategy of deterrence only plays into the Soviet's hands, allowing them to exploit their counterforce and defensive capabilities to achieve escalation dominance.

Instead, the anti-classicals argued, extended deterrence requires a decisive capability to prevail in a limited nuclear war. Because the Soviets are demonstrably brutal and indifferent to human suffering (the Communist dictatorship had already killed millions of its own citizens after all), the threat to punish the Soviet population was not an effective deterrent. Against a coarse and aggressive opponent, what works is *deterrence by denial*, not *deterrence by punishment*. To control escalation, you must deny with brute force the opponent's attempts to hurt you. Doing so requires a *countervailing strategy* – or a "theory of victory" – that makes certain military defeat the overwhelming obstacle to Soviet adventurism.

As might be imagined, this train of logic produced a head-on collision with the partisans of classical theory. The anti-classical program produced two intense weapon procurement debates in the United States – one about *"second strike" counterforce* (or prompt-hard-target-killing) capabilities like the MX missile, the other about *strategic defenses* like the ABM and SDI. Defenders of the silo-busting MX, including Henry Kissinger, argued that

so long as the Soviets had to fear a counterforce attack in response to local aggression, their inhibition against such adventures would be considerable. [Henry Kissinger, *Years of Upheaval* (Boston: Little Brown, 1982), p. 999]

The same reasoning led anti-classical theorists to become staunch defenders of *territorial ballistic missile defenses* like SDI and the earlier ABM. An effective defense against ballistic missile attacks was, of course, the ultimate form of escalation dominance, since it took American societal assets out of hostage in any escalation game with the Soviets.

If escalation discipline is to be imposed upon the Soviet Union, even in the direst of situations, potential damage to North America has to be limited. Damage-limitation has to involve both counterforce action and active and passive defenses. [Colin Gray, "Nuclear Strategy: A Case for a Theory of Victory," in Steven E. Miller, ed., *Strategy and Nuclear Deterrence* (Princeton: Princeton University Press, 1984]

Summary of Anti-Classical Weapon Preferences

The anti-classical attitude toward a great number of weapon systems can be inferred from two basic design principles:

- Counterforce is Good
  Effective deterrence is achievable only through possession of a striking power that threatens destruction of substantially all the enemy's long range nuclear delivery capability. A threat to destroy a large number of Soviet citizens does not repre-sent effective deterrence of a Soviet attack on the US and provides no deterrence to other forms of Soviet aggression such as an attack against another NATO country. [Air Force Commander's Conference Briefing Paper, 1960]
  [The measure of] relative capabilities and crisis stability that most clearly brings out the stability or potential instability of the relationship assesses the relative counterforce capabilities of each side and the countervalue capabilities remaining to each side after a two-sided counterforce exchange in which all useful coun-terforce targets have been addressed. [Paul Nitze, "Deterring Our Deterrent," *Foreign Policy* 25 (Winter 1976–77)]
- National Strategic Defenses are Good
  If we replace MAD with a view of deterrence based on a more realistic assessment of Soviet strategic objectives, we arrive at a radically different assessment of the effectiveness required for useful defenses . . . . Defenses with far less than leakproof effectiveness can so raise the offensive force requirements for attacks on military targets that [such attacks] will appear unattractive. [Fred S. Hoffman, "The SDI in U.S. Nuclear Strategy," *International Security* 10, No. 1 (Summer 1985)]
  The U.S. deterrent would rest on a defensive capability to deny plausibility to any Soviet "theory of victory." Strategic defense promises to strengthen the stability of deterrence by imposing major new uncertainties upon any potential attack. [Keith Payne and Colin S. Gray, "Nuclear Policy and the Defensive Transition," *Foreign Affairs* 62, No. 4 (Spring 1984)]

These principles produced a set of weapons prescriptions that departed dramatically from the classical list (see Table 2.1). While everyone agreed that the United States needed a secure second strike for itself, the two sides disagreed fundamentally about systems that threatened the Soviet's nu-clear arsenal. The classicals opposed such technologies, while the anti-classicals promoted them.

Table 2.1. *Classical versus anti-classical weapons*

	CLASSICAL	ANTI-CLASSICAL
MX-like MIRVed Missiles (MX)	Bad for All	U.S. (Only) Should Build
Anti-Submarine Warfare (ASW)	Bad for All	U.S. (Only) Should Build
Strategic Defense Initiative (SDI)	Bad for All	U.S. (Only) Should Build
Civil Defenses	Bad for All	U.S. (Only) Should Build
Anti-Satellite Warfare (ASAT)	Bad for All	U.S. (Only) Should Build
Invulnerable Platforms for Retaliatory Forces	Good for All	U.S. (Only) Should Build

The Classical Rejoinder

Classical writers attacked the anti-classical program by arguing that the quest for nuclear superiority would be costly, futile, and destabilizing. Such efforts would be expensive, particularly on the defensive side, because a nuclear offense costs much less to build than does the defense to negate it. The classical *action-reaction model* of the arms race implied that the Soviets would constantly upgrade their offensive forces to preserve a secure second strike.[9] To assume that the Soviets would simply stand still while we negated their retaliatory threat committed *the fallacy of the last move*. The more counterforce and strategic defense we built, the more they would expand their offense or take countermeasures to negate our damage limiting capabilities. The condition of mutual vulnerability is a fact of life that couldn't be eliminated by a technological fix. Unless we stopped seeking military superiority, the arms race would go on indefinitely and the probability of nuclear war would be needlessly increased.

To counter the arguments that MAD did not provide credible extended deterrence, the classical theorists designed a theory of limited war that did not require destabilizing weapons or military superiority.[10] They pinned

9 The following passages capture the classical attitude:
   "The Soviets have it within their technological and economic capability to offset any further damage limiting measures we might undertake, provided they are determined to maintain their deterrent against us. It is the virtual certainty that the Soviets will act to maintain their deterrent which casts such grave doubts on the advisability of our deploying the Nike-X [ABM] system." Robert McNamara, cited in Office of Technology Assessment, *Strategic Defenses* (Princeton: Princeton University Press, 1986), p. 46.
   "If you say to American strategic planners that we're going to make it harder for your weapons to penetrate, they don't say 'Well, we'll abandon the weapons.' They say 'We'll buy more,' or 'We'll design better ones.' The Soviets do exactly the same thing." McGeorge Bundy, "The McNeil/Lehrer News Hour," 3/12/85.
10 A classic formulation appears in Thomas Schelling's *Arms and Influence* (New Haven: Yale University Press, 1966). Schelling's ideas are elaborated in Robert Jervis' *The Illogic of American Nuclear Strategy* (Ithaca: Cornell University Press, 1984) and in his *The*

their argument on the *autonomous risk* that a limited nuclear war would spin out of control, whatever the participants' intentions. Even a limited countervalue response (dropping a bomb on one city, say) would set in motion an unpredictable escalatory dynamic that presented grave risks for everyone. Such *threats that leave something to chance* would provide ample deterrence against limited aggression, because both sides shared an overwhelming fear of nuclear catastrophe. Taking a step down the slippery slope toward the nuclear brink required neither battlefield nor counterforce superiority.

Because any extreme crisis and, even more, any use of force between the superpowers creates a chance of mutual destruction, military advantage loses most of its traditional meaning. . . . Armies do not have to be able to win in order to deter. As long as using force to change the status quo sets in motion forces that are hard to control, taking advantage of local military imbalances is extremely dangerous. [Robert Jervis, *The Meaning of the Nuclear Revolution* (Ithaca: Cornell University Press, 1989), p. 51]

Threats that leave something to chance are highly credible, because the uncertain dynamics of limited nuclear war make it impossible to preclude irrational behavior. In the presence of autonomous risk, incredible acts become all too possible. As Schelling puts it,

a country can threaten to stumble into war even if it can not credibly threaten to invite one. . . . If brinkmanship means anything, it means manipulating the shared risk of war. It means exploiting the danger that somebody may inadvertently go over the brink, dragging the other with him. [Thomas Schelling, *Arms and Influence* (New Haven: Yale University Press, 1966), p. 98]

The trouble with *nuclear warfighting doctrines*, according to classical critics, is that they lower the threshold of nuclear first use without providing a reliable mechanism to keep escalation under control. Because escalation dominance is technically unachievable at the strategic level – mutual vulnerability is a fact of life – basing a strategy on nuclear superiority is a political pipe dream. We would be better advised to concentrate on avoiding a nuclear war, rather than preparing to win one.

WHY NOT STOP HERE?

Dividing nuclear doctrines into classical and anti-classical categories is hardly an innovation on my part. Readers who know the nuclear debate will agree, I hope, that my rendition is familiar and conventional. Similar schemes appear in countless articles and monographs, and, I would guess, in most university courses about nuclear strategy. A neat division between

Meaning of the Nuclear Revolution (Ithaca: Cornell University Press, 1989). They are studied more formally in Robert Powell, *Nuclear Deterrence Theory: The Search for Credibility* (Cambridge: Cambridge University Press, 1990).

nuclear 'hawks' and 'doves' seems to organize a great deal of the expert debate, and provides a sense of the political controversies that surround weapon programs, arms control, and defense policy. When George Bush and Russian President Boris Yeltsin agreed to sign the START II treaty, the *Los Angeles Times* reported that:

Yeltsin has been mired for months now in a wrenching battle with the increasingly powerful *right-wing* elements of Russia . . . . After recent clashes with his *conservative* Parliament, Yeltsin wanted to "assert himself as the person in charge of defense policy." . . . But Sergei Baburin, a *hard-line* Supreme Soviet deputy, predicted that the Russian president's push for START II might help bring about his political demise. [*L.A. Times*, p. A12, 12/31/92] [Emphasis added]

Even today, long after the Cold War has been declared finished, perennial strategic dichotomies like "hardliner–softliner" continue to dominate our perceptions of nuclear politics. As long as one understands the arguments of the competing schools of thought, is there really any need to go further?

If we accept the basic distinction between classical and anti-classical thinking, as I certainly did before my study began, an immediate difficulty is finding a way to explain what drives the contending points of view. The two nuclear doctrines contain so many interconnected arguments – about the nature of the adversary, about the probability that deterrence might fail, about what deters, about what is technologically possible, about the relative importance of central and extended threats, about what is credible, and more – that it is very hard to tell, simply by reading the debate, which elements are fundamental to each position, and which are driven by deeper considerations. These ambiguities quickly become exasperating because they make it difficult to understand what factors might change people's thinking or how political events affect the climate of nuclear opinion. To calculate how the end of the Cold War will influence the nuclear arms race, for example, it seems essential to know whether nuclear weapons preferences rest on images of the Soviet Union or whether they reflect more abstract considerations that don't depend at all on the enemy's attributes – or even whether an enemy exists.

Such questions seem so basic and elementary that one would think they must have been settled long ago. I believe that just the opposite is true. In the chapters ahead, I'll present lots of evidence that we never got the morphology of nuclear preferences right – or to put it another way, that my wholly conventional classification provides a terrible model of how real political actors think and reason about nuclear strategy. Without understanding the players' preferences, of course, it becomes very difficult to untangle the arms racing game they were playing during the Cold War. Neither would it be evident how the momentum of the arms race was broken, or what the new armaments game might be. Why nuclear preferences have for so long been misconstrued – and even neglected – is an interesting problem in its own right, and one I'll say more about later on. For now, let me suggest two reasons that seem especially important.

The Prescriptive Orientation of Deterrence Theory

While nuclear deterrence theories contain many empirical assumptions, their orientation is highly prescriptive. The usual purpose is to justify a design for nuclear forces and a doctrine that prescribes their use. An odd feature of such theories is that they scarcely acknowledge the nuclear debate they're embedded in – at least in the following sense. When Albert Wohlstetter writes in "The Delicate Balance of Terror" that ". . . to deter an attack means being able to strike back in spite of it. It means, in other words, a capability to strike second . . .," he implicitly assumes that deterrence has an inherent logic, apparent by reflection alone, and rationally compelling to all (perhaps after some instruction). To defend his prescriptions for designing nuclear forces, Wohlstetter appeals to *universal principles*, not to empirical evidence that describes how people actually think and reason about deterrence. Of course, contrary opinions necessarily violate the universal principles. They are dismissed as "confused."

Since Sputnik, the United States has made several moves to assure . . . that we will match or overmatch Soviet technology and, specifically, Soviet offensive technology. . . . This has meant confusing deterrence with matching or exceeding the enemy's ability to strike first. [Albert Wohlstetter, "The Delicate Balance of Terror," *Foreign Affairs* 37 (January 1959)]

When theorists on all sides adopted the same strategy of argument, the fact of the nuclear debate quickly got lost from theoretical view. Notice how the prolific anti-classical writer Colin Gray defends his preferred strategy with a formalistic, axiomatic proposition like Wohlstetter's (notice too the title of the book in which his essay appears!):

The authoritative idea at the heart of the countervailing strategy is the proposition that deterrent effect is maximized when a potential enemy anticipates the defeat of his arms. [Colin S. Gray, "Nuclear Deterrence and Technological Change," in Roman Kolkowicz, ed., *The Logic of Nuclear Terror* (Boston: Allen & Unwin, 1987), p. 173]

And what about the classical proposition that deterrence must be mutual? For Gray, these claims are "an error" and a "fashionable rationalization":

It would be an error to equate a condition of offense dominance necessarily with acquiescence in the theory that mutual vulnerability is either extant . . . or desirable. . . .

By the end of the twentieth century, the . . . equation in the United States of nuclear deterrence (and indeed of deterrence more broadly) with the mutual vulnerability of societies will be seen to have been but a fashionable, doctrinal rationalization of a transient phase in the history of military technology. [p. 172]

Throughout the prescriptive literature, the idea that different people might legitimately understand deterrent stability in different ways is simply given no quarter. As a result, advice about force structures rarely anticipates domestic political resistance or incorporates political strategies to overcome it. Notwithstanding the intensely partisan character of national security politics, nobody's theory of deterrence portrayed a factionally divided Soviet adversary, or made force designs conditional upon which faction prevailed. Still less did they suggest how force designs might transform domestic coalitions on either side. The classical theory never even distinguished the two adversaries, who could just as well have been labeled X and Y. In all of these ways, prescriptive deterrence theories remain remarkably apolitical. Their cool logic and universal postulates stand in marked contrast to the fierce battles that actually developed about the H-bomb, ABM, MX, B1, B2, SDI, and SALT.

Still, the nuclear debate wore on year after year, without resolution. Even since the Soviet Union unexpectedly collapsed, disagreements run deep about how to achieve security after the Cold War. For someone schooled in party politics, like me, the partisan character of the nuclear debate stands out as a central feature of the arms race – and itself a key to understanding the larger problem of what deters. If it is true that people do not share a common understanding of deterrence, then the prescriptive theorist's analytical strategy becomes deeply suspect. Absent a consensus, it makes no sense to invoke *the logic* of deterrence to defend nuclear policies or arms control treaties. What deters must depend on how real political actors think and reason about strategy – and who controls decisions – not on an autonomous "logic" that seems right to the theorist.

A Focus on Nuclear Doctrines

As soon as we accept the possibility that deterrence has no universal logic, a careful empirical understanding of nuclear thinking becomes imperative. To understand what drives strategic preferences, a natural first step is to examine the competing arguments offered by nuclear experts. Many good surveys of the nuclear debate take this approach, including two recent volumes called *Analyzing Strategic Nuclear Policy* and *Nuclear Arguments*. Steven Kull follows a similar path in the absorbing interviews with defense officials reported in *Minds at War*. These surveys try to uncover the roots of competing strategic mentalities by exploring the rationales experts offer to support their policy positions.

While *analyses of rationales* are interesting and instructive, they also have their drawbacks. One trouble is that the field of view remains very much interior to the debate itself. By focusing on the experts' arguments for and against flexible response, SDI, or strategic counterforce, one gets no sense of the connections between nuclear thinking and the wider arena of partisan politics. Suppose it were true that nuclear hawks and doves are really just conservatives and liberals in disguise (as we'll see later, they aren't – but suppose they were). If the analyst simply addresses the nuclear arguments on their own terms, worrying mainly about whether or not they make sense, it will be easy to misconstrue the engines of controversy. What appear as disagreements about limited war or Soviet military doctrine would actually be driven by "ideological" differences that sustain a military debate, along with many others. Without seeking evidence that transcends the debate itself, we'll never see it for what it is.[11]

A second problem when arguments and doctrines become the object of study is that we quickly lose track of how particular individuals think and reason. The typical review of the literature, like the one in this chapter, provides little or no sense about whose views each "doctrine" represents – if anyone's. The same problem even appears in Steven Kull's *Minds at War,* which, unlike most strategic surveys, rests on an explicit scheme for sampling expert subjects. Kull's data provide an opportunity to break out of the usual mold, but the opportunity is lost when he organizes his chapters around controversial issues like hard-target-kill capability, strategic defenses, and war-winning strategies. Because rationales for particular policies become the "unit of analysis," rather than the respondents' individual belief systems, the transcripts of the interviews are "cut and pasted" in such a way that we can't tell which quotations go together. It then becomes impossible to reconstruct how particular respondents' thinking is structured across the different issues.[12]

11 Charles L. Glaser, *Analyzing Strategic Nuclear Policy* (Princeton: Princeton University Press, 1990); L. Eden and S. E. Miller, eds., *Nuclear Arguments: Understanding the Strategic Nuclear Arms and Arms Control Debates* (Ithaca: Cornell University Press, 1989); Steven Kull, *Minds at War* (New York: Basic Books, 1988).

Specialists in political psychology and public opinion studies ordinarily analyze the connections between political and social beliefs across many different issues. The pattern of connections defines the structure of *political belief systems.* Surveys of nuclear arguments by specialists in security studies rarely provide the same wide angle view, and therefore run the risk of overlooking deeper origins of the nuclear debate. Barry Posen's *The Sources of Military Doctrine* (Ithaca: Cornell University Press, 1984) and Jack Snyder's *Myths of Empire* (Ithaca: Cornell University Press, 1991) are two exceptions to the rule, seeking explanations for strategic preferences that range outside the military debate itself. Robert Putnam's *The Beliefs of Politicians* (New Haven: Yale University Press, 1973) and Robert Axelrod's, *Structure of Decision: The Cognitive Maps of Political Elites* (Princeton: Princeton University Press, 1976) are elaborate attempts to reconstruct the large-scale belief systems of working politicians.

12 Other recent studies that make doctrines and debates the focus of study, rather than the belief systems of individuals, include Lawrence Freedman, *The Evolution of Nuclear*

Making arguments, rather than people, the focus of study creates several problems. In the first place, such evidence doesn't establish that the "doctrine" actually describes how any particular person thinks. That the "classical" Albert Wohlstetter eventually became a strong defender of the SDI program while the "anti-classical" James Schlesinger remained lukewarm should give us pause. Do the doctrines we distill from the literature really describe individuals' political thinking, or are they simply composite sketches – conceptual models of the debate – that wouldn't stand up to empirical testing? Without making individual belief systems the object of study, we'll never know. A clear sign of trouble is that very few of us feel comfortable placing our own views in simple strategic pigeonholes.

A second problem appears when we try to draw inferences from imputed strategic doctrines to the politics of the arms race. Notice that my account of classical and anti-classical reasoning provides no evidence about the relative frequency of the two competing viewpoints. Is the classical view actually the politically dominant conventional wisdom, as we so often hear?

For many years there has been a broad consensus on strategic policy among academicians, professional strategists, and their intellectual clientele in the media, Congressional staffs, and in many parts of the Executive. A majority in all these groups agrees that the only proper strategic doctrine for the United States is Robert McNamara's "mutual assured destruction." [Edward Luttwak, "Nuclear Strategy: The New Debate," in E. N. Luttwak, *Strategy and Politics* (New Brunswick, N.J.: Transaction Books, 1980)]

How do we know that a majority of these groups held the classical view? Unless we track individual opinions, who could tell? Similarly, if we don't address how individuals draw connections among different issues, we can't infer who will ally with whom, when, and why. When doctrines are the object of study, it becomes very difficult to draw careful inferences about the factional politics of the arms race.

A final difficulty with analyses of doctrines and rationales is their focus on expert reasoning. When we survey the nuclear debate, as I have in this chapter, it is easy to forget that many players who influence nuclear policies have little or no strategic training at all. Military specialists certainly play an important role in the arms race, but so do voters, congressmen, apparatchiks, parliamentarians, protesters, and presidents. When so many influential players are manifestly not experts about nuclear issues, it is reason-

---

Strategy (New York: St. Martin's Press, 1983); Robert Jervis, *The Illogic of American Nuclear Strategy* (Ithaca: Cornell University Press, 1984); and R. Jervis, *The Meaning of the Nuclear Revolution* (Ithaca: Cornell University Press, 1989). The same pattern of analysis appears in most books about nuclear controversies. This kind of organization reveals the orientation of security studies toward policy making and prescription, rather than toward explaining nuclear thinking and politics. A political struggle over weapons policy is framed as a debate between competing positions, and the analyst often tries to settle "Who's right?"

able to wonder whether expert doctrines actually describe nuclear thinking as it arises in political life. Even the experts themselves often betray doubts that unsophisticated, emotional, amateurish, and irrational thinking may sustain people's preferences. Almost always though, the experts brush these doubts aside with an argument that a "rational" theory – their theory – should carry the day:

Even if one suspects that the politician, a rank amateur in strategic analysis, will be deterred where a professional strategic analyst would advise that he should not be, there remain good reasons for listening to the cautionary words of the professional. [Colin Gray, "Nuclear Strategy: The Case for a Theory of Victory," in Steven E. Miller, ed., *Strategy and Nuclear Deterrence* (Princeton: Princeton University Press, 1984), p. 25]

In these matters, to be sure, we are dealing fundamentally with conflicting intu- itions. There is no doubt that some people's intuitions are better than others, but the superiority of the former, though sometimes definable and explicable, may be difficult to prove. [Bernard Brodie, "The Development of Nuclear Strategy," in Steven E. Miller, ed., *Strategy and Nuclear Deterrence* (Princeton: Princeton University Press, 1984), p. 21]

. . . one of the advantages of an explicit theory of "rational" strategic decision . . . is that by showing the strategic basis of certain paradoxical tactics, it can display how sound and rational some of the tactics are that are practiced by the untutored and infirm. It may not be an exaggeration to say that our sophistication sometimes suppresses sound intuitions, and one of the effects of an explicit theory may be to restore some intuitive notions that were only superficially "irrational." [Thomas Schelling, *The Strategy of Conflict* (New York: Oxford University Press, 1960), p. 17]

Given the technical and logical complexity of nuclear doctrines, the possibil- ity that "real people don't think that way" has to be a genuine concern. Are the principles of deterrence really so self-evident that we can proceed as if they were universal? Is the persistence of the nuclear debate simply a matter of "confusion"? Can we afford to dismiss theorists of bounded rationality who argue as follows?

There is no reason to suppose that human behavior is guided by a few abstract princi- ples. . . . A strategy is not necessarily the result of conscious reasoning. A player guided by routine learning only also follows a strategy. Presumedly our motivational system is inherited from our animal ancestors. The power of imagination and reason- ing is a later addition to our biological heritage. . . . This means that rationality is in the service of a rather unsophisticated higher author. [Reinhard Selten, "Bounded Rationality," *Journal of Institutional and Theoretical Economics* 146 (1990)]

With these questions in mind, let's turn our attention next to how strategic amateurs might think and reason about deterrence, nuclear strategy, and the arms race.

3

An Introduction to Intuitive
Deterrence Theories

During the middle 1980's, public opinion polls reported that nearly 60% of the American population supported a program like SDI to provide a national defense against ballistic missile attack. Only 25% or so opposed SDI outright.[1] Since the majority view starkly contradicted the precepts of arms control theory and the ABM Treaty, it is salient to ask how the respondents' preferences arose.

Surely most of those interviewed were unfamiliar with the complex technological debate about SDI's engineering and economic feasibility. Nor could many have known much about the intricate analyses of deterrent stability that occupied professional strategists. Like most participants in the political arena, the poll respondents clearly did not possess the time or technical expertise to master such elaborate ideas. Instead, their preferences about nuclear defenses necessarily rested on simpler rules of thumb, historical parables, or gut feelings. Peace through strength; no more Munichs; power must be balanced; nice guys finish last; the best defense is a good offense – such commonplace adages are the ingredients of what could be called *intuitive deterrence theories*.

While we can be confident that most people in the political arena do not rely upon the complicated intellectual apparatus available to strategic experts, it is far less evident what calculations guide their intuitive thinking about deterrence and national security. The purpose of the chapters ahead is to explore how these intuitive theories take shape, and to understand what political consequences follow from them. In this way, we shall take another cut at understanding what drives the nuclear debate – not simply as it arises in the expert literature, but in the minds of ordinary people.

1 Polls touching upon SDI include CBS News/ *New York Times,* January 2–4, 1985; ABC News/ *Washington Post,* November 10–13, 1985; ABC News/ *Washington Post,* October 24–28, 1985; CBS News/ *New York Times,* October 25, 1984; CBS News/ *New York Times,* October 24–28, 1986; ABC News/ *Washington Post,* October 14, 1986; NBC News/ *Wall Street Journal,* October 14, 1986; CBS News/ *New York Times,* January 18–21, 1987; Gallup Organization, November 13–14, 1985; Yankelovich, Clancy, Shulman, September 8–10, 1986; *Los Angeles Times,* November 1–7, 1985.

Traditional deterrence theory has surprisingly little to say about such questions, perhaps because of its prescriptive orientation. Even though national security politics are highly contentious, nearly every writer in the prescriptive tradition proceeds as though deterrence has *a logic* – that is to say, a well-defined set of guiding principles presumed to be evident to all. These principles usually reflect the characteristics of nuclear weapons and a view of strategic motivation. Classical theorists, for example, trace the "reciprocal fear of surprise attack" and "crisis instability" to weapons technologies that create a first strike advantage. As Schelling and Halperin write in the opening passage of their seminal treatise on arms control:

The most mischievous character of today's strategic weapons is that they may provide an enormous advantage, in the event that war occurs, to the side that starts it. . . . At no time before in modern history did military technology make it so likely that the first moments of general war might determine the outcome. [Thomas C. Schelling and Morton H. Halperin, *Strategy and Arms Control* (New York: The Twentieth Century Fund, 1961), pp. 9, 10]

Stability, in the analysis that follows, has little to do with the imperfect rules of thumb that people might use to understand deterrence and everything to do with avoiding force structures that reward surprise attacks. The problematic issues in the classical view are primarily technological, not conceptual or political. The same pattern of analysis occurs in the anti-classical literature, even though the emphasis shifts from mutual deterrent stability to escalation dominance and battlefield superiority. In both theories, the strategic motivations of the players appear as self-evident axioms, while all the analytical effort is spent searching for appropriate arrangements of defense and offense. This approach is perfectly reasonable if one has to decide which kind of forces to buy or to control. No one would argue that first strike instabilities aren't important to understand. But an unfortunate side effect is that nuclear thinking gets shunted aside in the rush to address pressing policy decisions.

SOME CONSEQUENCES OF NEGLECTING INTUITIVE DETERRENCE REASONING IN PRESCRIPTIVE ARMS CONTROL

When the prescriptions of abstract deterrence theory were applied to arms control and national security policy making during the Cold War, the inattention of the strategic literature to intuitive deterrence reasoning became a serious problem. For the most part anyway, the prescriptions relied on the assumption that rational politicians would embrace the strategic logic divined by the expert. By assuming these precepts to be universally compelling, the political complexities caused by superficial, conflicted, or disparate thinking about national security disappeared.

The lack of strategic diversity among the inhabitants of such models seems ironic when we consider the difficulties faced by every administration in forging a coherent security policy with broad domestic support. More often than not, policy proposals that seemed eminently sensible to strategic experts have been foiled in the domestic political arena by opponents who did not share their vision of national security. The Joint Chiefs thwarted Kennedy's prized objective of a comprehensive test ban treaty. The Carter Administration could not secure ratification of SALT II. And the Reagan Administration's SDI program created as much rancor as the ABM, if not more. In much the same way, seemingly contradictory policies have been followed at the same time. The Nixon Administration agreed to ban ABMs but then deployed MIRVs. And many administrations espoused the classical idea that nuclear wars are unwinnable, even while American nuclear war plans were skewed toward counterforce targeting, preemptive attack, and damage limitation.[2]

All of this evidence, and the nuclear debate itself, is hard to reconcile with prescriptive models that postulate a coherent strategic world view. If deterrence has *a logic*, why do we observe so much political conflict about what it is?

The tendency of the early strategic theorists to underestimate such difficulties can be appreciated in an interesting discussion by the Israeli analyst Yehoshafat Harkabi, written during the middle 1960's. Harkabi laments about the complexity of nuclear weapons problems and their remoteness to the ordinary citizen. He then concludes that crucial decisions will inevitably pass into the hands of experts, undermining the democratic process, but nevertheless removing the inexpert from the field of play:

With problems of nuclear policy, . . . when heads of state determine policy, even they may not always be able to master the scientific and technical problems involved, and must rely on the opinions of a small number of experts who have accordingly become the oracles of today. . . . Cardinal problems for the welfare and future of the state and mankind, therefore, are no longer a subject for general public debate or deliberation in the formulation of solutions. As the man in the street comes to realize that the affairs of state are too perplexing for his understanding, he loses interest in them and becomes apolitical. An alienation between the citizen and the state is taking place. In issues of security and nuclear policy, it is expressed in the attitude, "Let the politicians break their heads over it." [Y. Harkabi, *Nuclear War and Nuclear Peace* (Jerusalem: Israel Program for Scientific Translations, 1966), p. 23]

2 Two revealing discussions are David Alan Rosenberg, "The Origins of Overkill: Nuclear Weapons and American Strategy, 1945–1960," *International Security* (Spring 1983) and Desmond Ball, "U.S. Strategic Forces: How Would They Be Used?" *International Security* (Winter 1982/1983). Aaron Friedberg, "A History of U.S. Strategic 'Doctrine': 1945–1980," *Journal of Strategic Studies* (December 1980), develops a "schizophrenic" model of U.S. strategic doctrine.

The trouble with Harkabi's account is that non-experts have occupied crucial positions of nuclear authority since the decision to bomb Hiroshima, including (ordinarily) the President of the United States, the Party First Secretary in the Soviet Union, and now the leaders of the Soviet successor states. In the United States, people with little or no strategic education shaped security policy at every level of the political system – as voters, as bureaucrats, as congressmen, and even as presidents. Here it is instructive to compare Harkabi's prediction with Lakoff and York's description of how SDI came into being:

> It was a decision reached by the President without prior review by the defense establishment, in the knowledge that such review would have been unfavorable, on the advice of an informal "kitchen cabinet" composed of political supporters. . . . Although many assumed the President must have been given the idea for SDI by his advisors, Reagan himself scoffed at the suggestion: "It kind of amuses me that everybody is so sure I must have heard about it, that I never thought of it myself. The truth is I did." [Sanford Lakoff and Herbert F. York, *A Shield in Space? Technology, Politics, and the Strategic Defense Initiative* (Berkeley: University of California Press, 1989), pp. 6–7]

Evidently, when expert prescriptions like the ABM Treaty conflict with the intuitive deterrence theories of influential political actors, serious political obstacles arise.

An interesting and instructive reflection of these snags is the undercurrent of frustration that wells up in the prescriptive deterrence literature when political actors don't embrace the prescribed "right answer." In his book *MX: Prescription for Disaster*, Herbert Scoville dismisses as "mindless" the argument that the United States should match the Soviets' heavily MIRVed ICBMs. Herbert York and Sanford Lakoff subtitle their deeply skeptical book about SDI *How the Reagan Administration Set Out to Make Nuclear Weapons "Impotent and Obsolete" and Succumbed to the Fallacy of the Last Move*. And many writers have invoked Hans Morgenthau's "fallacy of thinking conventionally" to describe their misguided political adversaries (whether domestic or foreign). The fallacy arises, it is said, when traditional military strategies are applied in the nuclear era without recognizing that "victory" no longer has meaning.[3]

The lament that players in the political arena have not understood the correct logic of deterrence, that their thinking is fallacious, conventional,

---

3 Herbert Scoville, Jr., *MX: Prescription for Disaster* (Cambridge: The MIT Press, 1981); Sanford Lakoff and Herbert York, *A Shield in Space? Technology, Politics, and the Strategic Defense Initiative* (Berkeley: University of California Press, 1989); Hans Morgenthau, "The Fallacy of Thinking Conventionally About Nuclear Weapons," in David Carlton and Carlo Schaerf, eds., *Arms Control and Technological Innovation* (New York: John Wiley & Sons, 1976). Further elaboration appears in Robert Jervis, *The Illogic of American Nuclear Strategy* (Ithaca: Cornell University Press, 1984) and *The Meaning of the Nuclear Revolution* (Ithaca: Cornell University Press, 1989).

and mindless, is good evidence that traditional deterrence theory has not captured very well the patterns of reasoning that drive national security politics. The frustration apparent in such titles as *The Illogic of American Nuclear Strategy*, *MX: Prescription for Disaster*, and *A Shield in Space?* suggests that nuclear policy should not rest simply upon an analysis of first-strike stability, battlefield utility, and technical feasibility – the traditional concerns of strategic experts. To the extent that non-experts occupy influential positions in the national security arena, which they surely do, their intuitive theories of deterrence must be reckoned with too. Otherwise, we will continue to be confounded when sensible proposals for arms control don't take hold in the political arena, when our nuclear policies don't produce their intended results, when other states behave "irrationally," and foreign leaders appear "undeterrable." These are the most important reasons, I believe, for taking intuitive deterrence theories seriously.

Interest in strategic heterogeneity and the origin of security doctrines increased noticeably during the late Cold War, in part because of the frustrations experienced by arms controllers, but also because of intellectual and political developments outside deterrence theory. A major impetus arose when the Reagan Administration brought a set of strategic precepts into the White House that departed markedly from the prevailing consensus. With that Administration's strong push for SDI, the MX, ASAT, ASW, and a strategy based upon "prevailing" in nuclear warfare, the heterogeneity of strategic thinking became an obviously salient problem. There developed an interesting literature during the 1980's pursuing the origins of military ideology, particularly dysfunctional "cults of the offensive" that were markedly destabilizing from the classical point of view. The focus in these studies was primarily on the doctrinal literature of military organizations, but their topical relevance was never far below the surface. The basic message was that military organizations often adopt doctrines with a strong offensive bias even when such doctrines are starkly inconsistent with the technology of warfare. This evidence belied any notion of a homogeneous strategic world view driven by technological imperatives alone. By showing that diverse influences beyond technology could shape strategic thinking – and deflect it from the received wisdom of stability theory – the new literature on military doctrine cast considerable doubt on the political realism of the prescriptive models.[4]

4 Important studies include Robert Jervis, "Cooperation Under the Security Dilemma," *World Politics* 30, No.2 (January 1978); Barry Posen, *The Sources of Military Doctrine: France, Britain, and Germany Between the World Wars* (Ithaca: Cornell University Press, 1984); Stephen Van Evera, "The Cult of the Offensive and the Origins of the First World War," *International Security* 9, No. 1 (Summer 1984); Jack Snyder, *The Ideology of the Offensive: Military Decision Making and the Disasters of 1914* (Ithaca: Cornell University Press, 1984); and David Alan Rosenberg, "The Origins of Overkill: Nuclear Weapons and

A second literature that has been critical of the prescriptive deterrence theories addresses the psychology of deterrence, the formation of perceptions about political adversaries, and the role of miscalculation in strategic interactions. The unifying theme in this literature is the psychological naiveté of deterrence theory, especially the tendency to overrate the cognitive sophistication of real decision makers in actual crises and wars. More realistic models, it is argued, require an understanding of signal reading, cognitive filtering, simplifying decision making heuristics, intelligence failures, and other psychological processes that undermine rational decision making.[5]

A third source of interest in competing strategic sensibilities arose in game theory, which became increasingly preoccupied with the impact of uncertainty in games of strategy. Traditionally, game theorists assumed that every player enjoys complete information about the opponents' "payoffs." The payoff structure of a game, it will be recalled, describes the players' goals and "world view" with numeric summaries of preferences over possible outcomes of the game. Most of the classical games that informed early deterrence theorists not only featured complete information about payoffs but included players with identical payoff structures (as in the Prisoner's Dilemma, Chicken, and the Assurance Game). Thus a dual symmetry pervaded early game theory and, with it, deterrence theory too. Players were similar in what they wanted and what they knew about each other.

Lately, game theorists have developed new methods of analysis that recognize the critical importance of uncertainty about the opponent's objectives (or *type*). These methods reflect a growing awareness that such uncertainty is crucial in problems involving threats and promises, credible commitments, signalling, bluffing, and deterrence. Many of the new models address the complexities inherent in such problems by representing opponents as a distribution of possible payoff schedules. In such models, coping with uncertainty about the opponent's type becomes a central element of strategy.

We needn't review the new literature here except to note the change of intellectual direction. Recent game theoretic work has rejected the earlier

American Strategy, 1945–1960," *International Security* 7 (Spring 1983). Steven Kull, *Minds at War* (New York: Basic Books, 1988), sets out explicitly to understand why policy makers "fail to adapt to nuclear reality."
5 Influential discussions include Robert Jervis, *The Logic of Images in International Relations* (Princeton: Princeton University Press, 1970), and *Perception and Misperception in International Politics* (Princeton: Princeton University Press, 1976); Alexander L. George and Richard Smoke, *Deterrence in American Foreign Policy* (New York: Columbia University Press, 1974); John D. Steinbruner, *The Cybernetic Theory of Decision* (Princeton: Princeton University Press, 1974); Robert Jervis, Richard Ned Lebow, and Janice Gross Stein, eds., *Psychology and Deterrence* (Baltimore: The Johns Hopkins University Press, 1985); and "The Rational Deterrence Debate: A Symposium," *World Politics* (January 1989).

ideas of political homogeneity and strategic symmetry by admitting a diverse cast of characters into the field of play.[6] But as soon as one entertains a multiplicity of types that the players can assume, the problem is how to define what the types might be. An interest in delineating competing strategic sensibilities is therefore much in keeping with the intellectual program of modern game theory. Characterizing the types that inhabit the national security policy making arena is another way of describing our objective here.

It should also be mentioned that game theorists and microeconomists have lately developed a serious interest in the strategic behavior of "boundedly rational" players. Herbert Simon introduced the concept of bounded rationality long ago, and the so-called behavioral decision theorists have since amassed considerable experimental evidence that reinforces Simon's doubts about theories driven by sophisticated optimizations. Formal theorists have now begun to take these arguments more seriously, focusing on strategic interactions among agents who have constrained computational abilities, finite memories, and other cognitive limitations. One interesting line of inquiry considers indefinitely repeated games among polymorphous populations of finite automata (machines with limited computing power, often defined by the strategy they play). When evolutionary selection winnows out ineffective machines, the survivors can be interpreted as successful strategic rules-of-thumb that have evolved during repeated plays.[7]

6 Useful reviews of recent game theoretic developments include Eric Rasmusen, *Games and Information: An Introduction to Game Theory* (New York: Basil Blackwell, 1989); David M. Kreps, *A Course in Microeconomic Theory* (Princeton: Princeton University Press, 1990) and *Game Theory and Economic Modelling* (Oxford: Oxford University Press, 1990); and Ken Binmore, *Essays on the Foundations of Game Theory* (New York: Basil Blackwell, 1988). The influence of these methods is evident in a number of recent political studies, notably Robert Powell's *Nuclear Deterrence Theory: The Search for Credibility* (Cambridge: Cambridge University Press, 1990). Robert Jervis' early works display a kindred spirit, devoting considerable attention to the role of uncertainties in strategic calculations and to the complexities created by competing models of deterrence. See *The Logic of Images in International Relations* (Princeton: Princeton University Press, 1970) and *Perception and Misperception in International Politics* (Princeton: Princeton University Press, 1976).

7 Robert Axelrod, *The Evolution of Cooperation* (New York: Basic Books, 1984), explores such problems by staging computer tournaments among competing programs. Formal theoretical treatments include Ariel Rubenstein, "Finite Automata Play the Repeated Prisoner's Dilemma," *Journal of Economic Theory* 39 (1986); K. Binmore and L. Samuelson, "Evolutionary Stability in Repeated Games Played by Finite Automata," University of Wisconsin, Social Systems Research Institute, 9029, November 1990; and Robert J. Aumann, "Cooperation and Bounded Recall," *Games and Economic Behavior* 1 (1989). For leads into the supporting literature, see Herbert Simon, "Theories of Bounded Rationality," in C. McGuire and R. Radner, eds., *Decision and Organization* (Amsterdam: North Holland, 1972); Daniel Kahneman, Paul Slovic, and Amos Tversky, eds., *Judgment Under Uncertainty: Heuristics and Biases* (Cambridge: Cambridge University Press, 1982); and David Bell, Howard Raiffa, and Amos Tversky, eds., *Decision Making: Descriptive, Normative, and Prescriptive Interactions* (Cambridge: Cambridge University Press, 1988).

Finally, international relations theorists have recently shown a growing interest in the interactions between domestic politics and international strategy. Recognizing the difficulties with "systemic" or third image explanations that rest solely upon universal strategic imperatives like the balance of power, these studies typically invoke domestic coalitional politics (and therefore strategic heterogeneity) to refine explanations of international behavior. These studies gained considerable impetus during the end of the Cold War, which raised such questions as how far the former Soviet empire will disintegrate and which political faction(s) will ultimately hold sway. Everyone sees clearly that future policy depends directly on the domestic struggles for power now under way, and the problem is how to understand the interaction between nuclear strategic policy and the revolutionary politics of democratization and ethnic nationalism.[8]

I have argued that intuitive deterrence theories are at once poorly understood and critically important in national security politics. Traditionally, deterrence theorists have assumed too casually that their calculations will be consistent with the reasoning used by actors in the political arena. But traditional deterrence theory can not explain the partisan character of national security politics, the persistence of the arms debate, the incoherence of security policy, oscillations between competing strategic doctrines, or the end of the Cold War. These patterns cast doubt on the guiding assumptions of prescriptive deterrence theory, particularly that deterrence has an intrinsic logic, evident to all. In the chapters ahead, I shall consider a large body of new data, gathered to shed light on intuitive nuclear thinking and the factional structure of nuclear politics. To appreciate what these measurements can tell us, it's important to understand the considerations that guided their design.

THE NUCLEAR THINKING DATA

The nuclear thinking data described below arise from a series of opinion surveys conducted between Fall 1988 and Spring 1993. The several hundred respondents in the samples include complete strategic novices, professional arms controllers, senior executives at major defense contracting companies, and government officials. I'll describe the samples presently, but first it would be useful to describe the questionnaire that each respondent completed.

8 Robert Putnam, "Diplomacy and Domestic Politics: The Logic of Two-Level Games," *International Organization* 42 (1988), has defended this program to international relationists, while George Tsebelis, *Nested Games* (Berkeley: University of California Press, 1989), makes a more general game theoretic argument. Two recent studies of the domestic origins of security policy include Bruce Russett, *Controlling the Sword* (Cambridge: Harvard University Press, 1990), and Jack Snyder, *Myths of Empire* (Ithaca: Cornell University Press, 1991).

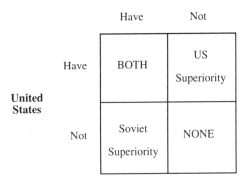

Fig. 3.1

Appendix 3.1 at the end of the chapter displays the survey question-naire. The questions on the first page elicit an ideological self-description, an assessment of the likelihood of nuclear war, and a characterization of the conflict of interest between the United States and the (then) Soviet Union. As we shall see, these items tap differences that are frequently invoked to explain competing schools of strategic thought. The heart of the survey appears on the second page, where respondents describe their preferences over possible outcomes of the arms race between the two nuclear superpowers. Each item describes an important policy problem in the arms race, including anti-submarine warfare, ballistic missile defenses like SDI, land-based MIRVed ICBMs like the MX, conventional force postures, and technologies to secure deterrent forces from preemptive attack. In each case, the respondents related their preferences by supply-ing numerical ratings in the four cells of Figure 3.1. The cells describe scenarios in which both sides acquire the weapon, one side or the other acquires it, and nobody does. The ratings range from 4 = BEST to 1 = WORST with ties allowed when the respondent perceives no difference among two or more outcomes.

While the matrix has a simple form, most people find that substantial thinking is needed to assign payoffs to the four cells. If one takes a moment to complete the questionnaire, it will become evident that many consider-ations bear upon these judgments including broad ideas about strategy and specific information about each weapon system. To appreciate the richness of the questions and the information they elicit, let's consider how several different individuals might approach them.

The Classical Arms Controller

First, let's assume the perspective of someone who embraces the classical philosophy of mutual deterrence and its ancillary model of arms control. For such a person, the guiding principle is to avoid "destabilizing" or "first-strike" technologies that erode mutual deterrence by undermining secure second strikes. Weapons that compromise either side's ability to retaliate after nuclear attack, it is argued, drive the arms race spiral and produce crisis instability. Not only do they compel one side or the other to build more nuclear forces (so as to secure a viable deterrent), but they create incentives to strike first if tensions escalate and war seems imminent. For these reasons, the classical point of view insists that destabilizing technologies be avoided. The classical attitude underlies the ABM Treaty, which bans ballistic missile defenses (for all practical purposes anyway) because they undermine the ability to retaliate in the event of nuclear attack. As Herbert Scoville puts it:

The ABM Treaty was a major security gain since it assured for the foreseeable future that any warhead launched in a retaliatory attack could travel unhampered on its way to its intended target. Thus mutual deterrence was guaranteed. [*MX: Prescription for Disaster* (Cambridge: The MIT Press, 1981), p. 92]

The same point of view informs the recent START II agreement, which eschews complete nuclear disarmament, and concentrates instead on de-MIRVing land-based ICBMs. In this way, the treaty strives to assure that neither nuclear arsenal presents a first strike threat to the other.

From the classical perspective, the first three weapons described in the questionnaire are all strategically suspect. Each one creates a potential damage limiting threat to the other side's retaliatory forces, and thereby erodes the stability of deterrence. Effective means of anti-submarine warfare (ASW) compromise the sea-based leg of the strategic triad, threatening the most secure platform that now exists for retaliatory nuclear forces. Partially effective ballistic missile defenses covering the entire national territory (like Reagan's proposed SDI) undermine both land-based and sea-based deterrents by absorbing retaliatory second strikes against "value targets." Highly accurate, multiple-warhead ICBMs threaten silo-based missiles, submarines in port, bomber bases, and C^3I facilities. MIRVed ICBMs (like the MX missile) would be the counterforce weapon of choice for anyone seeking a preemptive first strike, while themselves presenting a tempting target. From the classical perspective, then, the appropriate preference ordering is similar for each of these weapons. Arms control ("neither side has it") is best, while it is bad if one side, the other, or both sides add the weapons to their arsenal.

An interesting and more difficult question from the classical point of view is whether it would be just as bad if one side acquired destabilizing weapons as it would be if both had them. One argument might be that stability is greater when only one side lacks a secure second strike (rather than both), because the inferior party will never strike first knowing that devastating retaliation lies in store. Instead, only the superior party would have an incentive to strike first. If neither side had a secure second strike, on the other hand, then both would be tempted to preempt for fear that the other might do so first. By this reckoning, the cells with U.S. or SOVIET SUPERIORITY would rate higher than BOTH sides having the destabilizing weapon. Such preference profiles would look like this:

BOTH	US+
1	2
SOV+	NONE
2	4

CLASSICAL DOVE
TYPE I

Other reasoning about the reciprocal fear of surprise attack and crisis instability suggests another conclusion, however. What if the inferior party anticipates that the superior party will strike first while the lesser side's deterrent is inadequate? The inferior party might then decide to strike first itself – if it could limit damage by doing so. But if the superior party believed that its adversary was contemplating a first strike, it would have an incentive to attack preemptively too (regardless of its original intention). But then the inferior party's fears would be all the more salient, and its incentive to strike first would multiply. In this way, the mutual fear of surprise attack could arise when either side lacks a secure second strike. Such reasoning explains why the classical doctrine insists on the idea of *mutual* deterrence. As Thomas Schelling puts it:

The balance [of terror] is stable *only when* neither, in striking first, can destroy the other's ability to strike back. . . . If each side were confident that its own forces could survive an attack, but also that it could not destroy the other's power to strike back – there would be no powerful temptation to strike first. [*The Strategy of Conflict* (New York: Oxford University Press, 1960), p. 233–34] [Emphasis added]

If so, then it would be bad, and equally bad, if one side, the other, or both obtained the destabilizing technology:

BOTH	US+
1	1
SOV+	NONE
1	4

CLASSICAL
PURE DOVE

We don't have to settle which argument is correct, or which profile is a truer reflection of the classical attitude.[9] What should be clear are the range and subtlety of the considerations that can affect the preference orderings in the arms racing matrices. One should not be misled by the simplicity of the tables into thinking they are too prosaic to be strategically interesting. Far from it, in fact.

A Hard Core Anti-Nuclear Dove

A second important point emerges if we consider a hard core anti-nuclear dove whose basic objective is complete nuclear disarmament. Such a person would also resist programs like the MIRVed MX, just as the Classical Pure Dove did. The coincidence of preference raises the question whether the data might provide too little information to distinguish these very different attitudes?

I believe not. In this case, a congruence of outlook occurs about MIRVed ICBMs but the next item would likely produce very different responses. There the respondent must evaluate "effective technologies for protecting nuclear forces from preemptive attack." From the classical perspective, such stabilizing technologies are precisely what one wants to secure second strikes. It would therefore be best if BOTH sides acquired them and less desirable if only one side or neither did. From the classical perspective, the appropriate preference ordering is the inverse of the pattern for MX, SDI, and ASW.

By contrast, the anti-nuclear dove is far more likely to want nuclear forces dismantled than to have them protected. If nuclear threats are perceived to be an unreliable foundation for national security, and even a mortal peril, then one's attitude toward defending nuclear weapons will

9 Despite lots of recent effort, modern game theory provides no compelling theory to describe the process of interacting expectations and escalating fears described by models of crisis instability. As a result, nothing like a theoretical consensus exists about the relative stability of situations where one or both sides lack a secure second strike. Two sophisticated reviews of basic game theoretic difficulties are K. Binmore, *Essays on the Foundations of Game Theory* (New York: Basil Blackwell, 1988), and David Kreps, *Game Theory and Economic Modelling* (Oxford: Oxford University Press, 1990). Instructive works that reveal diverse approaches to understanding crisis instability include Daniel Ellsberg, "The Crude Analysis of Strategic Choices," RAND P-2183, 1959; Thomas Schelling, "The Reciprocal Fear of Surprise Attack," RAND P-1342, May 1958; Robert Powell, *Nuclear Deterrence Theory: The Search for Credibility* (Cambridge: Cambridge University Press, 1990); Dean Wilkening, Kenneth Watman, Michael Kennedy and Richard Darilek, "Strategic Defenses and First-Strike Stability," *Survival* (December 1985); Glenn A. Kent and David E. Thaler, "First-Strike Stability: An Extended Methodology," RAND Working Draft, WD-4019-AF, October 1988; and Barry O'Neill, "A Measure of Crisis Instability with an Application of Space-Based Antimissile Systems," *Journal of Conflict Resolution* (December 1987).

be quite unlike the classical view, which rests on the belief that disarmament would be destabilizing. The important point to notice is that the two items together reveal congruences and disparities of attitude that no single item could capture by itself. As we shall see, many subtle discontinuities of strategic thinking can be discerned by making comparisons across the several items.

Anti-Classical Nuclear Hawks

Finally, let's consider the perspective of a hardline nuclear hawk. Here the preference matrices will immediately reveal a very different attitude about SDI, MX, ASW, and the other damage limiting technologies. The hawk's guiding question is whether the weapon system promotes or impedes a war fighting capability. U.S. superiority is the most preferred outcome, while Soviet superiority is the most dreaded. A trickier question is whether arms control (nobody has it) is better than both sides having the weapon? Here again, many considerations might come into play, including one's faith in arms control treaties, the existence of threats beyond those posed by the Soviet Union, a comparison of the adversaries' technological sophistication, or a stake in defense contracting. With respect to SDI, Caspar Weinberger declared that this project would never be made a bargaining chip in arms control talks, that we were going to build SDI regardless of what the Soviets did, and that the best general strategy would be to capitalize on U.S. technological superiority. His preference ordering would therefore look very unlike any of the doves':

BOTH	US+
3	4
SOV+	NONE
1	2

ANTI-CLASSICAL
STRONG HAWK

Figure 3.2 summarizes how a sequence of four preference profiles readily distinguishes the classical and anti-classical types, and proponents of outright disarmament. The general point to notice is how competing deterrence theories induce distinctive patterns of preference over weapon deployments (on *both* sides of the arms race). While many further patterns of nuclear thinking are conceivable, it won't be easy to exhaust the opportunities for self-expression offered by the questionnaire. Given the four numerical scores from which the respondent can choose and the possibility of ties, there are more than 100 different patterns that each preference

	ASW	SDI	MX	INVULNERABLE
Classical Type	BOTH 1 / US+ 1 / SOV+ 1 / NONE 4	BOTH 1 / US+ 1 / SOV+ 1 / NONE 4	BOTH 1 / US+ 1 / SOV+ 1 / NONE 4	BOTH 4 / US+ 1 / SOV+ 1 / NONE 1
Anti-Classical Type	BOTH 3 / US+ 4 / SOV+ 1 / NONE 2	BOTH 3 / US+ 4 / SOV+ 1 / NONE 2	BOTH 3 / US+ 4 / SOV+ 1 / NONE 2	BOTH 3 / US+ 4 / SOV+ 1 / NONE 2
Disarmament Type	BOTH 1 / US+ 1 / SOV+ 1 / NONE 4	BOTH 1 / US+ 1 / SOV+ 1 / NONE 4	BOTH 1 / US+ 1 / SOV+ 1 / NONE 4	BOTH 1 / US+ 1 / SOV+ 1 / NONE 4

Figure 3.2 Expected preference profiles for respondents of different types

profile can assume. A collection of four such matrices, each for a different weapon, defines a very large space of potential responses, containing on the order of 150 million distinct sequences of profiles. As a result, it is possible to discriminate both gross and subtle differences in strategic perspective with far greater refinement than first appearances might suggest (or conventional survey questions would allow).

A GAME MATRIX

Readers familiar with scholarship on international relations and national security strategy will recognize the format of the matrices from a large literature that analyzes the arms race as a 2-person game between the nuclear superpowers. Such studies ordinarily begin with an argument that the arms race resembles some particular game like an Assurance Game (Stag Hunt) or the Prisoner's Dilemma. The analysis then describes the equilibrium behavior or strategic quandaries that follow from the assumed configuration of preferences. It is instructive, if a bit surprising, to discover that no one working in this tradition seems ever to collect empirical data about real players' preferences in nuclear "games." Instead, the payoffs are simply imputed according to the analyst's understanding of "the logic" of the situation. (The same kind of imputation occurs in many experimental games when the payoff matrix is fixed by the experimenter.) A basic objective guiding the design of the nuclear thinking questionnaire has been to collect more direct evidence about the game theoretic structure of the arms race (at least over the idealized binary choice set that most of the literature discusses).

It should be reemphasized that questions following the usual format of public opinion surveys ("Do you support SDI . . . strongly, . . . somewhat, . . . not at all?") fail to elicit enough comparisons to infer an individual's payoff schedule even in a simple 2x2 game matrix. Similar problems arise when we try to infer the preference orderings of statesmen and politicians, simply by reading their speeches or memoirs. Usually, some but not all of the relevant comparisons appear in such texts. As a result, the questionnaire items used here provide far richer information than is ordinarily available to describe the character of an individual's political support for each kind of weapon. By soliciting preferences in a form consistent with game theoretic analysis, we have a much sturdier basis for drawing inferences about political behavior from measurements of opinion.

A few examples will help make these advantages clearer. Consider the following patterns of preference about SDI (where, as usual, 4 is best and 1 is worst, the U.S. is the row player, and Soviets are the column player):

BOTH	US+
4	1
SOV+	NONE
1	2

BOTH	US+
4	3
SOV+	NONE
1	2

BOTH	US+
3	4
SOV+	NONE
1	2

Suppose further that all three respondents assumed at the time of the survey that the Soviets were committed to building SDI. (The Soviets' strategic choice Build is in the left column.) How would each person respond to a typical survey question that asked respondents to characterize their support for SDI along a scale from "very strong" to "none at all"? Given that the Soviets plan to build, each one prefers strongly that we build as well. If everything goes well in the survey, the first two respondents should register identical opinions, while the third one, seeing less difference between BOTH and SOV+, might indicate "strong" rather than "very strong" support.

Now consider how much information is lost in such a measurement process. The second and third respondents have an unconditional preference to build SDI, whatever the Soviets do. The first respondent, on the other hand, would oppose SDI if the Soviets abandoned the project. By measuring preferences as warmth toward the weapon system rather than as an ordering over strategic outcomes, the conventional survey item provides no information about which respondents would shift their position if the Soviet Union dropped SDI. Indeed, it misleadingly suggests that the first two respondents share a closer affinity of viewpoint, rather than the second two. The survey also conceals an interesting discontinuity in the political reasoning of respondents 2 and 3. Although both unconditionally prefer to build, the second respondent prefers that *both* sides have SDI while the third prefers outright American superiority. The rationale for supporting SDI seems clearly different. The two individuals' approach to bargaining with the Soviets or to campaigning for SDI would probably be different too.

These examples and others like them suggest three important advantages of a game theoretic measurement of preferences. First, it is possible to identify and distinguish far more political types with them than ordinary survey questions allow. Second, one can draw more direct inferences from the observed expression of preference to political behavior, using game theoretic techniques of analysis. Finally, the game theoretic format lends itself to rigorous testing of prescriptive deterrence theories, like the classical and anti-classical models, precisely because such theories prescribe configurations of nuclear weapon systems on *both* sides of the arms race.

CONTENT OF THE ITEMS

So much for the form of the questions. What about their content? The reader will notice first that many items focus on damage limiting (or second strike undermining) technologies that were the center of controversy in the Cold War arms debate. Almost everybody agrees that the U.S. must remain prepared to retaliate in the event of nuclear attack. Programs like hardening silos or building ballistic missile submarines have therefore enjoyed wide support. Technologies that threaten the other side's deterrent forces (like ASW, SDI, and MX) excite more debate and seem more likely to discriminate among competing points of view.

The questions can also be broken down in a second way that doesn't take the expert nuclear debate as a cue. Each question describes a "defensive" or "offensive" weapon, targeted at people or at other weapons. MIRVed ICBMs are people (and weapon) killers. INVULNERABLE platforms are weapon protectors. ASW is a weapon killer, and SDI is a people (and weapon) protector.

Notice finally that the questions focus on concrete policy issues for which real decisions have to be taken. While experts' arguments for nuclear policy choices often involve hypothetical scenarios about nuclear escalation, limited war, or surprise attack, our questions focus explicitly on the policy resultant of nuclear thinking, not the political rationale. This tack was taken because the cognitive output (or policy preference) ultimately determines behavior, and because it is hard to anticipate what rationales might underlie different respondents' positions. Rather than skewing the questionnaire toward those arguments that experts have invoked, our strategy is to give respondents as much freedom as possible to manifest their own patterns of nuclear reasoning. The format of the questions is at once politically neutral, comfortably accommodating diverse points of view, and directly relevant to arms race decisions. What remains to be seen is how well we can reason backwards from the observed sequence of policy preferences to the respondents' underlying conceptualization of deterrence and national security. It will be the purpose in chapters ahead to show that very rich inferences of this kind can be drawn.

VAGUENESS OF QUESTIONS

Occasionally (very rarely actually) respondents resist the vagueness of the questions. "What specifically does a good though not perfect ballistic missile defense mean?" they ask. They are told to answer according to their own understanding of what such a defense entails. Ruled out are completely ineffective defenses, prodigious defenses of the astrodome variety, and terminal silo defenses (alternatives that excite less controversy among competing schools of thought). After that, the respondents must "fill in the blank" by supplying their own image of SDI.

But why be vague? Why not ask about a national area defense based on a particular technology, with a particular capacity and a definite interception rate – especially since expert analysis often turns on such detailed considerations? One obvious reason is that no one knows what a missile defense might eventually look like, if it ever is built. As a result, people in the political arena must form opinions, channel support, or direct opposition to programs and legislation that are even more vague than our question. Votes to support research about SDI clearly did not turn upon a carefully specified engineering blueprint. Neither did the passionate political opinions that animated the Star Wars debate. SDI never had a definite engineering design, a clear strategic objective, nor any well defined cost. Necessarily then, people's political and strategic positions must reflect their own image of what a ballistic missile defense might someday involve. While some people's images may be technologically highly refined, most are probably quite unspecific and metaphorical. Ronald Reagan described SDI as a "shield that could protect us from nuclear missiles just as a roof protects a family from rain," even though the system he wanted to build included a heavy arsenal of exotic weapons orbiting over the Soviet Union. Whether one conceptualizes SDI as a shield or as an arsenal undoubtedly affects one's point of view.

Understanding how these notional sensibilities arise is a basic objective of our survey. If we were interested in the division of opinion on a specific proposal, then the questions would have to be written differently. But since we are trying to tap basic strategic intuitions and predispositions, asking narrowly specific questions seems counterproductive. Doing so would necessarily focus attention on a single image that may have no resemblance to the respondent's own. Instead, the questions have been designed to eliminate certain (usually non-controversial) possibilities, leaving the respondents broad latitude to invoke their own visions of nuclear systems and national security.[10]

SURVEYS VERSUS INTERVIEWS

A final question is why we have chosen to rely on survey questionnaires rather than depth interviews to discern patterns of nuclear thinking. No one would suggest that depth interviews aren't valuable. Rather, the surveys have complementary virtues – virtues, moreover, that have been underutilized for understanding the nuclear debate. Above all, such evidence allows systematic comparisons across large numbers of people and issues. Interviews, memoirs, testimony, and speeches, while rich in detail and highly suggestive, ordinarily do not address a consistent, stable, or explicit set of questions. They are hard to compare as a result. Such texts often contain enough elaborate detail that general patterns become hard to see. These difficulties are evident in the literature that dissects and classifies the expert nuclear debate. It almost appears that every analyst can produce a new classification, each based on different considerations, with categories that vary dramatically in number and kind.

Because the surveys invite greater data reduction, they can provide more reliable estimates of basic patterns in nuclear thinking. Such statistical stability comes at the expense of detailed description (unbiasedness). Readers familiar with statistical theory will recognize the familiar tradeoff between bias and stability as a pervasive dilemma in data analysis. The analytical strategy followed here approaches the tradeoff differently than is customary among international relations and security studies scholars. It offers hope, therefore, of providing new ways of perceiving a highly complex phenomenon. Above all, surveys allow us to deploy sophisticated data analytical methods to search for patterns. Doing so can reveal complicated multivariate relationships that would be extremely difficult to discern "by eye," simply by sifting through interviews or texts.

10 On the other hand, notice that every question describes a nuclear system in ordinary language, so that respondents do not have to decipher buzzwords like ASW or MIRV to understand what kind of weapon is meant.

All statistical analysis rests upon systematic, controlled comparisons. To understand better the rich variety of comparisons made possible by the nuclear thinking surveys, let's review the structure of the information we have collected.

Comparisons Within Matrices

A basic problem is to characterize the diversity of strategic viewpoints people bring to the nuclear debate. Journalists and scholars commonly draw distinctions between hawks and doves or hardliners and softliners. But are these distinctions politically meaningful or useful? Do they convey information or conceal it? What distinguishes people who reach opposed positions and how many politically distinct positions do they actually take? Are the basic differences ideological, informational, partisan, psychological, or what?

We have seen already that the comparisons across cells in any particular preference matrix can distinguish many different strategic attitudes. People motivated by anti-Sovietism, classical MAD thinking, employment in the defense sector, pacifism, or a sense that SDI would be economically ruinous will each respond differently to the item about nuclear defenses, for example. At the same time, the individual preference profiles define each respondent's game theoretic type with respect to an important strategic system. Such evidence is valuable for understanding the distribution of types in the political arena,[11] and for drawing inferences about the coalitional politics of the arms race.

Comparisons Across Matrices

The separate items in the questionnaire address important policy problems in arms control. Comparisons among the items allow us to identify general ideas about security and deterrence that organize preferences across dimensions of the arms race. If a classical MAD thinker tests each system according to whether it threatens or secures second strikes, then the responses on all the items will follow a coherent pattern. Likewise for the hawk whose measure of deterrence is battlefield superiority. But do people typically invoke such general organizing ideas or not?

Competing beliefs about deterrence and national security seem to exhibit amazing political durability. That they do so indicates their broad

---

11 Game theoretic models with incomplete information depend critically on how the distribution of political types is specified.

intuitive appeal and the difficulty of discrediting them. Could we ever convince Ronald Reagan, for example, that "peace through strength" didn't work? The wide appeal of Reagan's campaign slogan suggests that intuitive deterrence theories may rest upon a set of relatively fixed, high-level abstractions that are both hard to disconfirm and insensitive to political tides. If so, then a first priority will be to discover what these cognitive building blocks are, how many of them there are, and why different people latch on to different ones.

At the same time, it will be important to weigh how much influence broad organizing principles have in relation to more specific information about weapons systems and policy alternatives. Do a small set of anchoring ideas structure strategic opinions across a broad spectrum of issues, or do opinions fluctuate with the local details of each policy debate? Does the relative weight given to broad abstraction and contextual detail vary with the respondent's political sophistication or ideological position? Do there exist discernible populations of sophisticates and unsophisticates whose thinking varies in coherence, content, or stability? Such questions are particularly important for understanding the durability and cohesion of political coalitions in the national security debate and the impact of striking events like the demise of communism in the Soviet bloc. All of these questions can be studied by looking for coherent patterns in the respondents' preferences across the various weapon systems.

Comparisons Among Experts and Novices

Many fundamental problems turn on whether intuitive deterrence theories resemble expert reasoning or not. The question is critical for understanding the domestic politics of arms control, the efficacy of democratic controls over nuclear policy making, whether popular control of weapons policy is consistent with strategic stability, and whether the prescriptions of traditional arms control theory are politically tenable or not. Unraveling the implications of nuclear proliferation in countries where leaders are strategic neophytes also requires understanding whether traditional models of deterrence – each with its corollary theory of arms control – really capture the strategic beliefs and motivations of ordinary people.

The nuclear thinking samples include people with no formal exposure to strategic studies, advanced graduate students specializing in national security studies, professional arms controllers, strategic scholars, senior public officials, and high-level managers in major aerospace corporations. We shall therefore be able to compare patterns of reasoning across a broad spectrum of strategic sophistication, ranging from untutored neophytes to active professionals. Table 3.1 describes the various samples that comprise the nuclear

Table 3.1. *Surveys on nuclear thinking*

10/3/88	Nuclear Predicament Class, UCLA. Undergraduates.
10/29/88	CISA Conference on Unilateral Approaches to Arms Control, Cambridge, Massachusetts. Professional strategic experts.
3/1/89	Northrop Electronics. Lower, middle, and upper level managers.
10/2/89	Nuclear Predicament Class, UCLA. Undergraduates.
4/30/90	Graduate Seminar on Conventional Arms Control, UCLA. Advanced graduate students.
5/14/90	TRW Corporation. Senior Executives.
6/1/90	Graduate Seminar on Strategy, UCLA. Advanced graduate students.
10/1/90	Nuclear Predicament Class, UCLA. Undergraduates.
3/19/91	Professional Defense Analysts. RAND Corporation.
1/10/93	Nuclear Predicament Class, UCLA. Undergraduates.
5/93	Professional Defense Analysts. RAND Corporation.

Note: The nuclear thinking data can be obtained from the author in electronic or hard copy versions.

thinking dataset. By comparing responses across these samples, we shall be able to learn how the novice's reasoning departs from the expert's, whether a similar diversity of attitude arises in the two populations, and much more.

Comparisons Over Time

The data were gathered in nine waves, spaced at more or less regular intervals, between Fall 1988 and Spring 1993. Some populations were sampled repeatedly, creating a rolling cross-sectional design. We can therefore study whether support for the arms race unraveled with the end of the Cold War, how the transformation of the Soviet Union affected nuclear thinking, and whether experts and novices reacted differently to the epochal events of the period.

Comparisons Across Opinion Groups

In addition to the preference matrices, the data contain further information about political self-identification, the estimated probability of nuclear war, the conflict of interest between the U.S. and Soviet Union, and other attitudes. These items provide information about how nuclear thinking might be related to broader political orientations, about the origins of competing strategic sensibilities, and about political differences among groups spanning the political spectrum.

Appendix 3.1 *Nuclear thinking questionnaire*

Please answer the following questions honestly and straightforwardly, giving your best guess when you're not sure about the answer. Strive to give an accurate summary of your political views within the framework of the questions asked—even when you must oversimplify your true opinions (as you surely will sometimes).

1). How would you describe yourself politically? [Mark location on scale below.]

•----------------------•-----------------------•-----------------------------•--------------------------•

Far Left   Liberal   Middle of the Road   Conservative   Far Right

2). How likely is it that the United States will fight a nuclear war in the next four decades? [Indicate the probability in percentage terms with 100% denoting certainty and 0% denoting impossibility].

With the Soviet Union   _____ %

With Anyone   _____ %

3). People disagree about how to characterize the Soviet Union. Mark the position along the scale below that best captures your opinion.

•-----------------------------•-----------------------------------•--------------------------------•

| A major power sharing many interests in common with the U.S. | A formidable adversary but one that can be dealt with through tough diplomacy | A dangerous opponent that only respects military force | A mortal enemy bent on world conquest and destruction of the U.S. |

Appendix 3.1 *(cont.)*

How would you evaluate the following outcomes (some actual, others potential) of the arms competition between the United States and Soviet Union? Give numerical values to each of the four alternatives, assigning ties when the choices seem about equal. [Rankings like {4,3,2,1} or {4,1,1,1} are both perfectly o.k.]

4 = Most Desirable   3 = Next best   2 = Next to last   1 = Least Desirable.

A. How about a race to develop an effective means to search out and destroy ballistic missile submarines?

_____ Both Sides have it   _____ Only the U.S. has it
_____ Only the U.S.S.R. has it   _____ Neither Side has it

B. To develop ballistic missile defenses covering the entire national territory? [Suppose the defenses are less than perfect but not trivial either.]

_____ Both Sides have it   _____ Only the U.S. has it
_____ Only the U.S.S.R. has it   _____ Neither Side has it

C. To develop highly accurate, multiple warhead ICBMs like the MX?

_____ Both Sides have it   _____ Only the U.S. has it
_____ Only the U.S.S.R. has it   _____ Neither Side has it

D. To develop effective technologies for protecting nuclear forces from preemptive attack?

_____ Both Sides have it   _____ Only the U.S. has it
_____ Only the U.S.S.R. has it   _____ Neither Side has it

E. To develop large-scale conventional forces?

_____ Both Sides have it   _____ Only the U.S. has it
_____ Only the U.S.S.R. has it   _____ Neither Side has it

F. Do you believe that greater security against nuclear attack would be provided by . . .

_____ arms control agreements
_____ nuclear disarmament
_____ robust ballistic missile defenses from SDI
_____ better conventional forces

G. To create a stable nuclear balance of power, is it more important that . . .

_____ The forces of the U.S. and U.S.S. R. be kept equal
_____ The forces of the U. S. be kept superior to Russia's
_____ Some weapon systems be avoided altogether, by both sides

4

Competing Hypotheses About Nuclear Thinking

Before we study any dataset, it is always interesting to ask what patterns it ought to reveal. Doing so is the best test of what we really know, and a good check on concluding after the fact that we knew the answer all along. In the social sciences, the question is often much harder to answer than one might expect. I've asked many strategic experts to anticipate the contours of the nuclear opinion data, but few were confident in their answers – and not without reason. While the literature on strategy suggests a number of rough hypotheses, it lacks a well developed theory of nuclear preference formation. On the contrary, the literature paints so many different pictures of strategic players in the arms race that it's hard to know what to expect.

Broadly speaking, we can distinguish three families of models that might describe the structure of nuclear preferences. For short, these models might be remembered as "the one," "the few," and "the many."

MODEL I: UNITARY STRATEGIC NUCLEAR PREFERENCES

The simplest model of preference formation in the arms race would have every respondent converge to an intuitively obvious strategic world view. The classical deterrence literature rests on the idea that stable mutual deterrence will be everyone's guiding objective. If this basic strategic criterion were applied by all, or even by a considerable majority, we should discover a single dominant pattern of weapon preferences. Models that ascribe a common strategic motivation to whole countries predict a similarly simple result. To explain "Why the Soviets Think They Could Fight and Win a Nuclear War," for example, is to insist upon a considerable strategic uniformity, albeit of a kind very different than the classical type.[1] Fritz Ermarth embraces this analytical model when he describes the national strategic cultures of the Cold War. In his reading, Americans are classical thinkers, and Soviets are anti-classical:

1 Richard Pipes, "Why the Soviets Think They Could Fight and Win a Nuclear War," *Commentary* (July 1977).

The essence of U.S. doctrine is to deter central nuclear war at relatively low levels of arms effort ("arms race stability") and strategic anxiety ("crisis stability") through the credible threat of catastrophic damage to the enemy should deterrence fail. . . . Soviet strategic doctrine stipulates that Soviet strategic forces should strive in all available ways to enhance the prospect that the Soviet Union could survive as a nation and, . . . defeat the main enemy should deterrence fail. . . . The most influential factor that has inhibited lucid comparisons of U.S. and Soviet strategic thinking has been the uncritically held assumption that they had to be very similar, or at least converging with time. [Fritz W. Ermarth, "Contrasts in American and Soviet Strategic Thought," *International Security* 3, No. 2 (Fall 1978)]

Another variant of MODEL I arises in the game theoretic literature about nuclear strategy and arms racing. Here, too, the assumption of unitary strategic preferences is commonplace. To liken the arms race to a Prisoner's Dilemma or an Assurance Game, for example, is to impute a common preference ordering to both sides. Most game theoretic models of nuclear interactions rest upon symmetric payoff structures that imply a very high level of strategic homogeneity. The same assumption arises in numerous less formal models of international relations that invoke the balance of power, relative gains, and other overarching strategic rules of thumb to explain states' behavior.[2]

MODEL II: STRATEGIC POLARIZATION

Many readers would hesitate before wagering on unitary strategic preferences, simply because we observe so much political conflict about arms control treaties and weapons programs. If such discord is a fact of life, the question is how to characterize the antagonistic strategic beliefs that produce it. The most common explanations involve an opposition of polar strategic world views. The contrast in Chapter 2 between classical deterrence theorists and their anti-classical critics follows this pattern. Similar schemes abound in scholarship and journalism.

A typical classification of this kind appears in a recent survey of U.S. strategic doctrine by Aaron Friedberg. Unlike Ermarth, Friedberg argues that the "United States has had a strategic doctrine in the same way that a schizophrenic has a personality." U.S. strategic doctrine, he claims "has always contained two different strands." One is "more modern and assured destructionist," emphasizing "stability, equality, mutual vulnerability, the countervalue deterrent, the dangers of counterforce weapons, the catastrophic character of nuclear war, and a preference for sufficiency over

---

2 Even non-symmetric games in international relations typically ascribe strategic homogeneity to whole countries, even if the countries themselves have different types. For an interesting overview of the vast literature on symmetric 2x2 arms racing games, see Mark Irving Lichbach, "When Is an Arms Rivalry a Prisoner's Dilemma?" *Journal of Conflict Resolution* 34, No. 1 (March 1990).

superiority." The other strand is "traditional and military." It focuses on "war outcomes, on the importance of preparing to achieve sensible objectives should deterrence fail and the necessity of defeating the enemy." The traditional perspective entails greater interest in counterforce and countermilitary targeting, damage limitation, preemption, military superiority, and a strategy aimed at producing "victory" in the event of nuclear war.[3]

Friedberg's schizophrenic model of American policy has a long standing intellectual pedigree, echoing many similar contrasts in the earlier strategic literature. George Rathjens described the duality of American strategic thinking a decade earlier when he observed

. . . an inherent inconsonance in the objectives spelled out in our basic military policy, namely "to deter aggression at any level and, should deterrence fail, to terminate hostilities in concert with our allies under conditions of relative advantage while limiting damage to the US and allied interests." [George Rathjens, "The Dynamics of the Arms Race," *Scientific American* (April 1969)]

Rathjen's article analyzes the tension between enhancing deterrence and limiting damage after deterrence fails, concluding that "hard choices must be made between attempting to minimize the chance of war's occurring in a time of crisis and attempting to minimize the consequences if it does occur" (p. 184). The basic difficulty is that limiting damage in a nuclear war requires counterforce capabilities to destroy the opponent's nuclear forces or ballistic missile defenses to neutralize them. But such capabilities undermine the foundations of stable deterrence by negating the opponent's secure second strike.

Finally, let's recall the two modes of deterrence reasoning described by Albert Wohlstetter, a decade earlier still, in the aftermath of Sputnik:

Since sputnik, the United States has made several moves to assure . . . that we will match or over-match Soviet technology and, specifically, Soviet offensive technology. . . . The problem has been conceived as more or better bombers – or rockets; or sputniks. . . .This has meant confusing deterrence with matching or exceeding the enemy's ability to strike first. To deter an attack means being able to strike back in spite of it. It means, in other words, a capability to strike second. In the last year or two, there has been a growing awareness of the distinction between "strike-first" and "strike-second" capability but little, if any, recognition of the implications of this distinction for the balance-of-terror theory. [Albert Wohlstetter, "The Delicate Balance of Terror," *Foreign Affairs* 37 (January 1959)]

The two threads of reasoning appear again in Bernard Brodie's analysis of "The Anatomy of Deterrence" in *Strategy in the Missile Age*. Much like Wohlstetter, Brodie underlines "the sharp differences in character between a deterrence capability and strategy on one hand, and a win-the-war strategy and capability on the other" (p. 276).

---

3 Aaron Friedberg, "A History of the U.S. Strategic 'Doctrine' – 1945 to 1980," *Journal of Strategic Studies* (December 1980).

Wohlstetter, Rathjens, Brodie, and Friedberg appear to be describing a single, perennial discontinuity in outlook that separates people who prefer a strike-second nuclear posture, designed to eliminate first-strike instabilities (on the assumption that a nuclear war will be catastrophic and uncontrollable), and those who believe that the best deterrent lies in strike-first capabilities that maximize the outcome of nuclear war when it does occur (on the assumption that such a war really might happen). Much the same idea underlies many other famous distinctions in the strategic vocabulary, including:

- Thomas Schelling's distinction between brute force and coercion.
- Glenn Snyder's distinction between deterrence and defense.
- The Morganthau–Jervis distinction between "conventional" and modern conceptions of nuclear strategy.

Each contrast appears to specialize the everyday distinction between hawks and doves in the nuclear context. In every case, the central issues are whether nuclear weapons should be considered militarily usable or not, whether security should rest on mutual vulnerability or military superiority, and whether nuclear strategy should endeavor to deny the opponent's nuclear capability or accept it as a fact of life.

THE ORIGINS OF STRATEGIC POLARIZATION

While many theorists have noticed the basic conceptual divide between strike-first and strike-second mentalities, relatively little effort has been devoted to explaining its origin. Several possibilities come to mind, each plausible in its own way, but nevertheless resting on quite different mechanisms.

Images of the Enemy

In the preface to a recent edition of *The Logic of Images in International Relations*, Robert Jervis suggests that many disagreements about the fundamentals of deterrence can be explained "not by disputes about general theories of international interactions, but rather by different images of the Soviet Union, its intentions, and how it would respond to alternative American policies" (p. xi). Jervis' suggestion seems consistent with the vigorous debate about Soviet behavior and intentions during the Cold War, and about the trajectory of Soviet successor states afterwards.

Neo-conservatives in the Reagan Administration disagreed violently with defenders of arms control about Soviet geopolitical objectives, including whether the Soviets believed in mutual deterrence or not, whether they perceived a common interest with the West in arms control, whether they sought a war winning capability, and whether they could be deterred by the threat of urban destruction. Writers of the classical persuasion insisted that a security policy based on mutual deterrence was feasible because the Soviets shared an overriding common interest with the United States in avoiding nuclear war. Neo-conservatives argued that the Soviets were very hard to deter, that they were ruthless and aggressive, and inured to pain. Threats to destroy Soviet cities would fail to deter a regime that had already murdered millions of its own citizens. Instead, deterrence had to rest on a robust countermilitary or denial capability, creating a clear prospect of "defeat" in the event of Soviet adventures.[4]

The conservatives' descriptions of the Soviets coincide with the apparently universal impression Americans developed of Saddam Hussein. Like an aggressive wild animal who would never respond to threats of punishment, the "undeterrable" Hussein had to be physically contained, as if in a cage. Meanwhile, though everyone concurs that Russia has changed, the debate has shifted to what it will become. As before, sharp disagreements

4 The debate about Soviet strategic thought is ably surveyed in Sean M. Lynn-Jones, Steven E. Miller, and Stephen Van Evera, eds., *Soviet Military Policy* (Cambridge: The MIT Press, 1989), and Lynn Eden and Steven E. Miller, eds., *Nuclear Arguments: Understanding the Strategic Nuclear Arms and Arms Control Debates* (Ithaca: Cornell University Press, 1989). Interestingly, those who argued that the Soviets accept classical deterrence reasoning tended to emphasize the civilian leadership, while those who argued that they don't emphasized military writings. A good general survey of Soviet doctrine before the advent of the Gorbachev regime is David Holloway's *The Soviet Union and the Arms Race* (New Haven: Yale University Press, 1983). Surveys of Gorbachev's new thinking and recent developments include Seweryn Bialer, "The Passing of the Soviet Order?" *Survival* (March/April 1990); A. Alexiev and R. Nurick, "The Soviet Military Under Gorbachev," RAND Report R-3907-RC, February 1990; David Holloway, "State, Society, and the Military Under Gorbachev," *International Security* (Winter 1989/90); Allen Lynch, "Does Gorbachev Matter Anymore?" *Foreign Affairs* (Summer 1990); Arnold Horelick, "U.S.–Soviet Relations: Threshold of a New Era," *Foreign Affairs* 69, No. 1 (1989/90); Stephen Meyer, "The Sources and Prospects of Gorbachev's New Political Thinking on Security," *International Security* 13, No. 2 (Fall 1988). The recent literature emphasizes the political struggle between adherents of "conventional" nuclear ideas, and promoters of concepts like strategic stability, sufficiency, and defensive defense.

Robert Jervis' position can be found in *The Logic of Images in International Relations* (New York: Columbia University Press, 1989). He develops his argument further in *Perception and Misperception in International Politics* (Princeton: Princeton University Press, 1976), Chapter 3, and "Rational Deterrence: Theory and Evidence," *World Politics* (January 1989). Recent empirical studies that consider the role of perceptions about the Soviets in shaping foreign policy attitudes include Cheryl Koopman, Jack Snyder, and Robert Jervis, "American Elite Views of Relations with the Soviet Union," *Journal of Social Issues* 45, No. 2 (Summer 1989); Jon Hurwitz and Mark Peffley, "Public Images of the Soviet Union: The Impact on Foreign Policy Attitudes," *Journal of Politics* 52, No. 1 (February 1990); and Richard Herrmann, "The Power of Perceptions in Foreign Policy Decision Making: Do Views of the Soviet Union Determine the Policy Choices of American Leaders?" *American Journal of Political Science* 30, No. 4 (November 1986). These studies find that attitudes about the Soviets covary quite closely with other positions on foreign policy, though puzzling inconsistencies are common.

arise among people who espouse different security strategies. Some portray the Commonwealth of Independent States as a benevolent liberal democracy, while others emphasize the authoritarian Russian culture and the unlikelihood that democracy will endure.

Such debates are anything but new to the recent era, going back to the dawn of the nuclear age. Bernard Brodie had already described them during the 1950's:

Another attitude that gets in the way of understanding deterrence is the one which alleges that Soviet leaders, when faced with issues of peace and war, would be indifferent to the loss of individual cities and certainly of the populations (as distinct from the production capital) within those cities. The implication of this view is that a government or leadership imbued with that kind of indifference can be deterred not by considerations of loss in any graduated sense of the term, but only by the prospect of losing the war. [*Strategy in the Missile Age* (Princeton: Princeton University Press, 1959), p. 280]

Absolute Versus Relative Gains

A long standing dispute among theorists of international relations turns on whether states pursue relative or absolute gains. The question, as Kenneth Waltz puts it, is whether states ask "Will both of us gain?" or "Who will gain more?" Seeking to maximize relative advantage creates strategic interactions that are zero-sum, precluding cooperative behavior in arms control, in weapons decisions, and in war itself. Maximizing absolute gains to oneself, on the other hand, permits a cooperative pursuit of mutual interests, when they exist. The distinction is clearly relevant to the nuclear debate, where alternative prescriptions for strategy often turn on competing appraisals of the conflict of interest between the superpowers.[5]

Classical theorists emphasize the common interest both sides share in avoiding configurations of weapons that favor the first striker, in avoiding escalation after war begins, and in stabilizing the arms race. Anti-classical thinkers portray an intractable adversary and support strategies based on superiority, denial, and victory. The difference in perspective is strikingly captured by a story in Fred Kaplan's *The Wizards of Armageddon*. During a briefing about limited war strategies, which required withholding nuclear

5 Kenneth Waltz's description of the issues appears in *Theory of International Politics* (Reading, Mass.: Addison-Wesley Publishing Co., 1979), p. 105. Interesting recent discussions include Joseph Grieco, "Anarchy and Cooperation," *International Organization* (Summer 1988); Joseph Grieco, "Realist Theory and the Problem of International Cooperation: Analysis with an Amended Prisoner's Dilemma," *Journal of Politics* (August 1988); Robert Jervis, "Realism, Game Theory and Cooperation," *International Organization* (April 1988); Robert Powell, "Absolute and Relative Gains in International Relations Theory," *American Political Science Review* 85, No. 4 (December 1991); and Duncan Snidal, "Relative Gains and the Pattern of International Cooperation," *American Political Science Review* 85, No. 3 (September 1991).

attacks on Russian cities after war had begun, an appalled SAC Commander Thomas S. Power admonished the speaker, William Kaufmann:

"Why do you want us to restrain ourselves? Restraint! Why are you so concerned with saving their lives? The whole idea is to kill the bastards! Look. At the end of the war, if there are two Americans and one Russian, we win!" [Fred Kaplan, *The Wizards of Armageddon* (New York: Simon and Schuster, 1983), p. 246]

Kaufmann is said to have replied, "Well, you better make sure that they're a man and a woman."

Many aspects of the nuclear debate seem to depend on whether deterrence is understood to follow from the harm threatened to the aggressor in relation to its potential gains, or from the relative amount of damage suffered by the two sides (who "wins"). The second view reduces nuclear war and deterrence to a zero-sum interaction, while the first view admits a common interest in avoiding mutual catastrophe. Bernard Brodie tied these divergent ideas into his discussion of the deterrence and win-the-war philosophies. "We must notice," he writes,

that when we say that "maximum possible deterrence" probably depends on ability to win, we are implying, for the first time in the discussion, a comparison in the degree of damage likely to be suffered by each side. Prior to this point we were talking of deterrence as something resulting from a unilateral consideration of damage, that is, enemy estimate of damage likely to be suffered by himself. This is one of the issues that seems to provoke much confusion about deterrence. . . . What seems very difficult to grasp is that his gain cannot be measured simply in terms of damage to us, except insofar as that damage . . . terminates the threat to him. [*Strategy in the Missile Age* (Princeton: Princeton University Press, 1959), p. 279]

One reason that "those who are charged with defense planning" often underrate the importance of securing second strikes, argues Brodie, is that "they unconsciously reject the concept of deterrence based on retaliation."

They apparently feel that a force that lets itself take the first blow will not be strong enough to win a war, and they are by training, tradition, and often temperament interested only in strategies that can win. . . . They are either not interested in adjusting to a strategy of deterrence or they are convinced that a force not strong enough to win is not strong enough to deter. [pp. 282–283]

The polarization created by different estimates of Soviet motivations or by the opposition of relative and absolute gains both turn on disputes about the conflict of interest separating the nuclear adversaries. Whether those disagreements are driven directly by the image of the Soviets or by more abstract conceptions of politics is the larger question raised by the two ways of characterizing the debate.

The third item in our survey questionnaire asks the respondents to characterize the conflict of interest between the United States and Soviet Union (or later, Russia). At one end of the scale, the Soviets are described as sharing many interests in common with the United States. At the other, they are called a mortal enemy bent on world conquest. Compromise positions lie in between. If different conceptions of the superpowers' conflict of interest drive competing strategic sensibilities, the respondents' preferences about nuclear forces should covary with their location on this scale.

Nuclear Pessimists and Nuclear Optimists

Some people seem to believe that nuclear war is unimaginable while others consider it nearly inevitable (at least in the long run). Their difference in perspective – alternatively described by a subjective probability estimate that deterrence will fail, their "fear" of nuclear war, or their "faith" in deterrence – is another mechanism that might drive competing strategic sensibilities.

Classical writers typically portray nuclear warfare as such an unmitigated catastrophe that it would be "unthinkable." Given the manifest irrationality of fighting such a war, they tend to regard it as a remote possibility and to focus their energies on keeping the probability very small – above all, by avoiding destabilizing technologies. Even in the late 1950's, Albert Wohlstetter suggested these attitudes were becoming a general consensus:

We have heard so much about the atomic stalemate and the receding probability of war. . . . Is mutual extinction the only outcome of a general war? This belief, frequently expressed by reference to Oppenheimer's simile of the two scorpions in the bottle, is perhaps the prevalent one. . . . Many people have drawn the consequence of the stalemate as has Blackett, who states: "If it is in fact true, as most current opinion holds, that strategic air power has abolished global war, then an urgent problem for the West is to assess how little effort must be put into it to keep global war abolished." [Albert Wohlstetter, "The Delicate Balance of Terror," *Foreign Affairs* 37 (January 1959)]

Anti-classical writers, in marked contrast, portrayed the Cold War peace as fragile and perilous. They were preoccupied with scenarios in which deterrence fails – whether through a limited first strike on American silos or an attack on allies abroad. When it does fail, they argued, the last thing one wants is an arsenal of weapons that have no military utility on the battlefield and that leave the opponent's nuclear forces invulnerable to harm (i.e., a force that can only be used to punish the other side's population). Rather, an ability to limit damage with counterforce weapons and nuclear defenses is paramount. Such was the argument for ASW, ASAT, MX, SDI, MIRV, and many other systems that promoted "nuclear war fighting" abilities.

It is easy to appreciate how one's strategic preferences could turn on whether nuclear war seems improbably remote or menacingly proximate.

In one case, the objective will be to keep the probability low, while in the other case one must take steps to weather the storm.[6] As George Rathjens, Glenn Snyder, and many others have pointed out, the requirements for the two missions are often quite different.

An interesting question is whether some people are temperamentally inclined to be nuclear pessimists, and thereby impelled to prepare for the worst, while others are somehow optimists, and impelled to prepare for the best. Whether a person's sense of war's imminence turns on hard evidence about the adversary's behavior or psychological predispositions will evidently be hard to determine. Nonetheless, a case for the latter idea can be made simply by observing the ambiguity of most intelligence data. The literature on surprise attack suggests that intelligence evidence is never very hard, even on the eve of war. Rather than a clear, simple picture, there seems always to be an overabundance of noisy, conflicting signals supporting every point of view.[7] In such circumstances, people's sense of peril might be just as much a reflection of their own dispositions as an inference drawn from evidence. Like disagreements between bulls and bears on Wall Street or between "Cassandras" and "Pollyannas" on topics like global warming, the "energy crisis," or America's economic decline,

6 Daniel Ellsberg's model of crisis instability was among the first to show explicitly how the decision to strike first or not – and therefore whether to prefer strike-first or strike-second weapons – can turn directly on the estimated probability that deterrence will fail. See Daniel Ellsberg, "The Crude Analysis of Strategic Choices," RAND P-2183, 1959.

7 Ephraim Kam's *Surprise Attack* (Cambridge: Harvard University Press, 1988) is a recent study that shows how much latitude intelligence data allow the analyst in assessing the probability of war. Lawrence Freedman's *U.S. Intelligence and the Soviet Strategic Threat* (Princeton: Princeton University Press, 1986) tells a similar story about the assessment of nuclear forces during the Cold War.

An interesting side current in the Cold War nuclear debate turned on the commonplace observation that deterrence must eventually fail if there is some fixed (and independent) probability that nuclear war will occur in any given year. If the probability in each year is denoted by $p > 0$, then the total probability that war will occur within n years is $1 - (1 - p)^n$. What troubled people is that the total probability goes to 1 as n gets bigger. If p were only 1/100, the probability that nuclear war would happen in 40 years is already 1/3. McGeorge Bundy eventually pointed out the critical assumption in this deceptively persuasive argument, noting that there is no necessary reason to assume that the probability must remain constant from year to year. If it decreases at a regular rate, then the cumulative probability of disaster may be very small. See McGeorge Bundy, *Danger and Survival: Choices About the Bomb in the First Fifty Years* (New York: Random House, 1988), p. 615.

The distinction between "optimists and pessimists" plays an important role in Kenneth Waltz's influential review of the causes of war. See Waltz, *Man, the State and War* (New York: Columbia University Press, 1959). Julian L. Simon, "Resources, Population, Environment: An Oversupply of False Bad News," *Science* 208, No. 27 (June 1980) describes the infrequency with which many predictions of doom and gloom come true, and suggests reasons why they are nevertheless so common. Amos Tversky and Daniel Kahneman's "Availability: A Heuristic for Judging Frequency and Probability," *Cognitive Psychology* 5 (1973), and "Judgment Under Uncertainty: Heuristics and Biases," *Science* 185 (1974) are influential discussions of the conceptual difficulties people experience when estimating the probability of unlikely events.

the debate about "the nuclear threat" might be driven much more by gut feelings than by hard evidence.

The second question in the survey questionnaire is intended to discern this kind of difference among people. By eliciting an estimate of the probability of nuclear war over the long run (four decades), we might be able to distinguish nuclear pessimists from optimists and then test whether their strategic sensibilities diverge or not.

Left–Right Ideological Distinctions

It is commonplace to impute ideological motivations to contending strategic factions by labeling them "liberal" and "conservative." And it is certainly true in the United States that liberal Democrats have been more consistent supporters of arms control and more vocal opponents of systems like MX and SDI than have conservatives and Republicans. Such patterns raise the possibility that more general political and ideological orientations, arising outside the national security realm, generate cleavages about arms control and defense priorities.

One interesting characterization of such orientations is developed by Thomas Sowell in his recent book, *A Conflict of Visions: Ideological Origins of Political Struggles*. Sowell's model of political ideologies is driven by two competing "visions" of human nature – one "constrained" and the other "unconstrained." Visions, in Sowell's usage, are intuitive theories ("more like a hunch or gut feeling") that define "a sense of how the world works," "a sense of causation," and an "agenda for action."

The constrained vision emphasizes human limitations, both moral and intellectual, that limit choices and preclude ultimate solutions to social problems. Given man's imperfect rationality and foresight, the constrained vision seeks to advance human welfare by exploiting historically proven social institutions that mobilize and coordinate knowledge in a way that no single mind could grasp. Grand intellectual designs and social blueprints are, in this view, no substitute for moral traditions, the marketplace, and family values. "Man is better served by custom than understanding" because rationality is systemic, not individual – "an evolved pattern rather than an excogitated blueprint."

The unconstrained vision gives paramount importance to human reason. Experience, in this view, is greatly overrated in comparison to the power of the human mind. The unconstrained approach to human welfare is therefore to seek broad solutions to social problems through policy engineering, enlightened reasoning, and scientific progress.

Sowell surveys a variety of social attitudes that he imputes to these visions, including views about force and violence.[8] The direction of the analysis is evident in his observation that "war did not require an explanation within the constrained vision. Peace required explanation – and specific provisions to produce it. One of these provisions was military power" (p. 145). In the unconstrained vision, by contrast, war is not a reflection of human nature, but at variance with it. The fault is assigned to special reasons, including "imperfect institutions," "misunderstandings," and "emotions." Preferred solutions that reduce the probability of war include arms limitations, the quelling of nationalism, better communication, and negotiation.

Whether we agree or not that Sowell's distinction captures the essence of "liberalism" and "conservatism" – and one can only push such schemes so far before a host of complications and exceptions to the rule show up – his analysis raises the interesting possibility that basic strategic sensibilities might arise from considerations more abstract and general than the vicissitudes of the Cold War or the attributes of nuclear weapons. In a way that the previous explanations do not, his suggests that strategic intuitions will be systematically related to other political ideas and broader ideological orientations.

The first question on the survey asks respondents to locate themselves along a left-to-right ideological spectrum, providing direct evidence about the ideological origins of strategic preference. By including ideological position in a multivariate statistical analysis, along with the respondents' pessimism about the likelihood of nuclear war and their descriptions of the Soviet adversary, we may be able to disentangle the separate effects of each factor on strategic preferences. Without taking such steps, it's hard to see how the competing theories could be tested.

Parochial (Often Bureaucratic) Interests

Another popular explanation for strategic polarization invokes people's parochial interests to decipher their positions on national security questions. Many stories of this type distinguish "military" and "civilian" policy makers to account for hardline and softline trends of strategic thinking. The widely noted disparity between declaratory (civilian) strategic doctrine and actual targeting policy (for a long time controlled by military organizations) is often explained this way. Interservice rivalries, like the conflict between the Navy and SAC during the late 1950's, are another favorite explanatory tool. In this case, the Navy tried to slice itself a larger piece of

8 Thomas Sowell, *A Conflict of Visions: Ideological Origins of Political Struggles* (New York: William Morrow, 1987). Waltz develops a similar discussion in Chapter II of *Man, the State and War* (New York: Columbia University Press, 1954), "The First Image: International Conflict and Human Behavior."

the nuclear weapons pie by arguing for a minimal deterrence doctrine that made its Polaris submarines the centerpiece of U.S. strategy. The minimal deterrence mission required guaranteed retaliation against a finite number of Soviet cities, a mission that coincidentally was best suited to the Polaris's capabilities. SAC and the Air Force promoted a more sweeping countermilitary strategy, requiring thousands of warheads based on more accurate land based launchers and long range bombers.[9]

This hypothesis can be investigated in our data, at least glancingly, by comparing the views of academics and civilians with those of defense company managers and military analysts under contract with the Pentagon.

Irrational Consistency – a Relative of Strategic Polarization

In his book *Perception and Misperception in International Politics*, Robert Jervis describes an interesting mechanism that would surely impose great simplicity on strategic preferences even if it didn't produce a strictly dichotomous polarization.[10] Jervis describes people's tendency to dismiss tradeoffs and to overlook difficulties that detract from their preferred course. Invoking the human mind's impulse to reject inconsistent or dissonant ideas, he argues that "all considerations are seen as pointing to the same conclusion," all detractions are discounted or denied, so that "multiple, independent, reinforcing arguments" improbably converge on a single solution. Jervis calls this tendency "irrational consistency." A corollary pattern, he suggests, is that people commonly perceive their preferred policies as "a dominant strategy – i.e. one that is best no matter what the other state does" (p. 135).

9 Jack Snyder, *The Ideology of the Offensive* (Ithaca: Cornell University Press, 1984); Barry Posen, *The Sources of Military Doctrine* (Ithaca: Cornell University Press, 1984); Stephen Van Evera, "The Cult of the Offensive and the Origins of the First World War," *International Security* 9 (1984); and Jack Snyder, *Myths of Empire* (Ithaca: Cornell University Press, 1991), all develop these themes in their studies of military organizations and their strategic preferences. Edward N. Luttwak provides a close analysis of interservice rivalries and their pervasive implications in *The Pentagon and the Art of War* (New York: Simon and Schuster, 1985). Richard Betts confronts the arguments in his study *Soldiers, Statesmen, and Cold War Crises* (Cambridge: Harvard University Press, 1977), finding, however, tenuous support for them. He finds military officers frequently divided among themselves, sometimes less bellicose than civilians, but often motivated by parochial interservice differences. Classic discussions of bureaucratic processes in foreign policy decision making are Graham T. Allison, *Essence of Decision* (Boston: Little Brown, 1971), and Morton H. Halperin, *Bureaucratic Politics and Foreign Policy* (Washington: Brookings Institution, 1974).

10 Robert Jervis, *Perception and Misperception in International Politics* (Princeton: Princeton University Press, 1976). Irving L. Janis and Leon Mann, *Decision Making: A Psychological Analysis of Conflict, Choice and Commitment* (New York: Free Press, 1977), develop a similar discussion of "defensive avoidance," which they describe as the tendency of decision makers to ignore risks, to engage in wishful thinking, to exaggerate the prospects of success, and to deny personal responsibility in order to relieve the stress surrounding momentous decisions.

The argument doesn't imply that we must observe just two polar opposites, but it does weigh against conflicted, ambivalent, and middle-of-the-road positions. And, as Jervis points out, the unlikely coincidence that so many considerations converge on a single policy choice suggests that "policy preferences precede and determine at least some of the arguments made in favor of them" (p. 137).

Jervis' idea can be tested in the nuclear thinking data by observing whether or not respondents indicate preferences in the arms racing matrices that entail dominant strategies, and by considering the consistency of preference orderings across different weapon systems.

MODEL III: STRATEGIC DIVERSITY

A third class of models admits diverse patterns of strategic thinking and a multiplicity of political types. Some of these schemes derive from observing the nuclear debate, others from general models of political belief systems, and some from statistical reductions of public opinion data.

Converse's Model of Belief Systems

Philip Converse's seminal article "The Nature of Belief Systems in Mass Publics" has framed the debate about political belief systems for nearly three decades. Converse describes political ideologies as systems of ideas or attitudes that are bound together by *constraints*. The constraints in the system create interdependencies among the elements (measurable correlations in the static case; active covariation in the dynamic case). Some constraints are purely logical, but many are psychological or social. The more *central* elements of the belief system are those that are least likely to change when something in the system is perturbed (say by discordant information). Belief systems differ in the *range* of objects to which their elements refer. Systems that range widely and have political elements near their center are what Converse calls *ideologies*.

The central results in Converse's argument turn on his reasoning about the origins of the constraints. For most people, these tend to be "much less logical in the classical sense than they are psychological – and less psychological than social" (p. 209). Indeed, the shaping of large scale social belief systems into credible, apparently logical wholes "is an act of creative synthesis characteristic of only a minuscule proportion of any population" (p. 211). Rather than forging such complex schemes on their own, most people necessarily consume packages of ideas that have been disseminated by elites.

The trouble is that much of the signal becomes garbled during transmission. As ideologies are disseminated from elite to mass, the abstract principles that connect the elements together (the "whys" of the belief system) are the first to get lost. This leaves some people with a set of ideas that move together (for example, positions on SDI, abortion, and the death penalty), but without a rationale to connect them. Next to go is a knowledge of the elements themselves (of "what goes with what"). Converse's basic thesis is that the belief system crumbles rapidly during the process of social diffusion, leaving only a small fraction of the population with anything like a coherent political world view:

Very little information "trickles down" very far . . . as one moves from the elite sources of belief systems downwards on such an information scale. . . . The contextual grasp of "standard" political belief systems fades out very rapidly. . . . Increasingly, simpler forms of information about "what goes with what" (or even information about the simple identity of objects) turn up missing. The net result, as one moves downward, is that constraint declines across the universe of idea-elements, and that the range of relevant belief systems becomes narrower and narrower. Instead of a few wide-ranging belief systems that organize large amounts of specific information, one would expect to find a proliferation of clusters of ideas among which little constraint is felt. [Philip E. Converse, "The Nature of Belief Systems in Mass Publics," in David Apter, ed., *Ideology and Discontent* (New York: Free Press, 1964), pp. 212–213]

Converse's model implies a sharp discontinuity between the coherent, economical, abstract reasoning of political sophisticates and the disconnected, unmotivated, concrete thinking of unsophisticates. He buttresses his case with survey data that provide a direct contrast between congressional candidates and a national cross section of adults. The data suggest that, unlike the political elites, the mass public maintains political "attitudes" that are shockingly incoherent. Their answers to questions about foreign and domestic policy issues are hardly correlated at all, their responses to particular questions show little stability over time and betray no systematic philosophical or political underpinning. Instead, Converse observes,

the substantive conclusion . . . is simply that large portions of an electorate do not have meaningful beliefs, even on issues that have formed the basis for intense political controversy among elites for substantial periods of time. [p. 245] . . . It cannot therefore be claimed that the mass public shares ideological patterns of belief with relevant elites at a specific level any more than it shares the abstract conceptual frames of reference. [p. 231]

If Converse's reasoning and evidence are correct, then we should receive a rude shock when expectations derived from reading the professional strategic literature (Models I & II) are applied to data collected among strategic unsophisticates. Far from reflecting a cogent strategic logic, or even an ideological or political coherence, the data should assume a disorganized, fragmented appearance more properly described as noise than meaningful opinion. Only among the sophisticated, professional strategists in the sample should we observe coherent patterns like those described earlier.

John Steinbruner's distinction between "theoretical" and "uncommitted" thinking among public-sector decision makers follows the main contours of Converse's argument. Uncommitted thinking is characteristic of political appointees, new to the job. Their beliefs "are not stabilized by the weight of past experience" and "the pressure of inconsistency then produces oscillation over time between a number of belief patterns" (pp. 129–130). Theoretical thinkers, by contrast, "adopt very abstract and extensive belief patterns, patterns which are internally consistent and stable over time." Such people "actively impose an extensive pattern of meaning on immediate events," and maintain their belief systems "on grounds relatively independent of the reality principle" (pp. 130–132). As a result, information can be molded, ignored, or denied to produce confident, strong commitments to a single alternative even in the face of fluid, chaotic events (much like Jervis' irrational consistency). It is for this reason, Steinbruner wryly observes, that theoretical thinkers are commonly called "theologians" in the bureaucratic vernacular.[11]

Converse's model, it should be pointed out, has by no means enjoyed universal acceptance. It has been challenged, on one hand, by analysts who argue that beliefs are highly multidimensional, and therefore can not be expected to obey a simple left-to-right (or other unidimensional) structure. Others have argued that the survey items used to measure ideological thinking are themselves unreliable measures of attitude, contaminated by noise arising from vague, irrelevant, and ambiguous wording. When statistical corrections are made for the unreliability of the survey items, the apparent coherence of people's thinking increases dramatically. Much of the subsequent debate has therefore turned on esoteric questions of statistical methodology, with one school accepting "non-attitudes" as a legitimate description of mass political opinion and another pressing methodological fixes for Converse's troubling findings.[12]

---

11 See John Steinbruner, *The Cybernetic Theory of Decision* (Princeton: Princeton University Press, 1974).
12 Christopher H. Achen, "Mass Political Attitudes and Survey Response," *American Political Science Review* 69 (1975), develops a sophisticated methodological critique of Converse's analysis, suggesting that hazy questions are more responsible for his results than hazy minds. Richard G. Niemi and Herbert F. Weisberg, eds., *Controversies in American Voting Behavior* (San Francisco: W. H. Freeman, 1976), contains further discussion and debate. Converse develops his position in "Attitudes and Non-Attitudes: Continuation of a Dialogue," in Edward R. Tufte, *The Quantitative Analysis of Social Problems* (Reading, Mass.: Addison-Wesley Publishing Co., 1970). Recent developments appear in John Zaller, *The Nature and Origins of Mass Opinion* (Cambridge: Cambridge University Press, 1992). Studies that characterize the structure of foreign policy attitudes (not necessarily about deterrence *per se*) include Jon Hurwitz and Mark Peffley, "How Are Foreign Policy

"Schematic Models" of Political Cognition

Recently, theorists in social and political psychology have developed different explanations for the kind of evidence Converse observed in the electoral surveys. Recognizing the infrequency of systematic ideological thinking, they have focused on other cognitive processes and mental heuristics that give local coherence to people's thinking without necessarily providing a globally integrated world view.

One class of mechanisms that allow people with limited intellectual and informational resources to navigate in complex environments are called cognitive schemas. Schemas are mental prototypes, images, metaphors, "scripts," or categories that provide a frame of reference against which experience is compared and interpreted. In her recent study of the psychology of the Cold War, Deborah Larson describes an episodic "Munich script" and a more general (or categorical) "appeasement encourages aggressors" script that define a generic causal sequence to which many particular episodes can be referred (pp. 50–57). By matching (or assimilating) incoming experience to the stored schematic prototypes, the individual achieves an economical, routinized interpretation of the world that permits inferences to be drawn and predictions to be made. At the same time, the schema identifies salient aspects of the experience for storage in memory.[13]

Attitudes Structured? A Hierarchical Model," *American Political Science Review* 81 (1987); Ole R. Holsti and James Rosenau, "The Structure of Foreign Policy Attitudes Among American Leaders," *The Journal of Politics* 52, No. 1 (February 1990); and Eugene R. Wittkopf, "The Structure of Foreign Policy Attitudes: An Alternative View," *Social Science Quarterly* 30 (1981).

13 Good discussions of schema theory can be found in Deborah Welch Larson, *Origins of Containment: A Psychological Explanation* (Princeton: Princeton University Press, 1985); Shelley E. Taylor and Jennifer Crocker, "Schematic Bases of Social Information Processing," in E. Tory Higgins, C. Peter Herman, and Mark P. Zanna, eds., *Social Cognition: The Ontario Symposium* (Hillsdale, N.J.: Lawrence Erlbaum Associates, 1981); Terry Winograd, "A Framework for Understanding Discourse," in Marcel A. Just and Patricia A. Carpenter, eds., *Cognitive Processes in Comprehension* (Hillsdale, N.J.: Lawrence Erlbaum Associates, 1977); Robert P. Abelson, "Script Processing in Attitude Formation and Decision-making," in John S. Carroll and John W. Payne, eds., *Cognition and Social Behavior* (Hillsdale, N.J.: Lawrence Erlbaum Associates, 1976); William J. McGuire, "The Development of Theory in Social Psychology," in Robin Gilmour and Steve Duck, eds., *The Development of Social Psychology* (London: Academic Press, 1980); and Susan T. Fiske and Shelley E. Taylor, *Social Cognition* (Reading, Mass.: Addison-Wesley Publishing Co., 1984).

A related literature, sometimes called behavioral decision theory, studies the simplifying heuristics that people apply to characteristic problems in decision theory. The literature discovers systematic deviations from the prescriptive "right answers" and suggests interesting heuristic mechanisms to account for them. For useful reviews, see David E. Bell, Howard Raiffa, and Amos Tversky, eds., *Decision Making: Descriptive, Normative, and Prescriptive Interactions* (Cambridge: Cambridge University Press, 1988); Hal R. Arkes and Kenneth R. Hammond, eds., *Judgment and Decision Making: An Interdisciplinary Reader* (Cambridge: Cambridge University Press, 1986); and Daniel Kahneman, Paul

To the extent that political life is understood by canvassing a repertoire of cognitive schemas, either by direct matching, by analogy, or by assimilation, it is possible that opinions and attitudes might not look at all like the highly constrained ideologies that Converse searched in vain to find. Rather than a single guiding principle like rightness or leftness, any number of narrower schemas might organize political attitudes instead. (Of course, the spatial left-to-right representation of politics is itself a cognitive schema.) Political thinking could then assume a highly multidimensional structure, with some attitudes driven by one script or metaphor and other attitudes driven by another. Indeed, some schemas are said to be purely idiosyncratic generalizations drawn from the individual's own experience. In *Origins of Containment: A Psychological Explanation,* Larson describes Harry Truman's reliance on a "Boss Pendergast persona" to interpret other politicians' behavior throughout his later career (pp. 132–135). It follows that people can invoke quite different interpretations for a single event, drawing on categories and metaphors that are uniquely their own.

These analytical possibilities have made schema theory popular among specialists in political psychology who feel uncomfortable ascribing Converse's results (and others like them) to simple randomness and mental disorganization. Schema theory allows systematic explanations for disjointed, apparently fragmented political attitudes. It therefore enjoys wide currency among scholars whose factor analytic and similar multivariate analyses reveal complex, multidimensional structures in political attitude data.[14]

For present purposes, it is important to notice that Converse's model of popular belief systems and more recent social psychological models like schema theory all permit a diversity of political types to emerge in our data. Whether we should expect the diversity of opinion to be essentially random (or idiosyncratic), as Converse suggests, or driven by multidimensional, but nevertheless commonly shared cognitive schemas is an interesting ques-

Slovic, and Amos Tversky, eds., *Judgment Under Uncertainty: Heuristics and Biases* (Cambridge: Cambridge University Press, 1982).

14 Recent studies in political attitude formation that are friendly to the schema theorist's view of the world include Jon Hurwitz and Mark Peffley, "Public Images of the Soviet Union: The Impact on Foreign Policy Attitudes," *Journal of Politics* 52, No.1 (February 1990); Pamela Johnston Conover and Stanley Feldman, "How People Organize the Political World: A Schematic Model," *American Journal of Political Science* 28, No. 1 (February 1984); Richard Herrmann, "The Power of Perceptions in Foreign Policy Decision Making: Do Views of the Soviet Union Determine the Policy Choices of American Leaders?" *American Journal of Political Science* 30, No. 4 (November 1986); Robert Axelrod, "Schema Theory: An Information Processing Model of Perception and Cognition," *American Political Science Review* 67 (December 1973); and Susan T. Fiske and Donald Kinder, "Involvement, Expertise, and Schema Use: Evidence from Political Cognition," in Nancy Cantor and John F. Kihlstrom, eds., *Personality, Cognition, and Social Interaction* (Hillsdale, N.J.: Lawrence Erlbaum Associates, 1982).

tion. But either model militates against the compact, and highly coherent reasoning patterns described in Models I and II.

It is also noteworthy that both theories have much more to say about the structure of political attitudes than they do about their content. Converse's model suggests that unsophisticates' beliefs will be more unconstrained and narrow in range than the beliefs of sophisticates. It does not tell us what beliefs either group will maintain. Nor does schema theory have much to offer this way, since it allows any number of schemas to coexist, it admits wholly idiosyncratic schemas into the story (blurring the contrast with Converse's story), and it has little to say about which schema will be applied to particular events. Rather, the basic idea is that relatively simple heuristics, prototypes, or "lessons" will structure the thinking of unsophisticates about complex, unfamiliar nuclear policy problems. Such broad descriptions leave it to us to determine what schemas are applied in practice.

CONCLUSION

In light of the diverse possibilities we have surveyed, it is little wonder that strategic specialists would be hard pressed to anticipate the shape of our nuclear opinion data. As so often happens in social science problems, the difficulty is not a dearth of ideas but an overabundance of them, each plausible in its own way. With systematic and comparable data from a large set of respondents, we can now put the competing ideas to the test.

5

The Novice Strategists

We shall begin our exploration of the opinion data by studying three samples of undergraduates (N = 169) who enrolled in an introductory politics course at UCLA called "The Nuclear Predicament." The surveys took place in the first week of October during 1988, 1989, and 1990. Since the students completed the survey on the first day of class, their responses reflect the attitudes they brought into the course, not those they developed while taking it. For most students, the course provided a first exposure to the literature on nuclear deterrence and strategy.

Roughly speaking, the UCLA undergraduates come from the top 15% of high school seniors in California. On average they are more aware of public affairs than a typical citizen would be, but their political interest and sophistication vary considerably. Younger and better informed than the general adult population, the students resemble more closely those citizens who participate in the political arena as voters, organizers, and politicians. That resemblance makes them especially interesting to study. The respondents typify the politically active citizenry who affect nuclear policy in their roles as congressmen, bureaucrats, voters, and presidents, but who lack formal training or technical expertise in the subject.

Despite inevitable uncertainties about how far such evidence can be generalized, these samples have several virtues that make them especially valuable in a first study of intuitive deterrence reasoning. First, our ready access to the students made it possible to explore their nuclear thinking much more thoroughly than would ever be possible in an ordinary survey interview. One thing subsequent discussions and examinations made clear was that most students knew very little about nuclear issues when they enrolled in the course. Their historical knowledge about the Cold War, the Soviet Union, and the nuclear arms race was spotty, and the vast majority were unfamiliar with commonplace strategic concepts like central and extended deterrence, secure second strikes, threats that leave something to chance, countervalue and counterforce attacks, positive and negative control, first-strike instabilities, and escalation dominance. While bright, politically alert, and curious enough about nuclear affairs to take the class, they brought little substantive knowledge or analytical sophistication about nuclear policy with them. Instead, their positions could aptly be called untutored, intuitive, or notional.

A second virtue of these respondents was their ability to follow directions and to understand the questionnaire. Survey researchers generally live in dread that their questionnaires will elicit random noise, offered up by reluctant respondents who have a short attention span, who don't understand the questions, or who don't care to make an effort on the researcher's behalf.[1] The nuclear thinking questionnaire places considerable demands on the respondents – first in understanding what is asked, then in canvassing their opinions, and finally in recording preferences in the prescribed format. The students took their jobs much more seriously, I think, than a randomly dialed telephone pollee might. The care they took became evident in the questions they asked afterwards, and in the welcome absence of missing information on the questionnaires themselves. No one refused to complete a questionnaire.

Third, it is important to notice that the samples arise from a captive audience. Unlike the ordinary person contacted by a polling organization, the students had no real opportunity to opt out of the study because they felt ignorant about the subject matter, awkward about describing their thoughts to an interviewer, or too busy to bother. Put another way, the respondents did not select themselves into the sample after screening the content of the questionnaire and anticipating how they would do on "the test." This feature of the evidence seems especially advantageous when the subject matter under study is remote from everyday concerns.

Finally, sampling from the student population made replication feasible. As a result, we can trace the evolution of intuitive strategic thinking in a well-defined, stable population over a period of historic transitions. The three surveys discussed in this chapter span the years of the Cold War's demise, starting in the last days of the Reagan Administration and proceeding to the collapse of the Berlin Wall, the overthrow of Communist regimes in Eastern Europe, the reunification of the two Germanys, the development of U.S.–Soviet strategic cooperation, and then, unexpectedly, to the Persian Gulf Crisis.[2] Maintaining exact continuity in the questionnaire's

1 An influential discussion about response errors in political surveys is Christopher H. Achen, "Mass Political Attitudes and the Survey Response," *American Political Science Review* 69 (1975). Another interesting theory is John Zaller, *The Nature and Origins of Mass Opinion* (Cambridge: Cambridge University Press, 1992).
2 Later on, I shall describe additional samples of respondents, including more "Nuclear Predicament" students, collected after communism collapsed in the Soviet Union and the Commonwealth of Independent States replaced the USSR. Leaving aside these "fresh" data will provide an opportunity to investigate the robustness of conclusions drawn here

format and in the population studied entails a certain rigidity, to be sure, but a rigidity that is repaid by comparability. Above all, the data provide some hope of discerning the impact of these historic events on nuclear thinking, without confounding uncertainties about whether a single population is being studied.

To sum up, our novice strategists should be considered a sample of convenience, not a random sample of American adults. This aspect of the data may leave some people cold, especially those who have been trained to believe that only random samples are "scientific." Before dismissing the evidence out of hand, however, it should be remembered that virtually all social surveys and experiments rest upon self-selected samples of volunteers, not truly random samples from the adult population. Response rates in most national surveys are surprisingly low, casting serious doubt on their representativeness. Still, they often provide reasonable estimates of electoral outcomes.[3]

In the discussion to follow, the first priority will be to describe the patterns that arise in the novices' nuclear thinking, not to draw inferences about the shape of American public opinion at a particular time. Some readers will be satisfied at that. Others will be interested in how general the patterns really are. Is nuclear thinking among college students like nuclear thinking in other populations or not? Traditional statistical inferences are

from the earlier samples (an operation called "cross-validation" in the statistics literature). The new samples will also provide valuable evidence about the impact of the Cold War's demise on nuclear strategic preferences. Meanwhile, I'll continue to refer to the current CIS as the Soviet Union or the USSR, as it was called when these questionnaires were completed. Doing so will help us remember the context in which the data were gathered.

3 Many statisticians have pointed out how few samples in the social sciences are actually randomly selected, and how useful inferences can nevertheless be drawn from them. Donald Rubin puts the issue this way: "Almost never do we have a random sample from the target population of trials, and thus we must generally rely on the belief in subjective random sampling. . . . Most experiments are designed to be generalized to *future* trials; we never have a random sample of trials from the future but at best a random sample from the present; in fact, experiments are usually conducted in constrained, atypical environments and within a restricted period of time. Thus, in order to generalize the results of any experiment to future trials of interest, we minimally must believe that there is similarity of effects across time and more often must believe that the trials in the study are 'representative' of the population of trials. This step of faith may be called making an assumption of 'subjective random sampling.' . . . When investigators carefully describe their sample of trials and the ways in which they may differ from those in the target population, this tacit assumption of subjective random sampling seems perfectly reasonable." Donald B. Rubin, "Estimating Causal Effects of Treatments in Randomized and Nonrandomized Studies," *Journal of Educational Psychology* 66, No. 5 (1974), pp. 688–701. For further discussions, see Howard Wainer, ed., *Drawing Inferences from Self-Selected Samples* (New York: Springer-Verlag, 1986); Albert Gifi, *Nonlinear Multivariate Analysis* (New York: John Wiley, 1990); and Roderick J. A. Little and Donald B. Rubin, *Statistical Analysis with Missing Data* (New York: John Wiley, 1987). For a discussion of sampling problems in the National Election Studies, see James DeNardo, "The Strange Case of Surge and Decline," *UCLA Statistics Series*, No. 18 (1989).

unlikely to provide very convincing answers to such questions. Statistical tests that proceed from an assumption of random sampling (or that data are missing from a sample at random) are a poor substitute for actual replication of the survey experiment. As much as possible, then, I have tried to assess the stability of the results by sampling opinions from quite different groups, including professional nuclear experts and everyday people. These data give comfort that the students' schemes of nuclear reckoning share basic features in common with those of other groups. Indeed, after much trying, I can't think of any reason to dismiss their responses as atypical, uninteresting, or unenlightening. On the contrary, I shall argue later that the novice data typify nuclear thinking at every level of our political system, from bottom to top.

PATTERNS IN THE ARMS RACING PREFERENCE MATRICES

Let's begin with the basic patterns that arise in the novices' preferences about the four nuclear weapons systems described in the questionnaire. Recall that the first three items describe systems that evoke strident opposition from believers in classical ideas about stable mutual deterrence. Effective means of anti-submarine warfare (ASW) threaten the only component of the nuclear triad that is currently invulnerable to missile attack. Effective ASW would thereby undermine the most secure element of today's second strike forces. A national area defense that is less than perfect but not trivial is just the kind that maximizes the potential for first strike instabilities, according to opponents of SDI. Such a defense can admit a damaging preemptive attack while foreclosing effective retaliation. And finally, highly accurate, MIRVed ICBMs like the MX opened the "window of vulnerability" that so preoccupied the Reagan Administration. Such MIRVs are the counterforce weapon of choice among first strikers and nuclear warfighters.

The fourth item (INVULNERABLE) describes effective technologies for protecting nuclear forces from preemptive attack. Classical thinkers argue that *both* sides should have these, since everyone needs a secure second strike. From the classical point of view, the fourth item is simply the inverse of the first three. There is an important asymmetry, however, that such a description overlooks. The first three weapons systems produced intense procurement debates in the United States; the fourth one didn't. Classical thinkers oppose SDI, ASW, and MX because they tend to destabilize mutual deterrence. Anti-classical thinkers embrace these systems, arguing that the best way to deter military adventures is to threaten the other side's strategic and military capabilities. Everyone seems to agree, however, that the United States should have a secure second strike

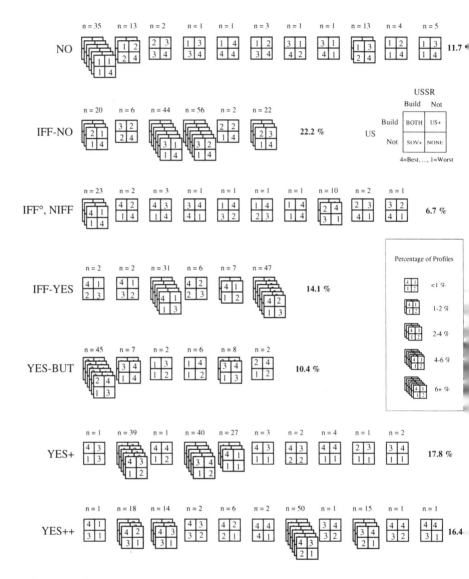

Figure 5.1 Observed political types in the novice samples – All Weapons Systems

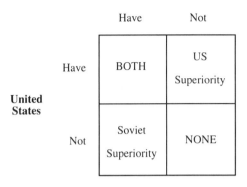

Figure 5.2

(except perhaps the advocates of outright disarmament). As a result, the first three issues have been more controversial, more widely debated, and more publicized.

With these considerations in mind, let's turn now to Figure 5.1, which collects all the preference profiles actually observed among the 169 novice strategists on the four nuclear items. The figure gives a clear view of the most striking pattern in the data.

DIVERSITY OF PREFERENCE

The most remarkable thing about Figure 5.1 is the proliferation of different political types it reveals. Each matrix in the picture describes a distinct preference ordering that appears in the data. I don't know of any prescriptive model of deterrence, or theory of the arms race, that anticipates anything like the diversity of types we see here. Recall that for each kind of weapon, the respondents rate four potential outcomes of the arms race (see Figure 5.2).

Altogether, we observe 60 different patterns of response in a total of 676 profiles (4 profiles from each of 169 respondents). A similar proliferation of preferences appears in every year of the study, and on every question. The number of times a profile appears in the data can be found above each matrix. Notice that the profiles appear in stacks that are proportional to their relative frequency in the data. To achieve some data reduction and make further analysis possible, we need to think right off about classifying all of these preference profiles into politically homogeneous groups.

A GAME THEORETIC ORDERING

A natural first idea is to order the profiles according to the intensity of political support they reveal for each weapon system. One such ordering is accomplished by considering the game theoretic implications of the preference patterns. To evaluate any particular profile, suppose that everybody shares it, both in the United States and in the Soviet Union, and then ask how the arms racing game between the superpowers would proceed.[4]

NO Profiles

Consider first an individual of the following type (from Row 1 in Figure 5.1):

USSR

BUILD NOT

		BOTH	US+
	BUILD	1	3
US		SOV+	NONE
	NOT	2	4

This person prefers unconditionally that the United States not build the weapon system. If the Soviet Union doesn't build, then the preference is 4 to 3 that the U.S. not build either. If the Soviet Union does build, the individual still prefers by 2 to 1 that we don't. In game theoretic parlance, *Not Build* is a (strongly) *dominant strategy*. Not building is the player's strictly best response to any strategy the Soviet Union might follow since it delivers a higher payoff than any other course of action, whatever the Soviets might do.

Now suppose that everyone maintained this pattern of preference on both sides of the arms race. The game between the two nuclear powers would look as follows:

USSR

BUILD NOT

		1	2
	BUILD	1	3
US		3	4
	NOT	2	4

---

4 For our purposes, it will be sufficient to consider the pure strategy equilibria in a simple one-shot game between the two sides. Real arms races clearly involve iterated play, great uncertainties, and tangled interactions with other political arenas. Analyzing these complexities is not required to appreciate the differences in preference structure that concern us here.

Here we have followed the usual convention of placing the row player's (USA) payoff in the southwest corner of each cell and the column player's (USSR) in the northeast. Notice that to express the same preference pattern from the Soviet point of view requires that we reverse the payoffs on the off-diagonal of the matrix. From their perspective, SOV+ becomes superiority for *us* and US+ becomes superiority for *them*. This game has a *dominant strategy equilibrium* at the strategy combination [*Not Build, Not Build*]. The strategy combination is also a *Nash equilibrium* since neither player can profit by deviating from it unilaterally. If such players controlled policy in both countries, the weapon system would never be built. In this sense, their pattern of preference entails strong opposition to the weapon and strong support for arms control.

In Figure 5.1, "NO" players are those respondents for whom *Not Build* would be a dominant strategy. Their preference profiles appear in the first row. In some cases *Not Build* is a strictly dominant strategy; in others it is weakly dominant. Weakly dominant strategies yield payoffs that are never smaller than any other strategy delivers, and are strictly greater for at least one strategy combination. It is therefore reasonable to expect players to follow dominant strategies of both kinds, when they exist.

IFF Profiles

The next three rows in Figure 5.1 describe IFF ("if-and-only-if") players. These people follow the maxim "If they have the weapon, we're going to have it too; otherwise, we don't want it." To see why the IFF types have been partitioned into separate groups, consider the following profiles:

	BUILD	NOT			BUILD	NOT
	BOTH	US+			BOTH	US+
BUILD	4	1		BUILD	3	1
	SOV+	NONE			SOV+	NONE
NOT	1	3		NOT	1	4

These two respondents are typical IFFs since they want the weapon when the Soviets have it and they don't want it otherwise. There is an obvious difference in political outlook, however, since the first person prefers both to neither, while the second prefers neither to both.

If we consider what happens when the two types encounter their Soviet mirror images, the following games arise:

USSR

	BUILD	NOT
US BUILD	4 / 4	1 / 1
NOT	1 / 1	3 / 3

	BUILD	NOT
BUILD	3 / 3	1 / 1
NOT	1 / 1	4 / 4

Neither side has a dominant strategy in these games, but there are two Nash equilibria in pure strategies, one at [Build, Build] the other at [Not, Not]. In the first game, the build equilibrium *Pareto-dominates* the arms control equilibrium since both players prefer BOTH to NONE. As a result, either side can guarantee its most preferred outcome simply by building first (knowing that the other side will then follow suit). BOTH sides building is therefore the most plausible outcome of the first game.

In the second game, arms control Pareto-dominates arms racing. If the two sides recognize the structure of the game, neither would have any incentive to build first and thereby disturb the Pareto-efficient equilibrium at NONE. In this sense, the first kind of IFF player manifests stronger support for the weapon than does the second player.

This example shows why it would be unwise to group all of the IFF types together, and why we should be reluctant to rely upon the Nash criterion alone to distinguish among the different profiles. Instead, Figure 5.1 reflects considerations of Pareto-efficiency as well. The row labeled "IFF-NO" contains IFF players who prefer the equilibrium at NONE to the one at BOTH. "IFF-YES" types prefer BOTH to NONE. And "IFF°" are indifferent between the two equilibria.[5]

YES Profiles

Finally, let's consider the YES respondents, who all have dominant strategies (either weak or strong) to build the weapon system. The YES players have also been partitioned into several groups, despite their shared enthusiasm for military procurement. Those called YES-BUT reach a dominant strategy equilibrium at [Build, Build] if they confront each other in an arms racing game. The equilibrium is *Pareto-inefficient*, however, and such players experience regrets if both sides follow their dominant strategies. Both prefer the outcome at NONE, where nobody builds, to the outcome at BOTH. The first profile in the YES-BUT row gives rise to the famous Prisoner's Dilemma. It is now widely appreciated that an equilibrium can be

5 Some additional types, to be described presently, also appear in the IFF° row.

sustained in the Prisoner's Dilemma at the cooperative, Pareto-efficient out-come, if the game is iterated indefinitely, if time horizons are "sufficiently long," and if there is incomplete information. Other scenarios lead back to the dominant strategy equilibrium at BOTH, so the obvious ambivalence in the preference profile becomes manifest in a politically interesting way.[6]

Among the YES+ players, the ambivalence just described disappears. These respondents not only have a dominant strategy to build, but the [*Build, Build*] equilibrium is Pareto-efficient as well. In other words, the YES+ types not only want to build, they feel better off having done so, preferring BOTH to NONE.

Finally, the last row of Figure 5.1 contains an interesting breed called YES++. These respondents share all the enthusiasms of the YES+ play-ers, but with an additional twist. All of them prefer outright Soviet superior-ity to an arms control agreement that leaves nobody with the weapon system! In this way, the YES++ players are even more ardent opponents of arms control than the YES+'s would be. For the YES++ers, arms control is the worst outcome imaginable. Most people I've talked to find the YES++ preferences to be absurd and suspicious, at least at first glance. These skeptics usually raise their eyebrows and dismiss the re-sponses as obvious mistakes or misunderstandings. Maybe they're right, but surely it's bad business to start an analysis by dismissing everything we don't understand as mistakes. Even if the world is noisy, it seems reason-able to take all the data seriously for now.[7]

As you move from top to bottom, the rows in Figure 5.1 indicate progres-sively stronger political commitments to the weapon systems, in the sense just described. Perhaps too much should not be made of the game theoretic rationale, since it does not rest upon a careful or realistic specification of how such games would actually be played. Nevertheless, the ordering seems clearly sensible. If we think about putting together coalitions in a typical weapons procurement or arms control battle, it would be hard to disagree that the dominant NOs are very different players from the domi-nant YESes, with the IFFs somewhere in between.

Table 5.1 and Figure 5.3 display further evidence about the diversity of

6 A second type of YES-BUT player also reaches a dominant strategy equilibrium at (BUILD, BUILD), but is indifferent between BOTH and NONE rather than preferring NONE out-right. For these individuals, the "-BUT" expresses a weaker kind of ambivalence.

7 In naming the profiles, I have borrowed terminology from Thomas Schelling's stimulating essay "A Framework for the Evaluation of Arms-Control Proposals," in Franklin A. Long and George W. Rathjens, *Arms, Defense Policy, and Arms Control* (New York: W. W. Norton, 1975). Schelling's framework is rich, and far ahead of its time. He discusses bargain-ing relationships among four basic political types that turn up in Figure 5.1, including a NO, an IFF, and two YESes.

Table 5.1. *Distribution of game theoretic types by year: novice samples*

All Games	Fall 1988	Fall 1989	Fall 1990	Total
NO	34	13	32	79
	10.9	7.39	17.0	11.7
IFF-NO	56	57	37	150
	17.9	32.4	19.7	22.2
IFF°, NIFF	3	9	20	32
	0.962	5.11	10.6	4.73
IFF-YES	41	24	30	95
	13.1	13.6	16.0	14.1
YES-BUT	26	28	16	70
	8.33	15.9	8.51	10.4
YES+	55	33	32	120
	17.6	18.8	17.0	17.8
YES++	82	11	18	111
	26.3	6.25	9.57	16.4
N.A.	15	1	3	19
	4.81	0.568	1.60	2.81
Total	312	176	188	676
	100%	100%	100%	100%

preferences in the novice samples. Table 5.1 shows the fraction of people in each game theoretic category over the three years. The marginal frequencies are quite similar after year, showing that the heterogeneity in Figure 5.1 is not an artifact of aggregating very different groups. Table 5.1 also shows that the collapse of communism in Eastern Europe did not dramatically reshape the distribution of preferences. Even after the Revolutions of 1989, the full spectrum of political types continued to appear. Figure 5.3 orders the profiles by their frequency of appearance in the data. With 169 respondents and 4 different weapons, we have 676 profiles altogether. The most popular profile occurred 56 times, the second most popular 50 times, and so on. We see that the responses are distributed widely across the elements of Figure 5.1, rather than concentrating on just one or two or three popular types as the prescriptive models of deterrence suggest they should. The 10 most common profiles (a whopping number, to judge

Type	Count	Cumulative %
[3 2 / 1 4]	56/676	8.3%
[4 3 / 2 1]	50	15.7
[4 2 / 1 3]	47	22.6
[2 4 / 1 3]	45	29.3
[3 1 / 1 4]	44	35.8
[3 4 / 1 2]	40	41.7
[4 3 / 1 2]	39	47.5
[1 1 / 1 4]	35	52.7
[4 1 / 1 3]	31	57.2
[4 1 / 1 1]	27	61.2
[4 1 / 1 4]	23	64.6
[2 3 / 1 4]	22	67.9
[2 1 / 1 4]	20	70.8
[4 2 / 3 1]	18	73.5

Type	Count	Cumulative %
[3 4 / 2 1]	15/676	75.7%
[4 3 / 3 1]	14	77.8
[1 2 / 2 4]	13	79.7
[1 3 / 2 4]	13	81.8
[2 4 / 3 1]	10	83.1
[3 4 / 1 3]	10	84.6
[1 3 / 1 4]	9	87.1
[1 4 / 1 2]	8	88.3
[3 4 / 1 4]	7	89.3
[4 1 / 1 2]	7	90.3

BOTH	US +
SOV +	NONE

Plus 36 further distinct types.
N = 169

Figure 5.3 Novice samples: most frequent political types – all weapons by most classifications of the strategic literature) cover only 61% of the observed responses. In all of these ways, preference diversity is a pronounced and stable pattern. Next we turn to some particular profiles that by their strangeness invite careful scrutiny.

PERVASIVE ANOMALIES

One of the most curious remarks during the generally curious Star Wars debate was President Reagan's suggestion that the United States would give the Soviet Union SDI if we got it first. Why, you might wonder, would the most anti-Soviet President of the Cold War period propose to give the "evil empire" blueprints to our national defense against a missile attack by them? Reagan's suggestion was so incongruous that many people dismissed it as politicking and sales pitching, including the Soviets. It comes as rather a surprise, then, to find that 7 of the 10 most popular profiles in our data express the same idea. As you proceed down the list in Figure 5.3, you'll discover that a large number of the novice respondents prefer that BOTH sides have the weapon system to outright American superiority (US+). From the classical perspective, such an idea is understandable if we are talking about systems that make second strike forces invulnerable. But here it occurs commonly for all the weapon types including ASW and heavy MIRVs. Neither classical nor anti-classical deterrence reasoning explains these views – or anticipates them in calculating a prescribed strategy.

A second anomaly are the curious YES++ responses. Recall that these individuals prefer outright Soviet superiority to arms control bans that leave nobody with the weapon. When such patterns appeared in pre-tests of the questionnaire administered in early 1988, I immediately suspected that my respondents must have reversed the rank orderings, using 1 to indicate "Best" and 4 to indicate "Worst." But oddly, few of these matrices make any more sense if you reverse the codings. Thereafter I took special precautions to emphasize the correct coding each time I administered the survey, repeating it aloud several times. I also included it directly above the weapons questions and called everyone's attention to it so that they could refer to it as they filled in their responses. But the YES++'s kept appearing, and on every type of weapon (see Table 5.2). There are 12 different kinds of YES++ in the data, comprising 16% of all the responses. In fact the second most common profile of all is a YES++. YES++ is the third most popular of the seven game theoretic categories. All of these patterns seem weird and hard to explain.

The anomalies don't stop there. How would you answer the following question about nuclear stability theory (taken from a midterm exam in the Nuclear Predicament class)?

Table 5.2. *Game theoretic type by weapon system*

All Games	Weapon System				
	ASW	INVULNERABLE	MX	SDI	Total
NO	20	12	23	24	79
	11.8	7.10	13.6	14.2	11.7
IFF-NO	42	19	50	39	150
	24.9	11.2	29.6	23.1	22.2
IFF°, NIFF	6	7	12	7	32
	3.55	4.14	7.10	4.14	4.73
IFF-YES	24	33	14	24	95
	14.2	19.5	8.28	14.2	14.1
YES-BUT	19	15	21	15	70
	11.2	8.88	12.4	8.88	10.4
YES+	30	43	17	30	120
	17.8	25.4	10.1	17.8	17.8
YES++	25	35	27	24	111
	14.8	20.7	16.0	14.2	16.4
N.A.	3	5	5	6	19
	1.78	2.96	2.96	3.55	2.81
Total	169	169	169	169	676
	100%	100%	100%	100%	100%

> Rank the following situations in order of stability:
> _____ Both sides have a secure second strike.
> _____ One side has a secure second strike and the other doesn't.
> _____ Neither side has a secure second strike.

That this question does not have a clear and definite right answer reveals an interesting soft spot in modern deterrence theory. I spent a long time debating with my fellow instructor in the course, Dean Wilkening, about the best response (apologies to former students). There was no disagreement about the most stable case (BOTH), but we couldn't agree about the correct ranking for the other two. He argued that it would be more stable if at least one side had a secure second strike than if neither did. In that case the inferior party would be deterred from striking first by the assured second strike of its adversary. The stronger side would therefore only strike

	BUILD NOT	
	BOTH	US+
BUILD	2	1
	SOV+	NONE
NOT	1	4

	BUILD NOT	
	BOTH	US+
BUILD	3	1
	SOV+	NONE
NOT	1	4

Figure 5.4 MIRVed ICBMs: unstable balance anomalies

first if it wanted to commit murder. I argued that both scenarios could be equally unstable, since the weaker side's temptation to preempt in a crisis could generate the mutual fear of surprise attack. Our debate went back and forth with no satisfying resolution, but nothing prepared us for the commonplace response by students that deterrence would be *more stable* when *neither side* had a secure second strike than when only one side did.

If we understand anti-submarine warfare and MIRVed ICBMs to describe *counterforce* or *strike first* weapons, as many experts do, then the survey questions about ASW and MX replicate the midterm exam question. And here again, over and over, the respondents find it more desirable that *both* sides should have these counterforce weapons than just one side or the other. Figure 5.4 shows some typical examples. The pattern is especially striking among the IFF-NOs, as you can see in Figure 5.1 and Table 5.2. With only one exception, the IFF-NOs actually prefer that both sides have MIRVs and ASW to unilateral American superiority! From now on, I shall refer to these profiles as the *unstable balance anomalies*, following the terminology in an interesting passage from Thomas Schelling's *The Strategy of Conflict*:

There is a difference between a balance of terror in which *either* side can obliterate the other and one in which *both* sides can do it no matter who strikes first. It is not the "balance" – the sheer equality or symmetry in the situation – that constitutes mutual deterrence; it is the *stability* of the balance. The balance is stable only when neither, in striking first, can destroy the other's ability to strike back. [*The Strategy of Conflict* (New York: Oxford University Press, 1960), p. 232]

Profiles that value mutual deployments of *first strike* weapons clearly defy the fundamental idea in classical theory that deterrence requires the ability to *strike second*. Of course, such preferences make no sense from an anti-classical perspective either (where military superiority is the key to deterring aggression).

Finally, let's consider what are perhaps the most bizarre responses of all, called NIFFs (not-if-and-only-if) in Figure 5.1. NIFF thinkers follow the procurement rule "If they don't have them, we should; but if they do get them, we'd be better off without them." The NIFF profiles can be found in the IFF° row of Figure 5.1, for lack of a better place to put them. The

NIFFs come in several varieties, and appear occasionally in every sample. A dialogue with a typical NIFF person might go like this:

Q: What do you think about SDI?
A: Well, the best thing would be unilateral American superiority where we had it and they didn't, but after that I suppose I'd choose Soviet superiority. Both having it is definitely worse than that, but neither having it would be a disaster.

Perusing Figure 5.1 will reveal many more anomalous, confusing, hard to understand responses in every category from NO to YES++. Some people rate Soviet superiority the best outcome of all. Lots of people call U.S. superiority the worst case. Others are indifferent between U.S. superiority and Russian superiority, as long as it's one or the other. After that they get unhappy. All of these delightful oddities bring us back to a basic question: Are the data themselves flawed and misleading, or is it our system of expectations about them that's defective?

IDEOLOGICAL SMEARING

In an effort to clarify the origins of the respondents' weapons preferences, I investigated next their relationship to the ideological self-descriptions and other background political characteristics elicited in the questionnaire. Figure 5.5, which describes the relationship between preferences about SDI and the novices' ideological self-descriptions, typifies what we find over and over again.

Although it is rather unconventional looking, Figure 5.5 is simply a scatterplot of preference profiles. Each matrix in the picture locates the preferences of a single individual in a two dimensional grid. Along the horizontal axis, moving from left to right, the game theoretic categories describe increasing political support for SDI. The vertical axis indicates the respondents' ideological self-descriptions. When several respondents fall in the same location on the grid, their preference profiles appear in a stack whose height measures frequency. As much as possible, I have tried to keep specific patterns of preference in vertical columns. This makes it easy to figure out what kind of people arrive at particular profiles. Moving horizontally reveals how people with a common ideology array themselves along the spectrum of political support for SDI.

By all that is right and good in political science, the data should form a diagonal pattern such that leftists and liberals oppose SDI while conservatives and rightists support it. The elevated peaks in the data are vaguely diagonal (an interesting feature that I'll return to later), but no right thinking person would call this picture anything but a mess. It shows people in every ideological category smeared across the whole game theoretic spec-

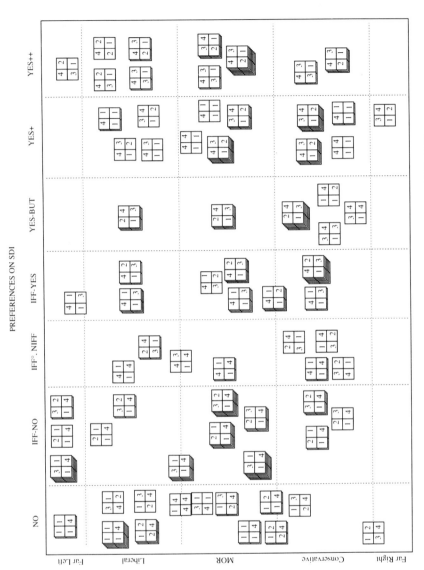

Figure 5.5 Ideological smearing: Novice samples, 1988,1989,1990

trum. Liberals take positions from NO to YES++, just like Middle-of-the-Roaders and Conservatives. Even the Far Leftists and Rightists are smeared, for heaven's sake.

Is it naive to expect that Figure 5.5 should have a diagonal pattern? Is it so implausible to think that strategic preferences might have an ideological basis? Was it pure accident that the conservative Ronald Reagan invested heavily in national defense and revived the ABM? Weren't his priorities disputed by liberal Democrats like Walter Mondale and Edward Kennedy? Does anyone object nowadays when hardliners in the Russian parliament are called "conservative"? To my way of thinking, the Liberal Hawks and Conservative Doves revealed in Figure 5.5 seem highly anomalous. Those who doubt that ideological labels like liberal and conservative have any meaning will be less surprised, I suppose.[8]

At the same time, the picture sheds new light on the anomalies discussed earlier. Here the vast majority of YES++ players prefer to give the Soviets SDI, should we obtain it first, and all of them prefer unilateral Soviet deployment of SDI to an arms control ban like the ABM Treaty. Not only are the YES++ profiles surprisingly numerous (14% of the total), but over 70% of them arise among people who call themselves middle-of-the road or conservative – again defying political common sense. Most of the NIFFs are also conservative, though we see a couple of liberal NIFFs too. There is even one lonely far rightist who is a dominant NO. This person prefers unilateral Soviet deployment to either American superiority or mutual deployment. Those who study Figure 5.5 more carefully will discover many other interesting puzzles too.

Is ideological smearing perhaps peculiar to SDI politics, reflecting the confusion surrounding that ill-defined system? Surprisingly the answer is no.

Figure 5.6 shows that similar patterns of ideological smearing appear for all four weapon systems.[9]

8 Bruce Russett describes smeared results like ours as commonplace in surveys about strategic defenses. The same disconcerting lack of ideological structure was discovered by Converse in the Michigan electoral surveys. Bruce Russett, "Democracy, Public Opinion, and Nuclear Weapons," in Philip Tetlock, Jo Husbands, Robert Jervis, Paul Stern, and Charles Tilly, eds., *Behavior, Society, and Nuclear War*, Vol. 1 (New York: Oxford University Press, 1989).

9 In constructing the scatterplots, I have followed the advice of John Tukey and Robert Abelson, who advocate assigning numbers to ordered categories so that powerful multivariate statistical methods can be applied to such data. The apparent arbitrariness of such assignments is less objectionable than one might suppose, if there is a strong *a priori* justification for the ordering (as game theoretic considerations provide here).

Tukey and Abelson propose coding schemes that are robust, meaning that the assigned scales will be strongly correlated with any "true" underlying scale that obeys the same rank order. It turns out that naive linear quantifications for ordered categories, like {1,2,3,4,5,6}, are not very robust. One does better by separating the extreme values from the rest of the

To take the analysis a step further, Table 5.3 describes simple linear regressions of the game theoretic types for each weapon system on all three background variables. POL ID are the ideological self-descriptions. USSR describes the respondents' descriptions of the conflict of interest between the United States and Soviet Union. LOGITPROB are the estimated probabilities of nuclear war (with anyone) during the next four decades, transformed to a logit scale.

The explanatory power of these regressions is incredibly poor, even for political survey data (where R^2 statistics often range between 30% and 50%). In three of the four regressions, the joint hypothesis that *all* of the regression coefficients are *zero* can not be rejected at conventional levels of significance. Figure 5.7 shows that the marginal distributions of the regressors are generally well behaved (the USSR variable is highly kurtotic, but otherwise the distributions show good dispersion and symmetry). There are no influential outliers, no obvious non-linearities, nor any appreciable collinearity in the data. There are, in short, no evident statistical pathologies to explain the strange results.

In plain words, these regressions say that knowing

1. How people describe their ideological position,
2. Whether they believe nuclear war to be very likely or virtually impossible, or
3. Whether they describe the Soviets as a power like us or a mortal enemy

---

pack as in {1,4,5,6,7,10}. The quantifications used here follow the latter pattern. The numeric scales for the political background variables and game theoretic types are defined as follows:

Political Identification –	Far Left = 0
	Liberal = 3
	Middle-of-the-Road = 5
	Conservative = 7
	Far Right = 10
Game Theoretic Type –	NO = 0
	IFF-NO = 3
	IFF°-NIFF = 4
	IFF-YES = 5
	YES-BUT = 6
	YES+ = 7
	YES++ = 10
USSR –	0 = "A major power sharing many interests in common with the U.S."
	3 = "A formidable adversary but one that can be dealt with through tough diplomacy."
	7 = "A dangerous opponent that only respects military force,"
	10 = "A mortal enemy bent on world conquest."

See Robert P. Abelson and John W. Tukey, "Efficient Conversion of Non-Metric Information into Metric Information," in Edward R. Tufte, ed., *The Quantitative Analysis of Social Problems* (Reading, Mass.: Addison-Wesley Publishing Co., 1970). Later on I shall employ techniques that provide statistically optimal quantifications of the categories.

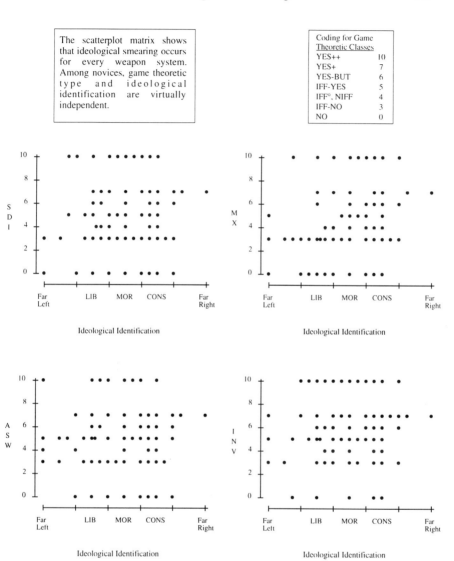

The scatterplot matrix shows that ideological smearing occurs for every weapon system. Among novices, game theoretic type and ideological identification are virtually independent.

Coding for Game Theoretic Classes	
YES++	10
YES+	7
YES-BUT	6
IFF-YES	5
IFF°, NIFF	4
IFF-NO	3
NO	0

Figure 5.6 Ideological smearing of game theoretic type

Table 5.3. Ideological smearing regressions

Dependent variable is ASWgame
169 total cases of which 1 is missing
R^2 = 1.7%   R squared (adjusted) = 0.0%
s = 2.934 with 168 - 4 = 164 degrees of freedom

Source	Sum of Sqrs	df	Mean Square	F-ratio
Regression	24.5826	3	8.19419	0.952
Residual	1411.94	164	8.60936	

Variable	Coefficient	s.e. of Coeff	t-ratio	prob
Constant	4.90883	0.7020	6.99	≤ 0.0001
Pol ID	0.080754	0.1305	0.619	0.5368
LogitProb	0.493875	0.3634	1.36	0.1760
USSR	0.042148	0.1261	0.334	0.7387

Dependent variable is INVgame
169 total cases of which 2 are missing
R^2 = 1.7%   R squared (adjusted) = -0.1%
s = 2.781 with 167 - 4 = 163 degrees of freedom

Source	Sum of Sqrs	df	Mean Square	F-ratio
Regression	21.3093	3	7.10309	0.918
Residual	1260.67	163	7.73415	

Variable	Coefficient	s.e. of Coeff	t-ratio	prob
Constant	5.34202	0.6700	7.97	≤ 0.0001
Pol ID	0.102841	0.1243	0.827	0.4093
LogitProb	0.184060	0.3445	0.534	0.5939
USSR	0.098452	0.1196	0.823	0.4115

Dependent variable is SDIgame
169 total cases of which 3 are missing
R^2 = 6.9%   R squared (adjusted) = 5.2%
s = 2.932 with 166 - 4 = 162 degrees of freedom

Source	Sum of Sqrs	df	Mean Square	F-ratio
Regression	103.921	3	34.6404	4.03
Residual	1392.54	162	8.59591	

Variable	Coefficient	s.e. of Coeff	t-ratio	prob
Constant	4.00685	0.7082	5.66	≤ 0.0001
Pol ID	0.227172	0.1306	1.74	0.0839
LogitProb	0.782547	0.3670	2.13	0.0345
USSR	0.127438	0.1267	1.01	0.3158

Dependent variable is MXgame
169 total cases of which 4 are missing
R^2 = 5.7%   R squared (adjusted) = 3.9%
s = 3.002 with 165 - 4 = 161 degrees of freedom

Source	Sum of Sqrs	df	Mean Square	F-ratio
Regression	87.7555	3	29.2518	3.25
Residual	1451.06	161	9.01277	

Variable	Coefficient	s.e. of Coeff	t-ratio	prob
Constant	3.55829	0.7238	4.92	≤ 0.0001
Pol ID	0.287731	0.1345	2.14	0.0339
LogitProb	0.586344	0.3771	1.55	0.1219
USSR	0.068844	0.1292	0.533	0.5948

Explanation: These remarkable regressions suggest that knowing whether novices call themselves liberal or conservative, knowing whether they think nuclear war is likely or virtually impossible, and knowing whether they think Russia is a mortal enemy or much like the US – all of that taken together – conveys virtually no information about game theoretic type on nuclear

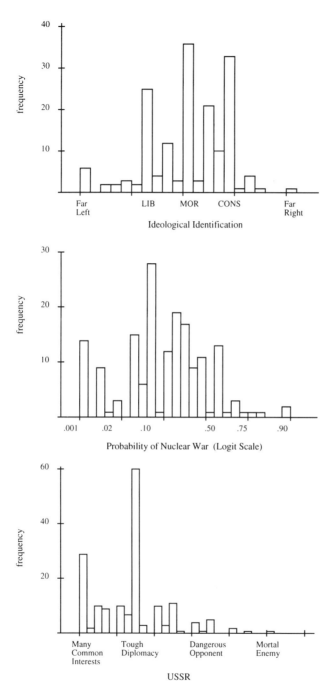

Figure 5.7 Distribution of novices on background variables

tells us *virtually nothing* about the strength of their support for any type of weapon. I believe that even hardened survey researchers, who quickly become inured to painful levels of noise, would be surprised by these results. After all, I didn't go to the trouble of measuring the explanatory variables because I thought they would be worthless and irrelevant. I chose the variables that seemed most likely to explain the factional structure of national security politics, given a close reading of the literatures on strategy and public opinion.

INSTABILITY OF GAME THEORETIC TYPE

It is interesting to consider finally whether the respondents' political positions on the various weapons systems are closely interrelated or not. Classical ideas about mutual deterrent stability suggest that the questions about ASW, SDI, and the MX should all elicit NOs, while the question about securing nuclear forces from preemptive attack (INVULNERABLE platforms) should elicit a YES. If classical thinking were the dominant perspective on the arms race, as many writers suggest, the observed game theoretic types should be highly stable from weapon to weapon, with INVULNERABLE having a political valence opposite to the other items. Anti-classical theory says all four systems are YESes. People with this point of view should take the same position on every question (presumably YES+). If the sample included both classical and anti-classical types, then the correlations among the first three game theoretic scales should be strong and positive (NOs go with NOs, and YESes with YESes), while the correlations involving INVULNERABLE would be attenuated toward zero (YESes on INVULNERABLE go with NOs and YESes alike on the other questions).

Table 5.4 shows the correlations among the respondents' game theoretic types on the four nuclear weapons systems (as usual, the game categories are scaled from NO = 0 to YES++ = 10 as described above). The correlations are a crude but familiar summary of how coherently the respondents' preferences are organized across various dimensions of the arms race. With the exception of the items on ASW and MX, which show a middling correlation, the rest of the relationships are slight indeed. The Pearsonian correlations hover around .25 in each case, indicating a very low level of linear covariation. The correlations involving the INVULNERABLE question look no different than any of the others, in either sign or magnitude. Nothing changes when we compute correlations among the ranks of the game theoretic categories (a procedure that is robust against monotonic transformations of the scales, and so does not assume linearity, and which is less affected by outliers or unusual values in the data). The summary statistics reflect a very high level of game theoretic instability from weapon to weapon.

Table 5.4. *Stability of game theoretic type across weapons: novices*

	ASW game	MX game	SDI game	INV game	Pol ID
Pearson Product-Moment Correlations					
ASW game	1.000				
MX game	0.460	1.000			
SDI game	0.260	0.244	1.000		
INV game	0.233	0.244	0.318	1.000	
Pol ID	0.073	0.205	0.188	0.103	1.000
Spearman Rank Correlations					
ASW game	1.000				
MX game	0.469	1.000			
SDI game	0.299	0.230	1.000		
INV game	0.229	0.233	0.323	1.000	
Pol ID	0.120	0.232	0.203	0.067	1.000

n = 169 cases, 5 missing

Coding for Game Theoretic Classes
YES++ 10; YES+ 7; YES-BUT 6; IFF-YES 5; IFF°, NIFF 4; IFF-NO 3; NO 0

To get a clearer picture of what's going on, Table 5.5 displays the full contingency tables of the respondents' game theoretic types for three typical pairs of weapons (all the pairs involving the MX missile). Neither of the first two pairings in the table involves the question about INVULNERABLE platforms for weapons. Both classical and anti-classical theory predict that the MX, SDI, and ASW items should elicit a consistent response (NO in the classical scheme and YES+ in the anti-classical). The rows and columns of each table are the game theoretic categories in which the respondents' preference profiles actually fell. The entries inside the table are the number of respondents who displayed each combination of game theoretic type. Far from finding everybody in the cells {NO, NO} and {YES+, YES+}, we observe responses all over the tables. All seven game theoretic categories are filled, and many respondents make substantial shifts in type from weapon to weapon.

To appreciate how much political volatility there is, consider the MX-SDI table a little more closely. Reading down the first column, we see that people who were NOs on the MX covered the entire spectrum on SDI. (The category N.A. indicates missing data.) Of the 23 MX NOs, 9 supported SDI at IFF-YES or better. In the first row, 11 of 24 SDI NOs expressed support for MX at IFF-YES or better. Of 30 YES+'s on SDI, 15

Table 5.5. *Novice sample: game theoretic consistency over weapons*

| | | | | MX-Game Type | | | | | |
	NO	IFF-NO	IFF°, NIFF	IFF-YES	YES-BUT	YES+	YES++	N.A.	Total
SDI-Game Type									
NO	7	4	0	1	2	2	6	2	24
IFF-NO	5	16	2	6	1	3	5	1	39
IFF°, NIFF	1	1	5	0	0	0	0	0	7
IFF-YES	2	12	3	6	1	0	0	0	24
YES-BUT	2	2	0	0	10	1	0	0	15
YES+	3	10	2	1	6	8	0	0	30
YES++	2	3	0	0	1	3	14	1	24
N.A.	1	2	0	0	0	0	2	1	6
Total	23	50	12	14	21	17	27	5	169
ASW-Game Type									
NO	10	3	0	0	1	2	4	0	20
IFF-NO	7	24	3	4	0	2	1	1	42
IFF°, NIFF	0	1	4	0	0	0	0	1	6
IFF-YES	1	11	0	8	0	1	3	0	24
YES-BUT	3	2	5	0	11	3	0	0	19
YES+	0	6	0	1	9	7	2	0	30
YES++	2	3	0	0	0	2	16	2	25
N.A.	0	0	0	1	0	0	1	1	3
Total	23	50	12	14	21	17	27	5	169

MX-Game Type

INVUL-Game Type	NO	IFF-NO	IFF°, NIFF	IFF-YES	YES-BUT	YES+	YES++	N.A.	Total
NO	4	2	1	1	1	1	2	0	12
IFF-NO	2	11	1	0	0	1	3	1	19
IFF°, NIFF	0	1	5	0	0	0	1	0	7
IFF-YES	4	15	2	9	1	1	1	0	33
YES-BUT	0	5	0	0	10	0	0	0	15
YES+	6	12	3	3	8	9	2	0	43
YES++	7	4	0	1	1	4	17	1	35
N.A.	0	0	0	0	0	1	1	3	5
Total	23	50	12	14	21	17	27	5	169

were politically hostile to MX. And so on. As a crude measure of consistency, we find 40% of the respondents remained in the same game theoretic category (these cases appear on the main diagonal of the table), while 60% changed type; 10% of the respondents shifted all the way from NO to YES. Finally, the most polarized respondents in the NO and YES+ categories appear to be the least consistent across items – contrary to all expectations.

The table comparing positions on MX and ASW shows somewhat more consistency than does MX-SDI (47% on the main diagonal) but provides very little support for either of the prescriptive deterrence theories we've considered. Contrary to classical expectations, only about one eighth of the novices express a NO to either weapon, and only 6 in 100 to both at once. YES+ respondents are hardly more numerous, on the other hand. Remarkably, (YES++, YES++) is a more popular combination than either of the prescriptive "right answers" at (NO, NO) or (YES+, YES+)!

The bottom table describes the novices' types for MX-IN-VULNERABLE. One would have expected from classical and anti-classical theorists alike that everybody should support systems to secure America's nuclear forces from preemptive attack. The YES responses are more common for INVULNERABLE platforms than for any other system, but 41% of the profiles nevertheless fail to reach a YES-something level of support. Only 13 out of 169 novices (7.5%) reach a classical configuration of YES on INVULNERABLE platforms and NO on MIRVed MX missiles.

Taking all the evidence together, there seems to be no reliable pattern of connection among the novices' political positions on the different weapon systems. What seems to be lacking is the ability to organize weapons technologies in strategically equivalent categories, like counterforce and countervalue, or offensive and defensive.

SOME TENTATIVE CONCLUSIONS

Before we try to unravel the complex and interesting puzzles raised by the novice data, it would be instructive to recall the expectations raised in the last chapter about what the data would look like. Many of those hypotheses seem woefully inadequate in retrospect, but that's often the way things turn out in social science. Usually, there are good reasons to support lots of different ideas and little evidence to narrow down the field.

Model I: Unitary Strategic Preferences

The models most grossly at odds with our data suggest that everyone shares a common understanding of nuclear deterrence so that weapon preferences

converge to a consensual game theoretic type. Prescriptive theorists typically invoke *the* logic of deterrence to argue that some weapons should be
deployed and others banned or controlled. In classical deterrence theory,
the idea that nuclears are an "absolute weapon" drives all the main results.
It follows that coercive threats of retaliation, not brute force, must be the
foundation of national security (since nuclear wars are "unwinnable"); that
we should defend weapons not people (to avoid arms races and crisis
instability); and that we should tolerate the other side's deterrent forces
(since deterrence must be mutual). If so, then people should respond nega-
tively to systems that undermine second strikes and positively to systems
that secure them. In similar fashion, anti-classical theorists argue that deterrence will be robust only when the adversary sees that aggression must lead
to defeat on the battlefield. Anti-classical theorists defend weapons that
promote battlefield superiority, and disdain those that don't. While the two
theories reach radically opposed prescriptions about weapons postures,
they share a common assumption that deterrence has an inherent logic,
evident to all. In this shared premise, both fail miserably to describe the
evidence. Whatever we believe *the* logic of deterrence to be, we shall find
our core prescriptions rejected at every turn, often by 80%–90% of the
respondents.

In the same way, the data belie any claim that the nuclear arms race has
been a Prisoner's Dilemma, or a Security Dilemma, or a Deadlock, or a
Richardsonian action–reaction process, or any other simple game with
unitary rational actors. Whatever pattern of preference we attribute to "the
United States" (or, no doubt, to "the Soviet Union"), we shall find glaring
disparities among real political actors and *lots* of them.

In the face of a perennial nuclear debate, one might wonder why a
working hypothesis of unitary strategic preferences remained the dominant
analytical approach throughout the Cold War.[10] I find it unlikely that any of
the leading theorists actually took their models literally, since, on the face
of things, people disagree violently about strategy. But the nuclear debate
by itself does not preclude using the unitary hypothesis as a reasonable
technical simplification – especially since it affords much more analytical
leverage than the alternatives. As long as *most* people accept the presumed
deterrence logic, such models can still be highly instructive representations

---

10 Fritz Ermarth makes the following interesting conjecture about the tendency of American
strategists to perceive strategic preferences as universal: "Explaining this particular expression of our cultural self-centeredness is itself a fascinating field for speculation. . . . It may
result from the fact that post-war developments in U.S. strategy were an institutional and
intellectual offspring of the natural sciences that spawned modern weapons. Scientific
truth is transnational, not culturally determined. But, unfortunately, strategy is more like
politics than like science." ["Contrasts in American and Soviet Strategic Thought," *International Security* 3, No. 2 (Fall 1978)]

of a more complex reality. The mere appearance of a strategic debate therefore does not invalidate the unitary actor models. One also needs quantitative evidence about the frequencies of various viewpoints. And there is really the catch. Reading the nuclear debate does not tell us how many people belong to the different strategic schools. Without individual-level preference data, nobody's working postulates could be refuted.

Our data suggest that *none* of the leading prescriptive and game theoretic models attains anything like a majority consensus for its presumed pattern of strategic preferences. The level of diversity is so great that *most* of the observed profiles can't be explained by *any* of the contending theories. We have, then, a much stronger result than that people disagree about strategy – something the nuclear debate already makes obvious. Rather, our data support the quantitative inference that *unitary models are not a reasonable analytical simplification*. However reasonable or necessary the unitary models appear, these data remain starkly inconsistent with their core simplification. Perhaps we can see better now why prescriptive theorists of all stripes so often find American nuclear strategy to be "illogical" and misguided.

Model II: Strategic Polarization

Almost equally at odds with the data are discussions that describe national security politics as polarized contests between "hawks" and "doves" – whether on ideological grounds, according to people's pessimism or optimism about the likelihood of war, or as a result of their understanding of the Soviet adversary. Neither do we find much evidence of irrational consistency, leading to unwavering (dominant) strategies. Some people have dominant strategies, of course, but a great many don't. And among those that do, few seem politically consistent across issues. Contrary to strategic polarization, we find preference diversity, pervasive anomalies, ideological smearing, and game theoretic instability. None of the predictors we gleaned from the literature seems to have anything to do with strategic preferences.

Model III: Strategic Diversity

Our data clearly favor models that allow a multiplicity of strategic preferences. But models of this type have very different rationales and implications. One kind rests on non-attitudes – diffuse, unconnected, unsystematic ideas, representing the remnants of garbled transmissions from elites to masses. Another kind relies on a system of multiple schemas – the conceptual categories or heuristics through which the world is screened and interpreted.

Those familiar with Philip Converse's seminal article on mass belief systems will have already noticed a striking resemblance between his results on grass-roots political thinking and our own data. The bizarre profiles, the lack of ideological structure in the novices' responses, and the pronounced instability from question to question all seem consistent with Converse's description of mass beliefs as "non-attitudes." Without some understanding of the esoteric conceptual schemes that organize experts' opinions, or lacking the "contextual grasp" to connect specific weapons technologies to general principles, the unsophisticated person's nuclear thinking becomes fragmented, politically self-contradictory, and anomalous from the expert's point of view.

Converse is careful not to suggest that the layperson lacks ideas about politics. Rather, he argues that these ideas are not linked together by commonly shared political concepts into coherent, wide-ranging cognitive systems:

. . . the configuration of political beliefs held by individuals simply becomes increasingly idiosyncratic as we move to the less politically sophisticated. While an equally broad range of belief elements might function as an interdependent whole for an unsophisticated person, we would find little aggregative patterning of belief combinations in populations of unsophisticated people, for they would be out of the stream of cultural information about "what goes with what" and would therefore put belief elements together in a great variety of ways. [Philip E. Converse, "The Nature of Belief Systems in Mass Publics," in David Apter, ed., *Ideology and Discontent* (New York: The Free Press, 1964), p. 239]

The result, Converse argues, will be a diversity of beliefs that is uncharacteristic among experts, a high level of instability in political thinking (over time and across issues), and the holding of opinions that, taken together, seem contradictory or "unnatural" to the sophisticated person. In all of these respects, his model seems consistent with our findings.[11]

Notwithstanding the good fit between Converse's model and our data, an

---

11 Much recent work in cognitive and social psychology would describe Converse's "non-attitudes" as *aschematic* or *piecemeal* thinking. Such thinking results from the unavailability of an integrated knowledge structure or system of conceptual categories through which political stimuli can be filtered and organized. Instead, problems are approached "element by element," without application of a schema. Another recent formulation invokes "idiosyncratic schemata" to explain why systematic patterns would not arise in aggregates of opinion data. Here the problem is not a failure to acquire or activate schemas, but that people apply their own personal (and dissimilar) schemas to the same issues. Converse himself concludes that longitudinal survey data "offer eloquent proof that signs of low constraint among belief elements in the mass public are not the products of well knit but highly idiosyncratic belief systems, for these beliefs are extremely labile for individuals over time." "The Nature of Belief Systems in Mass Publics," p. 241. For further discussions with political applications, see Susan T. Fiske, "Schema-Based Versus Piecemeal Politics"; Richard R. Lau, "Political Schemata, Candidate Evaluations, and Voting Behavior"; Pamela J. Conover and Stanley Feldman, "The Role of Inferences in the Perception of Political Candidates"; Ruth Hamill and Milton Lodge, "Cognitive Consequences of Political Sophistication," all collected in Richard R. Lau and David O. Sears, eds., *Political Cognition* (Hillsdale, N.J.: Lawrence Erlbaum Associates, 1986).

inconspicuous but worrisome glitch in the story raises doubts that we might be forcing the issue. While the novices' policy preferences appear to resemble those from "mass publics," don't college students stand near the pinnacle in Converse's hierarchy of political information? The answer, I believe, is that these undergraduates surely have more political awareness than the general adult population sampled by the Michigan survey researchers. But if so, shouldn't their opinions display the kind of organization and coherence that Converse finds among sophisticates? And if that is true, might there not be another explanation for their strange attitudes than cognitive disorganization?

On one hand, the odd results described above might be a signal that the survey instrument is itself unreliable and noisy. A better questionnaire might reveal systematic patterns in the students' thinking that our measures are too blunt to capture. On the other hand, how can we be sure that some kind of structure isn't lurking in the data already collected? Isn't it possible that we've missed something interesting by organizing the data analysis along game theoretic lines? Ordering the preference profiles by strength of political support is surely relevant for understanding strategic behavior and coalition formation in the arms race, but it might not be the best yardstick for measuring consistency in people's nuclear thinking.[12]

These arguments raise complex issues and require careful scrutiny. My immediate reaction to them is two-fold. First, though I confess to great ambivalence about a model that would portray these respondents as "people who, for lack of information about a particular dimension of controversy, offer meaningless opinions that vary randomly in direction . . ." (Converse, "The Nature of Belief Systems in Mass Publics," p. 243), I do not believe that such a model can be ruled out just by arguing that the students go to college. It simply does not follow from Converse's reasoning or evidence that college students' thinking must be well organized in every domain of politics. His surveys addressed general matters like the proper role of government in funding education, housing the poor, and dispensing foreign aid. The issues raised here seem far more technical and esoteric by comparison. If we asked typical college students for their opinions about controversial questions in brain surgery or computer operating system design, we wouldn't expect to find coherent, "natural" (to the expert), or stable responses. On such questions, most students will be ignorant about the underlying issues of dispute that separate expert schools of thought. For the same reasons, it is plausible that their views about "highly accurate,

12 Notice that most closed ended survey items order alternative opinions along some implicit, *a priori* scale like warmth of support for a candidate or party, leftness or rightness, or closeness to one's own preferred policy position. In this respect, there is nothing unconventional about the data analysis considered so far.

multiple warhead ICBMs like the MX" or "ballistic missile defenses covering the entire national territory" need not be stable or coherent either. Interpreting our data as non-attitudes can make perfectly good sense, if we are willing to believe that the undergraduate population is unsophisticated and uninformed with respect to the issues raised by the survey questionnaire. Compared to nuclear experts, such a description is, in fact, apt.[13]

The first point, then, is that a plausible case can still be made for interpreting the novice data as "non-attitudes," notwithstanding the students' general political sophistication. At the same time, the other hypotheses can't be ruled out either. The similarity between our results and Converse's seems remarkable, but the apparent disarray in the data may have other causes than fragmented thinking. This possibility returns us to the nagging question raised earlier. Couldn't there be some kind of structure lurking in the data that we've simply overlooked so far?

Here two strategies come to mind for breaking the impasse. If Converse's model of belief systems is essentially right, then the case for non-attitudes would be greatly strengthened by data from demonstrable nuclear experts that showed coherent, patterned responses to the same questionnaire. If the experts' preference profiles were strongly "constrained," then Converse's central theoretical claim would be confirmed and the plausibility of the non-attitudes hypothesis enhanced. Such data would also verify that the questionnaire is not inherently ambiguous or noisy. To pursue these possibilities, I collected a large body of data from nuclear experts using exactly the same survey instrument. Studying these data will prove later on to be highly instructive for anchoring our understanding of the unsophisticates' responses.[14]

Now suppose, on the other hand, that the chaotic-looking preference profiles in the novice samples are not really random at all. Imagine instead that some systematic cognitive process structures nuclear thinking through-

13 Those who doubt my judgment are welcome to read a large stack of term papers and exams written by the respondents. Converse himself is careful not to define an absolute scale of sophistication, based on education or other outwardly visible characteristics. His argument rests on relative levels of cognitive constraint. "For our purposes," he writes, "the specific elite sampled and the specific beliefs tested are rather beside the point. . . . A set of questions on matters of religious controversy should show the same pattern between an elite population like the clergy and the church members who form their mass 'public.' What is generically important in comparing the two types of population is the difference in levels of constraint among belief-elements." "The Nature of Belief Systems in Mass Publics," p. 229.

14 It is hard to see how one could ever decisively prove that random-looking responses from unsophisticates do not contain some hidden structure, whatever the expert data reveal. The notorious "random" number generator RANDU passed many tests for randomness, even though it produces output with subtle, but highly systematic patterns. See G. Marsaglia, "Random Numbers Fall Mainly in the Planes," *Proceedings of the National Academy of Sciences* 61 (1968), pp. 25–28.

out the population of unsophisticates, but in ways we've so far overlooked. Finding the footprints left behind by such a mechanism would be another way to break the impasse, this time by refuting the non-attitudes hypothesis directly. Identifying such footprints can be tricky, however, because even truly random data often appear highly structured, enough so to produce "statistically significant" results.[15] Making a convincing case against the non-attitudes interpretation therefore requires two things – direct evidence that statistically stable patterns exist in the data, and a plausible explanation for whatever patterns turn up. These requirements lead to a search for models that are consistent with the evidence we've seen so far, while producing distinctive signatures of their own. Such a search will occupy the two chapters immediately ahead.

One place to look for alternatives to Converse's account of mass political thinking are recent cognitive theories about social judgments. Of course, the left-to-right ideological thinking that Converse attributes to sophisticates is itself a good example of what people now call a cognitive schema.[16] That such organizing classifications allow people to sift through complicated evidence, to store and retrieve data, and to link different problems together is precisely how Converse distinguishes between sophisticated and mass political reasoning. The sophisticates invoke more wide ranging and general categorizations than do the novices, allowing them to address apparently disparate issues from a unifying point of view.[17]

What many contemporary political psychologists find hard to accept is not the style of Converse's model, but the yawning gap between a simple arrangement of sophisticates' beliefs along a left-to-right continuum and the hopelessly unpatterned, idiosyncratic, and even "meaningless" opin-

---

15 The large statistical literature on "data mining" and model selection shows how optimizing statistical fitting algorithms can easily capitalize on chance configurations that arise in truly random data, suggesting structure when none is there. For interesting reviews, see A. J. Miller, *Subset Selection in Regression* (London: Chapman and Hall, 1990), and Michael Lovell, "Data Mining," *Review of Economics and Statistics* 65 (February 1983).

16 Closely related concepts, not always clearly distinguished, include conceptual categories, heuristics, mental models, and default hierarchies. For an inventory of cognitive psychological terminology that is instructive and clear-headed, see John H. Holland, Keith J. Holyoak, Richard E. Nisbet, and Paul R. Thagard, *Induction: Processes of Inference, Learning, and Discovery* (Cambridge: The MIT Press, 1989).

17 Much of Converse's description of belief systems is, in fact, remarkably close to current definitions of schemas. The following passage might just as well have been taken from standard modern texts like Fiske and Taylor's *Social Cognition*: "The use of such basic dimensions of judgment as the liberal–conservative continuum betokens a contextual grasp of politics that permits a wide range of more specific idea-elements to be organized into more tightly constrained wholes. . . . With it, new political events have more meaning, retention of political information from the past is far more adequate, and political behavior increasingly approximates that of sophisticated 'rational' models, which assume relatively full information." Philip E. Converse, "The Nature of Belief Systems in Mass Publics," p. 227.

ions that Converse attributes to the masses (at least on the issues he studied). Couldn't mass opinion reflect systematic patterns of thinking that might not be unidimensional and homogeneous, but which nevertheless produce organized and predictable outcomes? As so often occurs in other fields, theoreticians resist the suggestion that the problem they care about is fundamentally unsystematic and unpredictable.

A search for alternative possibilities propels a recent wave of psychological modeling in social attitude studies, all drawing on the information processing perspective of cognitive science. Some attempts involve multiple schemas that become activated in different domains (or even simultaneously), some rely on mixtures of schematic and piecemeal processing, while others invoke combinations of consensual and idiosyncratic schemas. The trouble so far is that the conceptual foundations of the program seem more like a point of view than a rigorous completed theory. Certainly it is appealing to assume that people labor under severe cognitive constraints, and that they exploit mental shortcuts to cope with complexity. The hard part is discovering what system of mental shorthand they use, especially since many schemas appear to be domain-specific, plausible schemas can easily become horrifyingly complicated "tangled hierarchies," and no schema is directly observable. With new schemas appearing in the literature every day, it becomes more and more difficult to understand where the schemas come from, or which schemas from the burgeoning menu will be applied when and why. Building such an explanation for our data, then, is not a simple matter of lifting existing technology off the shelf.

These intellectual cross-currents in social and political psychology raise difficult questions about how to approach the novices' nuclear preferences. Should they be taken seriously, as the product of some comprehensible conceptual process, or should they be regarded as unstable, uninformative, uninterpretable noise? At this point, we have little basis for choosing one view or the other. Skeptics will say the data are all noise, coming from respondents who are so unsophisticated about nuclear policy that the questions make no sense to them. How can someone formulate a meaningful opinion about "systems like the MIRVed MX missile," if they have no idea what "MIRV" or "MX" signifies? Those who like to think that political thinking has some pattern or structure will shy away from such conclusions. Surely lots of people formed strong opinions about the "neutron bomb" without knowing much more about it than its name. Even more formed confident opinions about SDI, as if "SDI" were a well-defined system. Why should strategic novices' intuitions be random, even if they don't understand the details of the nuclear debate? Doesn't everyone place people, places, and things in mental categories and impute "default values" to them when better information is lacking?

In the next chapter, I shall try to defend the second point of view. There I develop a model of intuitive deterrence reasoning that explains novices' nuclear preferences as the outcome of a highly structured heuristic calculus. The model shows why we observe preference diversity, the political anomalies, ideological smearing, and systematic violations of prescriptive deterrence theory. The model also points to footprints in the data that will dispel any impression that all we have is noise.

6

The Intuitive Calculus of Nuclear Deterrence

The question now is how to make sense of the novices' strange nuclear preferences. One interesting approach is to seek mathematical models that can replicate *notional thinking* about deterrence and the arms race. I use the term notional to describe reasoning driven by intuition and gut feeling rather than careful instruction, considered reflection, or systematic calculation. The purpose of the model is therefore to mimic people's intuitive thinking about national security in a nuclear environment.

Putting forth the effort to construct such a model requires a certain leap of faith, of course, since the whole endeavor presupposes that some systematic process generated the novices' responses in the first place. Nothing in the data we've seen so far seems especially friendly to that idea, and some readers may have decided already that the students responded basically at random to questions they didn't understand – just as if they were asked to decipher a medieval Chinese text or some other incomprehensible thing. But even though people might be uninformed about weapons technology and strategic theory, does it follow that their intuitions about national security have to be random? The hunch followed here is "No."

Our prior knowledge that the novices were mostly unfamiliar with professional strategic theories certainly invites a model based on simple heuristic thinking. But the question then becomes how to generate the bizarre preference orderings, the proliferation of different types, and the ideological smearing – none of which seems simple or straightforward at all. In the models described below, complexity arises from the synthesis of simple ideas. We use bare bones, intuitive rules of thumb as building blocks and discover odd results when they are combined. To get a feeling for the possibilities, let's consider an interesting, though preliminary model that led the way to later ideas.

MODEL I: THE NUCLEAR DEBATE AS CROSSFIRE

The guiding idea in our first model is that laypeople (the public in "public opinion") observe a heated and polarized nuclear debate, get bombarded by arguments and evidence from experts on both sides, and reach summary judgments that reflect the relative credibility of the competing viewpoints.

The process can be likened to watching a debate about SDI on a TV show like "Crossfire" or "Firing Line." Here an articulate conservative spokesman, say William F. Buckley, Jr., engages a bleeding heart liberal in a sharpwitted rhetorical duel about arms control. After launching some highbrow insults at his guest, Buckley argues that SDI will provide a shield against nuclear attack from the Russians and other bad guys (seems like a good idea) and will eventually make nuclear weapons completely obsolete (a very nice idea). He buttresses his case with a learned-sounding historical discourse about the demise of the longbow. The arms controller retorts that SDI will cost a trillion dollars (not good), that it will be easily negated by simple countermeasures (seems bad), and will undermine the stability of nuclear deterrence (seems very bad). The viewer's opinion then emerges from the crossfire of competing claims.[1]

The relative weight given to the opposing lines of argument might de-

---

1 Some interesting recent discussions of political attitude formation that share a kindred spirit include Stanley Kelley's net score model in *Interpreting Elections* (Princeton: Princeton University Press, 1983) and John Zaller's two-message model in *The Nature and Origins of Mass Opinion* (Cambridge: Cambridge University Press, 1992). Each story involves a filtered flow of information and messages that produce ambivalent opinions. The amount of ambivalence varies across individuals, depending on their political predispositions and sophistication, their exposure to competing messages, and the relative salience of different issues.

  In Glenn Shafer's more general "constructive" theory of preference formation, people do not have a well-defined, preconceived "true preference" about many issues. When confronted with a choice or decision, they then "look to various arguments in an effort to construct one." Shafer's theory suggests why peoples' expressed preferences often appear self-contradictory, inconsistent, and unstable:

  > In fact, people generally do not have ready-made preferences. When asked to make choices, they look for arguments on which to base these choices. The ways in which the alternatives are described can suggest arguments and therefore influence these choices. This means that people's choices in response to one query may be inconsistent with their choices in response to another query, but this weak kind of inconsistency is inescapable for rational beings who base their choices on arguments. [Glenn Shafer, "Savage Revisited," in D. E. Bell, Howard Raiffa, and Amos Tversky, eds., *Decision Making: Descriptive, Normative, and Prescriptive Interactions* (Cambridge: Cambridge University Press, 1988), p. 203]

  In the same volume, James March describes how we "confound preferences":

  > Our deepest preferences tend often to be paired. We find the same outcome both attractive and repulsive, not in the sense that the two sentiments cancel each other and we remain indifferent, but precisely that we simultaneously want and do not want an outcome, experience it as both pleasure and pain, love it and hate it. [James G. March, "Rationality, Ambiguity, and the Engineering of Choice," in D. E. Bell, Howard Raiffa, and Amos Tversky, eds., *Decision Making: Descriptive, Normative, and Prescriptive Interactions* (Cambridge: Cambridge University Press, 1988), p. 44]

  March's discussion recalls the psychological idea of "approach–avoidance conflicts" and the everyday experience of ambivalence or "mixed feelings."

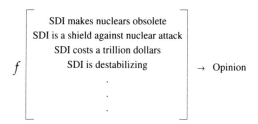

Figure 6.1 Crossfire metaphor: f is an evaluation (or judging) function that takes arguments from the nuclear debate as inputs and produces preferences as outputs.

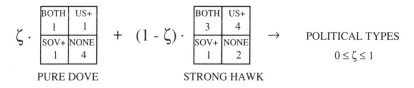

Figure 6.2 Crossfire formalization

pend on how likable or smart the debaters seem, the viewer's predispositions, the amount of "air time" given to the two sides, and many other factors that vary from viewer to viewer. Some people might dismiss Buckley as a bombastic pseudo-professor. Others might find the arms controller to be hopelessly deluded about the Soviet threat. But in general we could expect that both sides will score some points. Buckley's idea that SDI would blunt a nuclear attack seems believable and good, while the arguments that SDI will be very expensive and prone to countermeasures seem equally credible. Faced with a set of competing claims that all have some plausibility, we conjecture that many people will fashion preferences by drawing elements from both sides of the debate (see Figure 6.1).

If the Crossfire metaphor seems to make sense, the next step is to give some structure to the evaluation process. To formalize the polarized nuclear debate, we construct convex combinations of preference matrices that embody dovish and hawkish arguments (see Figure 6.2). At one pole is a PURE DOVE who rejects the weapon categorically and who supports rigorous arms control (like the ABM Treaty for SDI). At the other pole is a STRONG HAWK whose paramount objective is American military superiority. The STRONG HAWK is a YES+ player with a dominant strategy to *Build*. The HAWK's worst case scenario is enemy superiority. Equal deployments evoke preferences in between. Given a choice between BOTH and NONE, the HAWK chooses BOTH, arguing that we're going to have the weapon regardless and that we would never use it as a bargaining chip in arms control negotiations. Such was the position toward SDI of Caspar Weinberger and his close associates in the Reagan Administration.

In a speech to the World Affairs Council in Philadelphia, Weinberger said:

The Soviet Union has rejected the notion of deterrence through agreed mutual vulnerability. In fact, the Soviets have been modernizing and increasing their offensive arsenal and simultaneously stepping up their defensive programs – all with the clear aim of gaining a first-strike capability. [SDI therefore] stands alone as the right, and indeed the only thing to do – to remove the threat of mutual destruction, regardless of Soviet activities. [*N.Y. Times*, p. A13, 10/4/85]

Weinberger added that the worst case scenario would be a Soviet monopoly on defenses: "I can't imagine a more destabilizing factor for the world than if the Soviets should acquire a reliable defense against ballistic missiles before we do."

On the other hand, it would not be destabilizing if the United States got SDI first "because they're aggressive and we're not":

If we can get a system which is effective and which we know can render their weapons impotent, we could be back in a situation we were in, for example, when we were the only nation with nuclear weapons. [Caspar Weinberger, testimony before Senate Armed Services Committee, February 1, 1984]

Bear in mind that we had a monopoly on nuclear weapons for some years and never used them. . . . [They] know perfectly well that we will never launch a first strike on the Soviet Union. [Caspar Weinberger, speaking on NBC's "Meet the Press," March 27, 1983]

Weinberger's political ally, Kenneth Adelman, offered this assessment:

To kill SDI, in effect, would be to kill the goose that lays the golden eggs. . . . Logically and strategically, there is no better way to achieve greater security for both sides than a movement toward strategic defenses in combination with deep reductions in offensive arms. Defenses are not part of the problem in arms control – they are part of the solution. . . . I leave you with a question: Would you rather base our security on Western ingenuity or on Soviet integrity? [Quoted in Strobe Talbott, *Master of the Game* (New York: Alfred A. Knopf, 1988), pp. 252–53]

The convex combination forms weighted averages of corresponding cells in the two matrices.[2] As the scalar weighting parameter ζ varies between 0 and 1, the relative credibility (or plausibility or appeal) of the polarized elite positions shifts continuously from one side of the debate to the other. When $\zeta = 0$, the person attaches no credibility to the PURE DOVE's

---

2 Note on the convex operation: Any 2×2 preference matrix can be represented as a vector in a 4-dimensional space whose coordinates each represent one cell in the table. A convex combination of vectors **u** and **v** takes the following form:

position and 100% to the STRONG HAWK's. When $\zeta = 1$, the PURE DOVE's arguments carry the day. If ζ lies between 0 and 1, both sides of the debate have some credibility, producing a synthesis of the competing views. For enduringly controversial issues like nuclear strategy, we might expect to observe an entire spectrum of opinion – that is to say, people whose evaluations of the elite debate (ζ) run the gamut between 0 and 1.

To gain a surer feeling for the mechanics of the model, let's consider someone who is strongly inclined toward the dove end of the spectrum, who generally hates military spending, but who nevertheless feels drawn to the idea of SDI because it might prevent a nuclear catastrophe. All things considered, the person "buys" 70% of the anti-SDI arguments and 30% of the pro-SDI position (so that the credibility parameter $\zeta = .70$). Discovering the opinion such a person would register in our SDI preference matrix involves two steps (see Figure 6.3).

WEIGHTED AVERAGE STEP ($\zeta = .70$)

$$.70 \cdot \begin{array}{|c|c|} \hline \text{BOTH} & \text{US+} \\ 1 & 1 \\ \hline \text{SOV+} & \text{NONE} \\ 1 & 4 \\ \hline \end{array} + (1 - .70) \cdot \begin{array}{|c|c|} \hline \text{BOTH} & \text{US+} \\ 3 & 4 \\ \hline \text{SOV+} & \text{NONE} \\ 1 & 2 \\ \hline \end{array} = \begin{array}{|c|c|} \hline \begin{array}{l}.7*1+.3*3\\ =1.6\end{array} & \begin{array}{l}.7*1+.3*4\\ =1.9\end{array} \\ \hline \begin{array}{l}.7*1+.3*1\\ =1\end{array} & \begin{array}{l}.7*4+.3*2\\ =3.4\end{array} \\ \hline \end{array}$$

PURE DOVE   STRONG HAWK

RENORMALIZATION STEP

$$\begin{array}{|c|c|} \hline 1.6 & 1.9 \\ \hline 1 & 3.4 \\ \hline \end{array} \rightarrow \begin{array}{|c|c|} \hline \text{BOTH} & \text{US+} \\ 2 & 3 \\ \hline \text{SOV+} & \text{NONE} \\ 1 & 4 \\ \hline \end{array}$$

Figure 6.3

$$\zeta\mathbf{u} + (1-\zeta)\mathbf{v} \qquad (0 \le \zeta \le 1)$$

The convex combinations can also be written:

$$\zeta \cdot \begin{bmatrix} u_1 \\ u_2 \\ u_3 \\ u_4 \end{bmatrix} + (1-\zeta) \cdot \begin{bmatrix} v_1 \\ v_2 \\ v_3 \\ v_4 \end{bmatrix} = \begin{bmatrix} \zeta \cdot u_1 + (1-\zeta) \cdot v_1 \\ \zeta \cdot u_2 + (1-\zeta) \cdot v_2 \\ \zeta \cdot u_3 + (1-\zeta) \cdot v_3 \\ \zeta \cdot u_4 + (1-\zeta) \cdot v_4 \end{bmatrix} \quad (0 \le \zeta \le 1)$$

Notice that the same weights apply to all the cells in a particular matrix. Doing so makes

Once the convex combination is computed, the payoffs are renormalized to the format of the questionnaire – integer values with [4 = Best . . . 1 = Worst] and ties allowed if two alternatives have equal utility.

To derive the whole spectrum of opinion about SDI, repeat the same calculations for every value of ζ between 0 and 1. Doing so produces an interesting result:

	NO		IFF-NO		YES-BUT		YES-BUT		YES+	

BOTH	US+								BOTH	US+
1	1	2	3	2	4	3	4	3	4
SOV+	NONE								SOV+	NONE
1	4	1	4	1	3	1	3	1	2

PURE DOVE   STRONG HAWK

We get a spectrum of new political types as a synthesis of the strategic extremes.[3]

sense because the whole matrix, *taken together*, embodies the hawk or dove position. Geometrically, the convex combination defines a ray that connects the vectors **u** and **v** in $\mathcal{R}^4$. Preference profiles that lie along the connecting ray will be "generated" by the crossfire process. The operations presuppose that preferences can be measured on an interval-level utility scale, uniquely defined up to linear transformations. This assumption is standard in game theory.

3 Technical note on renormalization and rank order measurements: Some readers will notice that measuring preferences with integers, rather than as continuous, real-valued "temperature scales," entails a certain loss of information. Others might object that the heuristic model wastes information by making equivalent during renormalization all the convex combinations that share a common ordinal structure. And finally, some might feel uncomfortable that respondents whose "true" preferences don't fall on the convex ray will nevertheless get counted as "explained by the model" when their preferences share the same ordinal structure as points along the ray.

Let me suggest several reasons why losing some information about the intensity of preferences is more than repaid, in this problem anyway, by additional reliability in the recorded responses. First, the loss of information entailed by measuring preferences with integers is small from a game theoretic point of view. Many leading models in the literature (like the Prisoner's Dilemma, Chicken, and the Security Dilemma) are defined simply by rank orders of payoffs. If we are interested in the pure strategy Nash equilibria of an arms racing game, preference profiles that share a common ordinal structure are strategically equivalent. Second, our approach can be understood as identifying the ordinally-equivalent regions of $\mathcal{R}^4$ that certain convex rays pass through. If our basic substantive interest lies in understanding ordinal preference structures, then designing a model this way seems appropriate.

Another approach would be to study the *bundles* of convex rays formed from all possible order-preserving perturbations of generators like the STRONG HAWK. This approach can be justified by observing that any set of real-valued payoffs with the STRONG HAWK ordering is, substantively speaking, still a STRONG HAWK. It can be verified that order-preserving perturbations of the generators in these convex models have little effect on the families of profiles produced. The perturbations remain close to each other in $\mathcal{R}^4$ (once the

PROS AND CONS OF THE CROSSFIRE MODEL

The Crossfire model has certain problems, which I'll get to in a moment, but first let's discuss its virtues. Above all, the model seems to make sense. The idea that lay people form opinions by weighing and synthesizing arguments from the elite debate seems plausible – at least no less plausible than other political-psychological models like Jervis' irrational consistency or Converse's fractured diffusion. To appreciate what makes the Crossfire model distinctive, it is instructive to reflect for a moment about its connections to these other approaches.

What are people to think when they hear that SDI will defend against nuclear attack and that it will cost $1 trillion? Irrational consistency says that they will reject the idea that creates dissonance with their central beliefs. But another possibility is ambivalence – a simultaneous entertaining of politically inconsistent ideas. Such ambivalent or confounded opinions are the central feature of the Crossfire approach. It is true that the model admits highly polarized (or consistent or "constrained") opinions at the extremes where ζ approaches 0 and 1. Irrational consistency is therefore embedded in the Crossfire process as a degenerate special case. But obviously the Crossfire model wouldn't be interesting or necessary if everyone maintained opinions at the polar extremes.

Crossfire also bears a certain resemblance to Converse's diffusion model, relying as it does on the permutation or distortion of elite views within a mass audience. But the process of transformation seems different, at least at first glance. Rather than disintegrating into fragments during the diffusion stage, the elite formulas arrive intact but then get mixed together, producing preferences that look very different from the originating positions. Of course, once they have formed, the conflated preferences may look self-contradictory

best and worst cases have been scaled to some benchmark values). As a result, the rays connecting the perturbed generators pass through similar regions in the space of profiles (where ordinal rankings tend to be similar). The bundles of convex rays generated by the perturbations tend to "fill up" the regions of ordinally equivalent profiles. Our procedure can be understood as an approximation to this more elaborate alternative (that meets the second and third objections outlined above).

For these reasons, relatively little substantive information is lost either by measuring preferences as integers or by quantizing the outcomes of the convex procedure. Offsetting these losses is an important positive gain. Most respondents find it much easier to produce ordinal rankings over the cells in a matrix than to produce real-valued temperature readings (try it yourself). The directions required to elicit ordinal rankings are much simpler, and the responses are more reliable. As a result, measurements of preference rankings will be statistically more stable. Our models and measurements trade some bias (inaccurate or incomplete description) for stability (reproducibility and reliability). For further discussion about the virtues of rankings in political attitude measurement, see Henry Brady, "Dimensional Analysis of Ranking Data," *American Journal of Political Science* 34, No. 4 (November 1990).

(a.k.a. unconstrained, random, inconsistent, piecemeal, or aschematic) if we don't understand the confounding process that generated them.

Another contrast between the theories lies in the character of their predictions. Because the process Converse describes is basically destructive of elite views, his model mainly produces negative predictions about mass opinion. It tells us that the non-attitudes *won't look like* the highly constrained, stable, and wide ranging ideologies of elites, but it doesn't say much in a positive way about what they will look like. Because the Crossfire model rests on an explicit constructive procedure, forming preferences from mixtures of competing positions, it produces detailed, positive predictions about mass beliefs.

All of these considerations show that Crossfire relies on different mechanisms and produces different results than the other models, even though it shares certain important features in common. To my mind, it seems no less plausible or sensible than the other models. On the other hand, it seems no more plausible either. Each one makes sense in its own way.

If the Crossfire metaphor seems substantively sensible, it is equally important that the formalization seems faithful to the metaphor. Mathematical models ordinarily come with baggage of their own, some of it quite unwelcome. But this one seems to embody the substantive idea very well. The model creates an array of opinions that combine, with different emphasis, features of the polar extremes. Notice what happens in the sequence above as the HAWK's arguments begin to weigh on the PURE DOVE's steadfast anti-militarism. Initially, the DOVE's NO position gives way to an IFF-NO configuration. The DOVE's strong preference for arms control remains intact (NONE is best), but American superiority (US+) now becomes the second choice. BOTH becomes less preferred than US+ and more preferred than SOV+. In these ways, the new preference ordering inherits features from both of the parent profiles that generated it. The result is a politically ambivalent position, contingent on Soviet behavior. As the HAWK perspective receives progressively more weight, opinion shifts from IFF to YES-BUT. *Build* becomes a dominant strategy, but now with the well known ambivalences that reside in the Prisoner's Dilemma. That the fusion of disparate viewpoints should create political (if not psychological) ambivalence seems just right.

These interesting patterns suggest three further virtues of a more technical flavor. First, it is satisfying that the convex operation reproduces the game theoretic ordering derived earlier. That pleasant result provides an independent psychological rationale for the ordinal scale of political support developed in the last chapter. It also gives hope for substantial data reduction, if the dozens of opinion profiles can be mapped onto a one-dimensional game theoretic scale induced by the credibility parameter ζ. The result can be properly called a surprise, I think, because game theoretic considerations played no role in defining the convex procedure, and because the particular profiles that emerged from it were anything but self-evident before we started. Because it is hard to anticipate just what profiles a convex combination of matrices will produce, it is reassuring that a politically sensible sequence emerges from the process. Finally, the model has created a *family* of preference profiles that we didn't know were related before. The family has a well defined birth-order (providing information about the latent credibility parameter ζ), and well defined parents or generators. Crossfire has therefore given us several things we didn't know we had when we started: it produces new derivatives from familiar raw material, it reproduces the game theoretic scale, and it reveals family ties among profiles that otherwise seem disparate and unconnected. That the model produces non-obvious results shows that the formalization creates analytical leverage. Such leverage is welcome because we have many non-obvious patterns in the data to explain.

These points bring up a final and more important virtue – the model produces results that begin to look like real data. From a pair of simple generators, there emerge new political types along an ordered spectrum that includes NOs, IFFs, YES-BUTs, and YES+'s. That such complexity can arise from a simple cognitive process is certainly encouraging, since we know that a complex strategic calculus is unlikely to describe the reasoning of our respondents. But even more than the generic game theoretic categories, the model produces specific political profiles, all of which appear in the data. Such results should not be dismissed casually, unless we have a better explanation for profiles that depart from the expert prescriptions. The Crossfire explanation certainly could be wrong, but it seems much more interesting than dismissing such profiles as noise or nonsense, which of course is no explanation at all.

So much for the considerable virtues of the Crossfire model. It has defects too, both theoretical and empirical. If we include the generators with the rest of the family, then the model covers 153/676 or 22.6% of the profiles observed on the four weapons items. This performance is fair, I suppose, but nothing to write home about. Of the responses, 77% remain to be explained, including all of the IFF-YESes, the NIFFs, the YES++'s, and most of the profiles in the other game theoretic categories. The Crossfire family includes only five members, leaving 55 profiles unaccounted for. All in all, the fit to the data leaves much to be desired.

At the same time, the story underlying the Crossfire scenario has certain suspect features as well. First of all, it exploits expert opinions to generate everyone else's. As we all know, however, most people pay very little attention to the national security debate. ("Crossfire" and "Firing Line" are not exactly the highest rated shows on television.) On the other

$$f \begin{bmatrix} \text{Security Heuristic} \\ \text{Weapon Heuristic} \end{bmatrix} \rightarrow \text{Opinion}$$

Figure 6.4 An intuitive deterrence theory: f is a "combining function" that takes two heuristic rules of thumb as inputs and produces preferences as outputs.

hand, it is not clear why elite instruction is necessary to form an opinion about national security issues in the first place. Listen to any radio talk show during the Gulf War and you heard people asserting strong opinions about strategy that seemed to rest on nothing more elaborate than everyday rules of thumb ("If we let Saddam Hussein walk out of Kuwait scott free, then he'll cause more trouble later." "The United States should not act like a bully." "Giving the sanctions more time to work would have saved a lot of bloodshed." "Bush blew it when he didn't take out Hussein when he had the chance.") Formulating these ideas surely didn't require a Harvard tutor. And let's not forget what Ronald Reagan said about SDI: "The truth is, I thought of it myself." A third difficulty is that the Crossfire metaphor never makes clear why elite opinion should be any more polarized than lay opinion. Why should elites be immune to the ambivalences experienced by novices? Don't they hear the same conflicting points of view? Finally, the model provides no explanation for the generators themselves, which happen to be two of the most commonplace members of the family (accounting for 75 of the 153 "hits" in the novice data). In all of these respects, the model seems incomplete or unconvincing.

These concerns led to a long search for better models. Those considered all shared Crossfire's basic idea of fusing or commingling simple ideas, but they developed in different directions. What follows is that particular model I shall defend as most instructive about intuitive deterrence reasoning. Like all models, it does not fit the data perfectly. But it does capture many subtle patterns in the preference profiles, especially considering its stark simplicity and basic plausibility.

MODEL II: THE INTUITIVE DETERRENCE CALCULUS

In the new model, the "experts" disappear from the story and the generators become even more primitive strategic intuitions. In this way, an intuitive deterrence theory becomes available to everyone, politically attentive or not. The interplay of strategic intuitions is governed by a simple heuristic calculus that can be written schematically as in Figure 6.4.

The Security Heuristic

First let's consider the *Security Heuristic*, which describes the relationship between the opposing arsenals required to produce security. The security heuristic comes in two basic flavors:

SYMMETRY   STRENGTH

BOTH	US+
4	1
SOV+	NONE
1	4

BOTH	US+
2	4
SOV+	NONE
1	2

SYMMETRY Flavor. The primitive intuition underlying the SYMMETRY heuristic is that international stability (or stable deterrence) requires "balance." People who invoke this kind of thinking believe that security must be mutual, that power must be balanced, and that mismatches in military capability produce aggression. Fearing that the strong will attack the weak ("power abhors a vacuum"), they seek stability by making capabilities equal. These ideas define the SYMMETRY flavor of the security heuristic. According to this rule of thumb, the most favorable outcomes lie along the main diagonal of the arms racing matrix where the two sides are militarily balanced.

It is important to realize that the SYMMETRY heuristic entails an implicit notion of political symmetry as well. Whether we are superior to them (US+) or they are superior to us (SOV+) doesn't matter. Both cases are *equally* bad. The tacit idea that instabilities arise from the imbalance of forces *per se* implies a fundamental geopolitical equivalence between the players, regardless of their institutional or ideological differences. In this conception of deterrence, there is no distinction between "us" and "them." The two sides are treated interchangeably and the players' labels are irrelevant (as in symmetric games or classical deterrence theory or realist balance of power theory).

STRENGTH Flavor. The STRENGTH flavor of the security heuristic rests on another primitive strategic axiom – the weak don't attack the strong. So long as we remain strong relative to our adversaries, they'll understand that aggression is fruitless. Or, as Ronald Reagan put it so beautifully during his 1980 presidential campaign, "peace through strength." The STRENGTH heuristic appeals to people who believe in the survival of the fittest, in the "law of the jungle," that "winning is everything," or that it's a "dog eat dog" kind of world. Formally speaking, the STRENGTH heuristic is defined in the matrix above. The best case is U.S. superiority, the worst case is Soviet superiority, and cases that leave the two sides equal lie in between.[4]

---

4 With respect to the intermediate outcomes (BOTH and NONE), any utility value between 4 and 1 would capture the theoretical idea of STRENGTH. The main results discussed below are quite insensitive to the particular numerical choice made here.

Here the distinction between "us" and "them" becomes all-important in an interesting dual sense. Reagan's maxim says that if we are strong, the world will be stable and peaceful – first, because they will be deterred, and, second, because we are not aggressors ourselves. If we are not strong, however, there will be no peace because they will use their strength to pursue aggression and expansion. Equality of forces is better than inferiority certainly, but leaves us on a level playing field against a more aggressive adversary. In these ways, peace through strength involves both a military and a political asymmetry between the players. Because we are superior politically and morally, we can also be superior militarily without creating instability. The opposite conclusions apply to "them."

In both flavors of the security heuristic, we see an interesting parallelism between the preferred distribution of military capabilities and the political descriptions of the players. In one case, the strategic idea of strength commingles with a parallel idea of political or moral superiority. In the other case, the balance of power idea coexists with a conception of geopolitical symmetry. Given their great abstraction, their simplicity, and their reach across both military and political dimensions, it appears reasonable to interpret the security heuristics as something like a strategic "world view." They are very general political intuitions that describe stable distributions of power. At the same time, it is easy to see how such abstract intuitions could drive complex, lower level debates about what deters the enemy, the nature of Soviet and American societies, the feasibility of arms control, the causes of war, and many other detailed questions.[5]

The Weapon Heuristic

Next we turn to the weapon heuristic, which describes the *contents* of the nuclear arsenals rather than their relative size. The weapon heuristic also comes in two flavors:

GOOD WEAPON (Stabilizing)			BAD WEAPON (Destabilizing)	
BOTH	US+		BOTH	US+
4	2		1	2
SOV+	NONE		SOV+	NONE
2	1		2	4

5 For a review of the age-old debate in international relations about the relative war proneness of systems characterized by "parity and preponderance," see Jack S. Levy, "The Causes of War: A Review of Theories and Evidence," in P. E. Tetlock, J. L. Husbands, R. Jervis, P. C. Stern, and C. Tilly, eds., *Behavior, Society, and Nuclear War*, Vol. 1 (New York: Oxford University Press, 1989). An interesting formal study is Robert Powell, "Stability and the Distribution of Power," Working Paper, University of California, Berkeley, May 1993.

GOOD Weapon Flavor. A GOOD or stabilizing weapon is one that makes us better off as it proliferates. In the best case everyone has it, in the worst case nobody has it, while partial deployments lie somewhere in between. The name "good weapon" sounds like an oxymoron perhaps, but many examples can be found in the literature of nuclear strategy. In classical deterrence theory, systems that secure second strikes and promote crisis stability are good weapons that everybody should have. Arms controllers routinely propose that both superpowers deploy early warning systems, allow enemy spy satellites to orbit over their national territories (open skies), install permissive action link mechanisms on their nuclear weapons, and develop robust systems of C³I. All of these measures are intended to diminish trigger happiness by securing second strikes and diminishing the prospect of first strikes.

In his book *Disturbing the Universe*,[6] Freeman Dyson argues that defensive weapons are morally superior to offensive weapons. Such moral reasoning supports his case for a national security of self-defense, and a list of weapons preferences "that go flatly against the strategic thinking which has dominated our policies for the last forty years":

> Bombers are bad. Fighter airplanes and antiaircraft missiles are good. Tanks are bad. Antitank missiles are good. Submarines are bad. Antisubmarine technology is good. Nuclear weapons are bad. Radars and sonars are good. Intercontinental missiles are bad. Antiballistic missile systems are good. [*Disturbing the Universe*, p. 143]

Dyson's reasoning closely resembles Ronald Reagan's, when the former President embraced SDI as a pure good thing – "a shield that could protect us from nuclear missiles just as a roof protects a family from rain." Reagan's rule of thumb for distinguishing good weapons from bad did not rest on whether they secured second strikes or not. Rather, SDI was good because "we are talking about a weapon that won't kill people." What most appalled Reagan were "those horrible offensive nuclear weapons."[7]

Promoters of "Defense-Protected Build-Down" and cooperative deployment supported SDI as a way to replace offensive nuclear forces with defenses. Gorbachev's doctrine of *defensive defense* sought to replace provocative blitzkrieg-type weapons with passive, nonthreatening defenses. Kenneth Waltz has even argued that the proliferation of nuclear weapons to third world countries would be a good idea, lending stability to conflictual regions. The same idea underlies the argument that nuclear weapons make war obsolete. Secretary of State James Baker argued vigorously that the new Commonwealth of Independent States should keep a large

---

6 Freeman Dyson, *Disturbing the Universe* (New York: Harper Colophon Books, 1979). See especially Chapter 13, "The Ethics of Defense."
7 *N.Y. Times*, "Excerpts from Reagan's Speech at Jersey School," p. A8, 6/20/86.

stock of nuclear weapons, and not disarm completely, which he claimed would be destabilizing. His views prevailed in the START II Treaty. And so on. All of these ideas rest on some underlying criterion, moral or strategic, that distinguishes good weapons from bad.

BAD Weapon Flavor. The fewer countries that have BAD or destabilizing weapons the better. Ask most people about chemical, nuclear, or biological weapons and the bad bell goes off immediately. For them, these nightmare weapons of mass destruction should not exist. As the weapons proliferate to more and more countries, the nightmare gets worse. Many people would far rather that nuclear weapons didn't exist at all than that we possessed them alone – even if proliferation were not a problem. They don't trust governments and politicians and generals and submarine crews to handle them wisely. They don't like threatening innocent women and children with annihilation. They don't like killing machines. Period.

THE INTUITIVE CALCULUS OF NUCLEAR DETERRENCE

With these building blocks in hand, an *intuitive deterrence theory* can now be described precisely. I shall argue that novices' preferences in the nuclear arms race arise by combining a general political intuition about stable distributions of power with a local intuition about the attributes of particular weapons. In this way, two simple heuristics define preferences about the relationship between nuclear arsenals and their contents. Formally speaking, the *intuitive nuclear calculus* computes convex combinations of the weapon and security heuristics, using one generator of each type.

In forming these combinations, I conjecture that both considerations will be relevant to most people, but in different measures. Intuitive deterrence theories are not scripted doctrines or well rehearsed formulas, but mental composites, fashioned from considerations that have different salience to different people. When both heuristics matter at once, the result can be "mixed feelings."

The plausibility of this proposal can be appreciated in the following examples:

- Virtually everyone is appalled by biological weapons, but evidence that the other side is producing them can generate intense political pressure to match. For those who want to build, the security heuristic outweighs the BAD weapon heuristic (notice that neither STRENGTH nor SYMMETRY counsels inferiority). For those opposed, the horror of the weapon decides the question. But either decision leaves most people uneasy. If we build them, what if they get used? If we don't build them, what if we wish later that we had?

- The same ambivalence surrounded The Bomb, which everyone justified by saying, "They might get it first" (not "It's a nice weapon to have.") The weapon itself seemed horrible, but the idea that Hitler might get it first seemed worse. For some people who worked on the bomb, the fear of Hitler outweighed the horror of the device, allowing peace of mind. Others found themselves wracked by anguish and guilt about opening Pandora's Box.

• Ronald Reagan ran for President on a platform of peace through strength, but he did not promise to build the biggest arsenal of nuclear missiles the world has ever known. Instead, he promised to develop SDI and rid the world of nuclear weapons. At Reykjavik, Iceland, in September 1986, Reagan surprised everyone by embracing Mikhail Gorbachev's proposal to eliminate *all* strategic nuclear weapons, including bombers and cruise missiles, after 10 years. Evidently, an abstract preference for strength was tempered by a strong aversion to nuclear weapons. A belief in STRENGTH does not imply that every weapon is GOOD.

• Principles of SYMMETRY pervade modern arms control theory, but arms controllers propose all the time that some weapons be banned and others deployed.

In all of these examples, we see two dimensions of judgment working at once – one describing the relationship between the two adversaries' arsenals and the other describing their contents. Which consideration weighs more heavily seems to vary from person to person. If you don't know anything about random subtractive defenses or densepack basing modes, then your attitude toward them (if you are called upon to express it) will be governed by general principles – by your strategic "world view." As you acquire a more definite impression of the weapon (accurate or not), the weapon heuristic presumably counts more heavily in your thinking. How much information is required to create an image of the weapon is hard to say. A picture of a mushroom cloud probably does it for nuclear weapons. Even the name alone may be enough. Whoever named the "neutron bomb" certainly knew how to create a nasty first impression. All we can say for certain is that people vary greatly in how much they know about nuclear weapons systems, and how they picture them. It therefore seems likely that images of the weapon and general strategic principles carry different weights in different people's minds.

Since the relative weight of the two considerations can't be fixed in theory, we use a spectrum of convex combinations to admit individual differences. The convex operation synthesizes general strategic intuitions with judgments about the particular weapon system. Interesting ambivalences arise when the two intuitions conflict. At the same time, a complex taxonomy of game theoretic types emerges in four basic families.

The [SYMMETRY + BAD Weapon] Family

Consider those individuals who adopt the SYMMETRY flavor of the security heuristic and a negative view of the weapon system under debate. Mixing the two intuitions together produces the following spectrum of preferences:

13	35	26	44	23

BOTH	US+							BOTH	US+
1	2	1	1	2	1	3	1	4	1
SOV+	NONE							SOV+	NONE
2	4	1	4	1	4	1	4	1	4

BAD	PURE DOVE	Unstable Balance Anomalies		SYMMETRY

Right away we see one familiar face. It is the PURE DOVE, whose position now emerges as the product of more primitive ideas. But as we discussed earlier, the PURE DOVE represents the orientation of classical deterrence theory toward second strike underminers like SDI or the Russian SS-18 (a heavily MIRVed, land-based ICBM). The classical attitude is to ban these destabilizing weapons outright in arms control agreements like the ABM Treaty and START II. There appears then to be a close relationship between classical reasoning and the symmetric deterrence calculus.

The connection becomes more obvious when we decompose the most famous classical formula of all:

$$\text{MAD} = \text{MUTUAL (Symmetry Principle)}$$
$$+ \text{ASSURED DESTRUCTION}$$
$$\text{(Weapon Principle)}$$

In the classical approach, *both* sides must have secure second strikes – not just the U.S. Otherwise there arise first strike instabilities and the *reciprocal* fear of surprise attack. The idea that deterrence must be *mutual* locates SYMMETRY as a core idea of the classical approach. The second part of the acronym defines the classical weapon principle. Assured destruction (or guaranteed retaliation) provides the criterion for distinguishing GOOD weapons from BAD. Anything that impedes second strikes, making retaliation less than assured in the event of a first strike, is a BAD or destabilizing weapon. The arguments that the SS18, MX, SDI, ASAT, and ASW are destabilizing all rest on this principle. Technologies that secure second strikes make deterrence stable. They are "GOOD weapons." Classical GOOD weapons include hardened silos, submarine basing, robust C^3I, PALs, and, in the nuclear thinking questionnaire, "effective technologies for protecting nuclear forces from preemptive attack." The classical prescription for stable force postures can therefore be derived from the SYMMETRY heuristic and a simple weapon heuristic.

In addition to the PURE DOVE, the [SYMMETRY + BAD] Family includes two other familiar profiles – the *unstable balance anomalies* discussed in the last chapter. By indicating that NONE is the best outcome, people who maintain such preferences make obvious their belief that the weapon is "BAD." The anomaly arises in the simultaneous belief that it will be more stable if both sides have the bad weapon than if only one side does – even if the one side is us! The model shows how these profiles emerge when the SYMMETRY principle begins to outweigh the BAD weapon heuristic. But this kind of thinking is precisely what we might expect among non-experts who lean more heavily on general principles and lack a sharp criterion to differentiate good from bad weapons. Suppose, for example, that the classical rule to secure second strikes were replaced with a vaguer intuition that merely identifies "nuclear-sounding" systems as BAD. An intuitive blending of SYMMETRY with this conception of BAD-ness could easily fail to reproduce the classical recipe, replacing MAD with a cruder "balance of power" scheme of deterrent stability.

The [SYMMETRY + BAD] Family is an interesting brood that includes both classical ideal types and anomalous variations of them. In both respects, the heuristic calculus performs well. The family is also empirically popular. Above each profile in the sequence is the number of times it appears in the 676 responses given to the four nuclear weapon items in the questionnaire. Altogether, the family covers 141/676 = 21% of all the responses in the novice dataset.

The [SYMMETRY + GOOD Weapon] Family

The other side of the SYMMETRY family includes weapons that are GOOD:

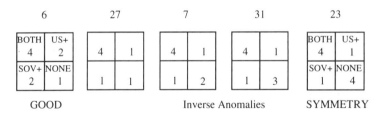

	6		27		7		31		23
BOTH	US+	4	1	4	1	4	1	BOTH	US+
4	2							4	1
SOV+	NONE	1	1	1	2	1	3	SOV+	NONE
2	1							1	4
GOOD			Inverse Anomalies					SYMMETRY	

The members of this family are simply mirror images of their BAD cousins, including the classical idea of good systems (everybody should have them) and a set of inverse anomalies (it's better that nobody have the GOOD weapon than just one side or the other). This side of the SYMMETRY family is also popular empirically, accounting for 15% of the novice responses. The total coverage of the SYMMETRY family (eliminating double counting of the SYMMETRY generator itself) is 212/676 = 31% of all the responses.

The [STRENGTH + GOOD Weapon] Family

Now we turn to the STRENGTH families. What happens when a believer in STRENGTH also believes that the weapon system is GOOD in the sense described by our formal generator?

	6		50		4		40		2	
BOTH	US+		4	3	4	4	3	4	BOTH	US+
4	2								2	4
SOV+	NONE		2	1	1	1	1	2	SOV+	NONE
2	1								1	2
GOOD		NICE HAWK				STRONG HAWK		STRENGTH		

The result is another important family that includes two of the most fre-quently observed profiles in the data. One is the familiar STRONG HAWK whose position now emerges from simple intuitions as the PURE DOVE's did earlier. The intuitive nuclear calculus therefore produces both Crossfire generators as special cases. The family also contains the anomalous NICE HAWK described in the last chapter. Recall that NICE HAWKs prefer to give the weapons to the Soviet Union if we get them first, and even prefer Soviet unilateral superiority to an arms control ban. Such people have a dominant strategy to build, making them hawks, but seem unusually co-operative toward the other side, making them nice. They are also the most extreme adversaries of arms control (YES++'s).

The NICE HAWK is one of the most puzzling anomalies in the novice data, and not just because all YES+'s seem weird on the face of things. The NICE HAWK is also the second most common profile in the data and appears predominantly among people who call themselves Conservative and Middle-of-the-Road. The intuitive calculus makes all of these remark-able results comprehensible in a gratifying, straightforward way. The model explains in the first place how this strange amalgam arises from the interplay of two contradictory heuristics. NICE HAWKs have apparently absurd preferences because they are torn between politically inconsistent ideas – the GOOD weapon heuristic favors proliferation of the weapon while the STRENGTH heuristic favors superiority. When the GOOD heu-ristic begins to outweigh the STRENGTH heuristic – and people clearly have adopted a powerful "GOOD weapon" heuristic when, for example, they speak about SDI making nuclear weapons impotent and obsolete – then a pattern of niceness is superimposed on the impulse to dominate and overwhelm. The model also explains why NICE HAWKs turn up so often. The intuitions that support the profile are simple, down-to-earth, and commonplace. Finally, the NICE HAWKs appear mainly on the right wing of the political spectrum because the STRENGTH heuristic is concentrated there (an important point to which we'll return in much greater detail). In all of these ways, the model clarifies what seems at first to be bizarre (if the indicated preferences are intended) or inexplicable (if the responses are simply noise). NICE HAWKs illustrate the psychology of ambivalent preferences in an exceptionally striking way.[8]

8 The apparent contradictions in Ronald Reagan's nuclear strategies left many people at a loss to understand them. To share SDI with the evil empire, to pursue nuclear disarmament through a high-tech arms race – these ideas seemed too dotty to be taken seriously. But our data reveal that intuitive, conflicted, double-edged thinking is the norm to be expected in nuclear politics. Even Reagan's Soviet adversaries, who had stereotyped him as a superiority seeking hardliner, eventually concluded that he was not "acting" when he wavered about giving up SDI for complete nuclear disarmament. What convinced Gorbachev's close advisor, Aleksandr Yakovlev, was precisely the depth of Reagan's ambivalence:

> In Reykjavik I first saw Reagan's human hesitation about what decision to make, and it seemed to me he wasn't acting. I saw his internal hesitation, his batting back and forth in his mind what to do. On the one hand, as it seemed to me, he was interested in the idea of universal disarmament, on the other hand sticking to the idea of such a funny toy as SDI. . . . In this man I saw that his professional ability to put on an act somehow wavered. He could be seen from a different angle as a human being. [Don Oberdorfer, *The Turn: From the Cold War to a New Era* (New York: Poseidon Press, 1991), p. 209]

Like many other American strategists, Brent Scowcroft was dismayed by the "enthusiastic confusion and mixed purposes" in Reagan's quest for nuclear disarmament. Much more than the newspaper writers and second guessers, Scowcroft identified the sharing impulse as a telling signature of Reagan's point of view, refusing to dismiss the anomaly as insincere. The "confusion," he argued, rested in the notion

> that the principal barrier to world peace was posed not by the existence of an ambitious and expansionist totalitarian state but rather by the existence of nuclear weapons, period. Some Administration officials began to describe nuclear weapons almost as the antinuclear movement describes them, as a sort of deadly virus – a common enemy of man.
> . . . The Administration's approach to strategic and nuclear matters was best signalled by one feature of its new policy; the United States would give SDI technology or its benefits to the Russians. If all nuclear weapons are like a virus, this makes perfect sense. If, on the other hand, they are instruments of state power – . . . if Soviet nuclear weapons are in a different category than, say, British or French ones – it does not.
> Almost all supporters of the Administration policy have regarded the President's persistence about giving SDI technology to the Russians as an embarrassment. It appears clear after Reykjavik, however, that it is at the heart of the Administration's position. [Brent Scowcroft, John Deutch, and R. James Woolsey, "A Way Out of Reykjavik," *N.Y. Times Magazine* 1/25/87]

Scowcroft's analysis captures beautifully the basic mechanism in our intuitive calculus. He claims that Reagan identified the principal barrier to world peace as "the existence of nuclear weapons, period" not "the existence of an ambitious and expansionist totalitarian state." In our terminology, we would say that Reagan's preferences about nuclears attached substantial weight to the BAD weapon heuristic, and relatively little weight to the STRENGTH heuristic (which rests on a clear distinction between us and them, the good guys and the bad guys). Framed in this way, one can see a cognitive parallel to the debate about gun control. There, too, some people identify guns as the problem, while others seek to deter the criminals who use them.

Alternative Generators for the [STRENGTH + GOOD] Family

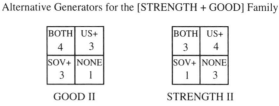

BOTH	US+
4	3
SOV+	NONE
3	1

GOOD II

BOTH	US+
3	4
SOV+	NONE
1	3

STRENGTH II

[STRENGTH + GOOD] RELATIVES

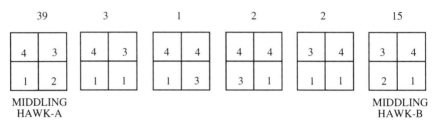

| 39 | 3 | 1 | 2 | 2 | 15 |

4	3	4	3	4	4	4	4	3	4	3	4
1	2	1	1	1	3	3	1	1	1	2	1

MIDDLING
HAWK-A

MIDDLING
HAWK-B

Figure 6.5

A Brief Technical Aside

It will be noticed that the formal definitions of the STRENGTH and GOOD and BAD heuristics contain an element of arbitrariness. We have assigned values of "2" to the middle-ranked outcomes in each generator when any value between 4 and 1 would capture the same idea. What would happen if these assignments were changed, for example, by defining the heuristics as in Figure 6.5?

The first point to emphasize is that the convex procedure is highly stable under these local perturbations of the generators. The resulting families are very similar, sharing many profiles in common. But the invariance is not perfect. Instead there emerge a handful of new profiles that bear a close family resemblance to the ones derived above. The close relatives include two very popular profiles that combine features of the STRONG and NICE HAWKs. Each of the MIDDLING HAWKs manifests one form of niceness – either the willingness to transfer the weapon to the Soviets or a preference for Soviet unilateral superiority over arms control – but not both. The one called type A is a YES+ while the type B is a YES++.

If we insist on a unique formal definition for each generator, the [STRENGTH + GOOD] family covers 15% of the responses in the data. A more liberal definition that allows the two perturbed generators into play produces an extended family covering 27% of the responses. The strict definition has the virtue of simplicity, making the theory seem more tidy. The tidiness is achieved, however, only by pretending that the generators are uniquely defined. Since later data analysis will show that responses in the extended family display many non-trivial forms of homogeneity, I find it more useful to live with the arbitrariness than to assume it away. Other people might favor the aesthetic considerations, choosing a simpler theory over a theory that explains slightly more.

The [STRENGTH + BAD Weapon] Family

The fourth and last of the basic families combines the STRENGTH and BAD weapon heuristics. These heuristics produce a variety of popular profiles, including the Prisoner's Dilemma configuration of preference. Notice how even those who embrace STRENGTH can arrive at a dominant strategy to disarm. This result shows us why the terms STRENGTH and HAWK should not be confused.

13	13	1	45	2

BOTH	US+							BOTH	US+
1	2	1	3	1	4	2	4	2	4
SOV+	NONE							SOV+	NONE
2	4	2	4	1	4	1	3	1	2

BAD			PD	STRENGTH

Once again, the family can be extended by tolerating perturbations of the basic generators. If we use the narrow definition, the family covers 11% of the observed profiles. The extended family covers 19%.

STRENGTH RELATIVES

5	22	7	0	8	15

BOTH	US+										
1	2	2	3	3	4	1	4	1	4	1	4
SOV+	NONE										
1	4	1	4	1	4	3	4	1	3	2	3

PROS AND CONS OF THE INTUITIVE NUCLEAR CALCULUS

Like the SYMMETRY families discussed earlier, the STRENGTH families produce both the politically familiar and the politically bizarre. The

STRONG HAWK captures our canonical idea of the political hawk, but the NICE HAWK, the YES++'s, and the MIDDLING HAWKs seem strange – too strange, some people have told me. Such skepticism is understandable perhaps, but not because I have simply introduced a model that gives odd results and declared it to be true. It has to count in the model's favor that I have collected three independent samples, separated widely in political time, in which the NICE HAWK (and closely related YES++'s) consistently shows up among the most popular profiles on four very different weapon items. Who would have predicted that result? And who would have guessed that seven of the ten most common profiles would indicate a preference that the United States transfer weapons to the Soviet Union if we get them first – and this before anyone was talking about the end of the Cold War? Five of those seven have now been explained by the model. The unstable balance anomalies occur over 100 times in 676 profiles, including both positive and negative flavors. Such evidence doesn't prove the model is true but certainly gives ample reason to take it seriously.

So does external evidence like Ronald Reagan's proposal to give the Soviet Union SDI. That the most anti-Soviet President of the Cold War should offer to give the blueprints of our national defense to the "evil empire" is a remarkably strange occurrence. Who predicted, or even imagined, that the most "hawkish" President in memory would agree in Reykjavik to complete nuclear disarmament? Neither anomaly seems so strange if we believe that Reagan understood SDI as a way to eradicate nuclear weapons from the face of the earth. With a powerful GOOD weapon heuristic like that, SDI becomes something like a cure for cancer – a technology we would gladly share if we found it first, and which we would be delighted to have the Soviets discover first. The nuclear calculus shows how the absurdity of Reagan's position is only apparent, notwithstanding his obvious belief in "STRENGTH." Rather than dismissing his behavior as insincere or irrational, the evidence suggests we should question instead the hackneyed stereotypes that conditioned our expectations about him.[9]

9 Don Oberdorfer reports that Reagan's ambivalent strategic philosophy, combining a commitment to military strength and an "abhorrence of the nuclear threat," confused even his closest aides and supporters. Like many skeptics outside the Administration, they too stereotyped their boss as a "hawk," only to be shocked by his behavior:

Reagan, who sponsored the most massive peacetime military buildup in U.S. history, was no secret dove. He was, however, deeply opposed to the possession and use of nuclear weapons, despite the fact that they had become the central ingredient in U.S. military power. Reagan stated his anti–nuclear weapons views on many occasions but, strangely enough, it was a shock when they later surfaced in negotiations with the Soviet Union. Most officials in the administration, as well as much of the public, did not take his anti–nuclear weapons statements seriously because they seemed dreamy and impractical for the U.S. president, especially one with Reagan's anticommunist policies and hard-edged oratory. [Don Ober-

Finally, the heuristic nuclear calculus has vastly outperformed the Crossfire model with only a slightly larger set of generators. If we eliminate double counting, the four basic families cover 60–76% of the observed profiles, depending on whether we insist on unique definitions for the generators or accept the extended families. This performance seems highly satisfactory given the simplicity of the model, its political realism, and its psychological plausibility. Perhaps more impressively, only a tiny handful of the profiles predicted by the model *failed to appear*, even in a relatively small sample of 169 novices. That result is extraordinary given the large number of previously unnoticed, theoretically neglected, slightly weird, and even bizarre profiles that the model produces. It also underlines an important point to which we shall return later – the model is not "overexplaining" simply by proliferating a zillion profiles that cover every possibility, whether they occur or not. Of the 111 logically possible profiles for each weapon, the notional calculus *does not* predict about 65. In fact, some of these excluded profiles do appear in the data and should be explained. We still haven't accounted for the single most popular profile of all, nor do we have any inkling about the strange family of NIFFs discussed in the last chapter.

MODEL III: MODEL II + HIGHER ORDER HEURISTICS

To address these remaining shortcomings, I've enhanced the basic model by allowing more complicated ideas to enter as "higher order heuristics."

Example I: Another Notion of a "BAD" Weapon

Consider the following ideas:

- SDI is a great concept and a much better approach to national security than nuclear deterrence. (SDI is a GOOD weapon.)
- The technology for SDI doesn't work.

There is certainly no reason that a person couldn't entertain both ideas at once, even though they support inconsistent conclusions about SDI. If so, then the person's weapon heuristic would be necessarily more complicated than the GOOD generator discussed earlier. The first idea corresponds to the GOOD weapon notion, while the second idea introduces a different concern. If we meld the two together, we get a *higher order* weapon heuristic.

dorfer, *The Turn: From the Cold War to a New Era* (New York: Poseidon Press, 1991), pp. 25–26]

The idea that SDI doesn't work, or is unaffordable, defines the following *POISON PILL* generator:

BOTH	US+
1	1
SOV+	NONE
4	4

POISON PILL

A POISON PILL is a weapon we don't want at all, either because it is ruinously expensive or because it is technically infeasible. Such objections define another idea of badness, since the evil effects of the weapon fall squarely on whoever acquires it. By contrast, the evil effects of destabilizing weapons cross national borders, increasing with the number of proliferators. If SDI is a great idea strategically (a GOOD or stabilizing weapon) but still a waste of money (POISON PILL), then we can derive the second order weapon heuristics called SWEET POISONs as follows:

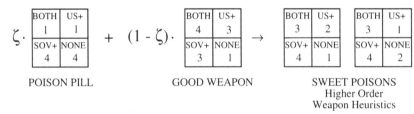

| | POISON PILL | | GOOD WEAPON | | SWEET POISONS Higher Order Weapon Heuristics |

When combined with the security heuristics in the usual way, either of these SWEET POISON flavors of the weapon heuristic defines essentially the same weird and interesting family of profiles. The SWEET POISON Family appears in Figure 6.6.

Prominent among the SWEET POISON Family are the NIFFs (NOT-IF-AND-ONLY-IFs). The NIFFs, you will recall, prefer that we have the weapon when they don't, and that we not have the weapon when they do!? Such preferences seem absurd at first glance but make a lot more sense if you believe that these generators produce them. The desire to have the weapon when they don't comes from the STRENGTH heuristic, which impels people to seek superiority when it's available. At the same time, the idea that the weapon will be an expensive white elephant supports a preference that we not build, especially if the other the side is going to have it. In that case, why wreck your economy with a system that doesn't work. The political advantages of superiority are no longer available, and the POISON PILL will simply erode the other guy's strength. "Why not let the other guy spend himself into the ground?" is an idea about SDI that was

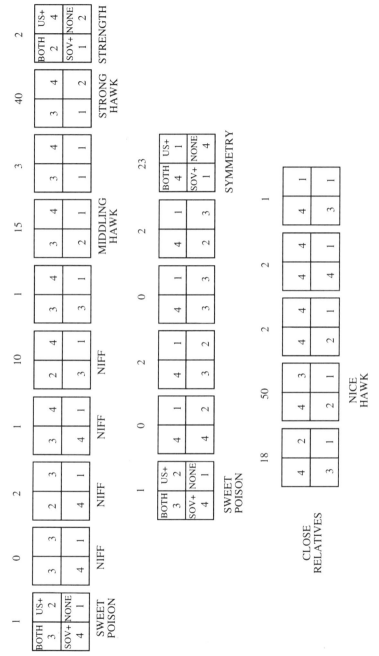

Figure 6.6 The SWEET POISON family

commonplace among Soviet analysts who supported a strategy of *asymmetric response* to President Reagan's initiative. A strategy of not matching the other guy's folly seems fine if you're convinced that SDI really is a white elephant. If you harbor doubts about being left in the dust, then a lot of ambivalence can result.

Such ambivalence is striking in the NIFF end of the SWEET POISON family. These profiles are so bizarre that they leave most people at a complete loss to explain them. The NIFF respondents generally place a high priority on Soviet "superiority" with U.S. superiority either slightly ahead or slightly behind. What the model succeeds in making clear is how the respondents are torn between three conflicting ideas (GOOD Weapon, POISON PILL, STRENGTH), which interact with strange results. The SWEET POISON profiles are not commonplace in the novice data, but they do turn up with striking regularity (roughly 6% of the profiles, excluding overlaps with other families). That virtually all of the SWEET POISON types show up in the data, even including the NIFFs, is a remarkable result. Even more remarkable is how particular respondents produce different members of the family on the various weapons questions. This is powerful evidence that the family structure produced by the model truly has an underlying psychological basis.

Example II: A Higher Order Security Heuristic

A second example of a higher order security heuristic arises in the following pair of ideas:

• Deterrence must be mutual.
• I don't like Communists at all. They are political thugs.

The first idea taps into the military dimension of the SYMMETRY heuristic, while the second idea taps the political or moral asymmetry of the STRENGTH heuristic. To the extent that we can imagine people holding both opinions at once, a synthesis of the two simpler intuitions seems reasonable. Modeling the synthesis with a convex combination of the SYMMETRY and STRENGTH generators produces an interesting result, as shown in Figure 6.7.

The higher order heuristic SYMMETRY + STRENGTH locates the most preferred outcomes along the main diagonal, revealing a disdain for military superiority. In this respect, the point of view is characteristic of the SYMMETRY family. But a sense of anti-Sovietism or political superiority asserts itself on the off-diagonal, where equality is refused. There is an evident unwillingness to equate our superiority with theirs.

When we introduce the new security flavor into the intuitive calculus, another very popular family emerges (see Figure 6.8). Disregarding over-

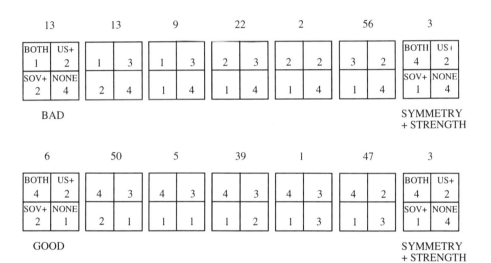

Figure 6.7

Figure 6.8 The SYMMETRY + STRENGTH family

laps with the other families, we have explained an additional $109/676 =$ 16% of the responses. By appending the two higher order heuristics to the basic model, we have now explained virtually every profile in the novice data. Of the diverse profiles the extended model supports, only 5 have failed to appear.

DISCUSSION

We now have a model that accounts for the novice preference profiles by combining simple strategic and political intuitions, suitably defined, in a weighted average. The basic idea of the model is that people apply two different heuristics to problems of nuclear strategy, one describing stable configurations power, the other describing the weapons themselves. We have seen how a very few heuristics of each kind can produce an amazing diversity of preference profiles, ranging over a broad game theoretic spectrum. Some of the profiles are consistent with traditional taxonomies of the arms debate (the PURE DOVE and STRONG HAWK). Others follow conventional theoretical templates like the Prisoner's Dilemma and Assurance Game. But most can't be pigeonholed so easily. Many seem politically bizarre.

The psychological interpretation of the pervasive anomalies and preference diversity turns on the ambivalence that arises when people embrace politically inconsistent notions. Many profiles like the NIFFs or YES++'s seem absurd at first glance because they appear self-contradictory or inconsistent with "self-evident" political truths. When the novices' preferences fail to conform with "axiomatic" benchmarks like

• Don't give your weapons to the enemy,
• Hawks are mean and nasty, or
• Military inferiority is dangerous,

they strike us as nonsensical, stemming from either mistakes or garbled thinking.

What our ingrained expectations fail to recognize is how natural and widespread equivocal thinking becomes in a political debate characterized by sharp partisan divisions, fundamental uncertainties, and great technical complexity. Under such conditions, lots of ideas seem intuitively plausible on both sides of every issue. If we have a cognitive mechanism that mingles the politically disparate notions together, then a potential for surprises exists. Our model makes evident how simple heuristic building blocks can easily produce anomalous preference structures, if they are combined rather than processed through a cognitive consistency filter. While the results may defy common sense, they are anything but unsystematic or incoherent. A better description would be ambivalent.

In one sense, the nuclear thinking data seem consistent with Converse's broad idea that mass publics don't put political ideas together "the right way" – at least relative to the norm of expert prescriptive theories. The novices' ideas do not seem constrained by the same threads of reasoning that experts might use. On the other hand, nothing about the heuristic nuclear calculus supports the idea that their thinking is unconstrained, random, or idiosyncratic. The term "non-attitudes" is a misleading description of the novices' strategic ideas. Instead, we have seen how a single highly structured cognitive algorithm can reproduce all the elaborate diversity of their political preferences.

No one would argue that we have "proved" that the intuitive nuclear calculus is true, or that other explanations couldn't account for the same evidence (though I have no idea what they would be). What we do have, I believe, is persuasive evidence that both the model and the data deserve to be taken seriously. By providing a plausible mechanism that can reproduce all the profiles in the data (and virtually only those profiles), I have shown that the unsophisticates' preferences do not have to be interpreted as noise, as nonsense, or as "garbage," even despite the bewildering patterns they reveal. This is not to insist that there is no noise or error in the data. Some respondents probably did make mistakes in reading the questions or in representing their actual preferences. What the model does show is that we do not *require* an explanation based on noise or error to account for the apparently absurd profiles we've observed.

At the same time, any model that can account in one stroke for the amazing proliferation of types, for the bizarre anomalies and the traditional archetypes, on both sides of the nuclear debate, also deserves high marks. Since many of the profiles seem outlandish, since their diversity has never been recognized in any theory of deterrence or the arms race – classical or anti-classical, normative or descriptive, formal or historical – and since no other model of political preference formation comes even close to predicting the detailed structure of the data, the intuitive nuclear calculus can not be dismissed casually.

Still, several reservations remain to be addressed. Because the model was not invented independently of the data, it is imperative to ask whether we have "capitalized on chance" or "mined the data" or "overfitted" the model in a way that conveys a spurious sense of fit. It is also necessary to investigate whether other models might fit the data equally well. A third concern is whether the patterns we've seen can be generalized beyond our samples. These issues will be addressed in the chapters ahead. First, I shall attempt to validate the model with a battery of statistical tests. Then, I turn to cross validating the model on independent samples of evidence drawn from different populations. Of special interest are data from a variety of professional nuclear experts. Whether their thinking departs systematically from the novices' is a basic question for later on.

To sum up, the intuitive nuclear calculus seems highly promising at the moment, but its status must remain tentative and provisional until it can be tested further and validated on fresh data.

7

Statistical Tests of the Intuitive Deterrence Calculus

While the intuitive calculus makes strong predictions that have now been confirmed by the novices' odd preference profiles, the model certainly did not arise independently of the evidence on which it was tested. Rather, the profiles came first and the model evolved by looking for a way to explain them. Because this search may have "capitalized on chance," it is important to check whether the theory can explain new features of the data that weren't considered in the model building phase.

Our model of nuclear thinking lends itself to independent validation because its matrix generators are not pure formalisms, selected by fit to the data alone. To be included in the model, each candidate heuristic required a plausible political interpretation. The key point to notice is that the specific substantive interpretations like "STRENGTH" or "GOOD weapon" impose far more stringent demands on the evidence than a simply formal description of the matrices would require. The convex operation by itself merely defines whether a preference profile should be present or absent in the data. The political and psychological interpretations of the model have broader implications, creating the opportunity for some interesting validating tests.

The primary concern in this chapter is whether our description of nuclear reasoning is consistent with the *sequence* of profiles collected from each respondent. A basic feature of the heuristic calculus is the way it produces families of profiles – not just singletons. With four profiles from each respondent, we can test whether preferences about different weapons obey the *family structures* predicted by the model.

HEURISTIC ORIGINS OF NUCLEAR PREFERENCES

Many of these tests turn on an obvious asymmetry between the security and weapon heuristics. The security heuristic, it will be recalled, reflects a broad political intuition about stable arrangements of power. The two basic flavors, SYMMETRY and STRENGTH, embody competing strategic world views. They reflect political assessments of the adversaries, and military judgments about what deters. The weapon heuristic addresses the contents of the nuclear arsenals. To the extent that people are mindful of differences between offensive and defensive weapons, between nuclear and conventional weapons, between counterforce and countervalue weapons, or between expensive and cheap weapons, the weapon heuristic captures a second element of national security policy preferences. When combined, the security and weapon heuristics produce an intuitive analogue of what we call a "deterrence theory" in the ordinary sense. They define preferences about the relationship between the nuclear arsenals and their contents.

Although nothing in the mathematical structure of the theory differentiates the security and weapon heuristics (each is a vector in $\mathfrak{R}^4$), there is a telling political difference between them. As the nuclear debate shifts from MX to SDI or ASW, the weapon heuristic can surely change flavor to reflect the different characteristics of each system. The theory would be nonsensical, however, if one's strategic world view changed from weapon to weapon. In Converse's terminology, the security heuristic has to be more *central* in the strategic belief system than is the weapon heuristic.

Because the weapon heuristic can be fluid and the security heuristic can't, the model requires a strong and particular form of consistency to appear in each novice's nuclear preferences. The profiles elicited about ASW, SDI, MX, and INVULNERABLE might be uncorrelated with political self-identifications. They might fluctuate wildly in game theoretic type. They might make little sense to the nuclear expert. But if the theory is right, the same flavor of the security heuristic ought to apply in every case.

Naturally, the appearance of such consistency would be something of a revelation at this stage of the game, given the chaotic appearance of the data we've seen so far. Without it, however, the substantive rationale for the model would collapse and the successful predictions of the last chapter would begin to look much less convincing. If the data do exhibit the kind of consistency predicted by the intuitive calculus, on the other hand, we would have powerful evidence against a theory of random response (or unreliable instrumentation) and much greater confidence that the confusing diversity of preferences, the ideological smearing, the game theoretic instability, and the pervasive anomalies are explicable results of a systematic cognitive algorithm.

The basis for these consistency tests is Figure 7.1, which codes all of the observed profiles according to the heuristic combinations that generate them in the nuclear calculus (the numbers above the profiles are simply identifying labels). The coding scheme exploits the broad definitions of the generators discussed in the last chapter. It would be nice if each profile that appears in the data could be assigned to a unique pair of generators in the

WEAPON HEURISTICS:

GD = GOOD WEAPON   BAD = BAD WEAPON   SYM = SYMMETRY   STR = STRENGTH   MIX = SYMMETRY + STRENGTH MIXTURE   POIS = SWEET POISON

SECURITY HEURISTICS:

NO

1	2.33	2.5	2.67	2.68	2.75	2.9	2.95	3	3.30	3.50	2.70	2.85
1 1 / 1 4	1 2 / 2 4	2 3 / 3 4	1 3 / 3 4	1 4 / 4 4	1 2 / 3 4	3 1 / 4 2	3 1 / 4 1	1 3 / 2 4	1 2 / 1 4	1 3 / 4 2	2 1 / 3 4	1 2 / 4 3
BAD+SYM	BAD	BAD	BAD	BAD	POIS+STR	SWEET POISON	POIS+STR	BAD+STR BAD+MIX POIS+STR	BAD+STR BAD+MIX POIS+STR	BAD+STR BAD+MIX POIS+STR	POIS+SYM POIS+MIX	

IFF-NO

4.25	4.3	4.33	4.67	4.7	4.75	4.1
2 1 / 1 4	3 2 / 2 4	3 1 / 1 4	3 2 / 1 4	2 2 / 1 4	2 3 / 1 4	3 1 / 2 4
BAD+SYM	BAD+SYM	BAD+SYM	BAD+MIX	BAD+MIX	BAD+STR BAD+MIX	POIS+SYM POIS+MIX

IFF°

5	5.05	5.06	5.1	5.2	5.3	5.5	5.9	4.9	4.85	4.95
4 1 / 1 4	4 2 / 1 4	4 3 / 1 4	3 4 / 4 1	1 4 / 3 2	1 4 / 2 3	1 4 / 2 3	2 4 / 3 1	2 3 / 4 1	3 2 / 4 1	1 3 / 4 2
SYMMETRY	SYM+STRG MIXTURE	SYM+STRG MIXTURE	POIS+STR	BAD+STR	BAD+STR	BAD+STR	POIS+STR	POIS+STR	SWEET POISON	

IFF-YES

6	6.25	6.3	6.33	6.5	6.1
4 1 / 2 3	4 1 / 1 3	4 2 / 2 3	4 1 / 1 2	4 2 / 1 3	4 1 / 3 2
POIS+SYM	GD+SYM	GD+SYM	GD+SYM	GD+MIX	POIS+SYM

	US+
BOTH	
SOV+	NONE

4=Best, ..., 1=Worst

YES-BUT

7	7.3	7.4	7.45	7.5	7.55	7.6	7.7	7.9
2 4 / 1 3	3 4 / 1 4	1 3 / 1 2	1 4 / 1 2	3 4 / 1 3	3 4 / 2 3	2 4 / 1 2	1 4 / 1 1	4 4 / 1 4
BAD+STR	BAD+STR	BAD+STR	BAD+STR	STRENGTH	STRENGTH	STRENGTH	STRENGTH	STRENGTH

YES+

8.1	8.2	8.25	8.3	8.5	8.6	8.7	8.8	8.93	8.95	8.9	8.75
4 3 / 1 3	4 3 / 1 2	4 4 / 1 2	3 4 / 1 2	4 1 / 1 1	4 3 / 1 1	4 3 / 2 2	4 4 / 1 1	2 3 / 1 1	3 4 / 1 1	2 4 / 1 1	4 2 / 1 1
GD+MIX	GD+STR GD+MIX	GD+STR	GD+STR POIS+STR	GD+SYM	GD+STR GD+MIX	GD+STR GD+MIX	GD+STR	POIS+STR	POIS+STR	POIS+STR	GD+MIX

YES++

9.2	9.3	9.4	9.45	9.5	9.6	9.7	9.72	9.8	9.85	9.9
4 1 / 3 1	4 2 / 3 1	4 3 / 3 1	4 3 / 3 2	4 2 / 2 1	4 4 / 4 1	4 3 / 2 1	3 4 / 3 2	3 4 / 2 1	4 4 / 3 2	4 4 / 3 1
POIS+STR POIS+MIX	POIS+STR	GOOD	GOOD	GOOD	POIS+STR	GD+STR GD+MIX POIS+MIX	POIS+STR	POIS+STR	GD+STR	GD+STR POIS+STR

Figure 7.1 Heuristic codes for observed nuclear preference profiles

model. Unfortunately, a one-to-one correspondence does not always exist. Though virtually all the profiles in the table are covered by the model, some arise in several different heuristic families. The NICE HAWK (Profile 9.70), for example, can be generated by pairing STRENGTH + GOOD or the STRENGTH–SYMMETRY MIXTURE + SWEET POISON. As a result, this profile can not be assigned to a definite family tree. Other profiles can be traced to one parent but not both. Such ambiguities should not be interpreted as a weakness of model unless we believe that only one line of reasoning can support each pattern of preference.[1] The ambiguities do rob us of information and statistical power. Fortunately, there remain many profiles with a clear family ancestry. They provide, I believe, ample leverage to discern whether the consistency required by the model appears in the data or not.

OBSERVED HEURISTIC COMBINATIONS

The question now is whether the intuitive calculus is really consistent with the game theoretic instability and ideological smearing we observe. Our interpretation of the evidence requires that the security and weapon heuristics be separate considerations, one of which is fixed and the other fluid. If the mathematical decomposition of the preference profiles shows that individuals apply different flavors of the security heuristic from weapon to weapon, the formal model would no longer make sense. If the weapon heuristic were not fluid, on the other hand, there would be no way to explain the political volatility of individual preferences. To be consistent with the model then, the individual sequences of preference profiles should exhibit two key characteristics: (1) the imputed weapon flavors should fluctuate from weapon to weapon, while (2) the imputed security flavor remains stable.

Whether the mathematical decompositions of the profiles in Figure 7.1 are consistent with these substantive political requirements remains to be seen. Obviously, nothing about the convex weighting scheme guarantees that real data must follow these patterns. Data generated by the prescriptive deterrence theories (classical and anti-classical) would not show unconstrained variability in the weapon heuristic. Under those schemes of reckoning, the security and weapon heuristics would march in step together, producing a far smaller set of preference types. Randomly generated data, on the other hand, would not exhibit a stable security flavor, since nothing would constrain the profiles to a single family tree. Such data would also show types the model can not explain.

---

1 I have already discussed how the classical MAD thinker and a believer in total disarmament could arrive at identical preferences about the MX missile or SDI.

Table 7.1. *Novice samples: heuristic mixtures over weapons*

Weapon Heuristic	Security Heuristic				
	SYMMETRY	MIXTURE	STRENGTH	Unclear	Total
INVULNERABLE					
BAD	27.7	33.3	29.2	6	22.5
GOOD	61.7	62.5	27.1	82	58.0
SWEET POISON	2.1	0	35.4	0	10.7
Unclear	8.5	4.2	8.3	12	8.9
Total	100%	100%	100%	100%	100%
Total n	47	24	48	50	169
ASW					
BAD	57.4	53.3	30.6	27.9	41.4
GOOD	29.8	43.3	28.6	55.8	38.5
SWEET POISON	2.1	0	32.7	0	10.1
Unclear	10.6	3.3	8.2	16.3	10.1
Total	100%	100%	100%	100%	100%
Total n	47	30	49	43	169
MX					
BAD	61.1	66.7	45.2	35	52.1
GOOD	20.4	27.3	16.7	47.5	27.2
SWEET POISON	1.9	0	31.0	0	8.3
Unclear	16.7	6.1	7.1	17.5	12.4
Total	100%	100%	100%	100%	100%
Total n	54	33	42	40	169
SDI					
BAD	58.2	50	37.8	18.9	40.2
GOOD	30.9	45.8	32.4	60.4	42.6
GOOD POISON	1.8	0	24.3	3.8	7.1
Unclear	9.1	4.1	5.4	17.0	10.1
Total	100%	100%	100%	100%	100%
Total n	55	24	37	53	169

Table 7.1 displays the combinations of security and weapon heuristics imputed to the respondents for each of the four nuclear weapons systems – MX, SDI, ASW, and INVULNERABLE PLATFORMS. The basic weapon flavors, it will be recalled, are GOOD, BAD, and SWEET POISON. The basic security flavors are SYMMETRY and STRENGTH, and the higher order mixture SYMMETRY + STRENGTH. Profiles coded unclear can't be attributed uniquely to a single pair of generators.

We can observe from the marginal totals of Table 7.1 that the GOOD and BAD flavors of the weapon heuristic account for over 90% of the codable profiles, while the SYMMETRY and STRENGTH flavors cover roughly 80%. As a result, a large number of novices fall into the four basic families (SYMMETRY + GOOD, STRENGTH + GOOD, STRENGTH + BAD, SYMMETRY + BAD). The entries inside the tables reveal that the security and weapon heuristics intermix rather freely, though certainly not independently in the statistical sense. Note that the percentages in each cell are computed by column to allow comparisons among groups who follow different security heuristics. Believers in STRENGTH do not find every weapon GOOD. Far from it in fact. Usually only 30% or so of the STRENGTH types follow the GOOD heuristic. Neither do believers in SYMMETRY invariably find the damage limiting weapons BAD and the second strike securers GOOD (as classical theory suggests). It is true, however, that the SYMMETRY types are considerably more likely to regard the "warfighting" systems as destabilizing – typically exceeding the promoters of STRENGTH by margins of 60% to 40%. The novices who use the higher order heuristic SYMMETRY+ STRENGTH apply the weapon heuristics with frequencies more like those of the pure SYMMETRY types than of the STRENGTH types. Finally, the SWEET POISON weapon flavor appears virtually always within the STRENGTH family.

Comparing the heuristic mixes across the weapons is also interesting. Systems that secure nuclear forces from preemptive attack are by far the most likely to be called GOOD. The MX receives the most BAD notices, while SDI and ASW lie in between. But more importantly for our purposes, the weapon heuristic marginals are much more unstable across items than are the security marginals – just as the theory predicts.

So far, the mathematical decomposition of the profiles by heuristic generator has survived its first test. The security and weapon heuristics covary in politically plausible ways, but not nearly as strongly as the prescriptive theories would suggest. At the same time, the weapon heuristic shows more instability across the weapons than does the security heuristic, at least in the aggregate. To see if the appearance is valid, we need to look now at the conditional distributions in the data more carefully.

HEURISTIC VOLATILITY ACROSS WEAPONS

Table 7.2 shows how consistently the weapon heuristic was applied in each possible pairing of the nuclear weapon systems. Table 7.3 repeats the display for the security heuristic. There is much to be learned from studying how consistently the heuristics have been applied across the different weapon combinations.

The six crosstables in Table 7.2 reveal considerable instability in the weapon heuristic, as we conjectured. The simplest measure of volatility is the percentage who apply the same weapon flavor in each pairing of nuclear systems. These respondents fall on the main diagonal of the tables, running from northwest to southeast. On average, about 55% of the respondents are consistent in this crude sense. The rate of pairwise consistency shows little variation from table to table. A problem with the raw percentages, however, is that they don't take account of the marginal totals in the tables. Even if the two preference profiles were statistically completely independent, some fraction of the respondents would fall on the main diagonal simply by chance. Comparing the total fraction, p_{ii}, in each diagonal cell with the "chance agreement" expected under independence is the basic idea of the κ statistic reported below each table. The proportion expected simply by chance is given by the product of the marginal proportions $\{p_{i+}\}$ and $\{p_{+i}\}$. The statistic κ expresses the difference between the actual and chance agreement as a fraction of the maximum value the difference could achieve, given the marginal totals:

$$\kappa = \frac{\sum_i p_{ii} - \sum_i p_{i+} p_{+i}}{1 - \sum_i p_{i+} p_{+i}}$$

When every case falls on the main diagonal, $\kappa = 1$. The measure of agreement statistic has been used most often to measure how consistently different observers react to a stimulus. Within the social science literature, values greater than .70 or so indicate strong agreement and those below .40 poor agreement.[2]

Table 7.2 shows that the measures of agreement for the weapon heuristic flavors are conspicuously low for every pair of weapons on the questionnaire. In some cases they are statistically indistinguishable from zero. They should be compared to the same measures for the security heuristic in Table 7.3 where the level of consistency across questions is sharply higher. The κ statistic averages nearly .70 for the security heuristic compared to only .24 for the weapon heuristic. The differences are sharp and statistically reliable

---

2 Further discussion of the κ statistic can be found in Yvonne M. Bishop, Stephen E. Fienberg, and Paul W. Holland, *Discrete Multivariate Analysis* (Cambridge: The MIT Press, 1975), Chapter 11. For a multinomial sampling model, where only the total sample size is fixed and the marginal totals are random variables, the maximum likelihood estimate of κ is found by substituting the observed proportions x_{ij}/N for the cell probabilities p_{ij}. Bishop, Fienberg, and Holland provide an approximate asymptotic variance for κ, determined by the delta method. The statistic κ can also be defined conditionally, measuring agreement on two items given that the row variable assumes a certain value. In that case, the measure becomes:

$$\kappa_i = \frac{p_{ii} - p_{i+} p_{+i}}{p_{i+} - p_{i+} p_{+i}}$$

Bishop et al. derive the asymptotic variances for these statistics as well. The conditional measures of agreement for the novice data will be discussed presently.

Table 7.2. *Novices: weapon heuristic consistency over weapons*

	BAD	GOOD	SWEET POISON	Unclear	Total
		MX Weapon Heuristic			
INVULNERABLE					
BAD	31	4	1	2	38
GOOD	52	31	6	9	98
SWEET POISON	2	9	6	1	18
Unclear	3	2	1	9	15
Total	88	46	14	21	169

Summary statistics, excluding those who are UNCLEAR.
Percentage on Main Diagonal—47%
κ Measure of Agreement (Asymptotic S.E)— .19 (.06)
McNemar Symmetry χ^2 (Prob Value)— 42.08 (pr = .000)

	BAD	GOOD	SWEET POISON	Unclear	Total
		ASW Weapon Heuristic			
MX Weapon Heuristic					
BAD	51	28	3	6	88
GOOD	10	30	4	2	46
SWEET POISON	2	2	8	2	14
Unclear	7	5	2	7	21
Total	70	65	17	17	169

Summary statistics, excluding those who are UNCLEAR.
Percentage on Main Diagonal—64%
κ Measure of Agreement (Asymptotic S.E)— .39 (.07)
McNemar Symmetry χ^2 (Prob Value)—9.39 (pr = .02)

	BAD	GOOD	SWEET POISON	Unclear	Total
		SDI Weapon Heuristic			
INVULNERABLE					
BAD	28	9	0	1	38
GOOD	34	50	6	8	98
SWEET POISON	4	9	4	1	18
Unclear	2	4	2	7	15
Total	68	72	12	17	169

Summary statistics, excluding those who are UNCLEAR.
Percentage on Main Diagonal—56%
κ Measure of Agreement (Asymptotic S.E)— .26 (.07)
McNemar Symmetry χ^2 (Prob Value)— 19.13 (pr = .001)

Table 7.2 (*cont.*)

	BAD	GOOD	SWEET POISON	Unclear	Total

ASW Weapon Heuristic

INVULNERABLE

	BAD	GOOD	SWEET POISON	Unclear	Total
BAD	26	9	1	2	38
GOOD	41	43	8	6	98
SWEET POISON	1	9	7	1	18
Unclear	2	4	1	8	15
Total	70	65	17	17	169

Summary statistics, excluding those who are UNCLEAR.
Percentage on Main Diagonal—53%
κ Measure of Agreement (Asymptotic S.E)— .21 (.07)
McNemar Symmetry χ^2 (Prob Value)— 20.54 (pr = .000)

SDI Weapon Heuristic

MX Weapon Heuristic

	BAD	GOOD	SWEET POISON	Unclear	Total
BAD	43	36	2	7	88
GOOD	16	22	6	2	46
SWEET POISON	2	6	4	2	14
Unclear	7	8	0	6	21
Total	68	72	12	17	169

Summary statistics, excluding those who are UNCLEAR.
Percentage on Main Diagonal—50%
κ Measure of Agreement (Asymptotic S.E)— .14 (.07)
McNemar Symmetry χ^2 (Prob Value)— 7.69 (pr = .05)

SDI Weapon Heuristic

ASW Weapon Heuristic

	BAD	GOOD	SWEET POISON	Unclear	Total
BAD	41	24	1	4	70
GOOD	19	35	6	5	65
SWEET POISON	4	7	5	1	17
Unclear	4	6	0	7	17
Total	68	72	12	17	169

Summary statistics, excluding those who are UNCLEAR.
Percentage on Main Diagonal—57%
κ Measure of Agreement (Asymptotic S.E)— .27 (.07)
McNemar Symmetry χ^2 (Prob Value)—2.46 (pr = .48)

Table 7.3. *Novices: security heuristic consistency over weapons*

Security Heuristic	Security Heuristic				
	SYMMETRY	MIXTURE	STRENGTH	Unclear	Total
	MX Security Heuristic				
INVULNERABLE					
SYMMETRY	39	4	2	2	47
MIXTURE	2	16	2	4	24
STRENGTH	5	4	25	14	48
Unclear	8	9	13	20	50
Total	54	33	42	40	169

Summary statistics, excluding those who are UNCLEAR.
Percentage on Main Diagonal—81%
κ Measure of Agreement (Asymptotic S.E)— .70 (.06)
McNemar Symmetry χ^2 (Prob Value)— 2.62 (pr = .45)

	ASW Security Heuristic				
MX					
SYMMETRY	37	3	9	5	54
MIXTURE	3	21	3	6	33
STRENGTH	2	1	26	13	42
Unclear	5	5	11	19	40
Total	47	30	49	43	169

Summary statistics, excluding those who are UNCLEAR.
Percentage on Main Diagonal—80%
κ Measure of Agreement (Asymptotic S.E)— .69 (.06)
McNemar Symmetry χ^2 (Prob Value)— 5.45 (pr = .14)

	SDI Security Heuristic				
INVULNERABLE					
SYMMETRY	37	2	0	8	47
MIXTURE	5	13	0	6	24
STRENGTH	7	3	28	10	48
Unclear	6	6	9	29	50
Total	55	24	37	53	169

Summary statistics, excluding those who are UNCLEAR.
Percentage on Main Diagonal—82%
κ Measure of Agreement (Asymptotic S.E)— .72 (.06)
McNemar Symmetry χ^2 (Prob Value)— 11.29 (pr = .01)

Table 7.3 (*cont.*)

Security Heuristic	Security Heuristic				
	SYMMETRY	MIXTURE	STRENGTH	Unclear	Total

ASW Security Heuristic

INVULNERABLE					
SYMMETRY	30	7	6	4	47
MIXTURE	2	14	3	5	24
STRENGTH	6	3	28	11	48
Unclear	9	6	12	23	50
Total	47	30	49	43	169

Summary statistics, excluding those who are UNCLEAR.
Percentage on Main Diagonal—73%
κ Measure of Agreement (Asymptotic S.E)— .58 (.07)
McNemar Symmetry χ^2 (Prob Value)— 2.78 (pr = .43)

SDI Security Heuristic

MX					
SYMMETRY	41	0	2	11	54
MIXTURE	7	18	1	7	33
STRENGTH	3	0	24	15	42
Unclear	4	6	10	20	40
Total	55	24	37	53	169

Summary statistics, excluding those who are UNCLEAR.
Percentage on Main Diagonal—86%
κ Measure of Agreement (Asymptotic S.E)— .79 (.05)
McNemar Symmetry χ^2 (Prob Value)— 8.20 (pr = .04)

SDI Security Heuristic

ASW					
SYMMETRY	37	1	2	7	47
MIXTURE	9	15	1	5	30
STRENGTH	6	2	26	15	49
Unclear	3	6	8	26	43
Total	55	24	37	53	169

Summary statistics, excluding those who are UNCLEAR.
Percentage on Main Diagonal—79%
κ Measure of Agreement (Asymptotic S.E)— .67 (.06)
McNemar Symmetry χ^2 (Prob Value)— 8.73 (pr = .03)

in every combination of the weapons. Even for pairings of highly dissimilar systems like the MX missile and INVULNERABLE platforms, the vast majority of respondents – typically 80% – adhere to a single security flavor (and therefore to a stable world view). Of those who aren't consistent, only a handful strongly discredit the theory by using SYMMETRY on one question and STRENGTH on the other. The rest combine the higher order mixture SYMMETRY+ STRENGTH with one of the pure types.

The evident coherence of the novices' strategic intuitions seems more remarkable when we remember the relative crudeness of the convex operations underlying the coding scheme,[3] the generic noisiness of social surveys, the extraordinary levels of ideological smearing in the data, and the game theoretic volatility of the individual profiles. Even despite the apparent chaoticness of the novices' preference profiles, the contingency tables in Table 7.3 are about as close to perfectly diagonal as real social science data ever get.

The pattern of consistency revealed in Table 7.3 (and of inconsistency in Table 7.2) is perhaps the most convincing evidence we've seen yet for the heuristic theory of nuclear preference formation. Were it true that the mathematical generators in the intuitive calculus simply fit the data opportunistically, without any substantial political basis, then it is hard to see why one kind of heuristic should exhibit so much stability and the other kind so little. If the novices' preference profiles were really random responses to inscrutable questions, then neither heuristic would be consistent across the different preference profiles. The prescriptive models of nuclear thinking do no better in explaining the results. The classical theory identifies SDI, MX, and ASW as strategically equivalent weapons (BAD). If the novices had followed this scheme of reckoning, then their weapon heuristic flavor should have been stable for all the pairs that included these systems. Instead, these pairs showed almost no consistency in an absolute sense, and even less agreement than the combinations that included INVULNERABLE platforms (the classical GOOD weapon). Anti-classical prescriptions are no more consistent with the data. Finally, if the novices' answers were trivially consistent – suppose they had answered every question the same way, just to avoid thinking – then both heuristics would have been stable in all the pairings.

The intuitive calculus imposes a subtler form of consistency on the data than does any of these alternatives. Like a random response model, it accommodates a large number of profiles and a high level of game theoretic volatility. But in stark contrast to a model of non-attitudes, the intu-

---

3 Recall that we've used the extended families, based on the looser definitions of the generators, to code the profiles. The high level of consistency that appears in the data vindicates the broad definitions of the generators defended in the last chapter.

itive calculus requires stability of world view. This pattern of reasoning restricts the profiles of each respondent to a single family tree in the space of convex combinations. That the data so consistently obey the restriction has to be counted as strong evidence in the theory's favor.

It is also interesting to consider the deviations from consistency in the tables. Here the theory suggests further predictions, albeit of a different kind. A basic principle in our cognitive algorithm is that the security heuristic should be unaffected by the local context of the arms debate. To the extent that the imputed security heuristic varies across the weapon items, the deviations from agreement should be simple noise. If so, they should be arrayed symmetrically about the main diagonal, with "mistakes" as likely to occur in one direction as another. To check, we can compute a statistical test for symmetry in the tables. Secondly, all respondents should adhere to their security heuristic with equal constancy, whether their view of the world is governed by SYMMETRY or STRENGTH or a MIXTURE of the two. As a result, the measures of agreement should be similar for respondents of every persuasion. These predictions can be checked with the conditional κ statistics described earlier.

The weapon heuristic flavor, on the other hand, should be sensitive to the characteristics of each nuclear system. How consistently the heuristic will be applied therefore depends on which questions are paired and what flavor of the heuristic we're talking about. Salient features of one weapon might be shared by other weapons too – or not. In the same way, people whose thinking exhibits one heuristic flavor might be affected by an aspect of a weapon that another group doesn't notice or care about. As a result, there can be no supposition that deviations from consistency will occur randomly or with equal frequency across weapon flavors and pairings.

To address these questions, I have computed two further statistical summaries. The McNemar Symmetry χ^2 tests the hypothesis that deviations from agreement are arranged symmetrically around the main diagonal (i.e., that $p_{ij} = p_{ji}$ for $\forall\ i \neq j$). The Symmetry χ^2 tests for the weapon heuristic display a pattern very unlike those for the security heuristic. Of the 6 weapon heuristic tables, 5 depart sharply from symmetry. The median of these χ^2 statistics is 14.26 [$\Pr(\chi^2_{3\,\text{d.f.}} > 14.26) \approx .002$]. For the security heuristics, the median of these χ^2 statistics is only 6.8, a value which does not achieve conventional levels of statistical significance. The deviations from agreement for the security heuristic are substantially more symmetric than those for the weapon heuristic.

To achieve a clearer picture of how symmetry breaks down, Table 7.4 presents conditional measures of agreement, computed separately for people in different heuristic families. The left side of the table shows

Table 7.4. *Novices: measures of agreement conditional on heuristic choices*

| | *Security Heuristic* | | | | *Weapon Heuristic* | | | |
	SYMMETRY	MIXTURE	STRENGTH		BAD	GOOD	SWEET	POISON
MX Conditional on INVULNERABLE				*MX Conditional on INVULNERABLE*				
κ_i	.751	.736	.626	κ_i	.654	.056	.288	
(S.E.)	(.09)	(.11)	(.10)	(S.E.)	(.135)	(.04)	(.12)	
ASW Conditional on MX				*ASW Conditional on MX*				
κ_i	.592	.708	.838	κ_i	.304	.437	.626	
(S.E.)	(.09)	(.10)	(.09)	(S.E.)	(.07)	(.11)	(.15)	
SDI Conditional on INVULNERABLE				*SDI Conditional on INVULNERABLE*				
κ_i	.894	.657	.627	κ_i	.551	.158	.178	
(S.E.)	(.07)	(.12)	(.09)	(S.E.)	(.12)	(.06)	(.10)	
ASW Conditional on INVULNERABLE				*ASW Conditional on INVULNERABLE*				
κ_i	.509	.653	.612	κ_i	.477	.08	.339	
(S.E.)	(.09)	(.13)	(.10)	(S.E.)	(.13)	(.05)	(.12)	
SDI Conditional on MX				*SDI Conditional on MX*				
κ_i	.901	.621	.845	κ_i	.154	.06	.269	
(S.E.)	(.06)	(.10)	(.08)	(S.E.)	(.06)	(.12)	(.14)	
SDI Conditional on ASW				*SDI Conditional on ASW*				
κ_i	.842	.511	.667	κ_i	.31	.221	.249	
(S.E.)	(.08)	(.11)	(.09)	(S.E.)	(.08)	(.09)	(.12)	

that all the respondents apply their security heuristic consistently, regardless of the world view they take. The first row of the table presents conditional measures of agreement between the INVULNERABLE platform and MX missile questions, grouped according to the security heuristic applied to INVULNERABLE. Those respondents who displayed a SYMMETRY profile on the INVULNERABLE question were much more likely than chance to do so on the MX ($\kappa_i = .751$). Those who applied the SYMMETRY + STRENGTH and STRENGTH flavors to INVULNERABLE were also highly consistent on the second question

(κ_i = .736 and κ_i = .626, respectively). The values of the conditional measures of agreement are high for every combination of weapons and statistically virtually indistinguishable for respondents with different strategic outlooks.

The computations for the weapon heuristic in the second column show a markedly different pattern. The measures of agreement are highly unstable from pairing to pairing (moving down the page) and also across flavors (moving across each row). In most cases, the patterns of consistency and inconsistency make good sense. Consider the responses to the MX, taking the INVULNERABLE profiles as given (row 1, column 2 in the table). People who found "effective technologies for protecting nuclear forces from preemptive attack" to be a BAD weapon were quite consistent in finding the MX a BAD thing too. Those who found INVULNERABLE platforms to be GOOD, however, displayed almost no consistency about the MX. This pattern seems highly plausible. People opposed to INVULNERABLE nuclear platforms (a basic idea in all deterrence theories) are not likely to support accurate multiple warhead missiles, after all. If one can't support a secure second strike, then it is unlikely that anything nuclear will seem very appealing. If so, we could expect to find the BAD heuristic from the INVULNERABLE question applied consistently to SDI and ASW as well, as it is in rows 3 and 4. People who find INVULNERABLE platforms to be a GOOD thing, on the other hand, need not agree about anything else. Classical and anti-classical thinkers all believe that U.S. forces should be secure from preemptive attack, but they disagree profoundly about systems like MX and SDI. As a result, we shouldn't expect the GOOD heuristic from the INVULNERABLE question to be applied consistently elsewhere. The data sustain this expectation too.

All of these calculations suggest that the security heuristic is applied much more consistently than is the weapon heuristic, both across weapons and by different political types. Still the evidence for consistency has been limited to pairwise measures of agreement, taking the weapons two at a time. To see whether the novice strategists applied the same security heuristic across the board, Table 7.5 summarizes information from the four-dimensional contingency table constructed from all four weapons questions. Of course, it becomes more complicated to measure consistency in such higher dimensional comparisons since there are many more ways that consistency can fail. Is a person more consistent when the SYMMETRY heuristic is applied to three items and STRENGTH to the last or when SYMMETRY is applied twice and SYMMETRY + STRENGTH twice? One could spend a great deal of time elaborating such scenarios and deriving measures for them, but I shall not do so here. Table 7.5 makes evident

Table 7.5. *Novice samples: Consistency of security heuristic across all four weapon profiles*

	All Clear	1 Unclear	2 Unclear	Total
All Alike	73%	57%	59%	65%
Minor Infraction	17%	19%	25%	19%
Severe Violation	10%	24%	16%	15%
Total	100%	100%	100%	100%
n	73	37	32	142 = 84 % of sample

Definitions: A "minor infraction" occurs when the pure security flavors, SYMMETRY or STRENGTH, occur with the higher order mixture SYMMETRY + STRONG. A "severe violation" occurs when the respondent uses SYMMETRY on one question and STRENGTH on another.

in a simple, straightforward way that most novices apply a single security heuristic to all four items on the survey.[4]

First consider those novices whose four profiles were "ALL CLEAR" (meaning that each profile could be assigned unambiguously to a definite heuristic family). Of these respondents, 73% applied a single security heuristic to all four weapons questions. None failed to use the same heuristic on less than three of four items. Among the 27% who showed one inconsistency, about a third committed a "SEVERE VIOLATION" by applying the SYMMETRY heuristic to one question and STRENGTH to another. The rest committed a "MINOR INFRACTION" by applying the higher order heuristic SYMMETRY + STRENGTH in combination with one of the pure types. In cases where 1 or 2 profiles can't be assigned to a definite family tree, we can still check consistency on the remaining profiles that are clearly codable. These respondents are nearly, but not quite, as consistent as the ALL CLEARS. Roughly 60% apply the same security heuristic to every item while perhaps 20% commit one severe violation. All together, around 65% of the novices display a consistent strategic world view on every single item and another 20% on all but one item.

4 Though some information is lost from the coding ambiguities, Table 7.5 includes 84% of the novice respondents. It should be added that even those novices with three or four UN-CLEAR profiles appear to manifest a high level of consistency. Only occasionally is it difficult to see an obvious pattern of similarity in their responses.

The intuitive calculus has passed a difficult test by revealing stable patterns of strategic reasoning in preference profiles that often seem politically chaotic and even nonsensical. The data show that a vast majority of novices address the nuclear puzzles with systematic strategic intuitions. At the same time, impressions about nuclear weapons technologies appear markedly less stable. Such instability should be no surprise among non-experts who haven't been trained to associate physical characteristics of weapons with strategic categories like counterforce or countervalue. Without some common accounting scheme to classify similarities and differences among weapons, impressions remain local and unsystematic. When the security and weapon heuristics are combined, the thread of strategic continuity provided by the security heuristic becomes much harder to see. Without a model to untangle the confounding effects of the two heuristics, it becomes all too easy to dismiss the resulting preference profiles as haphazard and implausible.

GAME THEORETIC VARIABILITY

It should be noticed that the diversity and instability of game theoretic type described in Chapter 5 follow directly from the simple cognitive dynamics in the model. Even though people's security heuristics are highly stable, variation in the weapon flavors (and in the convex weights applied to the security and weapon heuristics) produces rich game theoretic variety within the STRENGTH and SYMMETRY family trees. As a result, an individual's game theoretic type can shift dramatically across dimensions of the arms race, even when that person adheres steadfastly to a guiding strategic principle like "peace through strength." To the extent that the weapon heuristic moves idiosyncratically, the resulting volatility in political stance may strike the expert as bizarre, inconsistent, or unnatural reactions to "similar" weapon systems.

The same volatility will also confound efforts to reduce weapons politics to a simple contest between "hawks" and "doves." When used to describe preferences over procurement and arms control policies, such categories are far too impoverished to capture either the diverse heuristic recipes that can support a single game theoretic type, or the proliferation of types that arise among proponents of the STRENGTH and SYMMETRY world views. The conceptual confusion arises in both cases from trying to reduce political preferences to a single dimension, when they are generated by a two-dimensional cognitive algorithm. If nothing else, our data and reasoning show that the ubiquitous strategic dichotomy "hawk-dove" (and all its permutations) conceals far more than it explains, and should be avoided in serious discussions of armaments politics.

Table 7.6. *Novice samples: Choice of security heuristic by ideological self-description*

| Security Heuristic | Ideological Self-Descriptions | | | | | | | |
	Far Left	LIB	<MOR	MOR	>MOR	CONS	Far Right	Total
SYMMETRY	37	32	35	42	35	18	4	203
	61.7	33.3	43.8	29.2	25.7	13.6	14.3	30%
MIXTURE	7	17	10	19	25	29	4	111
	11.7	17.7	12.5	13.2	18.4	22.0	14.3	16%
STRENGTH	6	14	16	35	37	53	15	176
	10	14.6	20	24.3	27.2	40.2	53.6	26%
Unclear	10	33	19	48	39	32	5	186
	16.7	34.4	23.8	33.3	28.7	24.2	17.9	28%
Total	60	96	80	144	136	132	28	676
	100%	100%	100%	100%	100%	100%	100%	100%

EXTERNAL VALIDATION OF THE SECURITY HEURISTIC

The strong evidence we've discovered that laypeople approach the nuclear arms race with orderly strategic principles invites us to ask whether their intuitions have any systematic political foundation. The inter-item stability of the security heuristic is convincing internal evidence in favor of the intuitive calculus, but a world view (if it is one) should not be an island unto itself. Rather, we should expect basic strategic sensibilities to reflect broader political orientations. To the extent that the heuristic principles covary with independent measures like ideological self-identification, we can have greater confidence that generators like SYMMETRY and STRENGTH are not simply formalisms that happen to reproduce some important features of the data.

Table 7.6 and Figure 7.2 show that people's choice of security heuristic is strongly related to their position on the political spectrum. Here we have considered the profiles of all 169 novices on all four questions (676 profiles in all). The figure shows what fraction of the profiles drawn from each ideological neighborhood displays the various flavors of the security heuristic.[5] The frequency with which the novices invoke SYMMETRY

5 Percentages in the table are calculated over the entire 676 profiles. Percentages in Figure 7.2 are based on the 490 profiles that are not coded UNCLEAR (both normalizations are

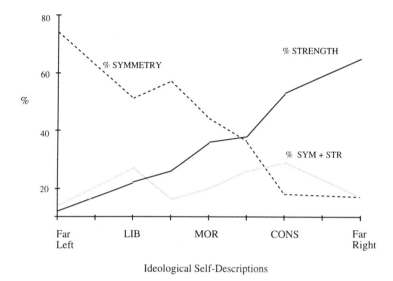

Figure 7.2 Novice samples: choice of security heuristic by ideological self-description

and STRENGTH varies sharply (and virtually monotonically) with political self-identification. Conservatives and far rightists understand deterrence to reside in STRENGTH by a clear majority. Liberals and far leftists find stability in SYMMETRY. Traveling across the political spectrum from far left to far right produces changes on the order of 60 percentage points in the fractions adhering to the competing heuristic flavors – a pronounced effect indeed. The higher order security flavor, SYMMETRY + STRENGTH, combines elements of both world views and is largely unrelated to political orientation (perhaps as we should expect).

THE CAUSES OF IDEOLOGICAL SMEARING

We can see now that basic strategic intuitions are not only consistently applied but ideologically highly polarized as well. This pattern undoubtedly explains why commentators so often identify the "hawk–dove" dichotomy with "conservative–liberal" thinking – such a connection does indeed arise on one dimension of the heuristic nuclear calculus. Why then do our unsophisticates' weapons preferences in the arms race appear so politically

interesting in their own way). Aggregating the four items helps to smooth out variation associated with the wording of each question. Nevertheless, patterns virtually identical to those in the figure appear for each separate weapon item.

unmotivated and ideologically smeared in Chapter 5? The answer provided by the model turns again on the multidimensional structure of nuclear preferences. The strategic world view embodied in the security heuristic may have ideological underpinnings, but the security heuristic does not determine preferences by itself. Instead, it interacts with a weapon heuristic that has very little political content or motivation. Formally speaking, the convex combinations in the model confound an abstract rule of thumb about stable configurations of power with concrete impressions about weapons. To the extent that the weapon heuristic flavor lacks a political foundation, then the politically systematic component of preferences can be masked by an overlay of more or less disconnected ideas. The result will be an array of opinion like the one observed for SDI in Figure 5.5 (and the other weapons in 5.6). Here a system of peaks in the data falls along the main diagonal in the picture. These peaks reflect the politically systematic effect of the security heuristic. But the diagonal structure in the data is heavily smeared by the politically unsystematic weapon heuristic.

To show more directly how this phenomenon works, I have computed the incidence of the several weapon heuristic flavors across the ideological spectrum. Figure 7.3 shows the results. The figure contains four separate panels, one for each weapon. The main point to notice is how little the choice of weapon heuristic flavor depends on political orientation. The fraction of profiles attributable to the GOOD, BAD, and SWEET POISON flavors is similar among liberals, middle-of-the-roaders, and conservatives. Few of the curves exhibit a marked trend and those that do display a sluggish rate of change (on the order of 15 or 20 percentage points at best over the whole ideological spectrum). For the hotly debated systems like SDI and MX, there is some slight ideological coloration in the weapon heuristic, but it pales in comparison with the stark polarization observed for the security heuristic. On the other hand, the level of the curves (as opposed to their slope) changes markedly from weapon to weapon. The novices clearly react to the descriptions of the weapons in the questionnaire, but not in an ideological way.

For people who have learned systematic rules for distinguishing among nuclear weapon systems, the lack of structure in these pictures might seem disconcerting. Two characteristic examples from the novice samples might make them easier to understand. We see that liberals apply a GOOD weapon heuristic to anti-submarine warfare nearly as often as conservatives do (somewhere between 30% and 40% of the time). But why should people who frequently express a preference for arms control, disarmament, and military symmetry embrace anti-submarine warfare as a good weapon? If one wanted to pursue a countervailing nuclear strategy, protect valuable shipping lanes, or exploit a clear technological superiority, there might be

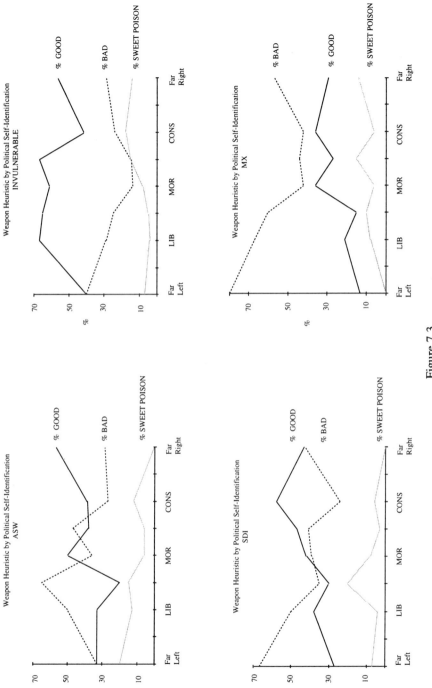

Figure 7.3

good reason, but these respondents clearly had no such aspirations. Later discussions with the liberal students unraveled the puzzle. What appealed to them was not the prospect of escalation dominance or a nuclear counterforce capability that might have appealed to conservatives. Such considerations never crossed their minds in fact. Rather the question evoked an image of "effective means to search out and destroy ballistic missile submarines." Described in these terms, ASW seemed to them like a way to destroy nuclear weapons or to render them "impotent and obsolete." The same appeal arises for SDI.

In much the same way, "effective technologies for protecting nuclear forces from preemptive attack" elicited more BAD weapon notices from liberals and far leftists than from any other group. Their objection was not to strengthening deterrence in the classical way – that issue hardly concerned them – but rather to "protecting" weapons they abhorred. In both examples, considerations that experts are trained to notice (like securing second strikes) didn't impress the strategic neophytes. On the other side of the coin, neophytes notice things about weapons that experts, by their training, no longer find salient. In both ways, the unsophisticates' reactions to the questions often strike experts as strange.

These examples raise the popular question whether the novices' preference profiles are highly sensitive to question wording and therefore unreliable measures of their "true" nuclear preferences. Such an objection contains a grain of truth, but largely misses the forest for the trees. In the first place, it misconstrues the evidence by disregarding the stable component of the nuclear opinions. Since the security heuristic is virtually unaffected by question wording (or by the local details of the nuclear debate), the nuclear profiles are certainly not determined in any thoroughgoing way by how the questions are phrased.

On the other hand, the model and data both suggest that the weapon heuristic is cognitively peripheral, politically unsystematic, and volatile. This pattern makes good sense because we don't expect neophytes to approach an esoteric debate with systematic ideas about its technical aspects. After even a few discussions with the novice respondents, it becomes obvious that the untutored layperson's impressions of nuclear systems have shallow roots and weak connections. Whether the GOOD weapon bell or the BAD weapon bell rings about SDI, for example, seems often to be controlled by scattered impressions and vague images – about the movie *Star Wars* or the woeful self-immolation of the space shuttle *Challenger*, say – rather than by some systematic scheme of reckoning. Whether a defense might be saturated, leaky, preferential, terminal, random-subtractive, or territorial typically has no effect on the layperson, who rarely anticipates the technical considerations that shape expert discussion.

As a result, the neophytes' preferences about security policy can be highly unstable, at least in one dimension. The relevance of framing, to use the popular psychological term, follows directly from the fluid quality of the weapon heuristic. To the extent that impressions about weapons are ill-formed and unstable, then the neophyte's reaction to survey questions, and more importantly to policy proposals, can surely be affected by how the issues are formulated.[6]

If lay opinion about nuclear weapons policy is sensitive to the wording of a survey questionnaire, then it will certainly be subject to manipulation through propaganda, persuasion, and salesmanship in the political arena. To the extent that the weapon heuristic is a more fluid element of nuclear thinking than the security heuristic, as our data suggest strongly, then we might expect the nuclear debate to focus on considerations of technical performance, feasibility, and cost – features of weapons that can turn unsophisticates' opinions around – rather than emphasizing questions of nuclear "grand strategy" where thinking is more stable, more polarized, and harder to change. While it is hard to imagine what evidence could have convinced Ronald Reagan that "peace through strength" might backfire by driving an arms race spiral or by feeding misperceptions about our intentions, many conservatives appear sensitive to arguments that SDI or the B2 Stealth Bomber are technically flawed and astronomically expensive. Our results also suggest why physicists and other technical experts are so often called upon to settle what appear to be essentially political disagreements in the nuclear debate. Their expertise addresses the most fluid dimension of nuclear preferences.[7]

---

6 An informative discussion about instabilities in survey response appears in John Zaller, *The Nature and Origins of Mass Opinion* (Cambridge: Cambridge University Press, 1992). Arguing that survey respondents typically harbor conflicted ideas about public policy issues – and we have certainly found plenty of ambivalence in our data – Zaller infers that many "opinions" expressed in sample surveys are skewed by the questionnaire itself. Zaller's model of survey response turns on the imperfect retrieval of "considerations" from memory. When asked to express an opinion, people make "attitude reports" based on the immediately salient considerations they can retrieve on the spur of the moment. To the extent that the latent distribution of considerations is mixed, the process of retrieval can be biased and unstable if the survey question makes some considerations more salient than others. In this sense, Zaller argues, few subjects hold a "true" or stable opinion. Another formulation might be that most people's "true" opinions are tentative and ambivalent.
   Stanley Kelley's theory of voting decisions in *Interpreting Elections* (Princeton: Princeton University Press, 1983) includes refined measurements of voters' ambivalence and shows how the instabilities they produce sometimes create spurious landslides. Shanto Iyengar and Donald R. Kinder discuss the agenda setting and priming effects of television newscasts in *News That Matters: Television and American Opinion* (Chicago: University of Chicago Press, 1987). These political manifestations of framing are consistent with a huge psychological literature on the subject.
7 Edward Luttwak writes as follows: "The word is much used in the common speech of Americans, but close scrutiny of executive statements, congressional hearings and debates,

HOMOGENEITY ANALYSIS OF THE PREFERENCE PROFILES

I now turn to statistically more advanced questions that the non-technical reader may wish to skip over. The discussion to follow will be important for specialists interested in public opinion data, but won't change the substantive conclusions presented so far.

That the intuitive calculus originated from a rather informal combination of data fitting and political theorizing leaves some people uneasy. They want to know whether another set of generators might fit the data better than ours does, and, if not, how to be sure. Couldn't the latent heuristic algorithm be extracted from the data by some formal statistical procedure like factor analysis? If not, how could other researchers replicate the results in their own datasets? Such queries largely boil down to the same interesting problem: is it possible to recover the intuitive deterrence calculus from preference matrix data using a fitting technique that does not rely on political criteria of reasonableness (like the one I used when selecting the generators in the model)?

A related set of questions concerns the statistical stability of the patterns arising in the data. Are those results sensitive to unusual cases or random features of the preference profiles? Do they describe typical behavior or has the fitting process capitalized unduly on chance configurations in the novices' responses? Could the fit be replicated on fresh data which contain different patterns of noise?

All of these questions lead quickly into non-standard statistical terrain. Classical multivariate techniques like factor analysis, discriminant analysis, and principal components all take as their point of departure a set of attitude measurements describing the subjects' location on a set of scales. In our survey, the respondents' preferences are recorded as matrices, not numbers, and the matrices have no natural metric or order. It is true that we earlier constructed a game theoretic ordering of the profiles to summarize the strength of political support for each weapon. That system of coding is politically interesting in its own right, but whether the profiles in each game theoretic category reflect a common pattern of nuclear thinking is highly doubtful. As things worked out, the game theoretic scales were abysmally unrelated to factors like ideological location and they were unstable across items. For purposes of describing the respondents' heuristic

military documents, academic writings, and of the vast quasi-academic literature produced by the defense-research industry reveals that sustained consideration of *strategy* is very rare in our public discourse. Most of what passes for strategy and the strategic is, in fact, . . . operational or tactical in nature, or even technical. In this great mass of words one may find much detailed discussion of individual weapons and forces, . . . but if one excludes a handful of writings, there is no strategy." "SALT and the Meaning of Strategy," in *Strategy and Politics: Collected Essays* (New Brunswick, N.J.: Transaction Books, 1980), pp. 91–92.

reasoning, there are no compelling *a priori* quantifications (numeric scales) for the preference matrices.

A data analytical scenario like ours can be addressed with generalizations of standard multivariate techniques that compute optimal quantifications of the data as part of the analysis itself. The very general and powerful techniques used here go by a variety of names, including multiple correspondence analysis, homogeneity analysis, and multivariate analysis with optimal scaling. Although these methods have attracted a lot of interest among statisticians, they remain unfamiliar to most social scientists. To give some idea of how they work, let me provide a brief survey of the particular technique used here, called HOMALS, or *homogeneity analysis by alternating least squares*.[8]

The basic objective in HOMALS is to seek out patterns of *homogeneity* or similarity in a set of observations. In our survey, the respondents provide a separate preference matrix for each of four nuclear weapon systems. These 2×2 tables assume 60 different patterns in the sample. To record this information requires a data matrix with four categorical variables (ASW, MX, SDI, and INVULNERABLE), each containing 60 unordered categories, for 169 subjects. Formally speaking, each variable, h_j , maps the set of *n* subjects into a finite set of k_j categories. (Here *j* = 1 to 4 indexes the four weapon systems, and k_j = 60 for all *j* is the number of different preference categories [i.e., distinct 2×2 profiles] observed for each weapon.) To put matters simply, the data matrix is a convenient way to store information relating *subjects* (respondents) to *categories* (distinct patterns of preference).

One can record such information in a so-called *indicator matrix*, consisting of dummy variables that define whether the *i*th subject falls in the *k*th category for weapon h_j. For our data, the indicator matrix **G** = (**G₁** | **G₂** | **G₃** | **G₄**) has dimension *169 × (60 × 4)* (subjects × weapon preference types x weapons) and looks like Figure 7.4.

The indices assigned to the different preference profiles (e.g., ASW 1 to 60) need not be numbers, of course, and the numbers shown here should not be confused with scales. They are simply labels to distinguish the different patterns of preference. The columns of the matrix describe the 60 possible 2×2 profiles for each weapon system (each column is a distinct preference *category*). The rows record which profiles each subject selected. With one profile per weapon (indicated by a 1), the rows of **G** sum to *m* =

---

8 The discussion here follows the treatment in Albert Gifi, *Nonlinear Multivariate Analysis* (New York: John Wiley & Sons, 1990), and John P. van de Geer, HOMALS, unpublished manuscript, Department of Data Theory, University of Leiden, The Netherlands, 1985. See also J.P. van de Geer, *Multivariate Analysis of Categorical Data* (Newbury Park, CA: Sage Publications, 1993).

	ASW	SDI	MX	INV
	1,2,...,15,16,...,60	1,2,...,15,16,...,60	1,2,...,15,16,...,60	1,2,...,15,16,...,60

$$
G = \begin{bmatrix}
10.00.. & 10.00.. & 10.00.. & 10.00.. \\
10.00.. & 00.10.. & 10.00.. & 10.00.. \\
00.10.. & 00.10.. & 10.00.. & 01.00.. \\
00.01.. & 01.00.. & 01.00.. & 10.00.. \\
01.00.. & 01.00.. & 01.00.. & 00.01.. \\
10.00.. & 10.00.. & 01.00.. & 10.00.. \\
00.10.. & 10.00.. & 00.10.. & 00.10.. \\
10.00.. & 10.00.. & 00.01.. & 10.00.. \\
.... & .... & .... & ....
\end{bmatrix}
$$

Figure 7.4 Indicator matrix in homogeneity analysis

4. The column totals of **G** record the marginal frequencies in each preference category for the four weapon variables h_j.

The general statistical question is whether the preference profiles tend to appear together in groupings that correspond to the heuristic families identified by our theory. To see how the HOMALS technique addresses such questions, consider the following geometric representation of the indicator matrix. Suppose we make a plot by first giving each of the 169 subjects a different label, x_i. Next assign separate labels, y_{kj}, to the 240 different weapon profile categories. These labels distinguish the 240 columns in the indicator matrix. The y_{kj} are just shorthand for everyday names like Prisoner's Dilemma profile on ASW, PURE DOVE on MX, or STRONG HAWK on SDI. Finally, let's scatter all these labels randomly in the plane (a two-dimensional space with coordinate axes). We use a two-dimensional space not just because the theory predicts that preferences have a two dimensional structure, but to obtain a graphical representation of the data. To keep track of which subjects go with which preference profiles, draw lines between each subject label and the four weapon preference labels the subject has selected. When we're finished we shall have represented all of the original information in a picture that looks something like Figure 7.5: Naturally the picture is an uninteresting mess because we've located the labels randomly in the plane. Thus far there is no data analytical gain, but a new feature has appeared in the representation of the data. We now have numerical scales for both the subjects and their preference profiles (each label is located along two separate coordinate axes).

The question now is whether the picture can be rearranged to represent the data in a more orderly and revealing fashion. Doing so will surely require reducing the clutter of lines. But to minimize clutter, we must keep

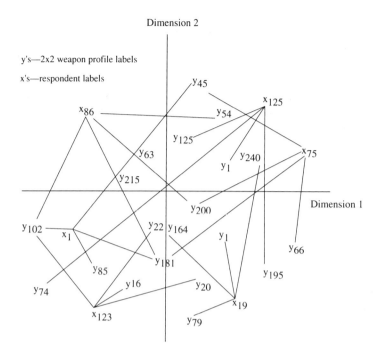

Figure 7.5 Graphical display of indicator Matrix **G**

the lines as short as possible. In other words, we must locate respondents as close as possible to the profiles they select, and the preference profiles as close as possible to the individuals who select them. Of course, one could make the picture trivially simple by collapsing all the labels to the origin. To avoid that uninformative result, we fix the overall size of the picture by centering the x's and giving them unit variance in each dimension. To minimize clutter under this constraint requires that labels of subjects who select similar preference profiles must lie near each other in the space, along with the preference profile labels they share in common. Respondents with disparate preferences must be kept apart. In this way, a search for *homogeneity* in the geometric sense separates the subjects into groups with commonly shared preference profiles. At the same time, the preference profiles are separated into groups that share common respondents. Profiles that tend not to be chosen by the same set of respondents become separated in space.

These geometric ideas essentially define the HOMALS algorithm. The technique computes optimal scales for the respondents and their preference profiles (that is, coordinates in p dimensional space for each subject and for each distinct weapon profile; here $p = 2$) so as to maximize homogeneity in the data. Notice that all the technique notices is whether respondents attach themselves to the same 2×2 preference profiles or not. (The only information available to the technique is the pattern of 1's in the indicator matrix.) What the categories "mean" politically, or what we think they mean, is irrelevant. Or to put the point another way, the technique chooses the scales for the preference profiles – we don't.

In practice, the HOMALS solutions are computed by an algorithm called alternating least squares. Beginning with an arbitrary assignment of locations for the subjects (the subject label coordinates are called *scores*), the 2×2 preference categories are then scaled or quantified (i.e., located in the plane) by averaging the scores (in each dimension) of the subjects who chose them. New scores are then computed for each subject by averaging the coordinates of the categories the subject has selected. The updated subject scores are then used to recompute the category quantifications, and so on, back and forth, until the alternating process converges (between steps the scores are orthonormalized to prevent collapse to the origin). The HOMALS subject scores and preference category quantifications are optimally scaled to make the data as homogeneous as possible in the geometric sense described above. The preference profiles are located at the centroids (average points) of the subcloud of subject points attached to them. Profiles selected by dissimilar groups are separated as much as possible in the space, while profiles attached to a common group of subjects lie close together.

The subject scores and category quantifications can be used to make a variety of enlightening plots, and to scale the data optimally for use in other multivariate statistical techniques. Important geometrical aspects of the HOMALS plots include the following:

- Respondents and their preference profiles are represented as points in a joint space.
- Preference profile labels lie at the center of gravity of the respondents who selected them.
- The distance between two subject points is related to the similarity of their preferences on the weapons items. Subjects with four identical profiles are plotted at the same location in space.
- Popular profiles are plotted nearer to the origin than are preference categories with low marginal frequency. Subjects with commonplace preference profiles lie closer to the origin than do subjects with unusual preferences.
- A variable more successfully *discriminates* among subjects to the extent that its category labels are separated farther apart in the plot. Along each dimension, the variance of the category quantifications for each optimally scaled variable is proportional to that variable's correlation with the subject scores (these correlations are called "*component loadings*").

The HOMALS technique has been applied with gratifying results to many kinds of problems and data. When given responses from a multiple choice exam, it will assign scores to the students that typically show correlations of .95 and more with the number of right answers – and this without knowing what responses are correct! Here the technique exploits the ability of the best students to find the right answers on the difficult questions, and of the worst students to find the wrong answers on the easy questions. In this way, the technique discovers patterns of homogeneity driven by the student's knowledge of the subject matter. When given archeological fragments and artifacts, exhumed from an ancient graveyard, the technique will put the artifacts and graves in serial order. Homogeneity arises in the data because new materials and motifs appear in graves of similar age, and persist forward in time but not backward.[9]

[9] Optional notes for technically minded readers:

The HOMALS algorithm minimizes the following loss function:
$$\sigma(\mathbf{X};\mathbf{Y}) = m^{-1} \Sigma_j \, \mathrm{SSQ}(\mathbf{X} - \mathbf{G}_j\mathbf{Y}_j)$$
where $\mathbf{X}$ is an $n \times p$ matrix of scores (or coordinates) for the subjects; $\mathbf{Y}_j$ is the $k_j \times p$ matrix of quantifications for the k categories of variable j; and $\mathbf{G}_j$ is the $n \times k_j$ indicator matrix for variable j, $j = 1$ to m. Here $m = 4$. The loss function describes the sum of squared distances in the p dimensional space between the individual points x_i and the category points of variable j that each respondent selects. The sums of the squared distances are averaged across variables, then the average is minimized. The minimization can be computed by alternating least squares. Doing so is equivalent to computing a Singular Value Decomposition on the matrix of bivariate marginals, $\mathbf{G}'\mathbf{G}$ (often called the Tableau de Burt). The optimal $\mathbf{Y}$'s are generalized eigenvectors of the Burt matrix.

An important special case of HOMALS is classical principal components analysis. In that problem, one seeks to replace a set of variables, again assumed to measure "the same thing," with scores that capture as much of their common variance as possible. The scores are chosen as weighted sums of the variables. Finding the optimal choice of weights and scores amounts to minimizing the departure from homogeneity in the loss function
$$\sigma(\mathbf{X};\mathbf{A}) = m^{-1} \Sigma_j \, \mathrm{SSQ}(\mathbf{X} - \mathrm{h}_j\mathrm{a}_j')$$
where the $\mathbf{h}_j$ are the variables, the $\mathbf{a}_j$ are weights to be selected, and the $\mathbf{X}$ are scores for the subjects. Here the differential weighting of the variables amounts to a simple linear transformation. In HOMALS, the variables $\mathbf{h}_j$ are first discretized into a number of categories. The weights are applied only after optimally transforming the variables by $\phi_j(\mathbf{h}_j)$, where ϕ_j can be any non-linear function of $\mathbf{h}_j$. For this reason, HOMALS is sometimes called Nonlinear Principal Components Analysis. The first HOMALS dimension is the first principal component of the data matrix after it has been scaled optimally. The optimal scales result from those transformations that maximize the first eigenvalue of the (transformed) correlation matrix.

HOMALS also linearizes bivariate regressions among the rescaled variables, if such linearizing transformations exist. Using HOMALS to rescale data optimally therefore lends highly desirable statistical properties to classical multinormal methods that assume linearity of regressions.

HOMALS and its generalizations have rich connections to a variety of classical and modern techniques, including canonical analysis, log-linear analysis, regression analysis, discriminant analysis, multidimensional scaling, and sliced inverse regression. For further discussions, see Jan DeLeeuw, "Multivariate Analysis with Linearizable Regressions," *Psychometrica* 53 (1988), pp. 437–454; J.L.A. Van Rijckevorsel and J. DeLeeuw, eds., *Component and Correspondence Analysis* (New York: John Wiley & Sons, 1988); M. O. Hill,

So much for the preliminaries. Let's now apply the HOMALS technique to the four nuclear preference items, ASW, MX, SDI, and INVULNERA-BLE. In this analysis, we include no information about the respondents' ideological self-descriptions, their game theoretic types, their heuristic choices, or anything else. The technique only sees the four preference profiles from each respondent, coded as nominal categories. It then seeks homogeneity of the geometric kind described above, considering only whether respondents select the same 2×2 profiles or not.[10]

Figure 7.6 plots the subject scores derived from a two dimensional HOMALS solution.[11] The respondents are separated in three or maybe four clusters, falling in a roughly triangular array. But what do the clusters mean? We know that subjects who share preference profiles in common lie in close proximity, but what characteristics define their common outlook?

The panels in Figure 7.7 seek to identify the sources of homogeneity in the data by highlighting subsets of respondents in the HOMALS plot according to their position on background variables in the survey. To the extent that liberals, or people who think that nuclear war is probable, or any other subset share a common scheme of nuclear preferences, its members will be located in the same region of the plot. The three rows in this figure consider the novices' ideological self-descriptions, their estimates of the probability of nuclear war, and their descriptions of the conflict of interest between the U.S. and the USSR. These variables emerged in Chapter 4 as the ones most promising for delineating the factional structure of the arms debate. They proved later to be unrelated to a game theoretic ordering of the profiles. Now they'll have another chance to redeem themselves.[12]

"Correspondence Analysis: A Neglected Multivariate Method," *Journal of the Royal Statistical Society, Series C (Applied)* 23 (1974), pp. 340–354; M. J. Greenacre, *Theory and Applications of Correspondence Analysis* (New York: Academic Press, 1984); M. Tenenhaus and F. W. Young, "An Analysis and Synthesis of Multiple Correspondence Analysis, Optimal Scaling, Dual Scaling, Homogeneity Analysis and Other Methods for Quantifying Categorical Multivariate Data," *Psychometrica* 50 (1985), pp. 91–119; and P.G.M Van der Heijden, A. De Falguerolles, and J. DeLeeuw, "A Combined Approach to Contingency Table Analysis with Correspondence Analysis and Log-Linear Analysis (with Discussion)," *Journal of the Royal Statistical Society, Series C (Applied)* 38 (1989), pp. 429–447.

10 Unlike the earlier tests of heuristic consistency, this analysis does not suffer any loss of information from ambiguous codings. Every profile influences the HOMALS solution, whether it can be assigned or not to a definite family tree in our model of the heuristic deterrence calculus.

11 A two dimensional solution makes sense here because our theory generates preferences with only two heuristics. Constraining the dimensionality of the solution is not restrictive in HOMALS because solutions are *nested*, meaning that the first dimension of a higher dimensional solution is the same as a one dimensional solution; the second dimension of a two dimensional solution is also the second dimension of a higher dimensional solution, and so on.

12 It is important to remember that these background variables haven't influenced the HOMALS calculations. Rather, we are using them *passively* to interpret what the solution means.

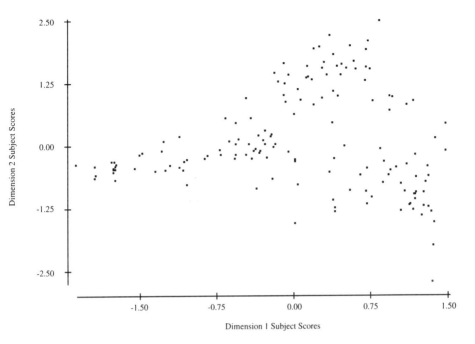

Figure 7.6 HOMALS – nonlinear principal components analysis of the 4 weapon profiles: two dimensional plot of subject scores

The first row of pictures shows where respondents from different parts of the ideological spectrum fall in the HOMALS space. Novices who are leftists and liberals gravitate toward the cluster in the southeastern corner of the plot while conservatives mainly reside along the northwestern ridge. Still, lots of liberal types fall along the ridge too. Those who place themselves in the middle of the road (anywhere between the liberal and conservative labels) fall all over the space. There seems to be some ideological structure in the HOMALS solution, but it is hardly pronounced.

The second row of pictures highlights the respondents according to their estimates of the probability of nuclear war during the next four decades. These estimates apparently have nothing to do with the clusters HOMALS identifies. Finally, the third row considers the novices' descriptions of the conflict of interest between the U.S. and the USSR. Those who call the USSR "a major power sharing many interests in common with the U.S." fall in every cluster, just like those who call the Soviets a "formidable adversary," a "dangerous opponent," and a "mortal enemy." If there is any pattern at all, it again occurs in the southeasterly group, which takes a kinder view of the Russians.

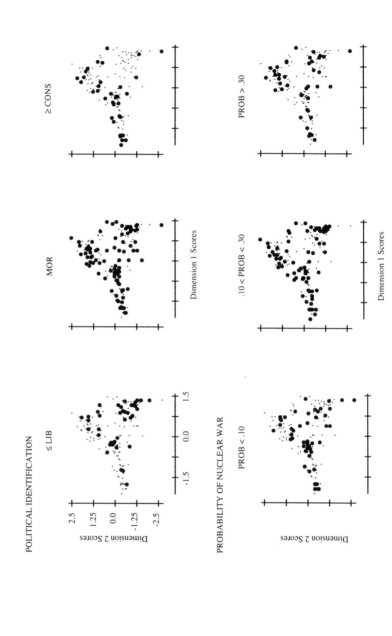

POLITICAL IDENTIFICATION

≤ LIB   MOR   ≥ CONS

PROBABILITY OF NUCLEAR WAR

PROB < .10   .10 < PROB < .30   PROB > .30

Dimension 1 Scores

Dimension 2 Scores

Dimension 1 Scores

Dimension 2 Scores

2.5 1.25 0.0 -1.25 -2.5

-1.5 0.0 1.5

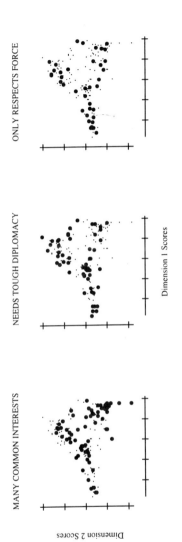

Figure 7.7 HOMALS – nonlinear principal components analysis of the 4 weapon profiles: subject scores grouped by background variables

Despite some ideological overtones, none of these variables accounts for the structure of the HOMALS plot very well. Perhaps the source of homogeneity in the preference profiles is game theoretic rather than ideological. To find out, Figure 7.8 highlights the respondents according to game theoretic type on the MX question. Here the results are more interesting but still mixed. Some of the game theoretic types reside in well defined neighborhoods, especially the unusual YES++'s in the north-central cluster in the picture. The YESes and the NOs are pretty clearly separated in the space, while the IFFs are not so much concentrated in a particular area.

The lower panel in Figure 7.8 shows another interesting way to study the solutions graphically. The Tukey boxplots show the distributions of the subjects' scores along the HOMALS first dimension, grouped by the respondents' game theoretic types. Several features of the boxplots invite attention. First, the median scores within the game theoretic categories follow a highly non-monotonic pattern along the first HOMALS dimension, indicating that it is not organized in a systematic game theoretic order. At the same time, we see that the scores for some game theoretic types show much more dispersion, and therefore less homogeneity, than do others (the longer boxes indicate greater spread along the first HOMALS dimension). Taken together, the diagrams in Figure 7.8 suggest that some game theoretic types are highly homogeneous, but that the HOMALS space as a whole is not organized in a game theoretic way.[13]

Now let's see how closely our model of heuristic nuclear thinking corre-

---

[13] Technical remark: The median scores within the game theoretic categories approximate the optimal quantifications (in dimension 1) that HOMALS would assign to the variable GAME TYPE. Recall that the optimal quantifications for a categorical variable are computed in HOMALS by averaging (dimension by dimension) the subject scores of respondents who fall in each category. Even though the variable GAME TYPE was not used actively in computing the HOMALS solutions shown here, the solutions can still be used to scale such *passive variables* (typically background variables about respondents that we use to interpret the solutions). In this case, averaging the subject scores within each game theoretic category (NO, IFF-NO, . . . , YES++) produces quantifications that make the scaled variable GAME TYPE maximally consistent with the patterns of homogeneity revealed in the preference profiles. The median scores shown in the last panel of Figure 7.8 are generally very close to the respondents' average score in each game category (and therefore to the optimal HOMALS quantifications in dimension 1).

The strength of relationship between a passive variable and the HOMALS subject scores depends on how widely separated the imputed category quantifications are. If the averages for the different categories of a variable are very similar, then the variable is not very strongly related to that HOMALS dimension. If the averages are very different, then the variable might be important for understanding what mechanism produces homogeneity in the data. Also relevant, of course, is whether the quantifications obey the *a priori* ordering of the categories. In the case of the respondents' game theoretic types, they don't, suggesting that the variable GAME TYPE does not organize the HOMALS first dimension.

The correlations between optimally scaled categorical variables (active or passive) and the subjects' scores are called *component loadings*. The component loadings can help identify variables that are strongly related to each HOMALS dimension.

sponds to the HOMALS solutions. Figure 7.9 highlights the HOMALS plot according to the security flavor imputed to each respondent on the MX question. (Remember that the security heuristic applied to one question is a good proxy for all the rest.) Here the results are dramatic. The groups isolated by HOMALS coincide amazingly well with the three heuristic families defined by our intuitive deterrence calculus. The southeastern cluster consists almost entirely of respondents who used the SYMMETRY heuristic. A tight central cluster corresponds to the SYMMETRY + STRENGTH group. Finally, the STRENGTH types are separated in two groups lying at either end of the ridge. These broad strategic heuristics partition the space almost perfectly. Each family lives in a distinct neighborhood, with hardly any overlap or smearing. Taken together, the neighborhoods fill the entire space. Were it not for the upper branch of the STRENGTH group, the three heuristic families would be arrayed in a neat monotonic order along the first HOMALS dimension. This interesting pattern raises the question why the STRENGTH family has been partitioned in two pieces.

Figure 7.10 highlights the HOMALS plot according to the weapon heuristic each novice applied to the MX question. The SWEET POISON types fall exclusively in the northern cluster; the GOOD weapon types lie farther south, spreading all along the first dimension; while the BAD weapon types lie along the bottom edge of the point cloud. In large measure, then, the weapon flavors align themselves from north to south along the second HOMALS dimension. But this pattern is just as the intuitive calculus would predict. The model generates nuclear preferences as a two dimensional phenomenon, driven by separate heuristics for the weapon system and for stable distributions of power.

Figure 7.11 features the STRENGTH group again, this time distinguishing novices who used the higher order weapon heuristic SWEET POISON from others who applied the simpler ideas of GOOD or BAD weapons. The weapon heuristic flavor discriminates neatly between the two subsets of the STRENGTH family.

The general topography of the HOMALS space is now clear. With the interesting exception of the [STRONG + SWEET POISON] cluster (including many YES++'s), the first HOMALS dimension aligns the novices by their choice of security heuristic. The second dimension taps the weapon heuristic. Figure 7.12 illustrates these patterns another way, showing the (conditional) distributions of the subject scores in each HOMALS dimension, grouped by the respondents' heuristic choices. The upper row of boxplots in Figure 7.12 shows how the security heuristic is strongly related to the scores in the first dimension and little related to those in the second dimension. The bottom row groups the scores according to the weapon

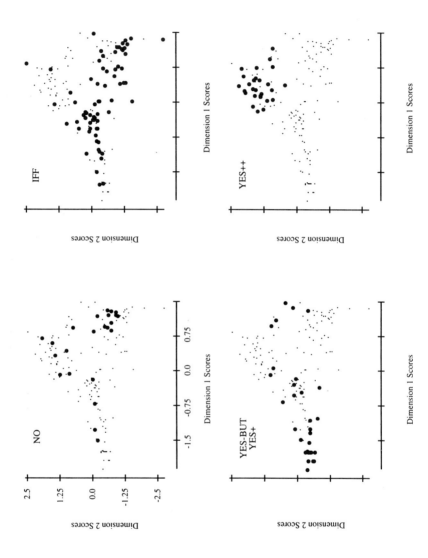

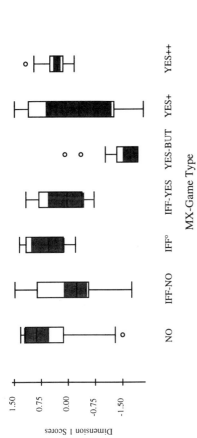

Figure 7.8 HOMALS – respondent scores highlighted by game theoretic type (MX), with (this page) Tukey boxplots of HOMALS respondent scores (1st dimension) by game theoretic type. Boxes span interquartile range. Gray zones are 95% confidence intervals around medians (central lines).

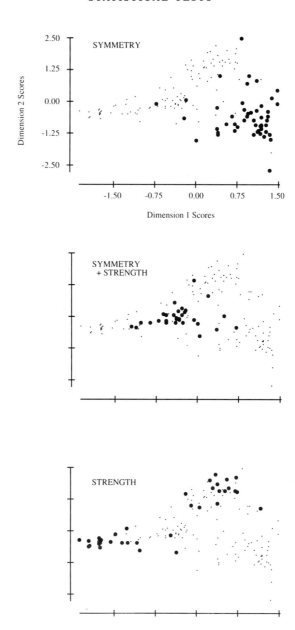

Figure 7.9 HOMALS – nonlinear principal components analysis of the 4 weapon
profiles: subject scores grouped by imputed security heuristic flavors

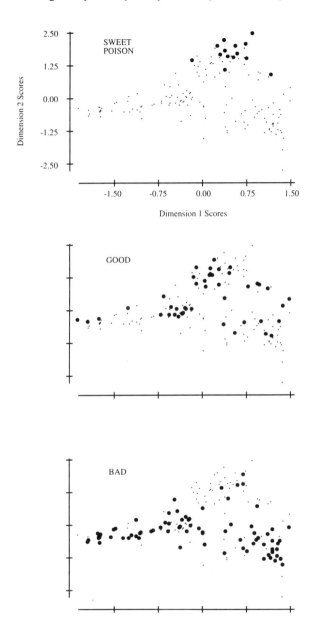

Figure 7.10 HOMALS – nonlinear principal components analysis of the 4 weapon profiles: subject scores grouped by imputed weapon heuristic flavors (MX)

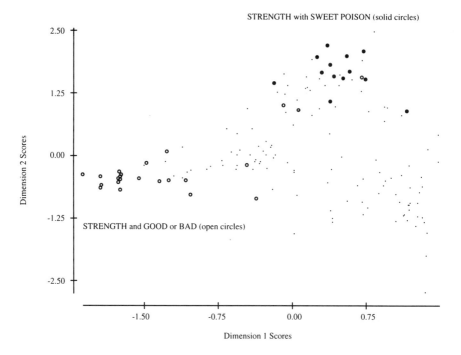

Figure 7.11 HOMALS – nonlinear principal components analysis of the 4 weapon profiles: subject scores for respondents using the STRENGTH heuristic (MX)

flavors, which are more related to the second dimension than they are to the first.[14]

The two dimensional HOMALS solution groups the novices almost perfectly according to the family structures of the heuristic calculus. If we return to Figures 7.9 and 7.10, the most widely separated clusters at the western and eastern borders of the pictures are the basic SYMMETRY and STRENGTH families, formed from combinations with the first order weapon heuristics GOOD and BAD. The two clusters in the middle of the plot correspond to the higher order heuristics in the model; the security heuristic mixture SYMMETRY + STRENGTH and the weapon heuristic SWEET POISON. Although these awkward appendages were unwelcome additions to the model, the picture makes clear that they are genuine

14 Recall that strength of relationship between variables and the HOMALS dimensions is revealed by how widely separated the average scores are across the categories. These characteristics define statistical measures in HOMALS like discrimination measures and component loadings.

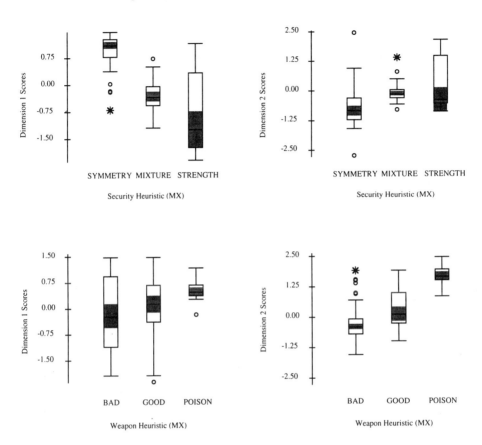

Figure 7.12 HOMALS – nonlinear principal components analysis of the 4
weapon profiles: subject scores by heuristic family (MX). The boxplots show
that the security heuristic is strongly related to the first HOMALS dimension
and not much related to the second. The weapon heuristic follows the opposite
pattern, showing a stronger relationship with the second dimension than the
first. The figures in the diagrams are Tukey boxplots. The line inside each box is
the median of the subject scores for respondents who displayed each heuristic
flavor. The boxes span the interquartile range (the middle 50%) of the ordered
subject scores. The gray zones are 95% confidence intervals for the medians.

sources of homogeneity in the data, not just noise. Their location in the
center of the picture is a nice representation of ideas that synthesize elements from each pole of the nuclear debate.

The correspondence between the theoretical and statistical groupings is
arresting when we consider that the HOMALS technique knew nothing

about the intuitive deterrence calculus when it scaled the subjects and their preference profiles. Rather, it discovered the heuristic families on its own, merely by grouping subjects together who shared profiles in common. On the other hand, the theoretical model emerged without any attention to patterns of homogeneity in the data. The original objective was merely to find generators that could replicate the table of observed types in a politically interpretable way. Remarkably, the two lines of analysis converged on the same result, reinforcing each other in the process. The statistical technique shows that the intuitive nuclear calculus is indeed the basic source of homogeneity in the novices' preference profiles, where homogeneity is now understood in the formally precise sense described by the HOMALS loss function. At the same time, the model of nuclear thinking clarifies what the statistical patterns mean. The nuclear heuristics explain the structure of the HOMALS solution with a precision and definiteness that conventional political variables in the survey don't come close to matching. Without the theory, we would be hard pressed to understand what the HOMALS plot captures. Without the statistics, we would be hard pressed to defend the model as an optimal description of the data. Taken together, the two lines of analysis are striking evidence that our intuitive deterrence calculus actually generates the non-experts' preferences in the nuclear arms racing game.

Before moving on – and I appreciate that many readers may be eager to do so – let's take a moment to reanalyze one last feature of the data. Figure 7.13 shows Tukey boxplots of the subject scores arrayed according to political background variables in the survey. When we separate the scores on each dimension, the effect of the background variables becomes much clearer than it was before. The upper row shows that ideological self-identifications are systematically related to the first HOMALS dimension but not at all to the second. This pattern confirms our earlier finding that the security heuristic is ideologically colored while the weapon heuristic isn't. The same pattern emerges in the second row, which groups the respondents according to how they rank U.S. superiority (relative to equality of forces or avoiding some weapons altogether) as a source of nuclear stability. The question is a direct probe of the respondent's security heuristic. It too lines up strongly with the HOMALS first dimension, and not at all with the second. Finally, the question characterizing the USSR shows some weak covariation with the first dimension and none at all with the second. All of this evidence is consistent with our interpretation of the first HOMALS dimension as a measure of the ideologically driven security heuristic. The second dimension captures the politically unsystematic weapon heuristic.

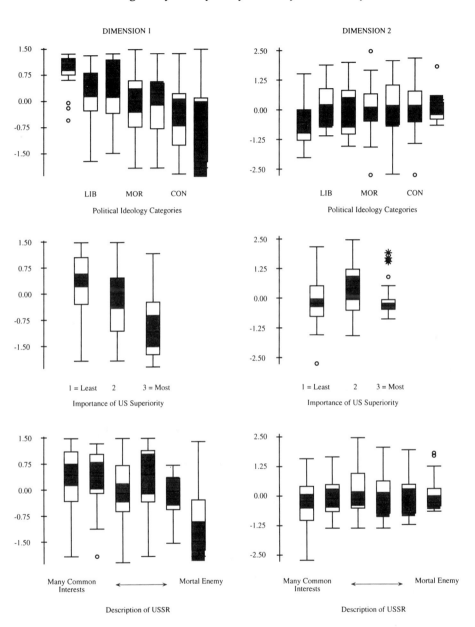

Figure 7.13 HOMALS – nonlinear principal components analysis of the 4 weapon profiles: subject scores grouped by responses to background survey questions

STATISTICAL STABILITY OF THE RESULTS

The question now is whether the patterns we've discovered are statistically stable or not. In classical statistical theory, this question amounts to asking whether repeated random samples from the same population would exhibit similar effects or not. In practice, the question is ordinarily answered not by taking new samples, but by assuming the existing one was drawn randomly from a known and stable probability distribution like the multinormal or multinomial. Given a detailed description of the parent probability distribution, actual replication becomes superfluous because the distribution of the sample statistics is already determined by theory.

Classical asymptotic techniques like the delta method can be used to derive confidence intervals and formal tests of significance for the HOMALS statistics, if one is willing to live with the strong probabilistic assumptions these methods require. Assuming we have drawn randomly from a known and stable population distribution seems rather heroic in our problem, however.[15] Instead, we employ a popular form of random resampling called *bootstrapping* to assess the statistical stability of our results. This approach is in keeping with an important program in modern statistics, which seeks whenever possible to replace strong probabilistic assumptions with computations.[16]

The bootstrap is simple to compute and explain, even if the statistical rationale for the technique is subtle and sophisticated. In order to simulate actual replications from the parent population, one draws repeated random samples (of size n with replacement)[17] from the empirical distribution in the sample. By recalculating the statistic of interest in each of the bootstrap pseudo-samples, one obtains, after many replications, a distribution that can be used to estimate the statistic's sampling distribution and standard error.

The bootstrap offers a simple yet powerful way to study the sampling properties of complicated statistics like the non-linear principal components estimates from HOMALS. If our categorical data happen to be a

15 The same objection applies to other *self-selected samples* of paid or willing volunteers that social scientists routinely analyze as if they were randomly drawn.

16 The bootstrap, the jackknife, and related perturbation methods have received intense study in statistics during the last 10 years. Basic surveys include B. Efron, "Bootstrap Methods: Another Look at the Jackknife," *Annals of Statistics* 7 (1979); D. V. Hinkley, "Bootstrap Methods (with Discussion)," *Journal of the Royal Statistical Society, Series B (Methodological)* 50 (1988); and T. J. DiCiccio and J. P. Romano, "A Review of Bootstrap Confidence Intervals (with Discussion)," *Journal of the Royal Statistical Society, Series B (Methodological)* 50 (1988). Applications to the HOMALS technique with comparisons to calculations by the delta method are discussed in Chapter 12 of Albert Gifi, *Nonlinear Multivariate Analysis* (New York: John Wiley & Sons, 1990).

17 The random resampling procedure typically results in some subjects being represented several times in any particular bootstrap pseudo-sample and some not at all.

random sample from a stable multinomial distribution, then the bootstrap pseudo-samples are related to the sample proportions in the same way that the sample proportions are related to the population parameters. The basic idea is that we could just as well have observed any of the random perturbations of the data as the one actually before us. On the other hand, the randomization methods like the bootstrap still provide interesting evidence about statistical stability even when we don't feel comfortable specifying a definite probability model for the original observations. To the extent that our n respondents seem equally important and interchangeable, it makes sense to check whether our statistical summaries remain stable when we perturb the sample randomly. Doing so clarifies whether the statistics are dominated by particular observations or clusters in the sample, or, alternatively, whether they provide good summaries of general patterns.

Figure 7.14 displays a plot of so-called *component loadings* from the nonlinear principal components analysis. The component loadings are the correlations between the optimally scaled categorical variables and the HOMALS subject scores (the loadings are computed dimension by dimension). The component loadings for each variable are represented as points in a two dimensional space with coordinates that describe the correlations with each HOMALS dimension.[18] To make the picture easier to read, we connect each point to the origin. Because variables with higher loadings discriminate better among subjects, these statistics suggest which variables determine each dimension of the HOMALS solution. Variables with longer component vectors discriminate better among the subjects. The direction of each vector indicates with which HOMALS dimension the optimally scaled variable is most strongly correlated.

Figure 7.14 shows the component loadings for both active and passive variables in our analysis. First consider the four weapons profiles that actually determined the HOMALS solutions. Without exception, their component loadings hover around .90 on both dimensions. That all four weapon variables load strongly and virtually identically on both HOMALS dimensions suggests that a similar, two dimensional scheme of reckoning determines nuclear preferences in each case. Nothing stands out to distinguish one weapon from the rest, or to suggest that one dimension is more important for understanding the profiles than the other. In these respects, the results confirm expectations from the intuitive calculus, which gives a symmetrical role to the weapon and security heuristics in determining preferences for all weapon systems.

The other vectors in the picture describe the component loadings for passive variables. Although these background variables haven't influenced

18 The squares of the component loadings are called *discrimination measures* in HOMALS.

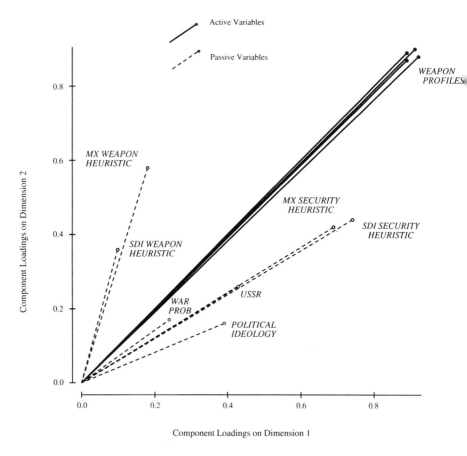

Figure 7.14 HOMALS component loadings

the statistical calculations, they can nevertheless be scaled according to the derived HOMALS solutions. Scaling the categories of political self-identification, for example, is accomplished by averaging the HOMALS scores of subjects who fall in each ideological category from far left to far right. If the computed averages are very similar across the categories of a passive variable, then the HOMALS dimension clearly does not depend on the differences the variable describes. If the category means are far apart, on the other hand, then the scores in that dimension are strongly related to the passive variable. Its component loading will then be high.

The passive variables with by far the highest loadings are the weapon and security heuristics derived from the intuitive calculus (here I've considered the heuristic choices on both the MX and SDI questions). The security flavors (SYMMETRY, STRENGTH, SYMMETRY + STRENGTH) are highly correlated with the first HOMALS dimension (loading $\approx$ .70) and modestly correlated with the second (loading $\approx$ .40). The weapon flavors (GOOD, BAD, SWEET POISON) show the opposite pattern, loading strongly on the second dimension (loading $\approx$ .60) and weakly on the first (loading $\approx$ .18). Similar patterns obtain when we consider the imputed heuristics from the SDI question instead of those from the MX. The loadings for the security heuristic are virtually identical in both cases. The weapon heuristic loadings are weaker for the SDI question, but in the same direction. Table 7.4 explains why the latter discrepancy appears. The weapon heuristic for the MX question transfers much more consistently to other weapons than occurs for SDI.

These results quantify the patterns revealed earlier in the graphical displays of the HOMALS solutions. The first HOMALS dimension corresponds strikingly well with the security heuristic and the second dimension with the weapon heuristic. In addition, Figure 7.14 shows the component loading for the political background variables. Ideological self-placement and description of the USSR load moderately on the security dimension (.39 and .43) and hardly at all on the weapon dimension (.16 and .26). Again we see that the security heuristic appears to be ideologically driven while the choice of weapon heuristic is largely unpolitical. The novices' estimated probability of nuclear war is virtually uncorrelated with either HOMALS dimension (.24 and .17).

Figure 7.14 captures in a single striking picture all of the main patterns we've located in the nuclear thinking data. The component loadings show how the intuitive calculus provides a much better explanation of nuclear preferences than do the conventional political variables derived from the literature. Not only are ideological identifications and perceptions of the Soviets weakly correlated with the preference profiles, they only address one dimension of a two dimensional cognitive algorithm. The result, as we learned in Chapter 5, is that conventional political categories ("liberals," "hardliners," "doves," "conservatives") translate very poorly into actual armaments preferences.

Since the HOMALS summary statistics describe the basic structure of the data so well, they are excellent candidates for a bootstrap study of stability. Figure 7.15 displays the results of 50 bootstrap replications from the original sample. Each panel shows the component loadings for the four weapons profiles, the weapon and security heuristics, and the political identification variable. The individual points in the graph describe the calculations from different bootstrap samples. One interesting wrinkle in the results concerns the interpretation of the two HOMALS dimensions. In

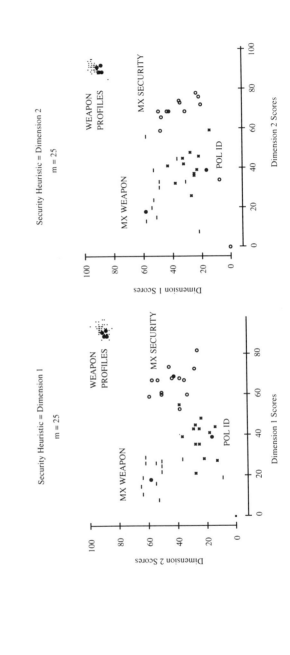

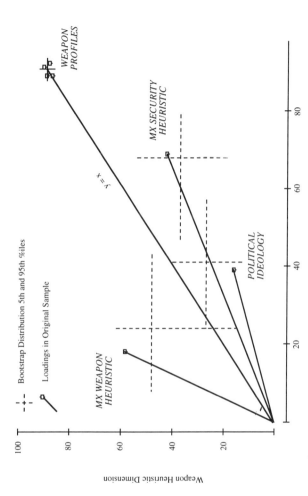

Figure 7.15 Bootstrap resampling study – HOMALS component loadings

STATISTICAL TESTS

half of the pseudo-samples (shown in the left panels), the security heuristic loads mainly on the first dimension. In the other half (shown on the right) the weapon heuristic loads on the first dimension. Given the symmetrical role the two heuristics play in the intuitive calculus, there is no reason to expect either one to enjoy a privileged role. The bootstrap results confirm this symmetry in a nice way. When the axes are reversed in the second panel (so that the security dimension is horizontal in both pictures), it becomes obvious that both patterns of solution describe the same structure.

In the bottom panel of Figure 7.15, I have superimposed the estimates from the original sample on the bootstrap distributions. (Here all the bootstrap estimates have been pooled, after making the axes conformable.) For each variable, the arms of the cross intersect at the average of the bootstrap estimates and extend to the 5th and 95th percentiles of the bootstrap distribution. The picture shows that the major patterns in the data are statistically highly stable, even for the passive variables that haven't influenced the HOMALS calculations. The 2×2 preference profiles that determine the solutions load strongly and symmetrically on both dimensions, while the weapon and security heuristics are clearly separated on either side of the 45° line. The political background variables consistently align themselves with the security heuristic, but with unimpressive loadings. The results indicate that a null hypothesis of zero loadings can be safely rejected in every case. More importantly, the calculations make evident that our original estimates have not been dominated by unusual cases or peculiar configurations in the data. In replication after replication, the same patterns emerge.

DISCUSSION

We began with the expectation that nuclear preferences should be organized in a simple way – if not consensually then mostly along ideological lines. That idea was rudely dashed by the ideological disarray, the individual volatility, the unexpected diversity, and the political strangeness of the novices' preference profiles. The patterns discussed in Chapter 5 take most people by surprise and propel a set of expectations that might be called Conversian. At first blush, the data seem so "unnatural" that a theory of random "non-attitudes" becomes hard to resist.

To build a counterargument, I have proceeded in two steps. First, I developed a model that shows how all of the preference profiles, from the standard issues to the true oddities, can be derived from a small set of simple heuristic building blocks. The heuristic calculus interweaves intuitive ideas about stable distributions of power with summary impressions of nuclear weapons to produce a rich tapestry of political types – and it does so without invoking reasoning that is implausibly complicated or esoteric.

The next step was to validate the heuristic calculus by showing it could explain features of the data that weren't anticipated when the model took shape. The theory predicts that each respondent's preference profiles should obey a particular family structure. Such predictions are non-trivial because the families produced by the three security generators contain profiles with little apparent political or game theoretic similarity. By making the heuristic origins of the profiles clear, the model reveals strong patterns of continuity in the novices' nuclear thinking (continuities that are highly obscure otherwise). Later, I demonstrated how these mathematically generated decompositions of the profiles covaried noticeably with ideological persuasion and other background variables. These relationships provided external validation of the model. Finally, I recovered the intuitive calculus from the preference profiles with a powerful multivariate statistical technique. The heuristic model accounted with remarkable precision for basic patterns of homogeneity in the data, even while predictor variables culled from the literature on nuclear strategy floundered to explain what was going on. A bootstrap analysis confirmed that the patterns created by the heuristic calculus were statistically highly stable.

We can think about theories of ideological polarization and chaotic non-attitudes as two extremes along a spectrum of possible structures that the lay reasoning about nuclear strategy might follow. By the lights of our results, each account suffers by overlooking one ingredient in the heuristic recipe that governs nuclear thinking. The security heuristic lends far more consistency and intellectual structure to nuclear preferences than a model of non-attitudes allows. The weapon heuristic, on the other hand, creates far more complexity, volatility, and smearing than a polarized taxonomy of hawks and doves admits.

By accounting for both facets of nuclear reasoning, the intuitive nuclear calculus does a better job of explaining the evidence before us. From the perspective of public opinion studies, the novice data are an interesting example of how a coherent and systematic cognitive algorithm can nevertheless produce survey responses that seem like chaotic "non-attitudes." From a political and strategic point of view, we see how simple, intuitive schemes of strategic reckoning can produce enormous political diversity and game theoretic complexity, even in small populations. The evidence suggests why the domestic politics of national security and the dynamics of the arms race are enormously complex problems. Whatever the pattern of nuclear thinking among experts, we know that strategic novices play a vital role in American political institutions, including the media, the electorate, the Congress, and the presidency. Decisions about national security therefore arise from the interplay of a complex cast of characters.

8

Expert Nuclear Reasoning

Do strategic experts think differently about nuclear affairs than the everyday person does? Are the experts' opinions more coherently structured and politically consistent? Are experts more likely to embrace the classical precepts of strategic stability and a philosophy of mutual secure second strikes? Are the experts' strategic opinions less influenced by ideological formulas and more attuned to scientific evidence about deterrence and the arms race? Are experts more dovish than novices and friendlier to arms control? Should we prefer that military officials and strategic experts be empowered to decide nuclear policy or should we be pleased when the democratically elected Russian and Ukrainian parliaments take control over a substantial fraction of the former Soviet arsenal? Such questions illustrate the rich variety of cognitive, political, and normative issues that arise when we compare how experts and novices reason about nuclear dilemmas.

THE SAMPLE OF EXPERTS

To address these questions, I collected opinions from 151 nuclear experts, using the same questionnaire that the novices completed. What distinguishes these respondents from other citizens is their professional immersion in nuclear weapons politics and policy making. The sample of experts includes senior corporate managers at two major aerospace and defense contracting firms in Southern California, professional defense analysts at the RAND Corporation in Santa Monica, senior government officials and academic specialists who gathered in Cambridge, Massachusetts, for a conference on arms control, and advanced graduate students in international relations and national security studies. Table 8.1 shows how the expert sample came together in several waves over a period spanning the end of the Cold War.

Table 8.1. *Surveys of experts on nuclear policy preferences*

10/29/88	CISA Conference on Unilateral Approaches to Arms Control, Cambridge, Massachusetts. Prominent strategic experts and defense officials. (N = 25).
3/1/89	Northrop Electronics. Lower, middle, and upper level managers. (N = 13).
4/30/90	Graduate Seminar on Conventional Arms Control, UCLA. Advanced graduate students. (N = 14).
5/14/90	TRW Corporation. Senior executives. (N = 11).
6/1/90	Graduate Seminar on Strategy, UCLA. Advanced graduate students. (N = 14).
3/19/91	RAND Corporation. Professional defense analysts. (N = 43).
5/15/93	RAND Corporation. Professional defense analysts (N = 31). (A validation sample not described in this chapter.)

Note: The views expressed by the experts do not represent the official or unofficial positions of the organizations that employ them. Their responses are anonymous expressions of personal opinions and preferences. Neither are the experts random samples of the employees in their organizations.

The nuclear thinking data can be obtained from the author in electronic or hard copy versions.

THREE HYPOTHESES ABOUT THE COGNITIVE STRUCTURE OF EXPERT OPINION

One thing is certain before we even look at the new data. When compared to the undergraduates at UCLA, these experts knew vastly more about nuclear technology, strategy, arms control, and the politics of national security. The question is whether their preferences about nuclear forces follow different patterns as a result. As usual we can discern several plausible hypotheses, all reasonable in their own way, but rather at odds with each other.

Hypothesis I: Elites' Opinions Have a More Parsimonious Structure

One influential line of argument suggests that political thinking among elites will display more coherence than mass opinion, more connectedness from issue to issue, more stability across time, and more resistance to change. An early defense of this position is Philip Converse's classic article on mass belief systems, which we have already reviewed at length. Converse argues that elites' beliefs are more "constrained" than mass opinion.

By learning the intellectual conventions and categories that define "what goes with what" in politics, elites form opinions that follow simpler, more predictable patterns than the fragmented, impressionistic thinking of the masses.

While Converse's study of mass belief systems focused on political and social reasoning, cognitive scientists' comparisons of experts and novices often reveal similar patterns. An instructive example are the clever experiments initiated by A. D. de Groot and refined by Herbert Simon to discover what makes chess masters more effective players than novices. One study focused on why the masters can remember the arrangement of pieces on the chess board so much better than novices manage to do. Do the masters simply have greater mental capacity or do they use similar mental capabilities more efficiently by learning better ways to store information? De Groot and Simon discovered that the masters' superior powers of recall disappear when the chess pieces are placed randomly on the board (and therefore at odds with the rules of game). The results showed how the masters exploit *domain-specific knowledge* of chess to encode and retrieve whole configurations of pieces, rather than storing them one or two at a time. When the chessmen no longer assume familiar patterns, the masters lose their conceptual bearings about "what goes with what" and do no better than novices at remembering the board.[1]

The experiments suggest that both groups labor with similar, highly limited capacities for short-term memory, estimated at something like 4 to 7 chunks.[2] What distinguishes the experts is their ability to compress more information into each chunk of available storage by organizing lots of specific facts into more general conceptual categories. In the same way, you would find it much easier to store and recall the letters below

L C N R U E A

if you perceived them as the word

N U C L E A R.

1 De Groot's original chess experiments are described in A. D. de Groot, *Thought and Choice in Chess* (The Hague: Mouton, 1965). This work is extended in a number of articles by Herbert Simon and his colleagues, including W. G. Chase and Herbert Simon, "The Mind's Eye in Chess," and W. G. Chase and Herbert Simon, "Perception in Chess," in Herbert Simon, *Models of Thought*, Vol. 1 (New Haven: Yale University Press, 1974).

2 A chunk is the underlying unit of short-term memory capacity proposed by the early cognitive theorist George A. Miller. When the chunk is measured in psychologically relevant units of recognition (like words or pawn structures in chess), rather than in "objective" units like bits of information, it appears that short-term memory has roughly constant capacity, whatever is being stored. See G. A. Miller, "The Magical Number Seven, Plus or Minus Two: Some Limits on Our Capacity for Processing Information," *Psychological Review* 63 (1956), and the articles by Herbert A. Simon, "How Big Is a Chunk?" and "The Information Storage System Called 'Human Memory' " in Herbert A. Simon, *Models of Thought*, Vol. 1 (New Haven: Yale University Press, 1979).

The representation of knowledge in hierarchies of increasingly abstract categories appears to propel cognitive development and expert learning in many other areas as well. Chi et al. asked experts and novices to sort physics problems by degree of similarity. While novices distinguished problems according to "relatively superficial features," experts learned to categorize problems by the underlying physical principles and solution strategies they involved. Categorization reduces demands on limited perceptual and storage capabilities, promotes inductive inference based on category membership, and simplifies the search for solutions in problem solving. The result is "more bang for the buck" when mental capacities are limited. As Edward E. Smith puts it, "If we see a particular child pet a particular dog at a particular time and a particular place, we code it as just another instance of 'children like dogs.' In doing this, we reduce a wealth of particulars to a simple relation between the categories 'children' and 'dogs' and free our mental capacities for other tasks."[3]

To sum up, a great deal of psychological argument and experimentation identifies expertise with the acquisition of parsimonious representations of problems and information in some domain. The idea is captured neatly in Converse's central thesis that cognitive constraint increases with information:

Economy and constraint are companion concepts, for the more highly constrained a system of multiple elements, the more economically it may be described and understood. . . . As one moves from elite sources of belief systems downwards on [the] information scale, . . . constraint declines across the universe of idea-elements, and the range of relevant belief systems becomes narrower and narrower. Instead of a few wide-ranging belief systems that organize large amounts of specific information, one would expect to find a proliferation of clusters of ideas among which little constraint is felt. ["The Nature of Belief Systems in Mass Publics," in David Apter, ed., *Ideology and Discontent* (New York: The Free Press, 1964), p. 213]

3 Edward E. Smith, "Categorization" in Daniel N. Osherson and Edward E. Smith, eds., *Thinking: An Invitation to Cognitive Science,* Vol. 3 (Cambridge: The MIT Press, 1990). An influential discussion of categorization can be found in E. Rosch, "Principles of Categorization," in E. Rosch and B. B. Lloyd, eds., *Cognition and Categorization* (Hillsdale, N.J.: Lawrence Erlbaum Associates, 1978). The problem solving experiments with physics students are reported in M. T. H. Chi, P. J. Feltovich, and R. Glaser, "Categorization and Representation of Physics Problems by Novices and Experts," *Cognitive Science* 5 (1981). More recent studies of "intuitive physics" include, M. K. Kaiser, J. Jonides and J. Alexander, "Intuitive Physics Reasoning on Abstract and Common Sense Problems," *Memory & Cognition* (1986); and M. K. Kaiser, M. McCloskey, and D. R. Proffitt, "Development of Intuitive Theories of Motion: Curvilinear Motion in the Absence of External Forces," *Developmental Psychology* (1986). Echoing the results of the chess and physics experiments, Susan Carey argues that cognitive differences between children and adults are best explained by the acquisition of *domain-specific* knowledge rather than the maturation of *domain-general* information processing capacity. See Carey, "Development," in Daniel N. Osherson and Edward E. Smith, eds., *Thinking: An Invitation to Cognitive Science,* Vol. 3 (Cambridge: The MIT Press, 1990).

It is easy to imagine how abstract categorization could make nuclear thinking among sophisticates much simpler to describe than the complex hurly burly we find in the novice data. In the framework of our discussion, the experts' nuclear doctrines might be understood as *meta-heuristics* that combine a political structure for deterrent stability and a rule for evaluating nuclear forces in a single package.[4]

Such doctrines would replace the complicated two dimensional calculus used by novices with a simpler composite rule for understanding nuclear policy problems. Where the security heuristic and weapon heuristic operated more or less independently among novices, they would become linked (or "constrained") among experts. By defining what properties make weapons GOOD or BAD, the doctrine would subsume specific nuclear systems (like MIRVs, terminal defenses, or neutron bombs) into more general strategic categories (like counterforce–countervalue, or offensive–defensive). As a result, the weapon heuristic would no longer be formed haphazardly, according to "superficial" aspects of each new system, or decided idiosyncratically by varying criteria of judgment. At the same time, by linking the weapon heuristic to a political philosophy of national security – SYMMETRY or STRENGTH – the nuclear doctrine would connect the separate dimensions of the novice's heuristic calculus. The effect would be to organize and simplify preferences across a wide spectrum of weapon technologies.

An obvious example of a unified nuclear belief system would be the classical MAD philosophy, which prescribes that deterrence must be mutual (SYMMETRY principle) and that nuclear forces should be designed to preserve secure second strikes (weapon principle). Notice how the classical doctrine defines a systematic dependency between the security and weapon heuristics where none may exist for novices. A similar integration of thinking would occur under other nuclear doctrines, too, including those that emphasize flexible response for credible extended deterrence, radical nuclear disarmament, or the moral superiority of defense over offense. Such doctrines produce rule driven, correlated opinions about diverse issues, including counterforce targeting, the B2 bomber, ASAT, theater nuclear forces, ASW, the MX, and nuclear disarmament. Like the expert in chess, the consumer of nuclear doctrines need not ponder the issues one at a time, but can address them as ensembles that embody more general concepts and principles.

4 Such a process resembles what Anderson calls a *composition of rules* in his formal model of cognition. See J. R. Anderson, *The Architecture of Cognition* (Cambridge: Harvard University Press, 1983). Holland et al. also emphasize how some forms of learning arise by combining existing, lower level rules into composites. See John H. Holland, Keith J. Holyoak, Richard E. Nisbet, and Paul R. Thagard, *Induction: Processes of Inference, Learning, and Discovery* (Cambridge: The MIT Press, 1989), for a discussion of *recombination*.

This view of expert reasoning suggests a number of specific hypotheses about the data we have collected. If the experts' preferences reflect a small set of general organizing principles, then their opinions should assume a simpler, more predictable structure (or *lower dimensionality*) than the novices' opinions display. In the expert data, one should be able to infer a great deal about a series of political positions from a knowledge of any one. Much more than for novices, the experts' nuclear preferences (measured here by game theoretic type) should be strongly related from issue to issue. At the aggregate level, the distribution of nuclear preferences should also become simpler. As the "illogical" combinations of heuristics used by novices are eliminated by the doctrinal filters, anomalous preference profiles should disappear and the observed diversity of types should diminish, perhaps dramatically.[5]

How strong these effects will be depends, of course, on how many nuclear doctrines coexist in the expert community. The limiting extreme would be a convergence of expert preferences to a single configuration (returning us to Model I). Such a result is frequently alluded to in the nuclear literature, where the classical mutual deterrence philosophy is commonly described as the "conventional wisdom" or mainstream opinion among experts in the United States.[6] Polarized distributions might appear if experts chose from two competing nuclear doctrines, like our classical and anti-classical theories, in the fashion described by Friedberg, Rathjens, Brodie, and Wohlstetter (as in Model II). Ideologically polarized distributions would occur if the competing doctrines varied in appeal to liberals and conservatives. Of course, a critical issue is how many people adhere to the different doctrines, not just how many doctrines there are. One could

---

5 As an alternative to the idea of doctrinal filters, we might prefer to consider the expert debate as a competition among arguments. All the arguments get aired, and then the fittest survive. Novices not exposed to the debate would, in this interpretation, be much more likely to base their preferences on "unfit" arguments and considerations, being unaware of the superior counterarguments. Expert preferences, by contrast, would be driven by a much smaller set of consensually held "survivors."

6 A typical example: "The dominant view of the workings of mutual deterrence has come to uphold three far-reaching dogmas:

One: our nuclear forces must be designed almost exclusively for "retaliation" in response to Soviet nuclear attack.

Two: our forces must be designed and operated in such a way that this "retaliation" can be swift, inflicted through a single, massive and above all prompt strike. What would happen after this strike would be of little concern for strategic planning.

Three: the threatened retaliation must be the killing of a major fraction of the Soviet population.

"Among Americans interested in nuclear strategy, only a minority now oppose any of these dogmas, and fewer still would reject them all." Fred Charles Ilké, "Can Nuclear Deterrence Last Out the Century?" *Foreign Affairs* 51, No. 2 (January 1973), pp. 267–285.

observe a sharply polarized debate in the nuclear literature, even when a preponderance of opinion favored one side or the other.

Hypothesis II: Experts Eschew Simple Solutions to Complex Problems

While the first hypothesis makes good sense, it would be a mistake to dismiss it as truistic or self-evident. In fact, an equally plausible case can be made for directly contrary conclusions. Since experts know far more about nuclear forces and the arms race, since they are regularly exposed to competing strategic arguments, and since their professional experience weighs against the hope for simple solutions to complicated problems, it is hardly obvious that the experts' political preferences should exhibit greater parsimony than the novices'. Rather, if expertise entails an awareness of complexity and an appreciation for nuance that novices don't share, one might expect to find that the *novice* is less attuned to trade-offs and complications, that the *novice* is more swayed by simplistic rules of thumb, and that the *novice* relies more on ideological formulas. By these lights, expert preferences could just as well reveal greater complexity, less correlation across different weapon systems, more ambivalence, less pigeonholing, and less ideological coloration than we observed among the novices.

A growing body of theoretical and experimental evidence suggests that there need not exist a simple monotonic relationship between expertise (or information) and conceptual parsimony. The recent theory of inductive inference proposed by Holland, Holyoak, Nisbet, and Thagard illustrates how cognitive scientists have gradually retreated from the idea that experts and novices can be distinguished simply as schematics and aschematics. In this model of human learning, conceptual categorization certainly plays a critical role, but feedback from the environment constantly impels the specialization of highly general categories when predictive failures occur. Constructing a mental model of reality therefore involves a continual struggle between two competing tendencies – one toward generalization and the other toward specialization.

The need to have useful rules to model the environment propels the system to generalize, but the rules may later produce erroneous predictions . . . [that are] often the result of an overgeneralization. [John H. Holland, Keith J. Holyoak, Richard E. Nisbet, and Paul R. Thagard, *Induction: Processes of Inference, Learning, and Discovery* (Cambridge: The MIT Press, 1986), p. 88]

If a prediction based on a strong rule fails, then [the system] creates a more specialized rule that includes a novel property. [p. 43]

[Doing so] always increases the complexity of the overall model. . . . Model construction is guided by two opposing pressures. The need for more accurate predictions favors the addition of further specialized rules, whereas the need for efficient prediction favors the addition of general rules to replace a larger number of specialized rules. [p. 37]

It follows that the level of generality and degree of parsimony in expert thinking will depend upon the intrinsic complexity of the problem and the availability of feedback from the environment.[7]

The theoretical recognition that wider knowledge may produce more specialized and complicated mental models gains added salience from psychological experiments showing that people often override high level generalizations when they acquire direct information about the specific object. Locksley and her colleagues found that social stereotypes (about assertive people, "day" versus "night" people, and the like) exerted a strong effect on subjects' perceptions and predictions when they had no other information to go on. The stereotypes were quickly overridden by "individuating" evidence, however, even when the evidence was largely irrelevant to the behavior being predicted. The results recall Kahneman and Tversky's earlier work showing that experimental subjects seem to ignore "base rates" in favor of specific information when drawing social inferences. In a typical study, subjects were asked to guess whether a thumbnail sketch described a lawyer or engineer after learning that the sketch had been drawn randomly from a pool that included 70 lawyers and 30 engineers (or vice versa). Surprisingly, if the description sounded even vaguely like a lawyer, the subjects guessed lawyer with equal probability, whether their universe contained 70% lawyers or 30%.[8]

Such evidence convinced Holland et al. to assume in their formal theory

---

7 The tension between generalization and specialization recalls the perennial divide between "lumpers" and "splitters" in academic life. Statisticians discuss the inferential dilemma as a tradeoff between bias and stability. More complex statistical models typically afford less biased estimates, but at a cost of greater statistical instability. Like everybody else, cognitive theorists are divided along similar lines themselves: for example, between the "generalists" who ignore the particular content of information in a search for universal cognitive processes, and "modularists" who view the mind as a holding company of discrete modules, specialized for different activities like language, music, visualization, and logic. For a panoramic survey in which this basic tension appears over and over, see Howard Gardner, *The Mind's New Eye: A History of the Cognitive Revolution* (New York: Basic Books, 1985).

8 For further information about the stereotyping studies, see E. Borgida, A. Locksley, and N. Brekke, "Social Stereotypes and Social Judgment," in N. Cantor and J. F. Kihlstrom, eds., *Personality, Cognition, and Social Interaction* (Hillsdale, N.J.: Lawrence Erlbaum Associates, 1981) or A. Locksley, C. Hepburn, and V. Ortiz, "Social Stereotypes and Judgments of Individuals: An Instance of the Base-Rate Fallacy," *Journal of Experimental Social Psychology* 39 (1982). For a discussion of the base rate experiments and later refinements, see D. Kahneman, P. Slovic, and A. Tversky, eds., *Judgment Under Uncertainty: Heuristics and Biases* (Cambridge: Cambridge University Press, 1982). Eleanor Rosch's experiments on categorization suggested that people exhibit a preference for middling generality (chairs) rather than superordinate categories (like furniture) or subordinate categories (like Adirondack chairs). On the so-called *basic level* in a categorical hierarchy, subjects learn names more readily, remember them better, and access them faster.

of inference that specialized rules will dominate general rules, whenever both are consistent with input from the environment. Their theory reflects a variety of evidence suggesting that highly generalized, "stereotypic schemas" give way to more specialized and elaborate mental models as people gain more information about their environment. If so, we might find our experts less likely than novices to lump diverse nuclear policy problems in strategic or ideological pigeon holes.[9]

Hypothesis III: Expert Theories Are Rationalizations for Novice Intuitions

A third hypothesis suggests that experts should display nuclear preferences essentially like the novices'. Arguments of this sort take the view that expert theories about politics are largely window dressing for bedrock intuitions that arise before expert learning occurs. Becoming a nuclear expert, in this interpretation, begins with a review of competing nuclear doctrines and culminates with an intellectual embrace of the one most consistent with the person's gut feelings and ideological prejudices. Experts might be able to muster more sophisticated rationalizations for their opinions, but stripped to their bare essentials (as in the game theoretic preference profiles), their positions would resemble the novices' in all important respects.

Steven Kull describes his recent book, *Minds at War*, as an effort to "learn how American defense policymakers rationalize certain defense policies that seem inconsistent with nuclear reality." Kull presents evidence that Reagan Administration officials could not sustain convincing arguments to support their nuclear policy preferences. Instead, their justifications for SDI, nuclear war-fighting doctrines, and first strike capabilities appeared mushy, self-contradictory, and logically shallow. Though he did not collect evidence outside the defense community, Kull nevertheless presents a bold conjecture that exemplifies the third view:

The problem itself is very much a systemic problem involving not only the American policymaking community but also the American public. . . . While there may be some specific points on which the policymaking community differs from the general public, it is very possible that members of the public would ultimately arrive at similar positions. . . . In short, my assumption is that defense policymakers

9 Several studies suggesting that conceptual parsimony need not increase with political expertise are reviewed in R. Lau and D. Sears, *Political Cognition* (Hillsdale,N.J.: Lawrence Erlbaum Associates, 1986). They include S. E. Taylor and J. D. Winkler, "The Development of Schemas," paper presented at the annual meeting of the American Psychological Association, Montreal (1980); and S. T. Fiske, D. R. Kinder, and W. M. Larter, "The Novice and the Expert: Knowledge Based Strategies in Political Cognition," *Journal of Experimental Social Psychology* 19 (1983).

reflect fairly well what might be called the collective psyche, complete with its tensions and contradictions. [Steven Kull, *Minds at War: Nuclear Reality and the Inner Conflicts of Defense Policymakers* (New York: Basic Books, 1988), p. 32]

Robert Jervis draws similar conclusions in his discussion of irrational consistency and the avoidance of value tradeoffs. Noting the tendency among nuclear debaters to insist – against all odds – that every consideration supports their preferred policy, Jervis infers that "policy preferences precede and determine at least some of the arguments in favor of that policy" (*Perception and Misperception*, p. 137). Jervis invokes the familiar political syndrome of "constant conclusions and changing rationales" to support his view that expert arguments are rationalizations for prior opinions (p. 138).

If expert theories in the nuclear debate are simply rationalizations for more basic intuitions, then we should not be surprised to find that the experts' nuclear preferences closely resemble the novices'. As A. J. P. Taylor has written: "Every expert is a human being, and technical opinions reflect the political views of those who give them."[10]

10 A. J. P. Taylor, *The Origins of the Second World War* (New York: Atheneum, 1962), p. 92, quoted in L. Eden and S. Miller, eds., *Nuclear Arguments* (Ithaca: Cornell University Press, 1989). Taylor's theme animates the skeptical analysis in Michael Salman, Kevin J. Sullivan, and Steven Van Evera, "Analysis or Propaganda? Measuring American Strategic Nuclear Capability, 1969–88," in the *Nuclear Arguments* volume.

Edward Luttwak suggests: "In the realm of military policy, debates are normally conducted by *ex post facto* arguments, which serve to support instinctual positions. Hawks and Doves are made so by their emotions rather than by their intellects, and strategy is for many a needless obstacle to the direct expression of views already determined." "SALT and the Meaning of Strategy," in *Strategy and Politics* (New Brunswick, N.J.: Transaction Books, 1980), p.105. Luttwak's analysis closely resembles that of Robert Jervis, *Perception and Misperception in International Politics* (Princeton: Princeton University Press, 1977).

The third hypothesis has a distinguished intellectual pedigree in social theory and philosophy, which return again and again to the theme that theories about social life can never be "objective," "scientific," and uncontaminated by political or cultural prejudice. One classic discussion appears in Karl Mannheim's *Ideology and Utopia: An Introduction to the Sociology of Knowledge* (New York: Harcourt Brace, 1959). For a helpful guide to the literature on political ideologies, see Robert Putnam, *The Beliefs of Politicians* (New Haven: Yale University Press, 1974). Steven J. Gould frequently argues that scientific theories should be understood as inescapably human creations that necessarily reflect the social prejudices and imperfect rationality of the human mind. A scalding example of his position can be found in *The Mismeasure of Man* (New York: W.W. Norton, 1985). Theodore Porter's *The Rise of Statistical Thinking 1820–1900* (Princeton: Princeton University Press, 1986) describes the pervasive influence of social and religious prejudices on the theoretical formulations of early statisticians. Benoit Mandlebrot, *The Fractal Geometry of Nature* (New York: W.H. Freeman, 1983), discusses the prejudices of classical mathematics, showing how numerous uncomfortable paradoxes have been swept under the rug by defenders of ancient geometric intuitions. In every case, these authors emphasize the intrusion of cruder intuitions into high theory. Such results support the basic argument in Thomas Kuhn's *The Structure of Scientific Revolutions* (Chicago: University of Chicago Press, 1962), which suggests that considerations of evidence alone rarely explain why scientific theories succeed or fail.

COGNITIVE COMPARISONS OF EXPERTS AND NOVICES

To help investigate these intriguing possibilities, we have a large array of nearly 1200 nuclear preference profiles. But finding the most telling comparisons between the experts and novices is no simple task. With 2 samples, 4 kinds of weapons, 60 different kinds of profile, 7 game theoretic categories, 3 background variables, and 6 heuristic flavors, one can form a huge number of contrasts between the two groups (e.g., what fraction of liberals have a PURE DOVE profile on MX and a YES+ profile on IN-VULNERABLE). In the face of such complexity, hard choices must be made. The approach I have found most instructive relies heavily on the model of nuclear reasoning presented earlier. Decomposing the two groups' preference profiles into familiar heuristic building blocks reveals many patterns of thought that otherwise would be hard to see. Other people would no doubt proceed differently, and discover things I haven't noticed.[11]

Table 8.2 contrasts the weapon heuristic flavors applied by novices and experts to the four nuclear systems described in the questionnaire. This table captures one of the most systematic and important differences between the two groups, and alerts us right away that the experts' nuclear preferences do not simply replicate the novices'.

The table suggests that experts apply classical criteria to nuclear weapons with far greater consistency than do novices. By heavy majorities (often 80–85% of the codable profiles), and by margins of 20 to 30 percentage points beyond the novice rates, the experts' profiles display the classical judgment that silo-based MIRVed ICBMs, anti-submarine warfare, and SDI are destabilizing (or BAD) weapons. By equally strong majorities, the

---

11 Technical remark: I have classified the experts' preference profiles according to the heuristic generators that produce them, using the coding protocols described in Figure 7.1. Less than a half dozen of the 600 expert profiles could not be accounted for by the generators in the model.

Fitting our model of nuclear reasoning presupposes that experts' preferences about the arms race, like the novices', rest upon two general considerations. One concern is the contents of the nuclear arsenals (the characteristics of weapons). The second concern is the political and military relationship between the adversaries (how power should be distributed). Beyond that plausible conjecture, there is no formal commitment that the two groups should think alike or that expert reasoning must be unsophisticated. We have already seen how canonical deterrence theories like MAD lie embedded in a much larger space of nuclear preferences generated by the convex combinations in the model.

 In her introduction to an edited volume on the nuclear debate, Lynn Eden describes "the assertions about Soviet intentions, the abstract mumbo jumbo of deterrence theory, and the conflicting and highly technical claims about weapon systems that seem to thread their way through every debate [about nuclear issues]." Eden's list of the considerations corresponds closely to the elements of the intuitive calculus. See L. Eden, "Introduction: Contours of the Nuclear Controversy," in L. Eden and S. Miller, eds., *Nuclear Arguments* (Ithaca: Cornell University Press, 1989), p. 3.

Table 8.2 *Choice of weapon heuristic flavors by novices and experts*

	MX		ASW		SDI		INVULNERABLE	
	Experts	Novices	Experts	Novices	Experts	Novices	Experts	Novices
BAD	72%	52%	69%	41%	58%	40%	17%	22%
GOOD	10%	27%	14%	39%	29%	43%	71%	58%
SWEET POISON	1%	8%	2%	10%	3%	7%	2%	11%
Unclear	17%	13%	15%	10%	11%	10%	10%	9%
Total	100%	100%	100%	100%	100%	100%	100%	100%
	n = 118	n = 169	n = 118	n = 169	n = 118	n = 169	n = 118	n = 169

Table 8.3 *Percentage who apply classical weapon heuristic flavors by pairs of weapons*

Weapon Pair	Prescribed Weapon Flavors	% Following Classical Prescription* Experts	Novices
MX - INVULNERABLE	(BAD, GOOD)	65%	37%
SDI - INVULNERABLE	(BAD, GOOD)	50%	24%
ASW - INVULNERABLE	(BAD, GOOD)	68%	28%
MX - SDI	(BAD, BAD)	69%	31%
MX - ASW	(BAD, BAD)	77%	37%
SDI - ASW	(BAD, BAD)	65%	29%

*Percentage of codable profiles

experts regard INVULNERABLE platforms for nuclear forces to be GOOD (here there is less disagreement with the novices). In every instance, the experts seem to embrace the general idea that a weapon is BAD if it compromises the ability to retaliate after a nuclear attack and GOOD if it enhances that ability. The experts also agree about how to apply the general principle to specific weapon systems. With the possible exception of SDI, where disagreement is greater, the experts categorize these weapons in a highly consensual way, following the precepts of classical arms controllers.

If anything, Table 8.2 understates how much the expert's reliance on the classical weapon categories exceeds the layperson's. Although a considerable fraction of novices arrive at the classical position on any particular system (typically 50–60% of those codable), far fewer stay with it from one weapon to the next. Experts, by contrast, apply the classical weapon flavors consistently. Table 8.3 groups the four nuclear systems in pairs, so that we can see the connection between responses to different items. When we compute the percentage of respondents who use the classical heuristic on both weapons at once, the experts come out far ahead of the novices in every case (typically by margins of 35 percentage points). This evidence suggests that a great many novices either don't know how to or don't wish to place weapons in the classical categories like counterforce and countervalue (or strike-first and strike-second). Experts, on the other hand, reliably follow classical prescriptions about which nuclear systems are BAD and GOOD.[12]

Unlike the novices, with their disorderly impressions of nuclear weapons systems, the experts evidently follow a simple rule when classifying them as

12 Tables 8.2 and 8.3 summarize information from more complete tables in the appendix of this chapter. The counterparts for novices appear in Table 7.2

GOOD or BAD. In Converse's terminology, the experts display a common understanding of "what weapons go with what." Given the partisan character of the nuclear debate, it is a bit surprising that these lessons travel across the entire political spectrum, unimpaired by ideological blinders. Figure 8.1 shows that experts adhere to classical weapon principles at higher rates than novices over the whole ideological spectrum. The rate of expert learning does not seem to depend on ideological persuasion either (the expert curves are essentially vertical displacements of the novice curves).[13] Instead, the experts adopt the classical weapon flavor at very high rates (typically 75–100%), on every item, with little variation by ideological position.[14] The experts' categorization of nuclear technologies largely follows a consensual pattern, in line with classical doctrine. In this respect, the data register a clear vote for HYPOTHESIS I, even in the strong form that predicts a dominant doctrinal consensus (Model I).

THE POLITICAL ARCHITECTURE OF DETERRENCE

The next question is whether the experts adopt classical reasoning about the security heuristic as well. Surely one of the most counterintuitive ideas in classical deterrence theory is mutuality: because deterrent stability requires mutual vulnerability, we should leave an adversary's missile platforms invulnerable to preemptive attack. It is easy to understand why *we*

13 One should not attribute too much significance to the distance between the curves in Figure 8.1. Many more novices display the classical weapon heuristic on any particular weapon than apply it consistently across weapons. The experts are much less erratic. The curves therefore understate the difference between the two groups. The telling pattern for our purposes is the consistent displacement of the expert curves in the direction of classical principles, regardless of the respondents' location along the ideological spectrum.

14 An interesting exception to these general patterns are the profiles for SDI, and to a lesser extent MX. Here the experts' weapon heuristics show noticeable ideological coloration. In general, the fraction displaying the classical weapon flavor changes very little from left and right. If we smooth the curves, the differential is roughly 25% for MX, and much less for ASW and INVULNERABLE platforms. For SDI, however, the partisan differential reaches 40 percentage points. It is interesting that the experts' weapon heuristics show ideological overtones on the same weapons that polarize novice judgments.

Remark on Relative Expertise of The Samples: Some readers come away from Converse with an impression that all college educated adults are political "elites." From this impression, they infer that our sample of college students must be nuclear experts too. The results about the weapon heuristic illustrate why I have resisted this conclusion. The evidence shows that very few UCLA undergrads understood basic ideas about first strike instability that people familiar with the nuclear debate appreciate universally. The expert profiles demonstrate the strong impression these ideas leave on those exposed to them.

Converse himself observes (with characteristic subtlety), "The ordering of individuals on this vertical information scale is largely due to differences in education, but it is strongly modified as well by different specialized interests." "The Nature of Belief Systems in Mass Publics," in David Apter, ed., *Ideology and Discontent* (New York: The Free Press, 1964), p. 213 (emphasis added).

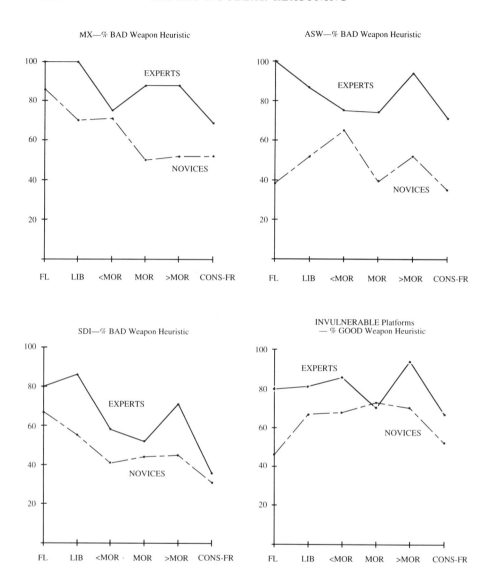

Figure 8.1 Percentage of experts and novices choosing classical weapon heuristic

need a secure second strike, but less obvious that *they* should have one too. Does expert training induce an appreciation that nuclear deterrence must be mutual? Do experts accept the logic of Thomas Schelling's position when he argues:

His own manifest invulnerability to our first strike could be to our advantage if it relieved him of a principal concern that might motivate him to try striking first. If he has to worry about the exposure of his strategic force to a surprise attack by us, we have to worry about it too. [*The Strategy of Conflict* (New York: Oxford University Press, 1960), p. 238]

To find out, we can compare the relative frequency of the security heuristic flavors in the two samples. If the classical theory of mutual deterrent stability has become the conventional wisdom among experts, their profiles should exhibit a much higher incidence of the SYMMETRY flavor than we observed among novices.

For all its plausibility, this conjecture finds no support in Table 8.4, which reveals a remarkable and surprising pattern. Whatever weapon system one considers, the experts and novices apply the various security heuristic flavors in *virtually identical proportions*.

Perhaps this striking similarity is mere coincidence, reflecting the fact that we haven't controlled the mixture of liberals and conservatives in the two samples. To address this possibility, Figure 8.2 displays the incidence of the security heuristic flavors among respondents with different political identifications. Amazingly, there is still no discernible difference between the two groups. Experts are no more likely than novices to associate deterrent stability with SYMMETRY. Neither are their intuitions about deterrence any less "ideological" than the novices'. In both samples, the preference for SYMMETRY or STRENGTH is sharply related to political orientation (the differentials between left and right range from 60 to 70 percentage points). Virtually identical proportions adhere to each conception of security across the whole political spectrum. Only the agnostic 20–30% who invoke the hybrid heuristic SYMMETRY + STRENGTH show no ideological coloration in their thinking. But even the agnostics appear with equal frequency in both samples.[15]

The data have led us to a strange and unexpected crossroads. To understand the cognitive consequences of nuclear expertise, it appears that we must accept two contradictory hypotheses at once. On the weapons dimension of the nuclear calculus, there is strong evidence in favor of HYPOTHESIS I. The novices' perceptions of nuclear weapons technologies appear disorganized, idiosyncratic, and "aschematic," while the experts' perceptions are highly organized along classical lines. Political ideology has

15 As might be expected, the experts apply their security heuristic with great consistency from weapon to weapon, just as the novices do. Further details appear in the Appendix.

Table 8.4 *Choice of security heuristic flavors by novices and experts*

	MX		ASW		SDI		INVULNERABLE	
	Experts	Novices	Experts	Novices	Experts	Novices	Experts	Novices
SYMMETRY	31%	32%	33%	28%	31%	33%	26%	28%
MIXTURE	18%	20%	14%	18%	27%	14%	17%	14%
STRENGTH	25%	25%	25%	29%	23%	22%	23%	28%
Unclear	27%	24%	28%	25%	19%	31%	34%	30%
Total	100%	100%	100%	100%	100%	100%	100%	100%
	n = 118	n = 169	n = 118	n = 169	n = 118	n = 169	n = 118	n = 169

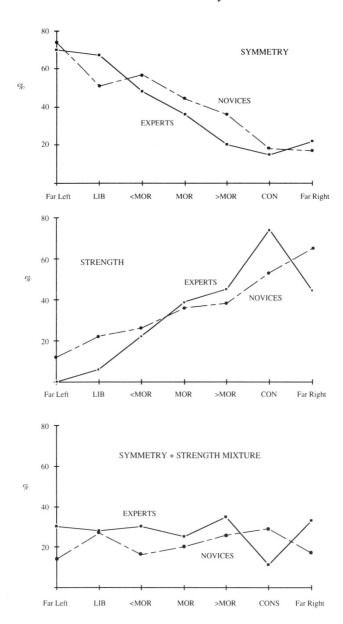

Figure 8.2 Choice of security heuristic flavor by political identification

little to do with how experts characterize nuclear systems. With the exception of SDI, their perceptions about weapons technologies are strongly consistent and non-partisan. Their judgments appear to reflect a broad "scientific" consensus.

With respect to the fundamental question of how to configure the opposing arsenals, however, it appears that expert training has little or no effect. The experts' intuitions about the political design of stable deterrence exactly replicate the novices'. In this basic sense, the data support HYPOTHESIS III. To use Kull's phrase, the "tensions and contradictions" that polarize the general public on questions of grand strategy remain undiminished in the expert arena. Expertise produces no convergence toward the classical, symmetrical conception of mutual deterrence. Neither does it attenuate the ideological element in people's strategic world view. Instead, the experts' security heuristics replicate the novices' down to fine details. Put another way, it is not clear whether "expertise" counts for anything on basic questions about stable arrangements of power.

POLITICAL CONTRASTS BETWEEN EXPERTS AND NOVICES

Let's move now from cognitive questions about nuclear thinking to the substantive political consequences of acquiring expertise. To study these questions, I shall consider the game theoretic profiles that finally emerge from each groups' deterrence calculus. Of basic concern is whether experts are systematically friendlier to arms control than novices might be. Whether expert opinion is politically more polarized, less diverse, less given to compromise, more predictable, or less adaptive in the face of change are also important questions. The interesting patterns revealed by the heuristic decomposition of preferences explain a great deal about the political and strategic contrasts between the two populations. In the political domain, as in the psychological, we shall discover systematic differences overlaid on patterns of fundamental similarity.

Diversity of Preference, Polarization of Opinion, and Anomalous Profiles

One of the most striking and surprising features of novice nuclear thinking is the diversity of preference types it produces on each weapon system. It is not clear from the evidence presented so far whether the expert sample should display a lesser or greater variety of game theoretic types. We know that experts display a much stronger consensus about the characteristics of nuclear weapon systems. On the other hand, their intuitions about stable arrangements of power look just like the novices'. While some aspects of the mutual deterrence doctrine are widely assimilated in the expert community, others are not.

Such observations leave doubts whether the experts' thinking is better considered *doctrinal* or *notional*. On one hand, it is possible that experts assimilate fully articulated doctrinal scripts that specify "right" answers to strategic problems and impose a common pattern of weapon preferences on those who accept them. If such doctrines were organized around the basic flavors of the security heuristic, SYMMETRY and STRENGTH, the expert community would fracture in two main blocs (with some marginal agnostics). One group's vision of national security would rest on parity and mutual deterrence, the other's on strength and escalation dominance. If experts in each camp adopted a heavily rehearsed standard line, we should see very little diversity of preference within factions, and sharp polarization between them. This pattern would certainly be expected from studying analytical typologies of the nuclear debate, which almost always describe a polarized competition among coherent nuclear doctrines.[16]

There are several important reasons to be wary about the doctrinal typologies as general descriptions of expert thinking. First, they are drawn overwhelmingly from published books and articles, which have been heavily filtered by editorial review and selection. Published sources may well display a level of organization and logical coherency that is far from typical among real experts and decision makers. At the same time, the classifiers themselves strive mightily to impose order on what seems like a messy phenomenon. One suspect practice is to focus on *exemplary texts,* rather than to examine representative samples of expert writing. Doing so naturally makes it easier to convey a sense of orderliness, but does not necessar-

---

16 For a good example, see Charles Glaser, "Why Do Strategists Disagree?" in L. Eden and S. Miller, eds., *Nuclear Arguments* (Ithaca: Cornell University Press, 1989). Glaser describes three main schools of thought, called Punitive Retaliation (MAD), Damage Limitation, and Military Denial. He even expresses doubts that three schools are too many, noting that "some readers of this essay have recommended combining the military denial school and the damage limitation school. . . . [Those who] dismiss the damage limitation school hold that only a few analysts really hold these views. . . . [Others] believe the military denial school simply packages the damage limitation school's beliefs for public consumption: its arguments are designed to justify many of the forces advocated more directly by the damage limitation school without alienating a public that is unwilling to strive for superiority and to engage in an all-out arms race" (p. 116).
   In the same volume, Salman, Sullivan, and Van Evera argue: "Nuclear balance assessments in the SALT era have sharply disagreed. Opinions on the poles have outnumbered those in the middle, and the gulf between the poles has not diminished over time." M. Salman, K. Sullivan, and S. Van Evera, "Analysis or Propaganda? Measuring American Strategic Nuclear Capability, 1969–88," in L. Eden and S. Miller, eds., *Nuclear Arguments* (Ithaca: Cornell University Press, 1989), p. 172.

ily provide a valid portrait of diversity.[17] Finally, doctrinal typologies do not support inferences about the relative frequency of different views. For all of these reasons, our data on experts' strategic preferences can provide better evidence about the cleavage structure of armaments politics.

In contrast to thinking doctrinally, it may be that experts merely extract arguments from the strategic debate, not organized conclusions about nuclear policy choices. Experts may depart from novices in the considerations that affect their thinking (as we have seen on the weapon heuristic), but continue to combine considerations in their own separate ways, just as the novices do. Such unscripted or notional thinking could support diverse patterns of preference – even among those who accept common heuristic principles – depending on the weights different considerations receive. In this case, we would expect expert opinion to follow the family tree structure of the heuristic calculus, falling in rich continuums of kindred types that include preference anomalies as well as conventional prototypes.

Either pattern of expert learning is consistent with the heuristic evidence presented so far. To make possible a systematic test, Figure 8.3 compares directly the set of preference profiles observed among the novices and experts. I appreciate that the intricate appearance of the preference maps in Figure 8.3 may discourage the reader from diving in. Like the ordinary topographical map, these pictures contain a very high density of information. Such maps come to life, however, as soon as one learns how to read them. And both can be highly absorbing, inviting the user to move back and forth between large-scale features of the terrain and minute local details. With a little practice, the reader will uncover many more interesting patterns than I shall have time to consider here.[18]

Here is a list of hints about how to read the preference maps and to recognize the patterns they contain.

- *Bold Versus Dimmed Profiles*
  Each page refers to a particular weapon system, but contains the entire set of profiles observed among the experts and novices. **Bold** profiles identify the prefer-

17 Glaser notes that "some analysts do not fit neatly into any of these schools" and that "analysts within a given school may disagree about policy." He defends his categories with two rather unconvincing arguments: 1) "these shortcomings are not necessarily serious if we view the schools as ideal types," and 2) "schools of thought are presented not so we will have categories into which all analysts will fit, but rather as a vehicle for understanding the overall contours of the debate." Glaser, "Why Do Strategists Disagree?" in L. Eden and S. Miller, eds., *Nuclear Arguments* (Ithaca: Cornell University Press, 1989), pp. 116–17.

18 For a discussion about the principles of statistical visualization that guided the design of these diagrams, see Edward R. Tufte's enlightening books, *The Visual Display of Quantitative Information* (Cheshire: Graphics Press, 1983) and *Envisioning Information* (Cheshire: Graphics Press, 1989). Also extremely helpful is William S. Cleveland, *The Elements of Graphing Data* (Pacific Grove: Wadsworth, 1985).

ences actually expressed for the given weapon, by a particular group. Dimmed profiles represent preference orderings that appear elsewhere in the data, but not for the weapon in question.

- *Expert Versus Novice Profiles*
  The expert profiles appear above the novices' in adjoining rows. Notice that vertically adjacent profiles match. When adjacent elements are bold, then experts and novices share the preference ordering in common. When both are dim, the two groups avoid the preference ordering. By scanning adjacent profiles, one can easily determine whether experts and novices reached similar preferences or not.
- *Elevations Denote Frequency*
  As a profile becomes more commonplace in either group, it appears in a taller stack.
- *Game Theoretic Ordering of Rows*
  The rows of the picture are arranged in game theoretic order, indicating increasing political support for the weapon as one moves down the page. The percentage of respondents in each game theoretic category appears on the right of each row.
- *Political Ordering of Weapons*
  Successive weapons enjoy increasing political support, as reflected by the percentage of respondents in the NO and YES+ categories.

These visual elements allow one to scan the pictures in many different ways:

- *Bold Versus Dimmed Scans*
  Following the patterns of light and dark allows one to see where opinion is concentrated along the game theoretic spectrum, whether opinion is polarized or scattered, and whether experts and novices think differently or alike.
- *Expert Versus Novice Scans*
  Item by item comparisons along the rows show whether experts and novices think alike about each weapon or not.
- *Elevation Scans*
  Scanning the picture for stacks shows where opinion is heavily concentrated, and whether either group converges to modal opinions. Clusters of stacks generally mean that many experts and novices think alike.
- *Top-to-Bottom Scans*
  Scanning the picture top to bottom for dark concentrations shows whether opinion aligns for or against a weapon.
- *Weapon-to-Weapon Scans*
  Scanning across weapons allows one to see how the weapon type affects the game theoretic landscape and the differences between experts and novices.

What follows is my interpretation of what the pictures reveal. Readers should form their own conclusions, and then compare notes.

To my eye, the dominant impression in every picture is that experts and novices form similar preferences. The correspondence between profiles is never one-to-one, but if the labels were removed from the margins, it would be hard to tell which group is which. There are two basic reasons the groups look so much alike. The first is that expert preferences are nearly as diverse as the novices'. Where the novices show 60 different profiles on the four questions, the experts show 48. The second reason is that many rows

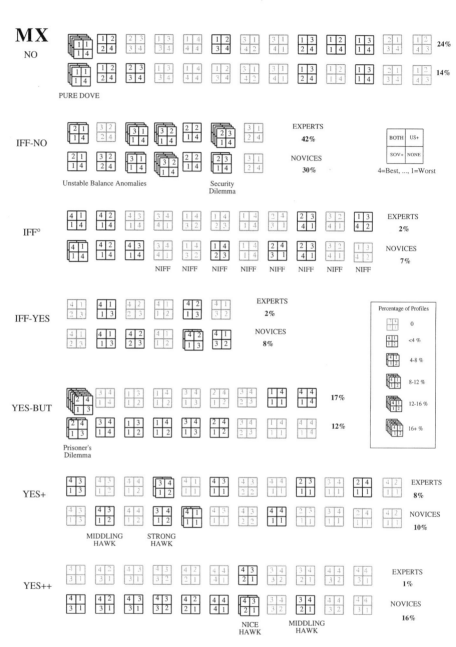

Figure 8.3 Expert and novice preferences compared

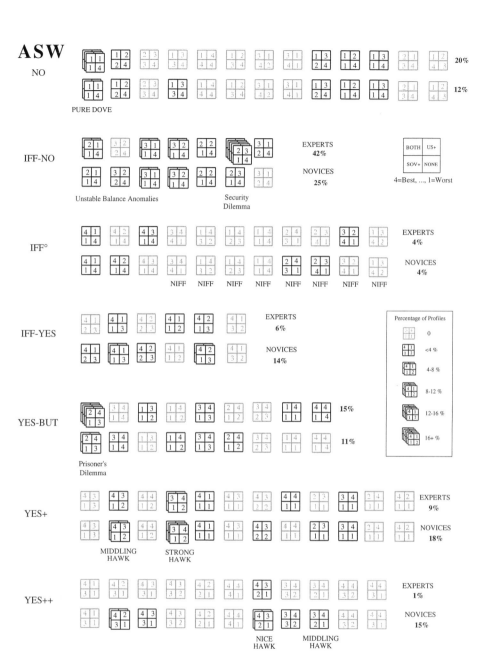

ASW

NO
PURE DOVE
20%
12%

IFF-NO
Unstable Balance Anomalies
Security Dilemma

| BOTH | US+ |
| SOV+ | NONE |

4=Best, ..., 1=Worst

EXPERTS 42%
NOVICES 25%

IFF°
NIFF NIFF NIFF NIFF NIFF NIFF NIFF NIFF
EXPERTS 4%
NOVICES 4%

IFF-YES
EXPERTS 6%
NOVICES 14%

Percentage of Profiles

	0
	<4 %
	4-8 %
	8-12 %
	12-16 %
	16+ %

YES-BUT
Prisoner's Dilemma
15%
11%

YES+
MIDDLING HAWK
STRONG HAWK
EXPERTS 9%
NOVICES 18%

YES++
NICE HAWK
MIDDLING HAWK
EXPERTS 1%
NOVICES 15%

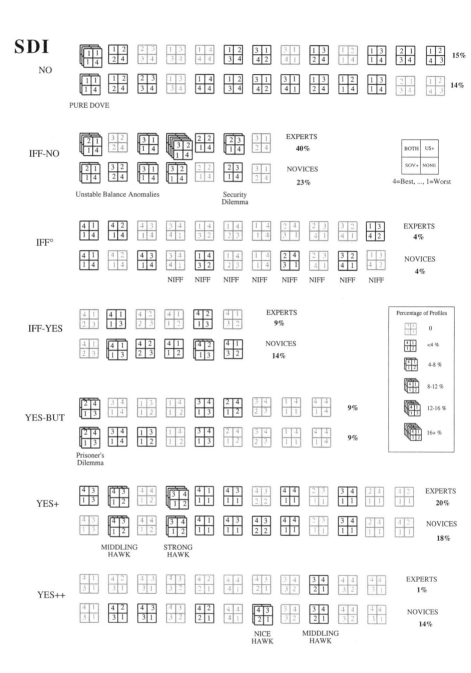

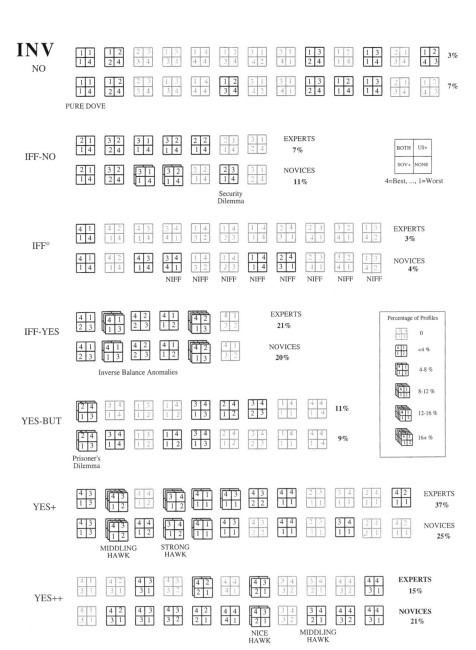

contain a high proportion of matches, in both dimmed and bold profiles. Expert opinion is no more concentrated at the profiles prescribed by strategic theory (classical or anti-classical) than is novice opinion. Experts absolutely do not exhibit a homogeneous pattern of preference as assumed in the Prisoner's Dilemma or Security Dilemma. Neither are they more polarized toward the extremes of the game theoretic spectrum. Experts are no more likely to pursue a single policy as a dominant strategy. Experts do not converge to a small set of modal doctrinal ideal types, nor do they concentrate in one or two game theoretic categories. Experts can not be partitioned into homogeneous factions of hawks and doves. Experts even display a great many anomalous profiles, particularly the "unstable balance anomalies," but also NIFFs, and the NICE and MIDDLING HAWKS.

All of this evidence persuades me that the experts' strategic reasoning is highly *notional*. By this term, I do not mean to imply that experts are irrational or uninformed. Rather, their pattern of thinking about the nuclear policy dilemmas is idiosyncratic and intuitive, like the novices'. Unlike the physicist or theologian, the nuclear expert clearly does not absorb a body of theory or doctrine that defines right and wrong answers to a range of basic questions (in this case, to the fundamental strategic question – what forces should we have?). The diversity of the expert profiles and their divergence from prescriptive "right answers" show that expert thinking is not scripted, programmed, or doctrinal. A better analogy might be a group of chefs who receive identical bags of groceries, pick out ingredients they find appealing, and then devise recipes of their own. The result will invariably be a great variety of dishes. When similar ingredients are selected from the bag, the dishes share family resemblances, but with many shades and variations according to the proportions used. Perhaps not all dishes are as good as others, but there is no agreement about which is best.

In the same way, the experts seem to rely on an intuitive – not rule driven – strategic calculus. They first select elements from the same bag of heuristic building blocks that novices use (albeit with somewhat less freedom on the weapon heuristic flavor). Then the heuristics are combined in proportions that vary from individual to individual. The result is a large variety of profiles that display two arresting properties. First, the experts' preferences satisfy the predictions of a mathematical model that combines heuristic ingredients in continuously varying proportions (as opposed to a few specific recipes). The intuitive nuclear calculus not only predicts that numerous profiles should occur, but that weird variations should coexist with conventional prototypes in predictable family structures. The second telling result is that expert profiles look very much like novice profiles. The similarity extends beyond the aggregate distribution of types to subtle and unexpected congruences of heuristic structure (for example, to the ideological structure in the security heuristic flavors of Figure 8.2). The inference that experts reason notionally is therefore supported by two kinds of evidence, one theoretical and the other empirical. Experts' preference profiles follow the patterns predicted by our cognitive algorithm, and they resemble the profiles of novices who have little or no strategic training. Readers with different tastes will no doubt attach different weights to the two kinds of evidence.

Taken together, the data in our two samples suggest that nuclear policy preferences at every level of the political system are largely the product of intuitive heuristic thinking. Certainly, the experts have accumulated an elaborate knowledge of nuclear technology. They've developed complicated models of arms races, played war games, designed computer simulations, and studied history. Their training clearly affects how experts categorize nuclear weapon systems. But all of this knowledge has not produced a consensus on fundamental questions about what deters, or what nuclear forces to build, or what kind of weapons to control. Instead, strategic expertise appears to have little effect on the intuitive, ideologically laden conceptions of deterrence that already appear in novices with no formal training at all. In a variety of different ways, expert nuclear opinion appears to rest upon the same intuitive calculus that novices use.

The force of these conclusions is greatly strengthened, I believe, by the appearance of anomalous profiles in the expert data. Since the fascinating *"unstable balance anomalies"* are especially suggestive, I'd like to examine them in closer detail.

Recall that in classical theory, what makes deterrence stable is not that both sides have the same forces, but that both have secure second strikes. Thomas Schelling draws this distinction carefully in *The Strategy of Conflict*, a book studied universally in the security community, and arguably the most influential book ever written about nuclear strategy. There he describes the difference between "a stable and an unstable balance":

It is not the "balance" – the sheer equality or symmetry in the situation – that constitutes mutual deterrence: it is the stability of the balance. The balance is stable only when neither, in striking first, can destroy the other's ability to strike back. [*The Strategy of Conflict* (New York: Oxford University Press, 1960), p. 232]

In this passage, we can see that the classical formula for stable deterrence involves both elements in our heuristic calculus at once. SYMMETRY by itself is not sufficient. Rather, deterrence is stable only when *both* sides avoid destabilizing, BAD weapons. Compared to the arcane twists and turns that deterrence theory can take, the idea that both sides should have a secure second strike stands among the most basic and elementary results in classical thinking.

Because the passage above portrays stability in absolute terms ("the balance is stable *only when* . . ."), the prescribed configuration of preference for "strike-first" or "counterforce" weapons appears to be the PURE DOVE:

BOTH	US+
1	1
SOV+	NONE
1	4

PURE DOVE

Such weapons should be avoided altogether, and it is equally bad when one side, the other, or both build them. Writing in the late 1950's, Schelling described anti-submarine warfare as a problem "we ought to hope is insoluble. If it were insoluble, . . . stable deterrence might be technologically possible" (p. 238). Later on, similar arguments were made about MIRV, the ABM, ASAT, and SDI.

Elsewhere, Schelling appears to introduce degrees of stability into the argument, depending on how many sides have strike-first capabilities:

The surprise attack problem, when viewed as a problem of reciprocal suspicion and aggravated "self-defense," suggests there are . . . military capabilities we might prefer not to have. Of course, it is *even better* if the other side does not have them either. [*The Strategy of Conflict* (New York: Oxford University Press, 1960), p. 231] [Emphasis added.]

Herbert Scoville draws similar conclusions about silo-busting, MIRVed ICBMs like the MX:

a theoretical countersilo capability . . . can be very destabilizing because of the appearance of a threat that it presents. The danger is multiplied many times when both nations have a potential countersilo capability. . . . [*MX: Prescription for Disaster* (Cambridge: The MIT Press, 1981), p. 79]

Although neither passage completely specifies preferences, a reasonable translation seems to be this: Compared to neither side's having strike-first weapons, it would be less stable if the U.S. (or Russia) got them, and even worse if both sides did. If the translation is right, the indicated preference ordering seems to be as shown,

BOTH	US+
1	2
SOV+	NONE
2	4

CLASSIC DOVE II

meaning that the situation improves steadily whenever second strike underminers disappear from either side's strategic forces.

However we read Schelling and Scoville, the overriding objective is clearly to remove destabilizing weapons from the nuclear arsenals. The first thing one notices in our data is how few experts display either of these classical NO profiles: only 13% for the MX and ASW, and 11% for SDI. More damaging still to a view that experts follow doctrinal scripts, the classical profiles are not even a majority response within the [SYMMETRY + BAD] family, whose heuristic structure is identical to the classical story!

5	40	27	26	9

BOTH	US+									BOTH	US+
1	2	1	1	2	1	3	1			4	1
SOV+	NONE									SOV+	NONE
2	4	1	4	1	4	1	4			1	4

BAD	PURE DOVE	Unstable Balance	Anomalies	SYMMETRY

Of the experts who combine the SYMMETRY and BAD flavors on MX, SDI, or ASW, roughly 60% indicate that it would be better that *both* sides had the destabilizing weapon than just one side or the other. By indicating NONE as the best outcome, these respondents clearly regard the weapon as a bad thing. But their profiles betray a strong intuition (Schelling might say a *naive* intuition) that balance is valuable *per se*, whatever weapons one is balancing. The intuition flies in the face of the classical formula, which rejects "unstable balances" as the worst case imaginable.

To see this point more clearly, it is instructive to recall Schelling's famous metaphor of crisis instability:

If I go downstairs to investigate a noise at night, with a gun in my hand, and find myself face to face with a burglar who has a gun in his hand, there is danger of an outcome that neither of us desires. Even if he prefers just to leave quietly, and I wish him to, there is danger that he may think I want to shoot, and shoot first. Worse there is danger that he may think that I think he wants to shoot. And so on." [*The Strategy of Conflict* (New York: Oxford University Press, 1960), p. 209]

Though neither party wants a shoot out, and both are symmetrically armed, they find themselves caught up in "the reciprocal fear of surprise attack," the antithesis of stable deterrence. As Schelling describes the problem, it appears that if he had gone downstairs without a gun, then the burglar would have followed his preferred course "just to leave quietly." Thus, even without balance, stability improves when either side eliminates its strike-first capability.

Herbert Scoville states the argument more directly, when he insists that matching a Soviet countersilo capability would be "mindless":

The whole concept of a balance in countersilo capability is irrational and should not be used as a criterion for the adequacy of strategic forces. A countersilo capability is a goal that neither side should seek regardless of the action of the other since it can only increase the risks of a nuclear disaster. Thus even if the Soviet Union does move in this direction, our answer should not be to match it. This would be a mindless response. [*MX: Prescription for Disaster* (Cambridge: The MIT Press, 1981), p. 79]

In the unstable balance anomalies, we see a group of experts (actually a majority of those who follow the SYMMETRY heuristic) who have accepted the *heuristic elements* of classical deterrence theory – that "strike-first" weapons like MX are destabilizing and that deterrence must be mutual – without accepting the political *conclusion* that destabilizing weapons should never be built, whatever the other side does (i.e. a NO configuration of preference with a *dominant* strategy not to build). From the perspective of our analysis, these experts evidently attach different weights to the two considerations than do Schelling and Scoville. The thrust of the classical argument is to eliminate "strike-first" weapons from the nuclear arsenals – not just to make the arsenals alike. To the extent that one would forgo such weapons even at the expense of balance ("the whole concept of a balance in countersilo capability is irrational"), greater importance is attached to the BAD weapon idea than to SYMMETRY. Likewise in our mathematical model. The two classical profiles emerge on the "left" side of the [BAD + SYMMETRY] family where the convex combination attaches more weight to the BAD weapon heuristic than to SYMMETRY. The anomalies deviate from classical reasoning by placing too much emphasis on balance. It is clearly as a corrective to this intuitive faith in the balance of power that Schelling introduces the idea of "unstable balances."[19]

In contrast to the classical formula, our experts combine these heuristic ideas in every possible proportion, as if they were independent and separable considerations. Their responses belie the same kind of intuitive heuristic thinking that we found among novices. Again, we observe the whole continuum of the [SYMMETRY + BAD] family (corresponding to every possible choice of convex weights), including profiles that are highly anomalous from the classical point of view. To the defenders of classical doctrine, these deviations from the prescribed recipe might appear misguided, or even "mindless." But they are far too common, even among highly intelligent, highly trained, full time strategic professionals, to be dismissed as unimportant or beside the point. The alternative weighting schemes are not simply

---

19 Notice, however, that the argument about "unstable balances" does not disavow the idea of symmetry or mutuality. Neither Scoville nor Schelling suggests that the problem changes in any way when the U.S., rather than Russia, possesses the BAD weapon. Deterrence must be mutual, and the labels of the players are irrelevant. Rather, the argument qualifies a prescription for symmetry by restricting it to a particular class of weapons (the GOOD, strike-second weapons). In our language, the argument combines a security and a weapon heuristic in a particular proportion.

aesthetically suspect. They have substantial political consequences as well, as we shall see later on. Where both classical profiles make not building a dominant strategy, the anomalies are IFF types. If the other side wants destabilizing weapons, then these respondents will build them too – for the sake of preserving balance!

Readers who feel uncomfortable with my interpretation might wish to argue that these experts actually accept Schelling's argument in the abstract, but don't believe it applies to the MX missile or to anti-submarine warfare or to SDI. Perhaps these systems have multiple strategic properties, so that experts don't see them as pure cases of counterforce or strike-first weapons.

Taking this position overlooks vocal opposition to SDI and the MX as destabilizers of mutual deterrence. The public record will show that many people did apply classical reasoning to these weapons. Nonetheless, let us leave the vocal and prominent critics aside, and confine our attention to the data at hand. To address the possibility that experts in the SYMMETRY camp really do accept Schelling's argument, at least in the abstract, consider the question about INVULNERABLE platforms ("effective technologies for protecting nuclear forces from preemptive attack"). This question expresses the paramount classical prescription without confounding it with specific technologies like mobile launchers or silo hardening. Without effective protection from preemptive attack, it follows *by definition* that second strikes can not be secure. The question therefore epitomizes the GOOD weapon classicists believe *both* sides must have.[20]

When we investigate the profiles for INVULNERABLE platforms, it turns out they replicate the unstable balance anomalies just as before, though now in the opposite direction. (Check the INVULNERABLE panel of Figure 8.3 in the IFF-YES rows.) While everybody in the [SYMMETRY + GOOD] family agrees that it would be best that both sides had invulnerable platforms, roughly 55% of these experts assert it is better that nobody have them than just one side or the other.

20 To take one example, Schelling describes invulnerable submarine platforms this way: "If the submarine proves to be for many years a fairly invulnerable site for anti-population missiles, we should perhaps view it not as an especially terrifying development but as a reassuring one. If in fact the best we can hope for is mutual deterrence and we only want the balance to be stable, then the polaris-type missile carried by a submarine of great mobility and endurance may be the kind of weapon system that we should like to see in adequate numbers on both sides. . . . True, it might seem more reassuring if we had the power to destroy the enemy's missile subs while he did not have the power to destroy ours, but . . . we perhaps should not even wish that we alone could have the 'invulnerable' nuclear missile submarine; if in fact we have either no intention or no political capacity for a first strike, it would usually be helpful if the enemy were confidently assured of this. His own manifest invulnerability to our first strike could be to our advantage if it relieved him of a principal concern that might motivate him to try strike first." [*The Strategy of Conflict* (New York: Oxford University Press, 1960), pp. 238–239]

	8		6		3		10		4

BOTH	US+							BOTH	US+
4	2	4	1	4	1	4	1	4	1
SOV+	NONE							SOV+	NONE
2	1	1	1	1	2	1	3	1	4

GOOD		Inverse Anomalies		SYMMETRY

Rather than embracing Schelling's idea that stability improves as the nuclear arsenals become more invulnerable to preemption, these experts obviously believe that stability resides in balance *per se*. Their intuition is so strong that they select *mutual vulnerability to preemptive attack* over *unilateral American deployment* of invulnerable platforms! As might be expected, the same respondents tend to produce the anomalies in both directions.

These patterns suggest that even when experts accept common heuristic principles, they still weigh and combine them in an unprogrammed, idiosyncratic, perhaps even unconscious fashion – not by consensual doctrinal formulas. Though the ingredients may be similar, the recipes vary dramatically. The results are preference profiles that remain close cognitive relatives, but drive politically antithetical behavior.

Similar patterns also arise among the numerous experts who haven't selected the classical heuristics. The tally on the INVULNERABLE question, which gets to the core idea in modern nuclear deterrence theory, is both remarkable and instructive. On this question, only 26% of our experts adopt a SYMMETRICAL conception of deterrence. Of these, 22% apply the BAD weapon heuristic to what one would have thought was the canonical GOOD weapon. This leaves only 20% of the sample in the SYMMETRY + GOOD group, and a good half of these reach an anomalous pattern of preference. Thus 90% of our experts reach non-classical preferences, spanning the whole game theoretic spectrum.

Only 52% of the experts support INVULNERABLE platforms at the YES+ level or better (i.e., as an unambivalent dominant strategy). The larger YES-something coalition amounts to 63% of the sample. It is fractured into 16 different patterns of preference, some of which indicate parity as the best choice, while others opt for American superiority. Quite a few say they would rather that both have INVULNERABLE platforms than just the U.S. have them, but that nobody's having them is better than Soviet superiority. Of the experts 35% indicate that they would not build secure weapon platforms in the United States if the Soviets didn't have them too. Roughly 33% say that both sides' having secure second strikes is not the best outcome. Altogether, the experts express 32 different patterns of preference about INVULNERABLE platforms. In every region of the game theoretic spectrum, we see a continuum of shadings and variations, not one standard line.

The data strongly refute the idea that a philosophy of mutual deterrence is the conventional wisdom among experts in the United States, or that any other nuclear doctrine is held consensually. A much better description of the experts' preferences is provided by our model of heuristic nuclear thinking, with its weird family trees, diverse political types, and loosely structured conceptual anarchy. In these respects, the experts look very much like the novice strategists for whom we had to invent the intuitive deterrence calculus in the first place. It appears, in short, that we are all amateur strategists.

POLITICAL DIFFERENCES BETWEEN NOVICES AND EXPERTS

The one exception to our basic conclusion lies in the respondents' understanding of weapon characteristics. Here the experts' knowledge and training clearly do matter. When we focus on the differences between the two preference maps, the experts' convergence to classical prescriptions for the weapon heuristic explains most of the dissimilarities that turn up.

Take the three systems considered destabilizing by classical theorists. Because experts largely understand MX, ASW, and SDI to be BAD weapons, the GOOD weapon anomalies virtually disappear in the expert sample. Most of these profiles appear in the strange YES++ category, which includes the popular NICE and MIDDLING HAWKS, and consistently draws 15% of the novice responses. This category contains by far the highest rate of mismatches between novices and experts. The YES++ anomalies form when the novice STRENGTH types apply the GOOD flavor to weapons experts consider BAD. With expert training, the YES++ profiles become extremely rare (fewer than 1%). But notice what happens on the question about INVULNERABLE platforms, which experts do consider stabilizing. Here, 15% of the expert profiles are YES++, including a stack of NICE HAWKS.

A related discrepancy between the two samples is the tall stack of expert profiles in the YES-BUT category (especially for MX and ASW). The stack occurs at the famous Prisoner's Dilemma. Why is this profile so much more common among experts than novices? The explanation turns again on the weapon heuristic. On MX and ASW, expert "hawks" ordinarily combine the STRENGTH and BAD flavors, resulting in many ambivalent YES-BUT responses. By comparison, many more novice hawks combine STRENGTH and GOOD. These respondents become YES+ and YES++'s. These tendencies produce fairly strong differences in the marginal frequencies of the several YES categories. Of the novices 25–35% fall in YES+ and YES++, compared to only 10% of experts. The expert hawks concentrate in YES-BUT, where they outnumber the novices. The differences are less pronounced for SDI and INV, because many more experts attach the GOOD flavor to ballistic missile defenses and INVULNERABLE platforms.

If we consider the SYMMETRY and SYMMETRY + STRENGTH families, similar effects occur. On MX, ASW, and SDI, the experts in these families overwhelmingly adopt the BAD weapon flavor, producing a high density of profiles in the NO and IFF-NO categories. Here, the experts outnumber novices by roughly 60% to 40%. Novices with similar conceptions of deterrence more often apply the GOOD weapon flavor, drawing them off into the more hawkish IFF° or IFF-YES configurations (where they outnumber experts). The differences are again less pronounced on SDI, because more experts adopt the GOOD weapon flavor.

If we sum up these effects, it becomes apparent that the experts' classical conception of weapon characteristics makes them systematically friendlier to nuclear arms control. Table 8.5 shows that despite having similar conceptions of deterrence, and similar cognitive styles, the two groups do not form politically equivalent distributions of preferences. Considerably more experts fall in the NO and IFF-NO categories, where the core constituency for limiting nuclear weapons resides. These categories contain the only players who reliably avoid destabilizing weapons when they confront an opponent of their own type. The core constituency for arms build-ups are the YES+ and YES++ types, who build as a dominant strategy against any opponent, even in iterated play. We can see that the expert's training about weapon characteristics has a considerable effect. While a clear majority of experts are core arms controllers for MX, ASW, and SDI, less than half the novices fall in that category.

IDEOLOGICAL UNMASKING, GAME THEORETIC CONSISTENCY, AND POLITICAL PREDICTABILITY

Our last set of comparisons addresses whether the experts' political positions are more stable and predictable across issues than the novices' proved to be. Studying the game theoretic consistency of the experts' profiles helps us understand the stability of political coalitions in the arms debate, the predictability of expert behavior, and the likelihood that expert policymakers send clear and consistent signals about their game theoretic type.

To help get started on these questions, I have coded the preference profiles in game theoretic categories from NO to YES++, and computed the rank order correlations between the respondents' positions on different weapons. Table 8.6 also contains correlations between the policy positions

Table 8.5 *Friendliness to Arms Control Among Experts and Novices*

| | MX | | ASW | | SDI | | INVULNERABLE | |
	Experts	Novices	Experts	Novices	Experts	Novices	Experts	Novices
Core Arms Controllers (NO and IFF-NO)	66%	44%	62%	37%	55%	37%	10%	18%
Core Arms Builders (YES+ and YES++)	9%	26%	10%	33%	21%	32%	52%	46%
	n = 118	n = 169	n = 118	n = 169	n = 118	n = 169	n = 118	n = 169

Table 8.6 *Spearman rank correlations among game theoretic types*

	ASW game	MX game	SDI game	INV game	Political ID
Novices					
ASW game	1.000				
MX game	0.469	1.000			
SDI game	0.299	0.230	1.000		
INV game	0.229	0.233	0.323	1.000	
Political ID	0.139	0.239	0.202	0.065	1.000
Experts					
ASW game	1.000				
MX game	0.646	1.000			
SDI game	0.535	0.565	1.000		
INV game	0.081	0.006	0.117	1.000	
Political ID	0.326	0.410	0.370	0.168	1.000

This table replicates Table VII, 'Constraint Between Specific Issue Beliefs for an Elite Sample and a Cross Section Sample, 1958," in Philip Converse, "The Nature of Belief Systems in Mass Publics," in David Apter, ed., *Ideology and Discontent* (New York: Free Press, 1964).

and ideological location. The correlations provide a crude but effective summary of game theoretic stability in the two samples.

The first thing to notice is how closely the pattern in this table matches the one Converse found. Compared to the novices, the experts are considerably more consistent from issue to issue and their opinions are more strongly correlated with political ideology. The predictable exception are the responses about INVULNERABLE platforms, which attract support from both ends of the political spectrum. These correlations wash out because the STRENGTH and SYMMETRY factions largely converge to the same position, making INVULNERABLE a poor predictor of other opinions. For our purposes, the interesting story resides in the experts' responses about MX, ASW, and SDI, which replicate Converse's results very closely.[21]

Converse inferred from his evidence that elites' opinions are more tightly organized in left-to-right ideological categories than are mass beliefs. But though our aggregate correlations look just like Converse's, the heuristic decomposition of individual profiles in Figure 8.2 suggests that ideology plays a virtually identical role among both sophisticates and novices. Ideo-

21 The INVULNERABLE correlations are closer to zero in the expert sample than among novices, because experts reach a stronger consensus on the GOOD flavor than do novices, and probably attach more weight to it.

logical thinking connects with strategic preferences through the security heuristic, and in essentially the same way for both groups. Why, then, does the role of ideology appear so much stronger for experts in the correlational analysis of preferences?

To see what's going on, recall the basic heuristic contrasts between the experts and novices. The security heuristic flavors, SYMMETRY and STRENGTH, occur in identical proportions and with the same strongly ideological coloration in both groups. The noticeable effect of expert training appears not on the security heuristic, but on the weapon heuristic (which is not politicized in either sample). Where the novices' intuitions about nuclear technologies are fragmented and idiosyncratic, experts organize weapons in a non-partisan, consensual scheme of strategic categories. The experts' nuclear calculus is certainly more constrained than the novices', just as Converse suggests, but the additional constraint is not ideological or political – it is essentially technical.

Ironically, this technical consensus makes the experts' strategic preferences *look* more ideological than the novices', even though ideology plays the same role in both groups. By creating a consensus about the weapon heuristic, expert training fixes movement along one dimension of free variation in the novices' heuristic calculus. But the idiosyncratic and disorganized weapon heuristic is precisely what *smears* and disguises the ideological element in the novices' preference profiles. Once the weapon heuristic becomes controlled by expert training, the ideological dimension of preferences – the strategic world view – is no longer concealed by noisy, unregulated intuitions. Sophistication does not add an ideological element to the nuclear experts' thinking. It *unmasks* that element by constraining confounding impressions about technical issues. As a result, the experts' game theoretic positions become more consistent from weapon to weapon and show a stronger correlation with ideological tastes. The result is curiously paradoxical. Precisely because the experts acquire an apolitical, non-ideological, "scientific" consensus on the technological dimension of their problem, they wind up looking more ideological than do the novices.

Whether this kind of ideological unmasking could explain other evidence like Converse's is an interesting question. In our data, it produces among the experts a markedly stronger relationship between the political background variables, all of which move together with ideological self-description, and nuclear preferences. Table 8.7 shows what happens when we regress our scale of game theoretic type on the three political background variables in the survey. Compared to the null results among novices, the strength of relationship is clearly stronger among experts (although the variation in expert preferences unexplained by political orientation remains very high). On every weapon item (except INVULNERABLE), the three background

Table 8.7 *Relationship of background variables to game theoretic type*

Experts			

Dependent variable is MX game
118 total cases of which 7 are missing
$R^2 = 33.7\%$ R^2(adjusted) = 31.8%
s = 1.999 with 111 - 4 = 107 degrees of freedom

F-ratio
18.1

Source	Sum of Squares	df	Mean Square
Regression	217.025	3	72.3
Residual	427.750	107	3.99766

Variable	Coefficient	s.e. of Coeff	t-ratio
Constant	1.02615	0.6440	1.59
Pol ID	0.432754	0.1214	3.56
logitprob	0.833041	0.3109	2.68
USSR	0.439380	0.1065	4.12

Dependent variable is SDI game
118 total cases of which 5 are missing
$R^2 = 26.0\%$ R^2(adjusted) = 24.0%
s = 2.057 with 113 - 4 = 109 degrees of freedom

F-ratio
12.8

Source	Sum of Squares	df	Mean Square
Regression	162.539	3	54.2
Residual	461.426	109	4.23327

Variable	Coefficient	s.e. of Coeff	t-ratio
Constant	2.61629	0.6577	3.98
Pol ID	0.255649	0.1246	2.05
logitprob	0.924178	0.3138	2.94
USSR	0.442868	0.1095	4.04

Dependent variable is ASW game
118 total cases of which 6 are missing
$R^2 = 28.8\%$ R^2(adjusted) = 26.9%
s = 1.968 with 112 - 4 = 108 degrees of freedom

F-ratio
14.6

Source	Sum of Squares	df	Mean Square
Regression	169.524	3	56.5
Residual	418.441	108	3.87445

Variable	Coefficient	s.e. of Coeff	t-ratio
Constant	2.75575	0.6292	4.38
Pol ID	0.253886	0.1202	2.11
logitprob	1.34144	0.3043	4.41
USSR	0.382799	0.1048	3.65

Table 8.7 (*cont.*)

Novices

Dependent variable is MX game
169 total cases of which 4 are missing
$R^2 = 5.7\%$ R^2(adjusted) = 3.9%
s = 3.002 with 165 - 4 = 161 degrees of freedom

F-ratio
3.25

Source	Sum of Squares	df	Mean Square
Regression	87.7555	3	29.25
Residual	1451.06	161	9.01277

Variable	Coefficient	s.e. of Coeff	t-ratio
Constant	3.55829	0.7238	4.92
Pol ID	0.287731	0.1345	2.14
LogitProb	0.586344	0.3771	1.55
USSR	0.068844	0.1292	0.533

Dependent variable is SDI game
169 total cases of which 3 are missing
$R^2 = 6.9\%$ R^2(adjusted) = 5.2%
s = 2.932 with 166 - 4 = 162 degrees of freedom

F-ratio
4.03

Source	Sum of Squares	df	Mean Square
Regression	103.921	3	34.6
Residual	1392.54	162	8.59591

Variable	Coefficient	s.e. of Coeff	t-ratio
Constant	4.00685	0.7082	5.66
Pol ID	0.227172	0.1306	1.74
LogitProb	0.782547	0.3670	2.13
USSR	0.127438	0.1267	1.01

Dependent variable is ASW game
169 total cases of which 1 is missing
$R^2 = 1.7\%$ R^2(adjusted) = -0.1%
s = 2.934 with 168 - 4 = 164 degrees of freedom

F-ratio
0.952

Source	Sum of Squares	df	Mean Square
Regression	24.5826	3	8.194
Residual	1411.94	164	8.60936

Variable	Coefficient	s.e. of Coeff	t-ratio
Constant	4.90883	0.7020	6.99
Pol ID	0.080754	0.1305	0.619
LogitProb	0.493875	0.3634	1.36
USSR	0.042148	0.1261	0.334

variables produce larger regression coefficients among experts than novices. (The joint hypothesis that the coefficients are equal in both samples
can be rejected in every case.)

Table 8.8 shows in greater detail how experts' game theoretic type becomes more consistent from weapon to weapon. This table may be compared to its analogue for novices (discussed earlier in Table 5.5). For the
weapons SDI, MX, and ASW, the experts are substantially more consistent
in their game theoretic position than novices. The pattern can be seen by
comparing the fraction of respondents who maintain a consistent game theoretic position from weapon to weapon (below each table I've computed this
fraction on the main diagonal for both samples). The pattern is reversed in
the pair MX–INVULNERABLE, which classical theory says should produce opposite positions. Here, experts show less game theoretic consistency
than novices, revealing again their higher commitment to classical weapon
categories.

To sum up, three important political differences between experts and
novices turn on how they formulate the weapon heuristic. The experts are
noticeably friendlier to arms control. The experts' game theoretic postures
toward controversial weapons issues are more consistent with each other.
And finally, the experts' postures toward weapons are more strongly related to ideological orientation. The experts' positions are therefore easier
to read and to predict politically.

CONCLUDING REMARKS

In matters of nuclear weapons, I have argued that we are all amateur
strategists. By this provocative statement, I mean that experts' preferences
in the nuclear arms race reflect the same intuitive strategic calculus that
controls novices' preferences. True, it appears that expert training alters
some proportions in the novices' heuristic recipes. But all the main
ingredients – not to mention the style of cooking – remain unchanged. Experts rely on the same heuristic rules of thumb that novices use, and they
combine them in the same intuitive, unstandardized, unprogrammed way.
The experts' strategic preferences consequently appear strikingly similar to
the novices' – somewhat more dovish perhaps – but still highly notional,
noticeably unlike doctrinal prescriptions, frequently anomalous, and remarkably disparate.

Because the same kind of cognitive algorithm operates in both groups, it
is possible to formulate mathematical models that capture a great many
patterns in the nuclear thinking data. Our formal heuristic calculus explains
why sophisticates and novices both display great diversity of type, why
neither group converges to conventional doctrinal prototypes, why both

populate the whole game theoretic spectrum, why both display a variety of anomalous preferences, why experts seem more ideological than novices but really aren't, why experts show more game theoretic consistency, why experts are somewhat friendlier to arms control, and why neither group can be lumped in polarized factions of "hawks" and "doves" as we so often try to do in political analysis.

I believe these findings have many far reaching implications, not only in security studies, but for game theory, public opinion and political psychology, and democratic theory. Let me briefly suggest some of the possible connections, without attempting anything like a complete or careful survey.

Because all strategic theory rests on a specification of political preferences, it is disconcerting to find that our guiding theories of nuclear strategy so badly misspecify the preferences of real political actors. The results make evident that competitions in weapons of mass destruction cannot be understood as interactions between homogeneous types (as in the Prisoner's Dilemma, the Game of Chicken, the Security Dilemma, or any game at all based on "unitary rational actors"). The data also cast grave doubts on a much larger class of theories that proceed by assuming the "structure of the game" is common knowledge. To the extent that our leading theories badly misspecify preferences, it is obvious that the preference structure of the arms race is not common knowledge. More likely, political actors develop disparate conceptual models of the game(s) they're in. I would conjecture, finally, that conventional theoretical models are similarly inappropriate for understanding alliance politics, "the balance of power," trade relations, imperialism, limited war, unlimited war, or grand strategy – in short, all of the cardinal problems in international relations. Such conclusions can not be dismissed by arguing that experts control decisions, not amateurs. Whether experts or novices pull the strings, we are all amateur strategists.

In the same way, the data strongly belie the idea that deterrence has an intrinsic logic, evident to all, as most prescriptive deterrence theories assume. Instead, policy prescriptions for arms control and force deployments must recognize that people disagree profoundly about what deters. Doing so will fix attention on the political dimension of strategy – on the competition among fluid, heterogeneous coalitions to control national security policy (in all countries involved). It will also shift attention from whether various weapon systems are "stabilizing" to how parallel coalitions supporting arms control can be fashioned in a stable cross-national equilibrium. All of the evidence suggests that much more attention should be paid to understanding how strategic preferences form, and to the political struggles that arise among antagonistic strategic factions.

The nuclear preference data also give pause about important ideas in public opinion studies and democratic theory. One influential line of argu-

Table 8.8 *Experts: game theoretic consistency over weapons*

MX

SDI

	NO	IFF-NO	IFF°, NIFF	IFF-YES	YES-BUT	YES+	YES++	N.A.	Total
NO	14	7	1	3	0	2	0	1	28
IFF-NO	2	34	1	6	1	3	2	0	49
IFF°, NIFF	0	0	3	0	0	0	0	0	3
IFF-YES	0	1	0	2	0	0	0	0	3
YES-BUT	0	5	0	0	8	7	0	0	20
YES+	0	0	0	0	0	9	0	0	9
YES++	1	0	0	0	0	0	0	0	1
N.A.	1	0	0	0	1	3	0	0	5
Total	18	47	5	11	10	24	2	1	118

% in Same Game Theoretic Category Experts 59% Novices 39%

ASW

MX

	NO	IFF-NO	IFF°, NIFF	IFF-YES	YES-BUT	YES+	YES++	N.A.	Total
NO	18	3	0	1	0	0	0	1	23
IFF-NO	5	37	1	1	5	0	0	1	50
IFF°, NIFF	2	0	2	0	1	0	0	0	5
IFF-YES	2	3	0	1	0	0	1	0	7
YES-BUT	1	3	0	0	12	3	0	1	19
YES+	0	2	0	0	2	5	0	0	10
YES++	0	1	0	0	0	0	0	0	1
N.A.	0	0	0	0	0	1	1	2	3
Total	28	49	3	3	20	9	1	5	118

% in Same Game Theoretic Category Experts 64% Novices 47%

	NO	IFF-NO	IFF°, NIFF	IFF-YES	YES-BUT	YES+	YES++	N.A.	Total
				MX					
Invulnerable									
NO	2	1	0	0	0	0	0	1	4
IFF-NO	1	7	0	0	0	0	0	1	9
IFF°, NIFF	2	0	2	0	0	0	0	0	4
IFF-YES	3	17	0	3	2	0	0	0	25
YES-BUT	0	3	1	0	7	2	0	0	13
YES+	12	11	0	0	10	7	1	2	43
YES++	6	10	0	0	1	0	0	1	18
N.A.	2	0	0	0	0	0	0	0	2
Total	28	49	3	3	20	9	1	5	118

% in Same Game Theoretic Category   Experts 25%   Novices 39%

ment holds that "elite" thinking is more coherently structured and rationally articulated than mass opinion, that much of what passes for "public opinion" trickles down through the media of mass communication, that mass politics often produce superficial or misguided policies, and that deliberative judgments and "enlightened preferences" deserve a privileged role in democratic decision making, particularly on technically complex questions.[22]

After studying the nuclear thinking data closely, I now find myself deeply wary about theories that characterize the everyday person's political preferences as less enlightened, less coherent, or less intelligent than the "expert's." In these data, I find no reason to describe the experts' preferences with normatively loaded encomiums like "enlightened" or "deliberative." "Ambivalent," "scattered," "idiosyncratic," "notional," "ideological," "unscientific," and "equivocal" seem like better descriptions to me. Also unpersuasive are the "top-down" models of opinion formation that portray mass beliefs as the disorganized or unreflective remnants of coherent elite transmissions. Rather, my evidence supports a "bottom-up" approach to understanding public opinion as the expression of primordial political intuitions and quasi-theories. The data suggest that *both* experts and novices use the same heuristic algorithm to generate nuclear preferences. The political divisions represented by our novice heuristic families seem almost impervious to assault by the experts' sophisticated mathematical models, computer simulations, and historical analysis.

22 Among recent studies, such ideas animate James Fishkin's stimulating proposal to conduct "deliberative opinion polls":

> We seem to face a forced choice between politically equal but relatively incompetent masses and politically unequal but relatively more competent elites. Institutions designed on the model of the deliberative opinion poll escape this dilemma. They embody political equality because everyone has an equal chance of being represented in the national sample of participants. But they also embody deliberation because they immerse a selected group of citizens in intensive, face-to-face debate. . . . [James Fishkin, *Democracy and Deliberation* (New Haven: Yale University Press, 1991), p. 2]

Fishkin defends his deliberative poll as an antidote to the direct-majoritarian mass politics of primaries, opinion polls, and media campaigns – a politics where, he says,

> instead of public opinions worthy of the name controlling leaders, preferences shaped by leaders and by the mass media too often are bounced back, without sufficient critical scrutiny and without sufficient information. . . . If the preferences that determine the results of democratic procedures are unreflective or ignorant, then they lose their claim to political authority over us. [pp. 19 and 29]

In much the same way, Larry Bartels proposes to measure the "political interests of ordinary citizens" by "imputing the observed preferences of relatively informed and intelligent survey respondents to their similarly situated but less informed and intelligent compatriots." Bartels calls the discrepancies between observed public opinions and imputed interests, "false consciousness." Larry M. Bartels, "Public Opinion and Political Interests," paper prepared for presentation at the Annual Meeting of the Midwest Political Science Association, Chicago, April 1990.

If my remarks strike you as unduly populist, let me add that I feel no more comfortable with arguments like that of Bruce Russett, who defends mass opinions about national security as "sophisticated" because they resemble expert theories of mutual deterrence. Here is how Russett describes some critical evidence for his case:

Americans' acceptance of the fact and theory of mutual deterrence shows in response to repeated questions about whether they prefer the United States to be stronger, weaker, or equal to the Soviet Union in nuclear weapons. . . . Most surveys have found a substantial majority saying only that they wished the United States to be equal. . . . Consistently fewer than 25 percent wanted the United States to be superior. . . .

Overall, we see in these survey responses a rather sophisticated and coherent understanding of the basic principles which many mainstream nuclear strategists have been trying to convey. [Bruce Russett, *Controlling the Sword: The Democratic Governance of National Security* (Cambridge: Harvard University Press, 1990), pp. 64–65]

It should be noticed that the nuclear thinking data support estimates virtually identical to those Russett extracts from commercial opinion surveys. Table 8.4 reveals that only 25% or so embrace the STRENGTH heuristic, while more than 50% embrace SYMMETRY (or the SYMMETRY + STRENGTH hybrid). I have taken pains to show, however, that the SYMMETRY heuristic *does not* ordinarily produce preferences consistent with a strategy of mutually secure second strikes (the classical theory of Schelling and Wohlstetter and presumably Russett's "mainstream"). On the contrary, a clear majority of those who embrace the SYMMETRY heuristic indicate strong support for "unstable balances" in MIRVed silo busters, SDIs, and vulnerable nuclear platforms (destabilizing systems for which "matching is mindless" according to Herbert Scoville). By not soliciting preferences over the relevant political alternatives – i.e., over the outcomes of the arms racing game – the conventional survey questions prove again to be highly limited and misleading. Far from establishing the sophistication of the respondents, Russett's evidence is fully consistent with the naive pursuit of a "balance of power" in destabilizing nuclear systems. Even worse, our data reveal that experts arrive at these unstable balance anomalies just as often as the novices do. The convergence of expert and novice nuclear preferences should not be taken as a source of comfort about democratic governance, but rather as a cause for humility and circumspection. Deliberation need not produce superior opinions when the problems we face become too complex.

In the next chapter I want to explore how our results about nuclear reasoning might revise traditional explanations of the arms race. Doing so will provide an opportunity to discuss the remarkable ending of the Cold War arms race that occurred while these data were being collected.

Appendix 8.1. Experts: Weapon heuristic consistency over weapons

Weapon Heuristic	Weapon Heuristic				
	BAD	GOOD	SWEET POISON	Unclear	Total
INVULNERABLE		MX			
BAD	18	1	0	1	20
GOOD	60	10	1	13	84
SWEET POISON	2	0	0	0	2
Unclear	6	1	0	5	12
Total	86	12	1	19	118

Summary statistics, excluding those who are UNCLEAR.
Percentage on Main Diagonal—30%
κ Measure of Agreement (Asymptotic S.E)— .04 (.03)
McNemar Symmetry χ^2 (Prob Value)— 60.1 (pr = .000)

	BAD	GOOD	SWEET POISON	Unclear	Total
INVULNERABLE		ASW			
BAD	16	3	0	1	20
GOOD	60	12	1	11	84
SWEET POISON	2	0	0	0	2
Unclear	4	2	1	5	12
Total	82	17	2	17	118

Summary statistics, excluding those who are UNCLEAR.
Percentage on Main Diagonal—30%
κ Measure of Agreement (Asymptotic S.E)— .01 (.04)
McNemar Symmetry χ^2 (Prob Value)— 54.6 (pr = .000)

	BAD	GOOD	SWEET POISON	Unclear	Total
INVULNERABLE		SDI			
BAD	14	5	0	1	20
GOOD	48	26	2	8	84
SWEET POISON	2	0	0	0	2
Unclear	4	3	1	4	12
Total	68	34	3	13	118

Summary statistics, excluding those who are UNCLEAR.
Percentage on Main Diagonal—41%
κ Measure of Agreement (Asymptotic S.E)— .05 (.06)
McNemar Symmetry χ^2 (Prob Value)— 38.9 (pr = .000)

Appendix 8.1 *(cont.)*

Weapon Heuristic	Weapon Heuristic				
	BAD	GOOD	SWEET POISON	Unclear	Total
_MX_		_SDI_			
BAD	64	15	2	5	86
GOOD	1	10	0	1	12
SWEET POISON	0	1	0	0	1
Unclear	3	8	1	7	19
Total	68	34	3	13	118

Summary statistics, excluding those who are UNCLEAR.
Percentage on Main Diagonal—80%
κ Measure of Agreement (Asymptotic S.E)— .43 (.10)
McNemar Symmetry χ^2 (Prob Value)— 15.25 (pr = .000)

_MX_		_ASW_			
BAD	72	10	0	4	86
GOOD	4	6	1	1	12
SWEET POISON	0	0	0	1	1
Unclear	6	1	1	11	19
Total	82	17	2	17	118

Summary statistics, excluding those who are UNCLEAR.
Percentage on Main Diagonal—83%
κ Measure of Agreement (Asymptotic S.E)— .38 (.11)
McNemar Symmetry χ^2 (Prob Value)—2.57 (pr = .46)

ASW		_SDI_			
BAD	60	16	3	3	82
GOOD	3	10	0	4	17
SWEET POISON	0	1	0	1	2
Unclear	5	7	0	5	17
Total	68	34	3	13	118

Summary statistics, excluding those who are UNCLEAR.
Percentage on Main Diagonal—75%
κ Measure of Agreement (Asymptotic S.E)— .36 (.10)
McNemar Symmetry χ^2 (Prob Value)—12.89 (pr = .000)

Appendix 8.2. Experts: Security heuristic consistency over weapons

Security Heuristic	Security Heuristic				
	SYMMETRY	MIXTURE	STRENGTH	Unclear	Total
INVULNERABLE		*MX*			
SYMMETRY	24	2	1	4	31
MIXTURE	4	10	3	3	20
STRENGTH	0	2	17	6	25
Unclear	8	7	6	21	42
Total	36	21	27	34	118

Summary statistics, excluding those who are UNCLEAR.
Percentage on Main Diagonal—81%
κ Measure of Agreement (Asymptotic S.E)— .71 (.07)
McNemar Symmetry χ^2 (Prob Value)—1.87 (pr = .60)

		ASW			
INVULNERABLE					
SYMMETRY	25	3	0	3	31
MIXTURE	5	9	1	5	20
STRENGTH	2	0	17	6	25
Unclear	7	5	10	20	42
Total	39	17	28	34	118

Summary statistics, excluding those who are UNCLEAR.
Percentage on Main Diagonal—82%
κ Measure of Agreement (Asymptotic S.E)— .72 (.08)
McNemar Symmetry χ^2 (Prob Value)— 3.50 (pr = .32)

		SDI			
INVULNERABLE					
SYMMETRY	25	4	1	1	31
MIXTURE	3	11	2	4	20
STRENGTH	0	4	19	2	25
Unclear	8	13	4	17	42
Total	36	32	26	24	118

Summary statistics, excluding those who are UNCLEAR.
Percentage on Main Diagonal—79.5%
κ Measure of Agreement (Asymptotic S.E)— .69 (.07)
McNemar Symmetry χ^2 (Prob Value)— 1.81 (pr = .61)

Appendix 8.2 *(cont.)*

Security Heuristic	Security Heuristic				
	SYMMETRY	MIXTURE	STRENGTH	Unclear	Total
<u>MX</u>	<u>SDI</u>				
SYMMETRY	30	4	0	2	36
MIXTURE	2	16	0	3	21
STRENGTH	0	4	19	4	27
Unclear	4	8	7	15	34
Total	36	32	26	24	118

Summary statistics, excluding those who are UNCLEAR.
Percentage on Main Diagonal—87%
κ Measure of Agreement (Asymptotic S.E)— .80 (.06)
McNemar Symmetry χ^2 (Prob Value)— 4.67 (pr = .20)

<u>MX</u>	<u>ASW</u>				
SYMMETRY	32	0	1	3	36
MIXTURE	1	12	1	7	21
STRENGTH	2	2	18	5	27
Unclear	4	3	8	19	34
Total	39	17	28	34	118

Summary statistics, excluding those who are UNCLEAR.
Percentage on Main Diagonal—90%
κ Measure of Agreement (Asymptotic S.E)— .84 (.06)
McNemar Symmetry χ^2 (Prob Value)—1.67 (pr = .64)

<u>ASW</u>	<u>SDI</u>				
SYMMETRY	31	5	3	0	39
MIXTURE	2	12	0	3	17
STRENGTH	2	3	18	5	28
Unclear	1	12	5	16	34
Total	36	32	26	24	118

Summary statistics, excluding those who are UNCLEAR.
Percentage on Main Diagonal—80%
κ Measure of Agreement (Asymptotic S.E)— .69 (.07)
McNemar Symmetry χ^2 (Prob Value)—4.49 (pr = .21)

9

The Factional Politics of Strategy and the End of the Cold War Arms Race

The complex and interesting patterns in the nuclear preference data inevitably raise wider political questions. What can the data teach us about arms race dynamics, arms control, nuclear proliferation, international cooperation, and international relations more generally? What do they suggest about the collapse of the Cold War and national security politics afterwards? Such questions invite a shift in focus from the psychological and cognitive foundations of nuclear preferences to their political and strategic consequences.

Because the data measure attitudes in a game theoretic format, they provide direct support for a positive political theory of national strategic behavior. The data show that the idealized players who inhabit deterrence theories and arms race models look very unlike real-world political actors – either experts or novices. Comprehending the implications for nuclear competition and cooperation, disarmament, and proliferation will require new theories to explain how this diverse cast of characters behaves and interacts.

The main purpose in this chapter is to suggest the kind of theoretical redirection that now seems necessary, given the structure of the preference data. If you consider that 40 years has already been spent refining arms racing models and deterrence theories with homogeneous, unitary actors, it becomes evident that the nuclear thinking data present a difficult theoretical challenge. As a first step down a long road, I want to sketch how a more realistic theory of the arms race might someday look. Without pursuing detailed game theoretic technicalities, which no doubt will be a delicate undertaking, I would like instead to fashion an explanatory template for some of the political dynamics that ended the Cold War. Doing so will illustrate how our fortuitously timed measurements shed new light on those historic events. At the same time, we'll discover many further avenues of inquiry for theorists and historians of the nuclear arms race, the Cold War, and international politics.

ELEMENTS OF A MULTILEVELED COALITIONAL MODEL OF THE
ARMS RACE

Element I: Heterogeneous Preferences

Every sample we've collected reveals surprising political heterogeneity. It follows that no analysis of the arms race can safely assume that deterrence has a logic, evident to all. Instead, nuclear preferences reflect disparate heuristic notions.

Intuitions that associate stable deterrence with SYMMETRY or STRENGTH seem especially deeply held, and define the major branches of expert and novice opinion. But many smaller branches grow off these main limbs. The novices' inconsistent perceptions of nuclear systems smear their ideologically colored world views. Experts perceive weapons more consensually, but still can't agree on how to weigh competing considerations. Without a persuasive nuclear doctrine to use for guidance, both experts and novices fall back on intuitive processing. Their heuristic calculus combines similar ingredients, but with much idiosyncratic variation in the blends. The result is preference diversity, even among highly trained experts who accept common strategic principles. It follows that what weapons get built, and what actually deters, depend critically on who holds the levers of political power.

Element II: Strategic Policy Arises from Factional Conflict

From the observation that nuclear preferences are highly diverse, even within small groups, it follows that domestic factional struggle must play a pivotal role in armaments politics – whether the nuclear powers are building up or building down. One should expect that people who harbor different conceptions of national security will coalesce into contending factions and compete for political power. This conclusion doesn't change whether experts or novices control decisions. Neither does it matter whether political power is concentrated in dozens of hands or dispersed over millions. We should still expect to see preference diversity, and therefore domestic political rivalry, affecting nuclear policy on all sides.

To some this point may seem self-evident, but one shouldn't underestimate its bite. If true, it follows that there can be no hope of explaining what coalitions form, when and why, without a detailed understanding of how nuclear preferences are distributed. So far as I know, such evidence virtually doesn't exist, for any country, during or after the Cold War.

Element III: Multileveled Interactions

What makes this factional game interesting and complicated is not just the diversity of players, but the interdependency between the domestic and international arenas. What weapons each country builds or dismantles surely depends on which strategic coalition holds sway (or how power is divided among several factions). But in general, the domestic balance of power will not simply reflect local parameters like the relative size, or political skill, or institutional position of the contending factions. The international environment matters too. This conclusion follows directly from our evidence, which shows that many players' policy preferences depend on the other side's actions. (The exceptions are people with unambivalent dominant strategies.) It follows that "who coalesces with whom" will reflect the adversary's behavior. But since the adversary's policy depends on factional alignments within its own political system, and those alignments reflect our policy, the domestic politics on both sides of the arms race become intertwined.[1] The flavor of the process is suggested by Kenneth Adelman's description of the Geneva Arms Talks of January, 1985: "Round and round we went," Adelman recalls, "both within the U.S. delegation and between the U.S. and USSR delegations." Reporters called George Shultz's Air Force Boeing 707 flight to the Geneva meetings, "The Ship of Feuds," because it contained "so many warring elements of the administration."[2]

Figure 9.1 portrays a multileveled, coalitional arms racing game, reflecting all three elements of our explanatory sketch. In either country, a domestic political struggle among competing strategic factions determines national policy in the arms race. The chosen policy then influences the domestic factional alignments in the rival state, and with them, its strategic move. And so on, back and forth. To understand the arms race and the possibilities for arms control, we must determine when such systems settle into a stable coalitional equilibrium, and what kinds of shocks can displace established patterns of behavior.

However plausible these explanatory elements might seem, there is no theoretical paradigm in security studies or international relations that successfully embraces all three. As we have seen in deterrence theory itself,

1 Don Oberdorfer, *The Turn: From the Cold War to a New Era* (New York: Poseidon Press, 1991), p. 104.

2 Don Oberdorfer, *The Turn: From the Cold War to a New Era* (New York: Poseidon Press, 1991), p. 102. Multileveled or hierarchical games locate politicians inside multiple arenas at the same time. Recent theoretical discussions include George Tsebelis, *Nested Games* (Berkeley: University of California Press, 1989); Peter Katzenstein, "International Relations and Domestic Structures: Foreign Economic Policies of Advanced Industrial States," *International Organization* 30 (Winter 1976); and Robert Putnam, "Diplomacy and Domestic Politics: The Logic of Two-Level Games," *International Organization* 42 (Summer 1988).

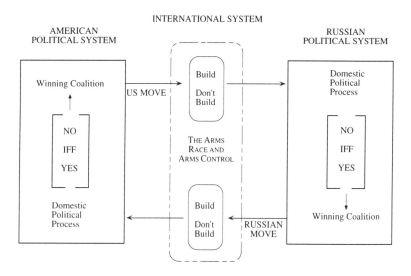

Figure 9.1 A multileveled, coalitional action–reaction model

the dominant pattern of explanation addresses the behavior of unitary state actors configured in an international system. Here the interactions between states are explained by international factors – in our problem, imperatives for security – while the disputes within states remain in the background. The focus rests entirely on the middle box in Figure 9.1 (the "international system"), while the domestic political systems are "black-boxed." To put the point another way, the state actor paradigm gains much of its theoretical leverage by specifying preferences in a way that eliminates domestic diversity. What Graham Allison described in 1975 as the "prevailing simplification" remains very much the norm today:

Weapons are the result of national strategic choice; governmental leaders select specific weapons and total force posture on the basis of precise calculations about national objectives, perceived threats, and strategic doctrine within the constraints of technology and budget.[Graham T. Allison and Frederic A. Morris, "Armaments and Arms Control; Exploring the Determinants of Military Weapons," in Franklin A. Long and George W. Rathjens, eds., *Arms, Defense Policy, and Arms Control* (New York: W.W. Norton, 1975), pp. 103–104.]

The same pattern of explanation – Allison's "Model I – The Rational Actor" or Waltz's "Third Image" – continues to dominate international relations theory more generally.[3]

3 For a revealing, unifying discussion of recent trends, see Robert Powell, "International Relations Theory: A Formal Approach," University of California, Berkeley, Working Paper, Fall 1991.

The major contending perspective focuses on the "bureaucratic" or the "domestic" politics of national strategy and behavior. This approach openly embraces preference diversity and the political struggle that goes with it – but not without a price. When approached on the level of concrete description, theory-building has mired down in what Allison described as the "hundred variables problem":

Evidently, there are at least one hundred important causal factors (and clusters of factors) involved in the process from which weapons emerge. No one, or group, of these factors dominates the outcome in a normal case. But simple analysis, prediction, and discussion require statements about the impact of single factors or clusters on the weapons outcome. Since other factors change significantly from one weapon to the next, specification of relations between a single factor (or group) and the outcome – "other things being equal" – becomes a difficult and perhaps even questionable enterprise. [Graham T. Allison and Frederic A. Morris, "Armaments and Arms Control: Exploring the Determinants of Military Weapons," in Franklin A. Long and George W. Rathjens, eds., *Arms, Defense Policy, and Arms Control* (New York: W. W. Norton, 1975), p. 122; see also Morton Halperin, *Bureaucratic Politics and Foreign Policy* (Washington: The Brookings Institution, 1974), Chapter 17, "A Complicated Reality"]

The process described in such accounts typically involves many organizations and institutions, often pursuing non-security objectives like budget maximization and political autonomy, with no clear logic to predict the outcome of their political struggle. To cope with this Pandora's Box of complexity, the domestically minded analysts have not only turned to "thick description" as a substitute for the more formal theories of the "third image" approach. They have accepted an alternative explanatory simplification. While taking an occasional bow to the prevailing state actor paradigm, they mainly attribute strategic policies to domestic factors, greatly downplaying the role of international interactions:

Analysts of arms races and proponents of arms control have tended to emphasize factors between nations as the primary determinants behind the arms race and the principal target for proposed cures. While actions of foreign governments . . . are obviously important, the analysis above suggests that the weapons in the American and Soviet force postures are *predominantly* the result of factors internal to each nation. [Graham T. Allison and Frederic A. Morris, "Armaments and Arms Control; Exploring the Determinants of Military Weapons," in Franklin Long and George W. Rathjens, eds., *Arms, Defense Policy, and Arms Control* (New York: W.W. Norton, 1975), p. 126] [Emphasis added]

In this way, a domestic explanation could be cast as an essentially parochial struggle among competing bureaucracies, sectors, ideologies, and interest groups. Doing so finesses the messy question of how "actions of foreign governments" affect the domestic balance of power, and how the resulting policy reactions feed back on the state who makes the original move. Instead, these explanations tend to focus on one country at a time, without entertaining complex interactions among several domestic political arenas at once.[4]

Because the bureaucratic and domestic models are not really multileveled in the sense described above, they have invited resistance in the discipline to what Allison called "the de-internationalization of international relations." With their heavy domestic accent and daunting complexity, they lacked appeal to both theoreticians, who value a rigorous approach, and policy makers, who want to know which weapons to buy, which weapons to ban, how to anticipate the other side's reactions, how to secure its cooperation, and how to deter unwanted behavior. As a result, the unitary state actor models played a leading role in security studies and arms control theory, from beginning to end of the Cold War.

Now let's consider how the nuclear preference data might contribute to the kind of multileveled, coalitional analysis of the arms race that so far has proved elusive. Before proceeding to the details, it is important to understand how these data provide new leverage in the problem. To appreciate the difficulties that ordinarily arise when analysts open the black box of domestic politics, consider Don Oberdorfer's description of the Shultz–Weinberger conflict over SDI, which came to a head before the foreign ministers meeting scheduled in Geneva for January 1985 :

> Weinberger was essentially a litigator and a fighter, and Shultz tended to negotiate in case of differences. Weinberger was . . . closer politically on most issues to Reagan's core supporters among conservatives. But on foreign policy questions, Reagan had a tremendous regard for Shultz. [*The Turn: From the Cold War to a New Era* (New York: Poseidon Press, 1991), p. 99]

Later we learn,

> Reagan sought to protect the SDI program at all costs, [while] Weinberger was all the more suspicious that Shultz would trade away part of Reagan's "dream" – and the Defense Department's fastest growing program. . . . Weinberger's basic point was that Shultz should not talk at all about the SDI program with Gromyko at the Geneva meetings, so that nothing could be given or traded away. [pp. 101–102]

This account clearly reveals a domestic political struggle taking place, and tries to specify the motivations that drive it (negotiation style, Rea-

---

4 See, for example, Graham T. Allison, *Essence of Decision* (Boston: Little Brown, 1971), and Morton H. Halperin, *Bureaucratic Politics and Foreign Policy* (Washington: The Brookings Institution, 1974). A recent study in this style is Jack Snyder, *Myths of Empire: Domestic Politics and International Ambition* (Ithaca: Cornell University Press, 1991). Snyder writes, in a characteristic passage:

> German overexpansion, rationalized by big stick strategic assumptions, is best explained as a result of the ideological blowback from the domestic political struggles characteristic of a late-developing society. German aggressiveness was not compelled by Germany's position in the international system; indeed, Germany's behavior was often wildly mismatched with the true incentives of the prevailing international order. [p. 108]

gan's dream, budgetary maximization, and so on). Like most descriptive studies, this one explains behavior by invoking a set of preferences and arguing that behavior follows from them – just as in the rational choice tradition. But to specify those preferences, Oberdorfer focuses on the politicians' reasons for a favored outcome, which can be as numerous as Allison's 100 variables. Which reasons count more heavily in deciding behavior is hard to see, and how to generalize from the particular episode is even less clear. By contrast, the preferences measured in this book specify rankings over the outcomes associated with national strategic policy choices. By rising above the underlying reasons for weapon preferences (whether psychological, organizational, ideological, financial, or political), we avoid the paralyzing 100 variables problem that a descriptive, motivational explanation invites.[5]

Besides being unwieldy, lists of reasons rarely establish the preference rankings that a rigorous analysis of strategic choice requires. It appears from Oberdorfer's description that Reagan and Weinberger have a dominant strategy to build SDI. But our data contain 30 different kinds of YES types, including YES+'s, YES++'s, and YES-BUTs. All prefer to build whatever the Soviets do, but a YES+ player would prefer arms control to Soviet superiority, a YES-BUT would prefer arms control to both sides' having SDI, and a YES++ would never accept arms control. Without more information, we can't tell from this description which of these very different profiles fit Reagan and Weinberger. To put the problem another way, we can't tell how these politicians will respond to various Soviet moves, or react to Soviet offers at the bargaining table.

Such information is critical if we want to understand *the strategy of conflict* in Thomas Schelling's sense:

To study the strategy of conflict is to take the view that most conflict situations are essentially bargaining situations. They are situations in which the ability of one participant to gain his ends is dependent to an important degree on the choices or decisions that the other participant will make . . . – in which the best course of action for each participant depends on what he expects the other participants to do. [*The Strategy of Conflict* (New York: Oxford University Press, 1960), pp. 7–9]

If we want to treat nuclear policy as a problem in strategy, as we clearly should, even a rudimentary analysis requires that we understand how preferences depend on the other side's move. It is amazing how rarely "domestic politics" accounts in international relations specify the dependency.[6]

---

5 This is not to argue that our preference data don't support rich inferences about the origins of the respondents' preferences. The point is rather that preferences need not be specified by referring to motivations.
6 The same criticisms apply to measurement scales in conventional opinion surveys. As we have seen, these scales do not address how policy preferences depend on the other side's behavior, and therefore cannot support a game theoretic analysis either.

I hope that the data presented in this book will help close the gap between our historical and theoretical understanding of the arms race. By depicting preferences in a way that is both theoretically constructive and empirically relevant, the stage is set for new models of international politics where politicians and voters have diverse strategic inclinations, where policies are made and contested by fluid coalitions, where power is distributed over many agents, where people need not share a common understanding of the game, and where domestic and international politics interact. Such an explanatory paradigm will find many applications in the nuclear arms race, but right now none seems more interesting than the puzzling demise of the Cold War itself. In the pages ahead, I want to suggest how one might use a multileveled coalitional model of security politics, informed by real data about nuclear preferences, to approach these startling events.

THE LARGE SCALE PATTERN OF THE NUCLEAR ARMS RACE

Understanding what broke the momentum of the nuclear arms race naturally requires some explanation for why it became stuck in a spiral of mutual buildups. Notwithstanding occasional interludes of détente and welcome respites like the ABM Treaty, the general pattern during the Cold War was that arms control worked poorly. How poorly can be gauged by the precipitous reduction in the nuclear arsenals since 1991. Both sides displayed little resistance to new technologies – including the H-bomb, ballistic missile launchers, MIRV, miniaturized "tactical" bombs, pinpoint guidance systems, ASW, cruise missiles, and stealth – whether those technologies were destabilizing or not. As a general rule, the weapon systems that didn't get built were either unaffordable or technically infeasible. Even the ABM, which was banned forever and didn't work, rose from the dead as SDI.

The question is why this costly and self-defeating behavior persisted so long. Suppose for the sake of argument that Soviet military policy was dominated in the pre-Gorbachev period by STRENGTH players, who were committed as a dominant strategy to building up the Soviet arsenal. Such a scenario has been suggested by many people, including those who've argued that the STRENGTH philosophy is intrinsic to Russian culture, that it reflected the totalitarian impulses of the Communist Party and their "garrison state," that it reflected the leading role of military officials in the Soviet Union, and that it was a legacy of disasters in two world wars. That the Soviets apparently devoted 25% of GNP to defense, even until their economy and political system collapsed, lends credibility to the conjecture.[7]

---

7 For a good introduction to a large literature, see Sean Lynn-Jones, Steven E. Miller, and Stephen Van Evera, eds., *Soviet Military Policy* (Cambridge: The MIT Press, 1989).

Table 9.1. *Game theoretic types for novices and experts*

	Novices	Experts			Novices	Experts	
	MX Missile				SDI		
NO	14%	24%			14%	15%	
IFF-NO	⌈30%	42%⌉		⌈23%	40%⌉		
IFF°	45% | 7%	2% | 46%	41% | 4%	4% | 53%				
IFF-YES	⌊8%	2%⌋		⌊14%	9%⌋		
YES-BUT	⌈12%	17%⌉		⌈9%	9%⌉		
YES+	38% | 10%	8% | 26%	41% | 18%	20% | 30%				
YES++	⌊16%	1%⌋		⌊14%	1%⌋		
Total	100%	100%			100%	100%	
Total n	169	118			169	118	
	ASW				INVULNERABLE		
NO	12%	20%			7%	3%	
IFF-NO	⌈25%	42%⌉		⌈11%	7%⌉		
IFF°	43% | 4%	4% | 52%	35% | 4%	3% | 31%				
IFF-YES	⌊14%	6%⌋		⌊20%	21%⌋		
YES-BUT	⌈11%	15%⌉		⌈9%	11%⌉		
YES+	44% | 18%	9% | 25%	55% | 25%	37% | 63%				
YES++	⌊15%	1%⌋		⌊21%	15%⌋		
Total	100%	100%			100%	100%	
Total n	169	118			169	118	

If our respondents are typical of the politically active population in the United States, then a coalitional explanation for why the nuclear arms race became stuck on the strategy combination [*Build, Build*] is already at hand. Under these circumstances, it follows from the frequency distributions in Table 9.1 that a large majority of Americans will support a policy to build all kinds of nuclear weapons systems, including those forbidden by established treaties and those considered destabilizing by deterrence theorists. Once the Soviets are committed to a nuclear buildup, what could be called the *Grand Arms Racing Coalition* in the United States includes not just the YES types, who prefer to build regardless, but all the IFFs, who prefer to build if the other side does. It is important to notice that the YESes by themselves are not a majority of our respondents. With respect to MX, SDI, and ASW, YESes are 25–30% of experts and 40–45% of novices. But the grand coalition of YES + IFF includes roughly 85% of novices and 75% of experts on each weapon, leaving the NOs in a highly isolated position.

If this large coalition succeeds in dominating policy, as seems probable in a democratic society, then the U.S. will commit itself to a military buildup. Doing so will cement a similar coalition of IFFs and YESes on the Soviet side, completing a multileveled action–reaction loop between the domestic coalitions. Unless something disturbs the distribution of preferences (like economic distress or institutional reform), the two sides will fall into an arms race supported by a stable coalitional equilibrium (such that no one in either country's controlling coalition would accept another policy, so long as the other side's policy remains in place).

Of course, the story works just as well in the other direction. If the United States appeared committed to *Build* in the early days of the Cold War, then a Soviet coalition of YES + IFF would be cemented in place. If that coalition were powerful enough to control policy, the arms race would again become locked on [*Build, Build*]. The general point is that when preferences are distributed as we find in our data, the accession in either country of a faction committed to strength, superiority, or military dominance can ignite an arms race that will be difficult to reverse, given the combined frequency of the YES and IFF types.

The Liberal's Dilemma

Our data reveal that the Grand Arms Racing Coalition is largely composed of people who reject classical ideas. This pattern already explains why so many weapons systems were proposed and even deployed that threatened the other side's ability to retaliate after a nuclear attack – including ABM, MIRVed ICBMs, SDI, ASAT, ASW, and more. On the other hand, neither the Grand Coalition nor its opponents are remotely monolithic or homogeneous. The arms debate will be vigorous, the clash of viewpoints sharp, and the politics of arms control contentious.[8]

Looking at things from the arms controller's perspective, one sees a cruel irony in the idea that a philosophy of mutual deterrence has become a general consensus in the United States (or even "universally").[9] If our data are right, this suggestion greatly overstates the political strength of people who seek to preserve *mutual* deterrence by avoiding counterforce weapons and territorial defenses. Even among experts, less than 15% of the profiles display the classical (NO) attitude toward weapons like MX, SDI, and ASW. And taken all together, committed opponents of the arms race are a

8 While the arms debate seems like an obvious and important feature of the arms race, it cannot be explained by unitary state actor models like classical MAD theory or the Prisoner's Dilemma.
9 Bruce Russett's *Controlling the Sword* (Cambridge: Harvard University Press, 1990) is a recent study that presents arguments and evidence for this view.

Table 9.2. *Game type by security heuristic: MX, ASW, SDI*

	SYMMETRY	MIXTURE	STRENGTH	Unclear	Total
Experts					
NO	40	0	1	28	69
IFF-NO	53	49	0	44	146
IFF°, NIFF	9	4	1	1	15
IFF-YES	7	14	0	0	21
YES-BUT	0	0	49	0	49
YES+	2	3	28	10	43
YES++	0	0	2	2	4
N.A.	0	0	4	3	7
Total	111	70	85	88	354
Novices					
NO	32	0	1	34	67
IFF-NO	60	50	0	21	131
IFF°, NIFF	19	4	1	1	25
IFF-YES	29	33	0	0	62
YES-BUT	0	0	55	0	55
YES+	16	0	35	26	77
YES++	0	0	27	49	76
N.A.	0	0	9	5	14
Total	156	87	128	136	507

small minority of experts and novices. NO profiles are only 15–25% of the total on MX, SDI, and ASW. With such a small base of support, arms controllers will be hard pressed to implement a classical strategic policy on their own.

The political weakness of arms controllers can be traced to several different patterns of nuclear thinking that depart from what is often misdescribed as the "conventional wisdom." First, more than 25% of all the people we surveyed embrace the STRENGTH heuristic. They reject mutuality out of hand, violating a basic axiom of the classical theory. Another 20% adopt a hybrid conception of security (the SYMMETRY + STRENGTH mixture), accepting balance as a guiding principle in the military realm but rejecting the idea of political symmetry. One can see in Table 9.2 that very few people who follow these heuristics arrive at a NO configuration of preference on the destabilizing weapon systems that were the main concern of arms controllers. A second difficulty appears among novices, who largely fail to grasp the logic of secure second strikes. As a result, novices frequently attach the GOOD weapon heuristic to weapons that experts consider BAD, eroding mass support for arms control. And finally, there are deviations from classical thinking within the [SYMME-TRY + BAD] family itself, resulting in the "unstable balance anomalies" (with IFF rather than NO profiles).

While the opposition of the STRENGTH faction is ideologically driven and more or less a fact of life for arms controllers, the anomalous SYM-METRY thinkers are a political bane. The trouble occurs when the intuitive appeal of military balance outweighs the BAD weapon heuristic, resulting in an "unstable balance anomaly" (an IFF type) rather than a classical NO preference ordering. Our data show that many liberals who accept classical intuitions about mutuality and destabilizing weapons still reach an IFF-NO preference on systems like MX and SDI. The IFF-NOs can support a treaty ban on weapons like MX and SDI as their first choice, but still vote to fund them if they believe the other side is committed to building.

The hedging behavior of the IFFs makes the momentum of the arms race hard to break by obstructing unilateral moves to kill BAD weapons outright. So long as the Soviets showed an inclination to build, the pivotal IFF types on the American side cast their lot with the YES players, funding military programs even for weapons they didn't like. Trapped in what might be called the liberal's dilemma, they greatly enlarged the coalition supporting the nuclear buildup. Their behavior replicates an interesting pattern called liberal pacification[10] in the literature of international relations. While liberals in the IFF-NO category would not engage in arms racing with likeminded adversaries, they readily arms race with opponents seeking STRENGTH.

Possibilities for Arms Control

This account identifies, I believe, the basic coalitional mechanism that explains why the Cold War arms race was prolonged and intractable. It does not yet explain the occasional successes of arms control during the long buildup or the ultimate undoing of the Cold War itself. To appreciate the possibilities for arms control in our scheme of explanation, one has to

---

10 Liberal pacification refers to the strong tendency of liberal democracies to avoid war with each other, even though they readily go to war with authoritarian states. So far the literature has devoted relatively little attention to the factional dynamics of democratic politics, and much more to the ideology of liberalism. The pivotal role of IFFs that we've observed in the arms race could perhaps be generalized to explain the larger pattern. For interesting discussions, see Michael Doyle, "Liberalism and World Politics," *American Political Science Review* 80 (1986); and Bruce Russett, *Controlling the Sword: The Democratic Governance of National Security* (Cambridge: Harvard University Press, 1990).

consider how mutually reinforcing winning coalitions can be assembled to support the policy *Not Build*.[11]

In diverse populations like those in our samples, there are several ways that arms control agreements or military build-downs can occur. One is to exploit institutional concentrations of power that allow minority factions to control military policy. Such possibilities existed on both sides of the Cold War, though probably more so on the Soviet side than the American. At least on the face of things, minority control is more difficult to achieve in a democratic system. But even in the United States, it would be no simple matter to place arms controllers in a controlling position when so much authority for procuring weapon systems is concentrated in military institutions.

A second strategy rests on mobilizing the large coalition that considers arms control more desirable than mutual armament. The set of profiles that rank NONE > BOTH includes not just the NOs, but the IFF-NOs and the YES-BUTs. For destabilizing weapons like MX, ASW, and SDI, this group includes 65–85% of our experts and roughly 50% of the novices. If the other side can present a credible threat to build when we do, and a credible promise not to build if we won't, this larger coalition can be formed. Such agreements are not necessarily stable, of course, because the YES players prefer to "break out" when they see an opportunity for unilateral advantage. If YES players hold a privileged institutional position, assembling this coalition will be difficult. A successful agreement requires careful monitoring, and that both sides remain convinced that their adversary can make good on the threat to match.

A third possibility relies on "bargaining from strength." If one side can achieve unmatchable qualitative or quantitative superiority over its adversary, then virtually everybody on the inferior side from the NOs to the YES+'s becomes a supporter of an arms control agreement. More than 95% of experts and 85% of novices rank NONE > INFERIORITY, the only exceptions being YES++'s. Such tactics are frequently defended by people who want arms control, but who believe their adversary is controlled by hawkish YES+ players. They are also used by people who don't want arms control, but who do want to mobilize support for building up. A

11 It should be noticed in the discussion to follow how a coalitional strategy for arms control (and for international cooperation more generally) departs from the approach suggested by analysts who portray the arms race as a particular social dilemma like the Prisoner's Dilemma or the Security Dilemma. In these games, the homogeneous players have preferences that make cooperation problematic. The impulse to defect is overcome by repeated play, through "education" about mutual interests, by hegemonic enforcers of social contracts, and by other manipulations of incentives. If our data are correct, these accounts misspecify the problem of securing international cooperation by misrepresenting the distribution of preferences. (They may be adequate descriptions of other problems.) In confrontations between two populations of heterogeneous types, the question is how to arrange in a stable equilibrium winning coalitions for cooperation.

basic problem is how to form a coalition on the superior side that will be willing to forgo its advantages, once they're achieved. The set of profiles in the NO and IFF categories prefer NONE to SUPERIORITY, and sometimes constitute a majority. But this coalition would not ordinarily preside over a buildup in the first place. In most cases, they would have to remove an entrenched coalition, dominated by YESes, to proceed.

Finally, one might consider a strategy of unilateral reductions to get the process of arms control started. By sending signals that one's policy had changed from *Build* to *Not Build*, it might be possible to induce reciprocation from the other side by realigning its domestic coalitions.

All of these stratagems played a role during the end of the Cold War. The rich possibilities created by preference diversity made for a politics of strange bedfellows and surprising turnabouts on both sides. To help gain a feeling for how a coalitional explanation of strategic cooperation would proceed, I would like to focus on the unilateral initiatives pursued by Mikhail Gorbachev and his colleagues. Doing so will provide a deeper understanding of the informational requirements that a multileveled explanation imposes, while revealing interesting political subtleties that surrounded Gorbachev's plan.

HOW THE ARMS RACE CAME UNGLUED

The beginning of the end for the Cold War was surely the advent of the Gorbachev regime in March 1985. That the critical turn occurred on the Soviet side, not the American, is a result that few Westerners would have predicted. It seems less surprising, perhaps, when one considers the isolated position of arms controllers in the United States and the diffusion of power in democratic institutions. These circumstances made it unlikely that the impetus to break the Cold War arms race could have originated on the American side. Instead, the concentration of political power in the Soviet system made it possible for their leaders to take steps that the Americans were immobilized from considering.

Those who met Gorbachev sensed right away that he and his colleagues were a new breed. After Brian Mulroney and George Shultz met Gorbachev at the funeral of Konstantin Chernenko, the Canadian Prime Minister asked Shultz when he thought "serious change" might begin in the Soviet Union. Shultz answered, "Today."[12] And indeed, within a few short months Gorbachev had already given evidence that major changes were afoot. In September 1985, the new Soviet Foreign Minister, Eduard Shevardnadze, proposed 50% reductions in the superpowers' offensive

12 Don Oberdorfer, *The Turn: From the Cold War to a New Era* (New York: Poseidon Press, 1991), p. 111.

nuclear arsenals. In October, Gorbachev announced in Paris that Soviet military policy would be governed by a new doctrine of "reasonable sufficiency." Then, in January 1986, he proposed the complete elimination of all nuclear weapons worldwide by the year 2000, including all the controversial intermediate-range missiles in Europe during the first phase.

Gorbachev's early proposals marked a sharp departure from Brezhnev's policy of "equal security," which prescribed that the Soviet Union should be able to match the combined strength of its potential adversaries. His desire for nuclear disarmament did not necessarily imply that Gorbachev was a NO player on nuclear forces, however. Rather he had a clear *quid pro quo* in mind. In return for drastic reductions in offensive forces, he wanted reciprocation from the United States. In particular, Gorbachev demanded a halt to all "research, development, and testing" of Reagan's Star Wars program. This demand quickly became the central preoccupation of Soviet arms controllers in their negotiations with the Americans.[13]

In a meeting in Moscow before the Geneva Summit of November 1985, Gorbachev told Robert McFarlane, "If you want superiority through your SDI, we will not help you. . . . We don't want war, but neither are we going to allow unilateral advantage" (Don Oberdorfer, *The Turn: From the Cold War to a New Era,* p. 136). At the same meeting, he told George Shultz:

> I don't want to play games, but if the American administration doesn't want to make a change then we'll go on forever [as before]. . . . Does the United States think that its present policies of exercising pressure and strength, that these policies have brought the Soviet Union back to the negotiating table? If that is the kind of thinking that motivates those around the President, then no success is possible. [pp. 131–132]

Gorbachev concluded by saying he would be willing "to reduce nuclear forces to zero on condition that the two sides prevent the militarization of space" (p. 137).

All of these remarks are consistent with the conjecture that Gorbachev's type on offensive nuclear forces was IFF-NO. Ideally, he wanted to see these systems eliminated altogether, but only if both sides went along. Unilateral American superiority was unacceptable (so NONE > BOTH > US+). On the other hand, his doctrine of reasonable sufficiency explicitly rejected the goal of Soviet superiority in favor of simple parity (so NONE > BOTH > SOV+ ≥ US+).[14] Gorbachev's initial overtures were not

---

13 Don Oberdorfer, *The Turn: From the Cold War to a New Era* (New York: Poseidon Press, 1991), p. 141. The Soviet obsession with turning off the Star Wars program lends credence to arguments that Reagan's strategy of "peace through strength" succeeded in bringing the Soviets back to the bargaining table, and, more broadly, in compelling them to seek economic relief from the arms race.

14 In his report to the Twenty–Seventh Party Congress, Gorbachev included the following principles among the keystones of his foreign policy:

premised on bargaining from strength, but rather on mobilizing those who preferred NONE to BOTH.

These preferences were consistent with Gorbachev's openly declared grand strategy to buy breathing room for domestic economic reform by turning off the arms race. As he told the top command of the Soviet armed forces in July 1985, "the foreign policy of the Soviet Union should be conducted in such a way that military tension in the world would be reduced and, at the same time, the security of the nation should be guaranteed."[15]

Gorbachev's reasoning seemed to follow these steps:

- A Soviet policy to *Not Build* would relieve the economic hemorrhage from the arms race, permitting a diversion of resources to domestic rebuilding.
- Maintaining the Soviet's hard won strategic parity required that the Americans accept an armaments policy of *Not Build* as well.
- A *Not Build* strategy in the U.S. would split the IFFs from the YESes in the Soviet Union, strengthening the coalition for *perestroika* and undermining the hawk factions bent on Soviet military superiority.
- Achieving an equilibrium in the arms race at [*Not Build, Not Build*] would diminish the probability of nuclear catastrophe.

The interconnection between domestic and international politics is explicit in Gorbachev's grand strategy for reforming the Soviet Union. On one hand, his bold plans for decelerating the arms race had calculated domestic effects. They also faced serious domestic obstacles in both the Soviet Union and the United States. It appears that Gorbachev was supported in his program by influential factions in the KGB and Soviet military who believed that economic stagnation had become a threat to national security. At the same time,

---

- "Security when one speaks of relations between the U.S.S.R. and the U.S.A. can only be mutual. . . . The highest wisdom is not in worrying only about oneself, or, all the more, about damaging the other side; it is vital that all should feel equally secure. . . . The modern world has become much too small and fragile for wars and a policy of strength. The aspiration to win military superiority can . . . bring no political gain to anybody." [SYMMETRY]
- "It is essential above all to considerably reduce the level of military confrontation. Genuine equal security is guaranteed not by the highest possible, but by the lowest possible level of the strategic balance, from which it is essential to exclude entirely nuclear and other types of weapons of mass destruction." [Nuclear weapons are BAD (even those on INVULNERABLE platforms)]
- "The nature of today's weapons leaves no state the hope of defending itself by technical military means alone – let us say with the creation of defenses, even the most powerful. . . . It is imperative to find a realistic solution guaranteeing that the arms race does not spread to outer space. The Star Wars programme cannot be permitted to be used as a stimulus to further arms race or as a roadblock to radical disarmament." [SDI is a BAD weapon or POISON PILL]

"Political Report of the CPSU Central Committee to the 27th Congress of the Communist Party of the Soviet Union, February 25, 1986," in Mikhail Gorbachev, *Selected Speeches and Articles* (Moscow: Progress Publishers, 1987), pp. 341–462.

15 Don Oberdorfer, *The Turn: From the Cold War to a New Era* (New York: Poseidon Press, 1991), p. 114.

he faced entrenched resistance from elements in the Communist Party apparatus and the military officer corps. On the American side, the conservative Reagan Administration was already embarked on a massive program of nuclear modernization. Gorbachev's grand strategy required that he obtain reciprocal arms reductions from the United States – no simple matter when American security policy was controlled by people who had expressed nothing but hostility toward arms control agreements between 1980 and 1985.

Gorbachev pursued his arms control program on two tracks. At first, he concentrated on renewed arms control negotiations with the United States, including the Nuclear and Space Talks that had just been revived in Geneva, and summit meetings with Ronald Reagan at Geneva in November 1985, Reykjavik in September 1986, Washington in December 1987, and Moscow in June 1988. These efforts produced the precedent setting INF treaty, which was the first to eliminate a whole category of nuclear forces. They did not, however, lead to a breakthrough on heavy intercontinental systems. After Reykjavik, Gorbachev increasingly relied upon dramatic unilateral initiatives to break the ice jam. Volumes could be written about both aspects of his strategy, but for present purposes I would like to concentrate on the second. Gorbachev's unilateral initiatives are perhaps the most noteworthy effort to secure international cooperation in the nuclear age, and an excellent laboratory for exploring how a coalitional explanation of cooperation departs from the usual paradigm.

THE COALITIONAL LOGIC OF GORBACHEV'S UNILATERAL INITIATIVES

The obvious political dilemma about unilateral initiatives is whether they will be exploited by the adversary, leaving the initiator with a "Sucker's Payoff." The first point to emphasize is that Gorbachev's unilateral initiatives did have a sensible coalitional basis, even though the advisability of such stratagems is very much debated in the theoretical literature on (international) cooperation.[16]

16 The rapidly evolving literature on the "evolution of cooperation" is filled with competing predictions about whether and when unilateral initiatives can establish cooperation. In most of the recent models, players have unitary and symmetric preferences, normally configured as a Prisoner's Dilemma, and play is iterated:

```
             BUILD    NOT
               2  |    1
   BUILD   2  |   4
               4  |    3
     NOT   1  |    3
```

In this game, both players prefer arms control to mutual buildups, but the cooperative outcome is hard to achieve because each side prefers superiority to arms control. To

The nuclear thinking data suggest Gorbachev's strategy was conceptually feasible, if hardly a sure thing, because the glue that held together the American Grand Arms Racing Coalition was Soviet behavior itself. If the Soviet Union by its unilateral actions could demonstrate a commitment to the policy *Not Build*, then the preferred policy of the large bloc with IFF profiles in the United States would swing to *Not Build* as well. So long as the political equation

$$NO + IFF > YES$$

obtained in the American political arena, Gorbachev's unilateral moves had the potential to fracture the large coalition that supported Reagan's military buildup. According to our data, the pivotal IFF bloc contained roughly 40–50% of experts and novices on the critical issues of SDI and MIRVed ICBMs. The potential coalition to stop the arms race (NO + IFF) was therefore a clear majority, including about 60% of novices and 70% of experts on these weapons (see Table 9.1). By inducing the IFFs to defect to a policy of military reductions, Gorbachev stood to circumvent the obstructive conservatives in Reagan's Administration and rescue a grand strategy that had come up empty handed at Reykjavik.[17]

To pursue the unilateral strategy he envisioned, Gorbachev had to overcome two obstacles. First, he needed to mobilize a controlling coalition in the Soviet Union that would accept the audacious idea of unilateral military reductions. Then, he needed to convince the Americans that his commitment to *Not Build* was genuine and durable. Simply changing Soviet policy was not enough, since doing so could be interpreted as a strategic retreat by YES players seeking to gather their strength. Even those who accepted Gorbachev's sincerity had to be convinced that his "liberal" faction wouldn't later be replaced by "hawks" who could exploit America's weakened position, if it reciprocated with concessions to the Soviets. The difficult problem was to alter the widespread perception that Soviet leaders were generally YES players in the arms race. In the discussion to follow, I

overcome the dilemma, the literature suggests numerous stratagems that restructure incentives, including lengthening time horizons, surrendering authority to hegemonic enforcers of contracts, and reconfiguring preferences themselves. Perhaps the most influential recent study has been Robert Axelrod, *The Evolution of Cooperation* (New York: Basic Books, 1984). See also Robert Axelrod and Robert Keohane, "Achieving Cooperation Under Anarchy: Strategies and Institutions," *World Politics* 38, No. 1 (October 1985).

17 Whether, in fact, NO + IFF > YES (politically, not necessarily numerically) is the central empirical question raised by our explanation sketch. Reconstructing the distribution of preferences in political institutions on both sides of the arms race should be the highest priority of political scientists and historians who gain access to the archives of the Cold War.

want to explore the nuclear thinking data for evidence about both critical elements in his strategy.

Mobilizing Support for Unilateral Initiatives

Within the framework of our measurements (which only recognize the discrete alternatives *Build* and *Not Build* along a continuum of deployments), we can already identify many different kinds of unilateral initiatives. A *unilateral build–down* actively dismantles nuclear forces. A *moratorium* is a commitment to stand still, even if the other side builds up. Both maneuvers can lead from superiority to parity, or from parity to inferiority. And finally, either kind of initiative can be applied to one of several weapons or to several weapons at once. Gorbachev therefore had many political options to consider. In a heterogeneous population, anticipating the levels of political resistance and support for each one was necessarily a complex calculation.

To get an idea about the potential feasibility of such measures, let's consider the unilateral build-down from the American point of view, taking the U.S. as the initiator. Doing so allows us to use the nuclear thinking data as a point of reference, testing how real experts and novices would respond to various initiatives. To the extent that nuclear thinking in the Soviet Union followed similar patterns, we might gain some insight about the domestic obstacles Gorbachev faced.[18]

What determines political opposition or support for unilateral initiatives? Presumably, people anticipate the outcome of making an overture to the adversary and then compare it to the results of holding back. Depending on the distribution of preference profiles, the kind of weapon, and the point of departure, winning coalitions might form around either course of action. The game trees in Figure 9.2 illustrate the simplest possible calculations that follow this general form. From an ongoing stream of interactions, the trees isolate a two period exchange in which one adversary takes the initiative (or not), and then observes a response from the other side. Of course, no one can know the opponent's reaction before the initiative occurs. The coalitions that align themselves for and against such maneuvers therefore rest on conjectures about the adversary's behavior. How such conjectures develop remains a mystery in games with uncertainty about the opponent's type (as surely exists here). To proceed, we consider all possible conjectures.[19]

18 It goes without saying that preferences may have been distributed differently in the Soviet Union than in our samples, so these inferences must be highly tentative until better data become available. At the very least, the calculations show what kind of information a coalitional explanation of unilateral initiatives requires, and may help to guide the collection of data from the Soviet archives.

19 Technically speaking, the term *conjecture* refers to beliefs that form off the equilibrium path in games of extensive form. The term is appropriate for this discussion, since I have not specified a solution concept or an explicit scheme for updating the players' beliefs. For

Figure 9.2 depicts a unilateral build-down by the United States, starting from an initial position of superiority (US+). If the United States builds down (in our dichotomous framework from *Have* to *Not Have*), the Soviets can *Not Build* (scenario I → NONE) or they can exploit the Americans by building up to superiority of their own (scenario II → SOV+). If the U.S. retains its weapon system, the Soviets can accede to continued American superiority by not building (III) or decide to match at BOTH (IV). To decide whether a build-down will be worthwhile, each American player must anticipate what path the game will follow after the alternative opening moves by the United States. Such a conjecture amounts to imputing a type to the opposing government (perhaps by calculating the net result of its domestic factional politics, perhaps by thinking of it as a unitary actor). The conjecture defines the anticipated paths along the upper and lower branches of the tree.

Optimistic conjectures are those that anticipate positive Soviet behavior after the Americans' unilateral initiative, resulting here in a "zero–zero" alignment of forces (scenario I). There are two different optimistic conjectures, depending on the predicted response when the U.S. *Holds*. In the first case (I:III), the Soviets decide not to build even when we keep the weapon, making their government in effect a NO player. In the second optimistic conjecture (I:IV), they refrain if we abandon the weapon, but build up if we keep it (as if they were an IFF type). Each conjecture defines a different pair of outcomes from which the United States must choose. Opposition to the unilateral initiative will come from people who prefer the anticipated outcome under *Hold* to the one under *Build Down*.

In Table 9.3, the upper pair of tables computes the fraction of experts and novices in our samples who would *oppose* a unilateral build-down of MIRVed ICBMs, SDI, and invulnerable platforms, if it were true that everyone formed an optimistic conjecture about the Soviet response. Above each table, one can see the outcomes defined by the conjecture and the set of game theoretic types who oppose building down. The important message in both tables is that when conjectures are optimistic, the coalitions that actively oppose unilateral build-downs of offensive weapons and ballistic missile defenses are a minority. Opponents of dismantling invulnerable platforms (i.e., of complete disarmament) remain a majority.

a discussion about the pivotal role of conjectures in games with incomplete information and the conceptual difficulties in modelling them, see Ariel Rubinstein, "Choice of Conjectures in a Bargaining Game with Incomplete Information," Chapter 6 in Alvin Roth, ed., *Game Theoretic Models of Bargaining* (Cambridge: Cambridge University Press, 1985). See also Rubinstein's "Comments on the Interpretation of Game Theory," *Econometrica* 59, No. 4 (July 1991). For a discussion of related topics, including *signalling* and *conjectural variation*, see Eric Rasmusen, *Games and Information* (New York: Basil Blackwell, 1989).

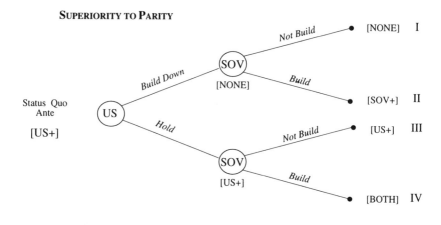

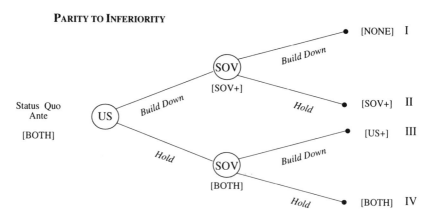

Figure 9.2 Opposition to unilateral build-downs (illustrative calculations from U.S. perspective)

The bottom row of the table provides similar calculations for pessimistic conjectures (where the opponent builds up after the initiator builds down). In the first of these scenarios, the Soviet Union builds up regardless of what we do (as if it were a YES player). In the second, less plausible scenario, they build up when we build down, and build down when we hold on (NIFF behavior). The critical pattern to notice here are the large (though not unanimous) majorities that line up against unilateral build-downs when people anticipate exploitation. Taken together, the data support the following basic political conclusion: Broad-based coalitions for unilateral build-

Table 9.3. *Opposition to unilateral build-downs (illustrative calculations from U.S. perspective)*

OPTIMISTIC CONJECTURES

Optimistic Conjecture 1 (I : III)
Build-down → NONE, Hold → SUPERIORITY

Optimistic Conjecture 2 (I : IV)
Build-down → NONE, Hold → BOTH

	Opposition Set: SUPERIORITY > NONE Virtually all YES				Opposition Set: BOTH > NONE Some NO, NIFF, IFF-YES, YES+, YES++		
	MX	SDI	INV		MX	SDI	INV
Experts	26%	30%	63%	**Experts**	12%	31%	73%
Novices	38%	41%	55%	**Novices**	35%	50%	67%

PESSIMISTIC CONJECTURES

Pessimistic Conjecture 1 (II : IV)
Build-down → INFERIORITY, Hold → BOTH

Pessimistic Conjecture 2 (II : III)
Build-down → INFERIORITY, Hold → SUPERIORITY

	Opposition Set: BOTH > INFERIORITY IFF + YES				Opposition Set: SUPERIORITY > INFERIORITY Some NO, Many IFF, YES-BUT YES+, Some YES++		
	MX	SDI	INV		MX	SDI	INV
Experts	72%	83%	94%	**Experts**	57%	65%	65%
Novices	83%	82%	90%	**Novices**	57%	55%	60%

downs can't be assembled without optimistic conjectures that the adversary will reciprocate. Table 9.3 shows that this conclusion is quite general. The only exception would be populations where NO players are by themselves an outright majority. In those instances, unilateral initiatives gain majority support even under pessimistic conjectures.[20]

20 Figure 9.2 shows similar calculations for a build-down that proceeds from parity to inferiority. The reader can verify that nothing in a story with dichotomous choices depends on the point of departure (the game trees support identical coalitions). The analysis for moratoriums requires a more complicated extensive form and that preferences be measured over a range of deployments. I would anticipate similar results in these problems, but the data I've collected are too crude to provide them.

Now let's return to Gorbachev's problem, adopting the working hypothesis that preferences in the Soviet Union and the United States resembled those in our samples. If so, our data affirm Gorbachev's unilateral strategy in two ways. First, the data suggest that Optimistic Conjecture 2 was an appropriate belief about the American political system (i.e., about the politically active population of novices and experts). From the Soviet point of view, an IFF conjecture was consistent with the pivotal role played by IFFs in the American Arms Racing Coalition (in our data, IFF + NO > YES and IFF + YES > NO). Second, the data suggest for the Russian side that a majority of experts and novices would support unilateral build-downs if an optimistic conjecture were adopted (again, assuming American and Soviet preferences are similarly distributed). Under conjectures that are consistent with the preferences in the data, Gorbachev's unilateral strategy therefore appears to be coalitionally feasible.[21]

The basic difficulty Gorbachev faced (under our hypothesis) was maintaining the optimistic conjectures about American reciprocity on which his domestic coalition rested. To sustain broad domestic support for a program of demilitarization – and to rescue his grand strategy – Gorbachev therefore needed reciprocation from the United States. Just weeks after taking power, he told the editors of *Pravda*:

Confrontation is not an inborn defect of our relations. It is rather an anomaly. There is no inevitability at all of its continuation. We regard the improvement of Soviet–American relations not only as an extremely necessary but also as a possible matter. But, of course, one cannot do without reciprocity here. ["Pravda Interview with Gorbachev on Relations with U.S.," *N.Y. Times* A10, 4/8/85]

Simply building down unilaterally and transferring resources to the domestic economy was not politically tenable. As Gorbachev insisted later at the 27th Party Congress, "We repeat again and again: the Soviet Union lays no claim to more security, but it will not settle for less."

Perceptions of the Soviet's Type

To secure the reciprocity he needed, it was not enough merely to change Soviet policy. Gorbachev also had to demonstrate a long term commitment to the policy *Not Build*. Otherwise, IFFs in the United States would antici-

---

21 To interpret these results carefully, several caveats must be remembered. We don't know how well our data represent American political activists. We don't know how well they represent Soviet opinion. And finally, there is nothing that guarantees that the majority viewpoint in society will prevail inside real political institutions. A safer conclusion would be that nothing in our data contradicts the actions Gorbachev took, nor suggests that unilateral initiatives must encounter insuperable domestic obstacles.

Those who feel uncomfortable generalizing from our samples of respondents will feel even less confortable with the existing literature on cooperation, which draws sweeping policy conclusions with virtually no direct evidence about preferences at all.

pate future Soviet exploitation, and continue to hedge by funding military programs that had long developmental lead times (including SDI). Table 9.3 suggests that unilateral initiatives were in fact well designed for this purpose. Since most YES players consistently oppose them, whatever conjecture is made about the other side's likely response, unilateral initiatives would appear to send a strong signal that YES players were no longer controlling policy in the Soviet Union.

Or did they? To find out, I expanded the nuclear thinking questionnaire in the Fall of 1990 to solicit conjectures about the Soviets' nuclear preferences. Each respondent was asked to "assume the perspective of the current leadership of the Soviet Union" and to evaluate the several nuclear weapons systems from the other side's point of view. The respondents then imputed preference profiles to the Soviets, just as they had done for themselves. Notice that the questionnaire did not ask about Gorbachev personally. The responses can therefore be interpreted as conjectures about the Soviet policy-making apparatus, not just his personal preferences (see Figure 9.3).

The data I shall describe here came from 47 novices in October 1990 and 43 experts in March 1991. Both surveys followed the INF Treaty of December 1987, Gorbachev's UN speech of December 1988 (where he announced large unilateral conventional force reductions), the Soviet's withdrawal from Afghanistan by May 1989, the collapse of communism in Eastern Europe during late 1989, and some Soviet–American cooperation in the Gulf Crisis. The surveys preceded by several months the abortive coup of August 1991. Both samples followed historic events that were widely heralded as ending the Cold War. Of course, they also followed 40 years of tension and hostility, and they occurred amidst reports of growing domestic upheaval in the Soviet Union.

When he went to Washington to sign the INF Treaty in December 1987, Gorbachev spoke repeatedly about "fears and prejudices inherited from the cold war" and the need for struggle against "long-held emotions and ingrained stereotypes."[22] During the same visit, Caspar Weinberger warned against euphoria about the Soviet leader. "I think it's awfully early to conclude this is a warm, caring, trusting man who's not going to do anything wrong. He's got claws and every once in a while those claws come out."[23] It remained far from obvious, even amid Gorbachev's glowing reception in Washington, whether American thinking about the Soviets had substantially changed or not.

Figures 9.4 and 9.5 present the basic patterns in the conjectural data I

22 "A Tempered Optimism – At the End of an Unlikely Journey, Reagan and Gorbachev Are Mindful of Differences," *N.Y. Times* A1, 12/9/87.
23 "Washington Summit Song Is Off Key for Weinberger," *N.Y. Times* A1, 12/12/87.

Now assume the perspective of the current leadership in the Soviet Union. How do you believe they would evaluate the following outcomes (some actual, others potential) of the arms competition between the United States and Soviet Union? Give numerical values to each of the four alternatives, assigning ties when the choices seem about equal. [Rankings like {4,3,2,1} or {4,1,1,1} are both perfectly o.k.]

4 = Most Desirable   3 = Next best   2 = Next to last   1 = Least Desirable.

A. How about a race to develop an effective means to search out and destroy ballistic missile submarines?

_____ Both Sides have it   _____ Only the U.S. has it
_____ Only the U.S.S.R. has it _____ Neither Side has it

B. To develop ballistic missile defenses covering the entire national territory? [Suppose the defenses are less than perfect but not trivial either.]

_____ Both Sides have it   _____ Only the U.S. has it
_____ Only the U.S.S.R. has it _____ Neither Side has it

C. To develop highly accurate, multiple warhead ICBMs like the MX?

_____ Both Sides have it   _____ Only the U.S. has it
_____ Only the U.S.S.R. has it _____ Neither Side has it

D. To develop effective technologies for protecting nuclear forces from preemptive attack?

_____ Both Sides have it   _____ Only the U.S. has it
_____ Only the U.S.S.R. has it _____ Neither Side has it

E. To develop large-scale conventional forces?

_____ Both Sides have it   _____ Only the U.S. has it
_____ Only the U.S.S.R. has it _____ Neither Side has it

Figure 9.3 The Soviet perspective on the arms race

collected. For each of the classically destabilizing weapons, the columns describe the respondents' own game theoretic types, while the rows show the types attributed to the Soviet leadership. If people simply projected their own preferences on the Soviet Union, the data would concentrate along the main diagonal of each table. In fact, very little projection or mirror imaging seems to occur. Instead, the table suggests that beliefs about the Soviets were pessimistic across the board, even after the dramatic unilateral measures Gorbachev had taken. The arrows inside the tables show the median conjecture among respondents in each game theoretic category. One can see that the modal estimates of the Soviets' type were largely independent of the respondents' own preferences, and almost always in the YES range. By large majorities, ranging between 60% and 70% on every weapon, respondents of every political stripe and level of expertise regarded the Soviets as YES players.

The likely consequence, shown by the boxes inside the tables, was that only a small fraction of our respondents preferred without hesitation that the United States reciprocate Gorbachev's initiatives. The boxes surround the set who (in a one shot game of complete information) would select the policy *Not Build*, given their beliefs about the Soviets' type. The NOs prefer not to build regardless of the Soviet Union's type. But since the NOs never exceed 23% of the total, the critical players are the IFFs. Of these, only a handful regard the Soviets as NO or IFF-NO players, and therefore inclined to a policy of *Not Build*. When the Soviets are perceived to prefer *Build*, the IFFs will select *Build* themselves. As a result, the coalition that clearly prefers reciprocation remains only 25–35% of these samples.[24]

I found these results surprising and discouraging at the same time. Since no one's beliefs seemed consistent with Gorbachev's actions, nor to rest on simple projections of type, I wondered whether the conjectures might be random or haphazard. One check was to code the imputed Soviet profiles by heuristic family to see whether their flavors matched the respondents' own. If the security heuristic flavors matched, we would at least have a projection of strategic world view (though not of game theoretic type). If the imputed preferences implied that the Soviets' security heuristic vacillated from weapon to weapon, on the other hand, the conjectures would be suspect. Table 9.4 shows the results for the question about MIRVed ICBMs (the same pattern occurs for every weapon). Once again the projection hypothesis simply doesn't fly. Instead, virtually everybody, regardless of preference for SYMMETRY or STRENGTH, attributed the STRENGTH heuristic to the Soviet leadership (for experts, 97% of the codable cases;

---

24 Such calculations assume that the Soviets share the respondent's perception of the game. If the Soviets could not be assumed to perceive the respondent's type accurately, the question would be whether their misperceptions were optimistic or pessimistic. Unless Soviet misperceptions somehow ran toward mistaking IFFs for NOs, there would be even less reason to anticipate them to play *Not Build*.

If our respondents took a long term perspective on the arms race, viewing it as an iterated game of infinite duration, it could be argued that the IFF-NOs should attempt an arms control agreement with YES-BUTs, since both groups prefer NONE to BOTH. The same argument could be made for YES-BUTs playing each other. If so, the coalitions supporting *Not Build* in our data would reach a majority of novices and experts on MIRVed ICBMs but not SDI. It goes without saying that the respondents' conceptions of these games, their time horizons, and their perceptions of Soviet beliefs remain very much in doubt, and need to be studied empirically.

MX

NOVICES' TYPE

← Conditional Medians

SOVIET TYPE	NO	IFF-NO	IFF°, NIFF	IFF-YES	YES-BUT	YES+	YES++	zip	total count
NO	1	2	0	0	0	1	0	0	4
IFF-NO	0	4	1	0	0	0	0	0	5
IFF°, NIFF	1	0	1	0	0	0	0	0	2
IFF-YES	1	1	0	0	0	0	0	0	2
YES-BUT	5←	6←	4←	2←	2←	0	0	0	19←
YES+	3	2	1	0	1	2←	0	0	9
YES++	0	0	0	0	0	1	2←	0	3
zip	0	0	1	1	0	0	0	1	3
total count	11	15	8	3	3	4	2	1	47

66%

Projectors (% on Main Diagonal) — 26%   % for whom *Not Build* is equilibrium choice — 38%
(1 shot games)

NOVICES' TYPE

ASW

SOVIET TYPE	NO	IFF-NO	IFF°, NIFF	IFF-YES	YES-BUT	YES+	YES++	total count
NO	2	1	1	0	0	0	0	4
IFF-NO	1	2	0	1	0	0	0	4
IFF-YES	0	0	0	2	0	0	1	3
YES-BUT	1	4←	1	4←	3←	0	0	13
YES+	4←	4	1←	1	2	5←	1	18←
YES++	0	0	0	0	0	0	1←	1
zip	0	0	1	1	0	1	1	4
total count	8	11	4	9	5	6	4	47

68%

Projectors (% on Main Diagonal) — 32%   % for whom *Not Build* is equilibrium choice — 26%
(1 shot games)

NOVICES' TYPE

SDI

SOVIET TYPE	NO	IFF-NO	IFF°, NIFF	IFF-YES	YES-BUT	YES+	YES++	zip	total count
NO	2	1	0	0	0	0	0	0	3
IFF-NO	3←	3	0	2	0	0	0	1	9
IFF-YES	0	2	0←	2←	0	0	0	0	4
YES-BUT	3	1	3←	2	3←	0	0	0	12←
YES+	0	1	0	1	1	7←	3←	0	13
YES++	0	0	0	0	0	1	2	0	3
zip	1	1	1	0	0	0	0	0	3
total count	9	9	4	7	4	8	5	1	47

60%

Projectors (% on Main Diagonal) — 38%   % for whom *Not Build* is equilibrium choice — 28%
(1 shot games)

Fig. 9.4 Novices' perceptions of games with Soviets–Fall 1990

EXPERTS' TYPE   ← Conditional Medians   **MX**

SOVIET TYPE	NO	IFF-NO	IFF°, NIFF	YES-BUT	YES+	zip	total count
IFF-NO	2	6	0	0	0	0	8
YES-BUT	7←	7←	0	5←	0	0	19←
YES+	1	3	0	4	4←	0	12
zip	0	0	1	0	1	2	4
total count	10	16	1	9	5	2	43

72% (YES-BUT, YES+)

Projectors (% on Main Diagonal) — 35%

% for whom *Not Build* is equilibrium choice — 37%
(1 shot games)

EXPERTS' TYPE   **ASW**

SOVIET TYPE	NO	IFF-NO	IFF°, NIFF	IFF-YES	YES-BUT	YES+	zip	total count
NO	2	1	0	0	0	0	0	3
IFF-NO	2←	6	0	0	0	0	1	9
YES-BUT	3	8←	0	0	8←	1	0	20←
YES+	0	2	1←	1←	3	1←	0	8
zip	0	1	0	0	0	1	1	3
total count	7	18	1	1	11	3	2	43

65% (YES-BUT, YES+)

Projectors (% on Main Diagonal) — 40%

% for whom *Not Build* is equilibrium choice — 33%
(1 shot games)

EXPERT'S TYPE   **SDI**

SOVIET TYPE	NO	IFF-NO	IFF°, NIFF	IFF-YES	YES-BUT	YES+	YES++	total count
NO	2	0	0	0	0	0	0	2
IFF-NO	1←	7	0	1	0	0	1	10
YES-BUT	1	4	1←	0	3←	4	0←	13←
YES+	0	3	0	1	1	8←	1	14
zip	1	0	1	0	0	2	0	4
total count	5	14	2	2	4	14	2	43

63% (YES-BUT, YES+)

Projectors (% on Main Diagonal) — 42%

% for whom *Not Build* is equilibrium choice — 28%
(1 shot games)

Fig. 9.5 Experts' perceptions of games with Soviets–Spring 1991

Table 9.4. *Attributions of Strategic World View: MIRVed ICBMs*

Attributed Soviet Heuristic	Respondent's Security Heuristic				
	SYMMETRY	MIXTURE	STRENGTH	Unclear	Total
Novices - October 1990					
SYMMETRY	23.1	16.7	20.0	10.0	19.1
MIXTURE	7.7	0	0	0	4.3
STRENGTH	57.7	66.7	60.0	50.0	57.4
Unclear	11.5	16.7	20.0	40.0	19.1
Total	100%	100%	100%	100%	100%
Total n	26	6	5	10	47
Experts - March 1991					
SYMMETRY	0	0	0	0	0
MIXTURE	0	0	0	5.9	2.3
STRENGTH	87.5	60.0	92.3	47.1	69.8
Unclear	12.5	40.0	7.7	47.1	27.9
Total	100%	100%	100%	100%	100%
Total n	8	5	13	17	43

for novices, 71%). The vast majority continued to attribute a deterrence philosophy to the Soviets that Gorbachev had explicitly disavowed. Neither do the conjectures about world view seem haphazard. Table 9.5 shows that the attributions of the STRENGTH philosophy were highly consistent from weapon to weapon.

While the basis and depth of these conjectures remain uncertain, two things are clear. The respondents are highly consistent in their perceptions of the Soviets, whether we compare experts and novices, liberals and conservatives, or NOs and YESes.[25] At the same time, it is evident that the conjectures are not mechanical replications of the respondents' own preferences or heuristic style. Most went out of their way to indicate that the Soviets had different preferences than their own. Even after Gorbachev acquiesced to the revolutions in Eastern Europe, it appears that not nearly enough Americans perceived the kind of fundamental change in Soviet politics to sustain a large coalition for reciprocation.

Our data suggest the difficult political obstacles that Gorbachev confronted after Reykjavik, and explain a great deal, I believe, about the

25 Of course, our single shot observations can't rule out the possibility that American perceptions did evolve during Gorbachev's tenure, even if only from YES+ to YES-BUT. However, a series of New York Times /CBS NEWS Polls shows that the fraction who believed "the Cold War is over" changed very little during the period November 1989 to October 1990, hovering between 35% and 45%. *New York Times* A12, 10/16/90.

Table 9.5. *Consistency of security heuristics attributed to Soviet leaders*

	SYMMETRY	MIRVed ICBMs - Novices MIXTURE	STRENGTH	Unclear	Total
Invulnerable Platforms					
SYMMETRY	6	0	0	0	6
MIXTURE	2	0	2	1	5
STRENGTH	0	0	22	2	24
Unclear	1	2	3	6	12
Total	9	2	27	9	47
Ballistic Missile Defenses					
SYMMETRY	5	0	0	1	6
MIXTURE	1	1	1	0	3
STRENGTH	0	1	22	1	24
Unclear	3	0	4	7	14
Total	9	2	27	9	47
		MIRVed ICBMs - Experts			
Invulnerable Platforms					
SYMMETRY	0	0	1	0	1
MIXTURE	0	1	0	0	1
STRENGTH	0	0	21	3	24
Unclear	0	0	8	9	17
Total	0	1	30	12	43
Ballistic Missile Defenses					
SYMMETRY	0	0	1	0	1
MIXTURE	0	1	1	0	2
STRENGTH	0	0	23	3	26
Unclear	0	0	5	9	14
Total	0	1	30	12	43

political dynamics that followed. In order to break the deadlock with the Reagan conservatives, Gorbachev sought to mobilize political pressure on the American Administration with a series of bold unilateral initiatives. But because American perceptions of the Soviets were deep-seated, the initiatives did not crack the Grand Arms Racing Coalition. The Reagan and Bush Administrations were then left free to pocket Gorbachev's concessions without reciprocation. When his own domestic coalition eroded as a result, Gorbachev confronted a difficult dilemma. Slowing down his initiatives and taking a tough line to win favor at home would only reinforce the old stereotypes he was trying to break down in the United States (while compromising his grand strategy). Advancing his initiatives to increase pressure on the White House, on the other hand, could either break the

Grand Coalition in the United States or destroy his own domestic position. With each succeeding failure to consummate the "grand compromise" in arms control, Gorbachev's political situation became more difficult. He found himself caught in an escalating spiral of unilateral concessions, desperately seeking to fracture the White House's supporting coalition before his own collapsed.

Gorbachev's program after Reykjavik began fairly auspiciously when he successfully concluded the INF Treaty in 1987. He got the ball rolling in March by reversing the Soviets' insistence on a comprehensive arms agreement, suggesting instead that the problem of medium range missiles in Europe be singled out, and that a separate agreement on it "be concluded without delay."[26] After further concessions on short-range missiles, deployments in Asia, and intrusive verification, Gorbachev finally secured an agreement in December 1987. The treaty provided for the global elimination of short and intermediate range nuclear missiles. Even though it required a steeply asymmetrical build-down – the Soviets gave up roughly 1700 warheads to the Americans' 500 – and provided for unprecedented levels of on-site inspection, the Reagan Administration still encountered sharp resistance from Republican "hardliners."

The INF Treaty no doubt helped Gorbachev's program on two fronts. By giving up a small measure of superiority, he addressed the Americans' perceptions of the Soviets' type. By obtaining a formal arms agreement, he hoped to fuel optimism in his own country about future reciprocation. Gorbachev defended his initiative as a way to "create an atmosphere of greater trust."

We would like the agreement on medium-range missiles to stimulate talks on strategic arms reduction linked with nonwithdrawal from the ABM Treaty, to prompt the opening of talks on conventional armaments and to speed up progress in the elimination of chemical weapons. ["Gorbachev Looking to More Accords," *N.Y. Times* A6, 3/3/87]

But despite the enthusiastic press coverage Gorbachev received during the treaty signing,[27] the INF Treaty did not effect a major agreement on strategic weapons before Reagan's farewell summit in June 1988.[28] Disagreements about SDI testing remained the basic obstacle.

Gorbachev responded to the deadlock after the Washington Summit with a series of escalating unilateral moves. In February 1988, he declared that

---

26 "Moscow, in Reversal, Urges Agreement 'Without Delay' to Limit Missiles in Europe," *N.Y. Times* A1, 3/1/87.

27 See "Gorbachev a Hit with American Public," *N.Y. Times* A1, 12/4/87, but also, "President Assails Conservative Foes of New Arms Pact," A1, 12/4/87.

28 See "Gorbachev Voices Irritation at Slow Pace of Missile Talks," *N.Y. Times* A1, 6/1/88, and "Gorbachev Criticizes Reagan, Seeing 'Missed Opportunities,' but Calls Visit a 'Major Event,' " A1, 6/2/88.

the Soviets would withdraw from Afghanistan. In July, he offered to dismantle the controversial Krasnoyarsk radar, if the Americans would agree to nonwithdrawal from the ABM Treaty. And finally, in the most portentous concession of all, he announced in December at the UN that the Soviet Union would unilaterally reduce its conventional forces by 500,000 men, including 6 tank divisions in Eastern Europe.

Through these bold efforts, Gorbachev hoped to undermine the supporting coalition that Reagan had assembled (and Bush inherited) behind advanced weapon technologies like SDI, B-2, MX, Trident II, the cruise missile, satellite-based ASW, and ASAT. His efforts produced considerable apprehension among Republican strategists, who feared that he might succeed in splitting the NATO alliance and fracturing their domestic support.[29] The incoming Bush Administration nevertheless held firm, beginning its term by putting arms control on hiatus while it undertook "a comprehensive review."[30]

While Bush remained immersed in study, the domestic pressure on him began to grow. In April 1989, the *New York Times* reported that "as startling actions and proposals by the Soviet Union spread around the world, pressures are mounting on the Bush Administration to abandon its passive posture and respond to Moscow's initiatives." Senator Pell argued that the Administration "should be much more responsive," suggesting that if "Gorbachev isn't able to show results, his vote of confidence may just fade away." George Kennan testified that the United States "should not allow these initiatives from the Soviet side to go unrecognized."

But Bush Administration officials insisted that there was "no need to rush." On one hand, they claimed that "American influence was marginal, and that Gorbachev had no choice but to continue the process of liberaliza-

---

29 During the Washington summit, one senior Administration official complained that "there was no real movement on human rights. No real movement on Afghanistan. And yet you see in the media all these euphoric people who shook Gorbachev's hand, and they are now convinced that he's for world peace." During the same visit, worried White House strategists assembled focus groups to study public reactions to Gorbachev's speeches and statements. They reported that the "place where the bottom fell out for Gorbachev was when he mentioned Lenin. It just dropped to zero. It put everything back in perspective that he's a Communist." "Officials Wonder When Glow Will Fade," *N.Y. Times* A9, 9/12/87.

30 The tenor of Bush's approach became evident after Gorbachev's UN speech, when the President-elect responded in a press conference: "But really, it is too early to give a full analysis because I just don't know yet. I'm one who has been – always been a little bit cautious, and yet I don't want to seem negative. So I'll just have to wait on that one. . . . And so I welcome the flexibility and innovative steps that Mr. Gorbachev has taken but understand that we are not going to rush in to some proposal just to be hitting his bid." "Transcript of Bush's Remarks on Domestic and Foreign Issues," *N.Y. Times* A8, 12/15/88. See also, "Bush Says Talks on Strategic Arms Must Be Delayed – Sees Need for Prudence," *N.Y. Times* A1, 12/15/88; "Gorbachev in London Chides U.S. on Arms Talks," A8, 4/7/89; "White House Says There Is No Hurry to Arrange Summit Meeting," A10, 9/15/89.

tion regardless of what the United States does." On the other, they confessed to fears that "what is happening with the Russians isn't permanent, that it might be reversed, and so they don't want to get overcommitted."[31] Both arguments revealed the prevailing sentiment that the Soviets were really YES players, whose conciliatory behavior was forced by events, not chosen "by preference." Reciprocation would not change Soviet behavior, but would weaken the United States' position later when the YES players recovered their footing.

In May 1989, Bush welcomed "the eclipse of communism" in one of his first major foreign policy addresses, and warmly praised Gorbachev for the first time. He announced his desire to "integrate the Soviet Union into the community of nations." Officials attributed the conciliatory tone to a

realization by Mr. Bush himself that he is losing the international public relations war with Mr. Gorbachev and . . . needs to offer a portrait of himself as a forceful but flexible leader able to match Mr. Gorbachev. ["Bush Wishes Gorbachev Well on Soviet Changes," *N.Y. Times* A1, 5/25/89]

But in the same speech, Bush also announced his commitment to develop the mobile MX, the Midgetman, and eventually to deploy a "comprehensive defensive system, known as SDI." He further declared that "the Warsaw Pact's massive advantage in conventional forces . . . far exceeds the levels needed to defend legitimate security interests," and that Gorbachev's unilateral reductions "even if implemented, are not enough to eliminate the significant numerical superiority." Far from pushing a treaty on strategic weapons, the Administration shifted its focus to extracting new concessions in conventional forces. With a new priority in place, the START talks again faded into the background.[32]

The events during the early Bush Administration revealed the difficult obstacles Gorbachev faced on the American side. Though he succeeded in mobilizing noticeable public pressure on Bush, perceptions of the Soviets lagged far behind their behavior. The coalition supporting the defense budget remained intact, allowing the White House to pursue its natural inclination for STRENGTH. On issue after issue, they pocketed Gorbachev's

31 Bush insiders said the "key debate centers on the question of potential American influence on Mr. Gorbachev's present and future courses of action. One camp argues that American influence is marginal, the other that what the United States does matters a lot." "U.S. Urged to Respond to Soviet Initiatives," *N.Y. Times* A8, 4/7/89. The debate boiled down to whether Gorbachev's group were IFF types or not.

32 "Excerpts from President's Address at U.S. Coast Guard Academy," *N.Y. Times* A7, 5/25/89. The National Security Adviser Brent Scowcroft was reported to be sympathetic to arguments that "the United States should not move quickly to cut strategic arms as long as the Soviet Union maintains important advantages in conventional weapons." White House officials also refused to embrace "a more conciliatory approach on limiting the testing and deployment of 'Star Wars' antimissile systems," expressing reluctance to "tackle an issue that is likely to be divisive within the Administration." "U.S. Places Priority on Cut in Troops, Not Missiles" *N.Y. Times* A8, 4/7/89.

concessions without compromising the modernization programs they held dear. Keeping SDI and a START treaty at arms length, the Reaganites in Washington pressed to eliminate every category of Soviet superiority they could (including short and intermediate range forces, conventional forces in Europe, the heavily MIRVed SS-18s, and mobile SS-24s).

Because he could not reshape perceptions rapidly, Gorbachev gradually became trapped in a vicious cycle. Until he could mobilize a countercoalition to compel American reciprocity, he remained stymied by the Reagan team's understandable belief that SDI (and strategic modernization) was the "goose that laid the golden egg." But to break down the stereotypes that sustained the American buildup, Gorbachev was impelled toward ever bolder concessions of his own. As Alexandr Bessmertnykh admitted at one point, "We cannot live with a deadlock, particularly at the present time."

The pace of Gorbachev's initiatives only increased in 1989. In February, the Soviets completed their withdrawal from Afghanistan. In June, free elections took place in Poland. In August, Solidarity took power, apparently with active Soviet consent. In September, Shevardnadze dropped the Soviets' long-standing demand that non-withdrawal from the ABM Treaty be included in any agreement on offensive strategic forces. And finally, the unilateral campaign reached an historic climax during the fall, when Gorbachev refused to intercede as the Soviet empire crumbled in Eastern Europe, culminating with the collapse of the Berlin Wall in November 1989.

Even the Soviets' offer to drop their demands about SDI and the collapse of the Warsaw Pact failed to produce a START agreement at the Malta summit meeting in December 1989. The President pledged to "smooth the path toward lifting trade restrictions" and called for reductions in chemical weapons – proposals that Gorbachev eagerly embraced as "tangible evidence of the President's commitment to perestroika." But there were no new treaties or specific accords.[33] After much pleading from Gorbachev, Bush did agree to accelerate progress on the START talks, targeting the summit meeting in June 1990 as a reasonable deadline.

The "Bush initiatives," as the White House labelled them, were better designed to address the President's domestic problems than Gorbachev's.

---

33 The *New York Times* reported that "the significance of the first summit meeting between the leaders seemed more in the tone than the substance. . . . For all the cordiality, the meeting did not produce any new treaties, or specific agreements, or even a joint statement." "Bush and Gorbachev Proclaim a New Era for U.S.–Soviet Ties; Agree on Arms and Trade Aims," *N.Y. Times* A1, 12/4/89. See also, "Bush Gives Gorbachev Economic and Arms Proposals," *N.Y. Times* A1, 12/3/89; "Bush Proposes Steps to Help Improve the Soviet Union's Ailing Economy," A5, 12/3/89; "U.S. Shift on Arms Talks – President Decides to Try to Complete Pact on Strategic Weapons Before June Summit," A5, 12/3/89.

One senior official said "the White House was anxious to relieve the pressure on Mr. Bush, both at home and abroad, to deal more boldly with the Soviet Union." But just two days after the summit concluded, front page headlines in the *New York Times* announced "Communist Party Begins to Splinter Under Gorbachev." As it turned out, the ascendancy of Gorbachev's factional rivals would soon delay the START treaty again.[34]

While Bush was able to sustain his domestic coalition by tossing crumbs to the Soviets, Gorbachev returned home from Malta to growing discord. When James Baker testified before the Moscow Parliament in February 1990, he encountered open hostility about American intransigence. One deputy told Baker,

In this country, we also have our hawks and doves, and the actions of the United States in Panama provided additional argument to our hawks, especially after our summit meeting in Malta. . . . ["Baker Braves the Gauntlet in the Moscow Parliament," *N.Y. Times* A1, 2/11/90]

The most heated exchange occurred when the former Army Chief of Staff, Marshal Sergei Akhromeyev, decried the Americans' failure to reciprocate Soviet concessions:

Mr. Secretary, the Soviet Union has been reducing its armed forces for the last two years by 500,000 men and its military budget by 14 percent. The United States has barely reduced its armed forces and is only slightly reducing its military budget. I have the impression that while improving relations with us in the military sphere you continue to insist on acting in respect to the Soviet Union from a position of strength. ["Baker Braves the Gauntlet in the Moscow Parliament," *N.Y. Times* A1, 2/11/90]

Baker replied that "relations are improving because the peace has been maintained through strength, Marshal." Reporters described Baker's reaction to unfriendly questions as a "stick-it-in-your-ear, we-won-you-lost tone."

The trouble was that each succeeding failure to contain the American's high-tech spending spree deepened fears in the Soviet Union that the United States was exploiting its concessions. Making matters worse, the early returns from Gorbachev's military cutbacks had done nothing to arrest a deepening economic crisis. And perhaps most forbiddingly, in the aftermath of large conventional reductions and an outright revolution in Eastern Europe, the Soviets suddenly faced a reuniting Germany without any buffer to hold them at bay.

Throughout 1990, Gorbachev's domestic position steadily deteriorated as ethnic and economic strife escalated, the Soviets' military position eroded, and no substantial concessions or treaties materialized with the West. As resentment grew, the YES players in the Soviet government

34 "Communist Party Begins to Splinter Under Gorbachev," *N.Y. Times* A1, 12/6/89.

began more boldly to challenge Gorbachev's strategy. Shortly after Baker's visit, progress toward a START agreement stalled when the Soviets intervened harshly in Lithuania and rebuffed an American proposal to ban land-based MIRVed ICBMs. The Soviets suddenly insisted that any agreement must cut submarine-based ballistic missiles, the heart of the American strategic arsenal, as well. The disagreement arose after reports in February that all the outstanding issues on START had been settled.[35]

These setbacks were widely interpreted to mean that military leaders had reasserted themselves at Gorbachev's expense. They also demonstrated how difficult it was for Gorbachev to reshape perceptions of the Soviet Union in an atmosphere of active factional struggle. Describing the mood in Washington, Senator Bob Dole wondered out loud:

Do we really know Gorbachev? How long is he going to be around? Should we just whack away at our defense budget? What are they doing? Where is their peace dividend? . . . People are thinking "Yeah, this is sort of a wake-up call." ["A Baltic Chill on Relations – Momentum is Slower in Superpower Talks," *N.Y. Times* 4/8/90]

But more fundamental than doubts about Gorbachev himself was the uncertain direction of factional politics in the Kremlin. As one senior Administration official put it:

We have no real idea just how much pressure he is under. For all the glasnost and democratization and perestroika, we know as little today about high politics in the Soviet Union as we did in the Brezhnev regime. It is as opaque to us now as it was 10 years ago in terms of who is doing what to whom, who is cutting what deals, where the pressure is, the interpersonal dynamics of the top dozen leaders. ["U.S. Shows Doubts About Gorbachev and Future Pacts," *N.Y. Times* 5/13/90]

Another official surmised that Gorbachev

. . . sees how much he is going to need the army. So he promotes Yazov to a marshal, makes several nice speeches about the military. [With the prospect of domestic turmoil] it is more important to know that when he beckons, the army will come than it is to ice a deal with George Bush. ["U.S. Shows Doubts About Gorbachev and Future Pacts," *N.Y. Times* 5/13/90]

With the durability of Gorbachev's supporting coalition in growing doubt, the pressure on Bush to conclude a major agreement on long range ballistic missiles dwindled. The June 1990 summit came and went without a treaty. Later that fall, the announcement that Gorbachev had won the Nobel Peace prize was greeted in the Soviet Parliament "with five seconds of lukewarm applause." Critics denounced Gorbachev's failed grand strategy, charging that he had "sapped Soviet strength and prestige by his liberation of Eastern Europe and slashing of the military." Said one deputy, "Even I could defend the interests of the Soviet Union in this way, by

---

35 *N.Y. Times*: "U.S. and Soviets Appear to Agree on Main Elements of Arms Treaty," A1, 2/11/90; "U.S. and Soviets Differ over Ban on Multiple-Warhead Missiles," A1, 4/8/90.

making concessions, unjustified concessions." Because he never mobilized enough pressure to extract major concessions from the Reagan–Bush group, Gorbachev found himself in the worst of all worlds. His unilateral cutbacks of the Soviet military had neither rejuvenated the Soviet economy nor induced reciprocity from the United States, leaving the Soviet Union weakened within and without.[36]

In the end, the START I agreement calling for 30% reductions in the strategic arsenals was signed on July 31, 1991, just days before the coup that removed Gorbachev from power. In the race to see whose domestic coalition would collapse first, the treaty arrived with too little too late.

The multileveled interactions between Gorbachev's international strategy for arms control and the restructuring of Soviet domestic life assumed historic proportions with the collapse of the Communist Party. While it is evident that a crumbling productive system and incipient economic chaos contributed directly to the fall of the Communists, there are several ways that the failure of Gorbachev's security strategy can be implicated in the latest Russian Revolution. First, the lack of reciprocity from the United States precluded truly major arms reductions that might have produced a significant peace dividend for Gorbachev. This link is the weakest, I believe, because it is doubtful that the Soviet war machine could have been converted in the short run to domestic consumer production. Second, the escalating spiral of concessions that Gorbachev fell into produced the fateful decision of December 1988 to withdraw Soviet conventional forces from Eastern Europe. This move clearly signalled the slackening of Soviet support for repressive puppet governments in the region, who then fell like dominoes within a period of months. Gorbachev's conventional initiative undoubtedly helped precipitate the revolutions of 1989, which in turn unleashed violent centrifugal forces within the Soviet republics. Finally, Gorbachev's unrequited concessions and the undoing of the Soviet empire deeply angered the STRENGTH factions in Moscow, who engineered the coup against him. The coup proved to be the undoing of the Communist Party, which collapsed completely when the plot unravelled.

Shortly after the August coup, the *New York Times* proclaimed that "with the precipitous decline in Soviet power and the crumbling of the Soviet economy, all of the political momentum is running against military spending."[37] In this pithy commentary on nuclear cooperation, one sees the ultimate political hurdle that Mikhail Gorbachev never overcame. In the

---

36 "Talks Fail to End Disputes on Long-Range Weapons," *N.Y. Times* 6/2/90; "Outlook Is Cloudy for an Arms Deal by U.S. and Soviets – Military Influence in Moscow Concerns American Aides," *N.Y. Times* A1, 2/6/91; "Gorbachev's Prize – Soviet Leader is Regarded as a Hero Everywhere but in His Own Country," *N.Y. Times* A12, 10/16/90.
37 "Battle Cry in Congress – Lawmakers Brace for a Fight on Arms," *N.Y. Times* A1, 10/1/91.

end, it took the collapse of the Warsaw Pact, the fall of the Communist Party, and the disintegration of the Soviet Union to convince Washington that the Cold War was over.

CONCLUDING REMARKS

In this chapter, I have tried to suggest how a new approach to measuring nuclear preferences might advance our understanding of basic strategic questions about nuclear cooperation and the arms race. I appreciate that many caveats can be raised about the measurements I have exploited here. Certainly, I have extrapolated liberally from a relatively small sample of respondents. Without further data, there is no way to know whether the extrapolations are valid. The nuclear thinking data measure preferences over ultimate outcomes in the arms race, posed as simple dichotomies (build a weapon system or not). Understanding the step-by-step logic of a nuclear build-down may well require more refined measurements about a full continuum of deployments. Our measurement procedure elicits preferences weapon by weapon, without recognizing interdependencies among them – say between preferences about SDI and the configuration of MIRVed ICBMs. The price to be paid for the extra realism, of course, would be greater complexity and statistical instability. It is naive to believe that more realism always produces deeper understanding and better forecasts. Nonetheless, the measurement techniques proposed here are still in their infancy. Much remains to be learned about doing them well.

With all these caveats in mind, I hope the detailed calculations in this chapter will at least give pause. The major lesson, I believe, is that without taking preferences seriously, there is no hope of understanding nuclear politics during or after the Cold War. Preference formation has been woefully neglected in international relations, even though the dominant models of explanation all reason from preferences to behavior. In the unitary state actor approach, theorists have been content to specify preferences axiomatically, as if they were self-evident. In the domestic politics approach, preferences have been specified anecdotally, and incompletely. The trouble is that nuclear preferences are too diverse and too complex to be specified casually. Our evidence shows that domestic conflicts about national security necessarily become linked across state boundaries because many people's preferred policy depends upon what the other side does. Without carefully constructed measurements that describe for how many people these dependencies exist, and on what issues, there is no hope of unraveling coalition formation within countries or the strategic interactions between them. To understand unilateral initiatives, the politics of arms control, the end of the Cold War, nuclear proliferation, or international cooperation, one has to count heads.

Chapter 10

Nuclear Thinking After the Cold War

Since communism collapsed in Russia and Eastern Europe, we take it for granted that the nuclear arms race has been radically transformed. But has national security increased or decreased since the Cold War ended? Is nuclear war more or less likely than it was before? What will remain of the Cold War arsenals in the future? That these basic questions remain clouded in uncertainty suggests how little we really understand about the transformation called "the end of the Cold War." Intuitively, we appreciate that great events happened, but what they mean politically is anything but clear. In this final chapter, I would like to address one important piece of the puzzle by investigating how nuclear thinking changed after the Soviet Bloc collapsed and the nuclear arms race ground to a halt.

From a strategic perspective, understanding the mechanism(s) that support the current respite in the nuclear arms race is a fundamental problem. Within the analytical framework explored in this book, two main explanations are plausible, each with very different implications. One possibility is that nuclear preferences have remained more or less fixed, while the coalitions that control nuclear policy have been rearranged. We learned in the last chapter that the strategy combination [*Not Build, Not Build*] can become a stable coalitional equilibrium when the coalitions NO + IFF secure a controlling position in both domestic arenas. Each side can then demonstrate a credible commitment to not building, and nobody in either controlling coalition will be motivated unilaterally to defect from a cooperative strategy. The nuclear thinking data suggest that NO + IFF is a sizable majority in the United States. It may be as well in Russia. Thus, explaining the current cooperative equilibrium does not necessarily require any shift in nuclear preferences.

The trouble, if this explanation is right, is that STRENGTH players with YES profiles have in the past dominated military policies. If the YESes should regain a controlling position in either country, the NO + IFF coalitions could be split, inverting the process that finally stopped the arms race. This possibility has worried writers and officials on both ends of the political spectrum, even from the beginning of the Gorbachev period. While conservatives invoke the specter of "Weimar Russia" to remind us that the benign coalition now governing Russia could be replaced by an uglier and more dangerous regime, liberals urge us to lend more support to the embryonic Russian democracy.[1] Both arguments suggest that the post-Cold War build-down rests on a reversible coalitional alignment held together by the "liberal" character of the Russian regime.

Unpleasant scenarios about Weimar Russia raise the question whether deeper changes in nuclear thinking – what Boris Yeltsin once called "personal perestroika" – might have reshaped the distribution of nuclear preferences that drove the Cold War arms race. Have the difficult economic hardships of the transition period, and the new political conditions in Europe, so transformed how people understand world politics and national security that nuclear weapon building has lost all appeal? Do the patterns of preference we observed before August 1991 represent political thinking that died with the Cold War? Or does essentially the same constellation of political types remain in the game, configured now in new policy coalitions that might still be rearranged in the future? Clearly, the more the distribution of preferences has shifted toward the NO end of the game theoretic spectrum, the more robust the current equilibrium will be against political shocks in the future. Indeed, if the NO coalitions become sufficiently large, then factional politics in Russia (or the U.S.) would no longer threaten the cooperative equilibrium. *Not Build* would be a dominant strategy for large majorities, and the Cold War nuclear arms race would literally be dead.

Inquiring whether there has been a shift away from YES thinking toward the NO and IFF-NO profiles raises larger questions about the cognitive foundations of the nuclear preferences and the roots of public opinion. Table 9.1 suggests that these core opponents of arms racing and weapons procurement come disproportionately from the SYMMETRY family. To skew the distribution of nuclear preferences against the arms race seems to require broader acceptance of the SYMMETRY philosophy of deterrence. But the security heuristics have strong ideological overtones among experts and novices alike. It could be argued, then, that the robustness of the nuclear peace ultimately depends on the cognitive foundations of nuclear thinking and the roots of ideology. Are people's strategic intuitions rooted in abstract general principles, or do they reflect political characteristics of the adversary and immediate political circumstances? Either hypothesis might explain the relationship we discovered between the security heuristic

---

1 In early 1992, Defense Secretary Dick Cheney advised lawmakers that "the possibility of an economic train wreck that would yield a very ugly regime in Russia can not be wished away." "Cheney Issues Warning on Defense Cuts," *L.A. Times* A15, 2/1/92. His warning is typical of a large body of analysis.

flavors and ideological orientation, but each carries different implications about the end of the Cold War.

An explanation of the first kind recognizes the strong cognitive parallels between SYMMETRY and STRENGTH, on one hand, and the core intuitions of liberalism and conservatism on the other.[2] The central idea of liberal theory is equality. From the fundamental principle that "all men are created equal," it is argued that everyone should enjoy equal rights, equal protection before the law, equal opportunity, and even equality of welfare. One-person-one-vote, affirmative action, progressive taxation, universal suffrage, free public education, busing, and draft lotteries are among the many leveling policies that derive from these arguments. It seems plausible that the SYMMETRY philosophy of deterrence would have strong intuitive appeal for those who believe that people everywhere are essentially the same, and that equality is morally the most persuasive arrangement for society.[3]

STRENGTH, on the other hand, seems consistent with the modern day conservative's belief in social hierarchy. The conservative supports laissez faire economic policies and minimal government so that the best and the brightest – the smartest, most entrepreneurial elements of society – can rise to the top, making everyone richer as they go. Social inequality and the maldistribution of wealth are accepted as necessary consequences of free market competition in which only the fittest survive. At the same time, the conservative wants aggressive police departments, freely available hand guns, and the death penalty to protect "decent folks" from the criminal element. Core curriculums in schools and universities defend basic Western values against the cultural assaults of outsiders. All of these positions reflect an intuition that not all people are created equal, that some people are better than others, and that everyone benefits when the cream has the "freedom" to rise to the top.[4] That superiority is a virtue in a nuclear competition between "us and them" seems like a natural corollary.

2 I use the terms in their contemporary sense, recognizing that historically they have different connotations.
3 One could equally well argue that liberalism is a philosophy that elaborates moral intuitions about social symmetry. The social and military philosophies would then be related to each other by the primitive social intuitions they share in common. For interesting discussions about the idea(s) of equality in liberal thought, see Amy Guttman, *Liberal Equality* (New York: Cambridge University Press, 1980), and Douglas Rae et al., *Equalities* (Cambridge: Harvard University Press, 1981). For discussions about intuitive foundations of liberal attitudes, see David Sears, Leonie Huddy, and Lynitta Schaffer, "A Schematic Variant of Symbolic Politics Theory, as Applied to Racial and Gender Equality" in Richard Lau and David Sears, eds., *Political Cognition* (Hillsdale, N.J.: Lawrence Erlbaum Associates, 1986) and Jennifer Hochschild, *What's Fair?* (Cambridge: Harvard University Press, 1981).
4 As Rae and many other political theorists have noticed, "the most profound difficulty for egalitarianism in all its forms arises from the persistence of human diversity." Douglas Rae et al., *Equalities* (Cambridge: Harvard University Press, 1981), p. 82.

If strategic heuristics are rooted in general social intuitions about equality and hierarchy, then it is not clear that the collapse of the Soviet Union will have changed nuclear preferences very much. If we don't expect conservatives to become liberals because the Cold War is over, then it isn't evident that STRENGTH partisans should suddenly embrace SYMMETRY. With the collapse of the Soviet threat, the watchword among many conservatives has been that "it's still a dangerous world out there." Because there are always bad guys on the loose, they argue, we must remain vigilant and maintain our military strength.

Another kind of explanation involves the image of the enemy in the choice of security heuristic. No one, not even the purest classical thinkers, advocated that mutual assured destruction should define our relationship with Saddam Hussein. In the Gulf War, virtually everyone preferred the kind of overwhelming superiority that allowed us to destroy his military machine before it could harm our vital interests. Likewise, no one advocates that we maintain overwhelming nuclear superiority against the Canadians or Italians. As Brent Scowcroft argued in a critique of Reagan's strategy, "Soviet nuclear weapons are in a different category than, say, British or French ones." Such observations suggest that the choice of security heuristic depends on political attributes of the adversary. But which attributes? And why should ideological identification intervene in how adversaries are perceived?

Much of the strategic debate about the Soviet Union turned on how much weight should be given to its totalitarian form of government. Classical defenders of mutual deterrent stability argued that the Soviets shared with us an overriding common interest in avoiding nuclear war, and that this common interest compelled them to accept mutual deterrence just as we did (or supposedly did). In the face of a global nuclear catastrophe, their form of government made little difference. But many conservatives argued that the Soviets were intractably aggressive precisely because of their totalitarian, Communist ideology. Because it prescribed a life and death struggle against capitalism, communism required the capability to fight and win a nuclear war. To deter Communists therefore required sufficient military superiority to overwhelm their strike-first forces.

In these examples, the relationship between security philosophy and political ideology appears to be mediated by thinking about the adversary's political system. The more similar (or palatable) the political system appears, the more plausible the SYMMETRY heuristic becomes, and *vice versa*. Because the Soviets' egalitarian, anti-market ideology was more congenial to liberals than it was to conservatives, it was easier for liberals to discount the Soviets' totalitarian politics in strategic calculations. Conversely, the more powerful the SYMMETRY heuristic's appeal, the easier it is to perceive common interests in the face of political differences. If these conjectures are on the right track, then the democratization of the Soviet Union might have had substantial effects on people's nuclear thinking and weapons preferences by making the SYMMETRY heuristic more popular.

Ordinarily, it would be difficult to untangle with survey data whether perceptions about the Soviet Union or general ideological predispositions controlled the security heuristics. The two explanatory variables tend to be confounded together, and no opportunity exists to manipulate them independently as we would in an experiment. During our study, however, fortune intervened by performing a social experiment of historical proportions. Because the regimes in Eastern Europe and the Soviet Union changed so dramatically as our rolling cross sections accumulated, it is possible to investigate how the collapse of communism affected basic strategic intuitions and the nuclear weapons preferences they support. In fact, the nuclear thinking data may be unique in affording these opportunities.

To allow comparisons before and after the Soviet Union collapsed in the Fall of 1991, I collected two additional samples in early 1993 – one of novices in January (the Nuclear Predicament undergraduate class again), and another of experts in May (professional strategic analysts at RAND Corporation). The surveys followed closely upon the START II agreement that dramatically reduced nuclear forces and largely eliminated the land-based MIRVed ICBMs that had been the heart of the Soviet arsenal. They occurred many months after the Communist Party had been overthrown in Russia, and a democratic regime created in its place. These events surely removed all doubts that the Cold War was over. The new samples therefore provide interesting evidence about the impact on nuclear thinking when the enemy is radically transformed. They also create an opportunity for statistical cross-validation of the results from earlier chapters.

HOW DID THE END OF THE COLD WAR AFFECT NUCLEAR PREFERENCES?

Let's begin by exploring how the heuristic calculations of novices and experts might have changed with the collapse of communism. Table 10.1 displays the novice respondents' choice of security heuristic in samples collected between October 1988 and January 1993. These calculations describe all the weapon profiles combined (four per respondent). Among novices, the frequency of the SYMMETRY heuristic increased noticeably between 1988 and 1990, while the percentage of profiles based on STRENGTH diminished. When I completed the first draft of this book, I was convinced by this evidence that a basic dependency existed between the character of the adversary's regime

Table 10.1 *Novices' choice of security heuristic by year (all weapon profiles combined)*

	1988 October	1989 October	1990 October	1988-1990 Total	1993 January	Grand Total
SYMMETRY	17.3	36.9	44.7	30.0	32.6	30.5
MIXTURE	18.3	17.0	12.8	16.4	18.0	16.7
STRENGTH	32.1	26.1	16.0	26.0	26.7	26.2
Unclear	32.4	19.9	26.6	27.5	22.7	26.5
Total	100%	100%	100%	100%	100%	100%
Total n	312	176	188	676	172	848

and the novice's strategic world view. As the opponent's political system became more like our own, the strategic principle of SYMMETRY became intuitively more plausible.

The hypothesis now appears far less compelling in light of new evidence gathered in 1993. Even though the Russian political system became much more like ours when the Communists fell from power in August 1991, the incidence of the security heuristic flavors in 1993 matched the average totals of the earlier period virtually exactly. As you can see, the popularity of SYMMETRY actually decreased between 1990 and 1993 – contrary to the hypothesized effect. One might be tempted by the table to argue that the main impact of Russian liberalization had already occurred between 1988 and 1989 (when the use of SYMMETRY increased most sharply). But why would the main effect appear before the Revolutions of 1989 swept Eastern Europe and the Communist Party fell from power in Russia? If the security heuristic reflects immediate political circumstances, shouldn't those events produce the larger movement in strategic thinking? To me, the most convincing interpretation of the table is that the collapse of communism had almost no effect on the strategic intuitions of novices. The movement we see in the table appears to be random fluctuation, from sample to sample, around a stable baseline.

Figure 10.1 shows how the relationship between the novices' ideological self-descriptions and their heuristic choices evolved over time. In this picture, the pattern in 1988, 1989, and 1993 is virtually identical, while the sample from 1990 stands apart as unusual. In fact, were it not for the two anomalous middle-of-the-road categories in 1990, we would say that all four samples look alike. There is in every year a robust relationship between ideological position and choice of the SYMMETRY heuristic, and the relationship shows little displacement, if any, over time. Taken to-

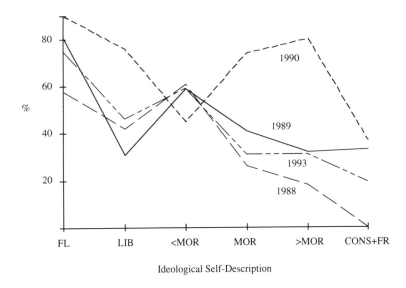

Figure 10.1 Percentage of novices choosing SYMMETRY flavor by ideological identification, over time

gether, the evidence suggests that heuristic nuclear thinking changed very little as the Cold War unraveled, even after the Soviet Union had unambiguously disintegrated. Instead, it appears that the novice's strategic world view is highly abstract and unresponsive to political events.

Did the experts' thinking respond more noticeably to the dramatic happenings? Figure 10.2 compares the expert samples collected before the Revolutions of 1989 to those collected afterward. The latter group includes the new set of responses from strategic analysts at RAND Corporation, collected in May 1993. Here again, one would be hard pressed to discern any flux at all in the heuristic frequencies. Not only do the two curves look very similar, but, if anything, the total incidence of the SYMMETRY heuristic *declined* after 1989. The impression of stability in the heuristic frequencies is only reinforced by the remarkable similarity between the expert and novice samples. Figure 10.3 shows that neither expert learning nor profound social revolutions appear to displace the strategic predispositions that already develop in young adults. The heuristic foundations of intuitive deterrence theories seem remarkably stable and robust.

These findings explain why we find very little movement in the distributions of game theoretic types for the various nuclear weapon systems. Because the end of the Cold War did not produce a mass embrace of the

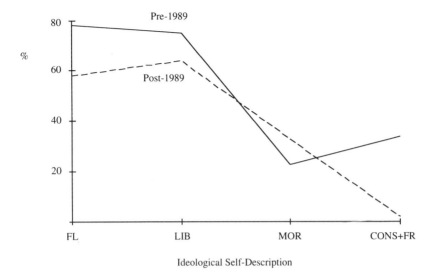

Figure 10.2 Percentage of experts choosing SYMMETRY flavor by ideological identification, before and after the Revolutions of 1989

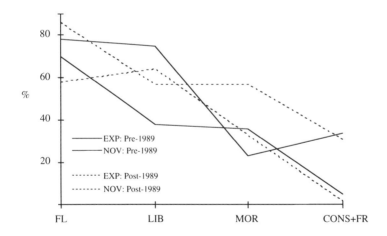

Figure 10.3 Choice of SYMMETRY flavor before and after the Revolutions of 1989

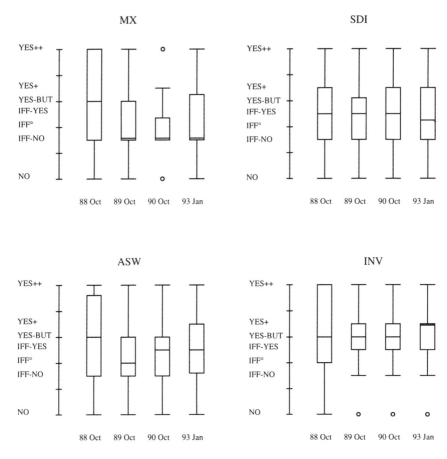

Figure 10.4 Novices: distribution of game theoretic types over the end of the Cold War

SYMMETRY heuristic, the core supporters for arms control (NO and IFF-NO types) have not become a dominant majority, nor even substantially more numerous than they were before. Figure 10.4 compares the distribution of game theoretic types, from NO to YES++, among novices, during the period from 1988 to 1993. In these Tukey boxplots, each box spans the middle 50% of the cases along the game theoretic spectrum (the interquartile range of the distribution). The line inside each box identifies the game theoretic type of the median respondent (or, the "median voter" if you wish). The whiskers emanating from the boxes extend (more or less) to the extremes of each distribution, excluding outliers that are identified by small circles. The pictures contrast the center, the spread, and the shape of each distribution, thereby revealing movements in political opinion about the various nuclear weapon systems.

Though the distributions in Figure 10.4 are not absolutely stable (how could they be in widely separated samples collected over a 5 year period?), they certainly do not betray any systematic trend toward nuclear "dovishness." Among the four weapon systems, a majority coalesces in the NO + IFF-NO categories only for the MX missile. The location of the median game theoretic type typically moves up and down a bit, with no clear direction or trend. Neither does the shape or spread of these distributions show any consistent movement. The sample of novices from 1988 appears to be the most diverse (the boxes are longest), and the most inclined toward YES profiles (at least for MX and ASW). Otherwise, the end of the Cold War seems to have little effect on the novices' inclination to support nuclear armaments building.

Figure 10.5 tells a similar story for the experts. If anything, the expert distributions become more hawkish, not less, after 1989. Figure 10.6 compares two samples of experts from the RAND Corporation, the first responding in March 1991 (well before the coup against Mikhail Gorbachev) and the second in May 1993 (after the START II Treaty was signed). The RAND comparisons are more telling, I believe, because they come from a single stable population. The pictures show virtually no movement in the distribution of types, except for SDI, which attracts more positive support in 1993 than it had in 1991. Table 10.2 shows the swing toward SDI comes from a sharp increase in the fraction of experts identifying territorial defenses as a GOOD weapon, an interesting legacy, perhaps, of the Scud-Patriot exchanges in the Gulf War.

To sum up, none of our samples sustains the idea that distribution of support for nuclear weapons systems has tilted toward the NO end of the game theoretic spectrum. The core constituency for arms control has not increased in size, among either experts or novices. Neither the preference profiles themselves, nor their underlying heuristic structure, suggests that the collapse of communism affected nuclear thinking. We cannot conclude, therefore, that the end of the Cold War arms race rests upon a massive redistribution of preferences. Instead, nuclear preferences, like the strategic intuitions that support them, have remained more or less fixed.

PERCEPTIONS OF THE RUSSIAN ADVERSARY

If the respondents' own nuclear preferences were not moved by the end of the Cold War, what about their perceptions of the other side? In the last chapter, we saw that both experts and novices overwhelmingly perceived

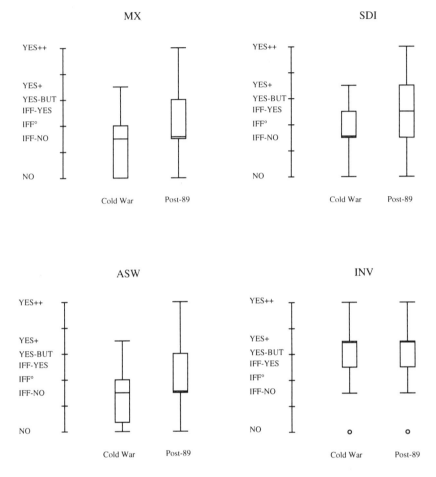

Figure 10.5 Experts' game theoretic types before and after the Revolutions of 1989

the Soviet leadership to be YES players in the arms race, even after Mikhail Gorbachev's concerted efforts to persuade Americans that the Soviet regime no longer understood security to rest on STRENGTH. These inferences were based on measurements collected in late 1990 and early 1991 that tapped respondents' conjectures about the nuclear preferences of Russia's "current leaders." With two additional samples from 1993, we can now explore the trajectory of these conjectures after the Soviet regime collapsed.

Figures 10.7 and 10.8 compare, for novices and experts, the game theo-

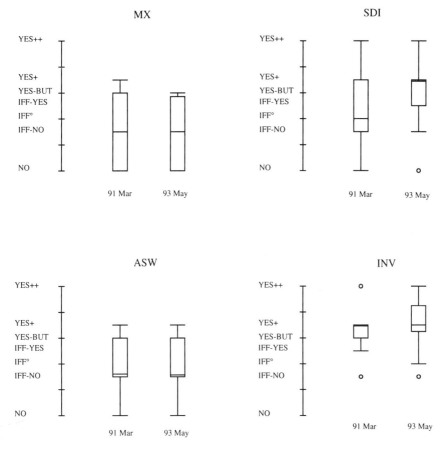

Figure 10.6 RAND experts: game types before and after the collapse of the
Soviet Union

retic types attributed to "the current leadership" in Russia, before and
after the overthrow of communism. The main movement in these conjectures occurs for the MX-like MIRVed ICBMs, which were banned from
both arsenals in the START II agreement. Both experts and novices were
considerably more likely to identify the Russians as NOs or IFF-NOs in the
later samples. Similar movements occurred for the anti-submarine warfare
capabilities, while the attributions for SDI and INVULNERABLE nuclear
platform remained largely unchanged.

To appreciate what drives these perceptions of the Russians' nuclear
preferences, we can decompose the imputed profiles into their heuristic

Table 10.2 *RAND Experts' choice of weapon heuristic for SDI, by year*

	March 1991	May 1993	Total
BAD	44.2	19.4	33.8
GOOD	34.9	71.0	50.0
SWEET POISON	7	0	4
Unclear	14.0	9.7	12.2
Total	100%	100%	100%
Total n	43	31	74

components. Tables 10.3 and 10.4 break down the profiles for the MIRVed ICBM missiles, showing the imputed security and weapon heuristics, and the resulting distributions of game theoretic types. Among the novices, the fraction who perceive the Russians as STRENGTH players is virtually identical, before and after the fall of the Communist Party ($\approx$ 71% of codable profiles). Neither is there very much movement in the imputed weapon heuristics, the main change being a slight increase in the POISON PILL profiles. As a result, the imputed distribution of game theoretic types changes relatively little. The fraction of the novices who place the Russians in NO and IFF-NO categories increases from 19% to 30%, while the fraction seeing them as YES players stays the same (66% to 67.5%). In this way, the distribution of perceptions becomes more polarized, with the main movement occurring from the IFF-YES to the IFF-NO range. Taken all together, the novices' perceptions of the Russians do shift after the end of the Cold War, but hardly in a dramatic fashion.

The experts, on the other hand, respond much more noticeably to the dramatic reductions in the nuclear arsenals, and the START agreement to eliminate land-based MIRVs. In May 1993, 48% of the experts imputed NO or IFF-NO profiles to the Russian leadership on the MX-like systems, where only 19% had done so in March of 1991. The experts' perception of the Russians as STRENGTH players also decreases quite sharply (from 97% of codable profiles to only 61%). The experts became more likely to read the Russians as SYMMETRY players (including the SYMMETRY + STRENGTH mixture) who understand the land-based MIRV as a BAD weapon.

One might wonder why the imputed distributions of game types changed so little for the other weapons, when more and more of the experts perceived the Russians as SYMMETRY players. The answer is *not* because the imputed security heuristic changed from weapon to weapon. The world view attributed to the Russians is highly stable across weapons, as we

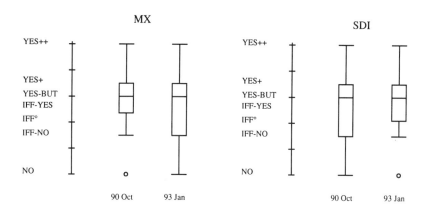

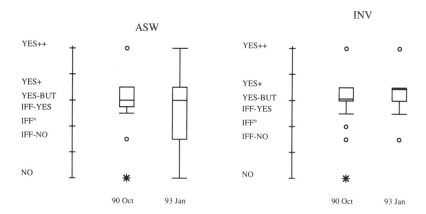

Figure 10.7 Game types imputed to Russian leaders, by novices, before and after the overthrow of communism

should expect. Instead, the wider attribution of SYMMETRY was some-times offset by countervailing movements in the weapon heuristic, as Table 10.5 illustrates for SDI. Not only did the experts themselves become more likely to perceive territorial missile defenses as a GOOD weapon, they became more likely to attribute the GOOD weapon flavor to the Russians as well. The combined movements in the security and weapon flavors more or less "canceled out," leaving the distribution of perceived game theoretic types no more dovish than before.

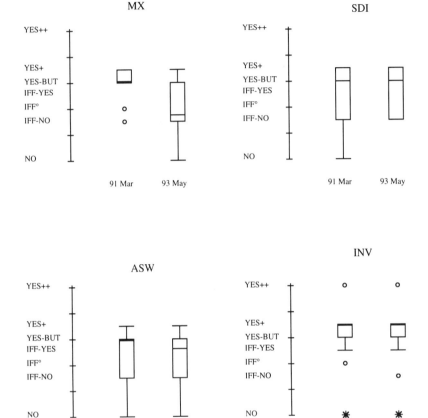

Figure 10.8 Game types imputed to Russian leaders, by experts, before and after the overthrow of communism

A FRAGILE NUCLEAR PEACE?

Our data suggest that the cooperative equilibrium we now observe in the nuclear arms race rests not on any fundamental change in nuclear thinking, nor upon any substantial redistribution of nuclear preferences. Rather, the main effect of the collapse of communism appears to be shifting perceptions of the *Russians'* nuclear preferences. These shifts are more pronounced among experts than novices, and may reflect the experts' greater awareness of Russian strategic behavior. Nothing about the results implies

Table 10.3. *Novices: game type and heuristics*
imputed to Russian leaders, MX-type missiles,
before and after the overthrow of communism

	October 1990	January 1993	Total
Novices: Russian Security Heuristic - MX			
SYMMETRY	19.1	2.3	11.1
MIXTURE	4.3	18.6	11.1
STRENGTH	57.4	55.8	56.7
Unclear	19.1	23.3	21.1
Total	100%	100%	100%
Total n	47	43	90
Novices: Russian Weapon Heuristic - MX			
BAD	53.2	53.5	53.3
GOOD	25.5	23.3	24.4
SWEET POISON	4.3	11.6	7.8
Unclear	17.0	11.6	14.4
Total	100%	100%	100%
Total n	47	43	90
Novices: Russian Game Type - MX			
NO	8.5	4.7	6.7
IFF-NO	10.6	25.6	17.8
IFF°	4.3	2.3	3.3
IFF-YES	4.3	0	2.2
YES-BUT	40.4	34.9	37.8
YES+	19.1	23.3	21.1
YES++	6.4	9.3	7.8
N.A.	6.4	0	3.3
Total	100%	100%	100%
Total n	47	43	90

that the current pattern of nuclear reductions will not be durable. But the fundamental conditions that drove the nuclear arms race – the preference structures that determined strategic choices during the intense Reagan buildup – remain largely intact. Because basic strategic intuitions are highly abstract (and perhaps "ideological," though the direction of the causal arrows is far from clear), dramatic changes in the international environment have had very little effect on the propensity to support nuclear weapons acquisitions. It follows that the robustness of the current equilibrium depends greatly on the continued ability of Russian leaders to

Table 10.4. *Experts: game type and heuristics imputed to Russian leaders, MX-type missiles, before and after the overthrow of communism*

	March 1991	May 1993	Total
Experts: Russian Security Heuristic - MX			
SYMMETRY	0	9.7	4.1
MIXTURE	2.3	19.4	9.5
STRENGTH	69.8	45.2	59.5
Unclear	27.9	25.8	27.0
Total	100%	100%	100%
Total n	43	31	74
Experts: Russian Weapon Heuristic - MX			
BAD	48.8	54.8	51.4
GOOD	27.9	16.1	23.0
SWEET POISON	2.3	0	1.4
Unclear	20.9	29.0	24.3
Total	100%	100%	100%
Total n	43	31	74
Experts: Russian Game Type - MX			
NO	0	22.6	9.5
IFF-NO	18.6	25.8	21.6
IFF°	0	3.2	1.4
YES-BUT	44.2	29.0	37.8
YES+	27.9	16.1	23.0
N.A.	9.3	3.2	6.8
Total	100%	100%	100%
Total n	43	31	74

prevail over those who might want to restore Russia's fading military strength and "superpower" status.

Figure 10.9 illustrates the logic of this argument by arraying the expressed nuclear preferences of experts and novices against the profiles they imputed to Russian leaders. The tables compare the game theoretic structure of the arms race before and after the fall of communism, here for the MX missile. The marginal totals in the tables show that the distribution of preferences changed very little among the respondents, while they perceived the Russians to become systematically more "dovish." Respondents enclosed in the boxes would be disinclined to build the MX-type system in a one-shot game with the Russians, given their beliefs about the Russians'

Table 10.5. *Experts: game type and heuristics imputed to Russian leaders for SDI, before and after the overthrow of communism*

	March 1991	May 1991	Total
Experts: Russian Security Heuristic - SDI			
SYMMETRY	2.3	6.5	4.1
MIXTURE	4.7	29.0	14.9
STRENGTH	60.5	51.6	56.8
Unclear	32.6	12.9	24.3
Total	100%	100%	100%
Total N	43	31	74
Experts: Russian Weapon Heuristic - SDI			
BAD	55.8	35.5	47.3
GOOD	32.6	54.8	41.9
GOOD POISON	2.3	0	1.4
Unclear	9.3	9.7	9.5
Total	100%	100%	100%
Total N	43	31	74
Experts: Russian Game Type -SDI			
NO	4.7	0	2.7
IFF-NO	23.3	29.0	25.7
IFF°	0	3.2	1.4
IFF-YES	0	6.5	2.7
YES-BUT	30.2	9.7	21.6
YES+	32.6	48.4	39.2
N.A.	9.3	3.2	6.8
Total	100%	100%	100%
Total N	43	31	74

political type. The fraction in the *Not Build* coalition increases substantially among the experts, from roughly 35% to 60%. Among the novices, little change occurs, with only one third or so preferring not to build. The table leaves the impression that the current nuclear peace is rather fragile and tenuous. Everything turns on newly formed impressions of the adversary, and·one is struck by the stubbornness of the old patterns of thought.

A CLOSING THOUGHT

The humbling lesson of the nuclear thinking data is that, in the face of great complexity, we are all amateur strategists. It is comforting to believe that

RAND Experts: MX — 93 May

Russia	Respondent's Type							
	NO	IFF-NO	IFF°	IFF-YES	YES-BUT	YES+	zip	total
NO	3	4	0	0	0	0	0	7
IFF-NO	4	4	0	0	0	0	0	8
IFF°	0	0	1	0	0	0	0	1
IFF-YES	0	0	0	0	0	0	0	0
YES-BUT	3	0	0	0	6	0	0	9
YES+	1	1	0	1	2	0	0	5
zip	0	0	0	0	0	0	1	1
total	11	9	1	1	8	0	1	31

64.5% 48% Not Build Coalition = 61%

Novices: MX — 93 Jan

Russia	Respondent's Type								
	NO	IFF-NO	IFF°	IFF-YES	YES-BUT	YES+	YES++	zip	total
NO	1	1	0	0	0	0	0	0	2
IFF-NO	2	6	2	0	1	0	0	0	11
IFF°	0	1	0	0	0	0	0	0	1
IFF-YS	0	0	0	0	0	0	0	0	0
YES-BT	3	6	1	1	1	2	0	1	15
YES+	1	1	0	0	3	3	2	0	10
YES++	0	0	0	1	0	2	2	0	4
total	7	15	3	1	5	7	4	1	43

30% 51% Not Build Coalition = 37%

RAND Experts: MX — 91 Mar

Russia	Respondent's Type						
	NO	IFF-NO	IFF°	YES-BUT	YES+	zip	total
NO	0	0	0	0	0	0	0
IFF-NO	2	6	0	0	0	0	8
IFF°	0	0	0	0	0	0	0
IFF-YES	0	0	0	0	0	0	0
YES-BUT	7	7	0	5	0	0	19
YES+	1	3	0	4	4	0	12
zip	0	0	1	0	1	2	4
total	10	16	1	9	5	2	43

60.5% 19% Not Build Coalition = 37%

Novices: MX — 90 Oct

Russia	Respondent's Type								
	NO	IFF-NO	IFF°	IFF-YES	YES-BUT	YES+	YES++	zip	total
NO	1	2	0	0	0	1	0	0	4
IFF-NO	0	4	1	0	0	0	0	0	5
IFF°	1	0	1	0	0	0	0	0	2
IFF-YS	1	1	0	0	0	0	0	0	2
YES-BT	5	6	4	2	2	0	0	0	19
YES+	3	2	1	0	1	2	0	0	9
YES++	0	0	0	0	0	1	2	0	3
zip	0	0	1	1	0	0	0	1	3
total	11	15	8	3	3	4	2	1	47

55% 19% Not Build Coalition = 38%

Figure 10.9 Imputed game type for Russians by respondent's game type, MX-like missiles the first great nuclear arms race subsided when we finally mastered its laws of motion. But the hallmark of the Cold War was intractable political controversy, not strategic consensus. After the Cold War, no less than before, we must accept strategic heterogeneity as the guiding premise in theories of national security. Otherwise, we shall find ourselves continually mystified by the democratization of nuclear authority that continues all around the world.

Index